Luminos is the Open Access monograph publishing program
from UC Press. Luminos provides a framework for preserving and
reinvigorating monograph publishing for the future and increases
the reach and visibility of important scholarly work. Titles published
in the UC Press Luminos model are published with the same high
standards for selection, peer review, production, and marketing as
those in our traditional program. www.luminosoa.org

The publisher and the University of California Press Foundation gratefully acknowledge the generous support of the Philip E. Lilienthal Imprint in Asian Studies, established by a major gift from Sally Lilienthal.

A

Philip E. Lilienthal (signature)

BOOK

Acquired Alterity

Acquired Alterity

Migration, Identity, and Literary Nationalism

Edward Mack

UNIVERSITY OF CALIFORNIA PRESS

University of California Press
Oakland, California

© 2022 by Edward Mack

Suggested citation: Mack, E. *Acquired Alterity: Migration, Identity, and Literary Nationalism*. Oakland: University of California Press, 2022. DOI: https://doi.org/10.1525/luminos.116

Names: Mack, Edward Thomas, author.
Title: Acquired alterity: migration, identity, and literary nationalism / Edward Mack.
Description: Oakland, California: University of California Press, [2022] | Includes bibliographical references and index. | This work is licensed under a Creative Commons CC BY-NC-ND license. To view a copy of the license, visit http://creativecommons.org/licenses
Identifiers: LCCN 2021028986 (print) | LCCN 2021028987 (ebook) | ISBN 9780520383043 (paperback) | ISBN 9780520383050 (ebook)
Subjects: LCSH: Japanese—Brazil—Bastos (São Paulo)—History. | Japanese language—Brazil—Bastos (São Paulo)—History. | Japanese literature—Brazil—Bastos (São Paulo)—History. | Japanese—Brazil—Ethnic identity. | Immigrants—Brazil—Bastos (São Paulo)—History. | BISAC: LITERARY COLLECTIONS / Asian / Japanese | HISTORY / Latin America / South America
Classification: LCC F2659.J3 M33 2022 (print) | LCC F2659.J3 (ebook) | DDC 981/.61—dc23
LC record available at https://lccn.loc.gov/2021028986
LC ebook record available at https://lccn.loc.gov/2021028987

31 30 29 28 27 26 25 24 23 22
10 9 8 7 6 5 4 3 2 1

CONTENTS

LIST OF ILLUSTRATIONS

MAPS

FIGURES

ACKNOWLEDGMENTS

Over the many years it took me to complete this book, I benefited from the professional and personal support of so many institutions and individuals that I fear important ones will be left out. Let me begin, then, by thanking anyone who does not find their contribution mentioned here. The omission is the result of failing memory and not a lack of gratitude.

Certain institutions played key roles in enabling this work: the University of Washington Japan Studies program and Simpson Center for the Humanities, the International Research Center for Japanese Studies (Nichibunken), the Japan Foundation, the Sociedade Brasileira de Cultura Japonesa (Bunkyō), the Museu Histórico da Imigração, and the Centro de Estudos Nipo-Brasileiros (Jimonken). Within each of those institutions were people who made my work there possible, including Hosokawa Shūhei, Célia Oi, Susumu Miyao, Katsunori Wakisaka, Negawa Sachio, Suzuki Masatake, and the members of both of the History and Culture of Japanese Immigration in the New Continent and the Comparative Study of Local Japanese Education team research projects at Nichibunken. Others, such as Michael Foster and Michiko Suzuki, made my time at those institutions so much more fun.

This project would not have been possible without Kasumi Yamashita, who brought me to Brazil and introduced me to so many amazing people, especially James Kudo and Erico Marmiroli. Many a lovely day was spent in Liberdade and the Bunkyo.

My thinking on these topics has benefited greatly by participating in an ongoing series of related symposia organized by Seth Jacobowitz and including many of the leading scholars on the Japanese diaspora (Zelideth Rivas and Jeffrey Lesser in particular), and on an ACLA panel organized by Lisa Hofmann-Kuroda and

ix

Andrew Leong, as well as at the various talks I have been able to give at universities in the United States, Japan, Brazil, Korea, Australia, New Zealand, and Canada. My thanks to all of the people who made these opportunities possible.

Throughout, a group of dear friends in Japan and Korea have been the source of invaluable support of all kinds: Kōno Kensuke, Kō Youngran, Gomibuchi Noritsugu, Cheon Junghwan, Tsuboi Hideto, Rimbara Sumio, and Hibi Yoshitaka among them. I cannot have asked for better friends on matters both professional and personal.

Many people have pressed me to finish my work with both supportive kindness and gentle snark, in different measures depending on the individual, over the past few years. Drew, Liz, Joe, Elisabeth, David, Rich, Gillian, Adam, Chris, Zev, Davinder, Ju, Jay, Alice, Brooke, and Zoe and so many other friends have been essential stalwarts (though, as Hal Bolitho once said, one man's stalwart is another man's thug.) My colleagues at the University of Washington have provided me with an ideal environment in which to pursue this work.

My thanks to Shintaro Hayashi, Leiko Gotoda, Jorge Takei, and Kenji Takemoto for allowing their family members' stories to appear in English translation and to the Yendo family for their generous cooperation.

Jennifer Robertson was instrumental in bringing this book to the University of California Press, and Sabine Frühstück, Enrique Ochoa-Kaup, Francisco Reinking, Bob Pease, Alexander Trotter, Paige MacKay, and Reed Malcolm have provided direction, support, and patience as it has made its way to publication. I would like to thank Anne Walthall for helping to fund the series New Interventions in Japanese Studies, making it possible to publish this book through the Luminos Open Access program.

Sienna and Jonah have been there with love, joy, companionship, and inspiration all along. I am so lucky to be your father.

MAP 1. South America. Map by Pease Press Cartography.

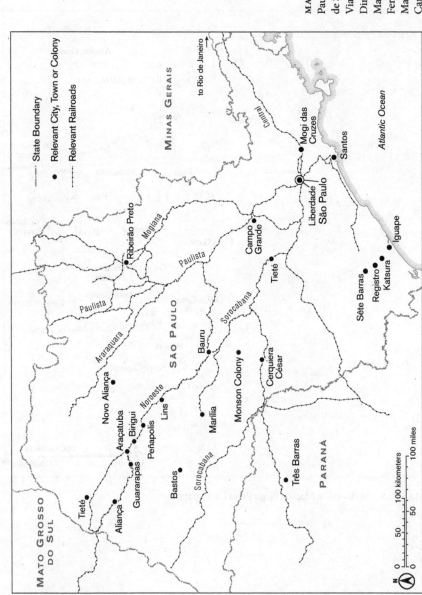

MAP 2. State of São Paulo. Based on Estado de S. Paulo, Secretaria da Viação e Obras Publicas, Directoria de Viação, Mappa da Viação Ferrea em 1–1–1932. Map by Pease Press Cartography.

Legend:
- State Boundary
- Relevant City, Town or Colony
- Relevant Railroads

MINAS GERAIS

to Rio de Janeiro

Central

Mogi das Cruzes

Santos

Liberdade
São Paulo

Iguape

Ribeirão Preto

Mogiana

Campo Grande

Paulista

Tietê

Sête Barras
Registro
Katsura

Atlantic Ocean

Paulista

SÃO PAULO

Araraquara

Bauru

Sorocabana

Novo Aliança

Noroeste

Lins

Cerquiera César

Monson Colony

Araçatuba
Birigui
Peñapolis

Marília

Guararapas

Bastos

Sorocabana

Três Barras

PARANÁ

MATO GROSSO
DO SUL

Tietê

Aliança

N

0   50   100 kilometers
0   50   100 miles

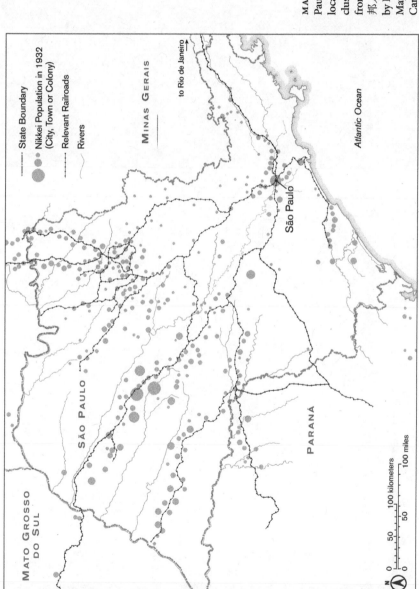

MAP 3. State of São Paulo. With approximate locations of population clusters in 1933 drawn from ブラジル在留邦人分布図, compiled by Burajiru Jihōsha. Maps by Pease Press Cartography.

Legend:

State Boundary

Nikkei Population in 1932 (City, Town or Colony)

Relevant Railroads

Rivers

MINAS GERAIS

to Rio de Janeiro

São Paulo

Atlantic Ocean

MATO GROSSO DO SUL

SÃO PAULO

PARANA

N

0   50   100 kilometers
0   50   100 miles

Introduction

In 1932, two stories were written in Japanese depicting the large-scale emigration from Japan to Brazil that occurred prior to the Second World War, and both went on to receive newly inaugurated literary awards. The stories were selected by writers and editors who thought them to be exceptionally valuable for a variety of reasons, both literary and social, and who utilized the awards not only to ascribe value to the texts discursively, but also to impact the dissemination, preservation, and reception of those texts through material means.[1] The result was that they reached significantly expanded reading communities and did so with an imprimatur of authority that signaled the works' particular significance to those communities.[2]

While the commonalities between these two works and the ways they reached readers are notable, their differences are even more telling. Though both were written in Japanese and thus could be thought to have been directed at a single imagined readership (perhaps "the Japanese"), the reality is that their readerships were quite different. One story was published in a prestigious magazine produced in Tokyo, which enjoyed some circulation and influence among intellectuals throughout the Japanese empire and the globe, not all of whom would have identified as "Japanese." The other was published in the city of São Paulo, Brazil, in a Japanese-language newspaper whose circulation was limited almost exclusively to one diasporic community, but which played a similarly central role in it. The differences between the material networks within which the stories were created, feted, and then circulated, and the experiences of their authors after these acts of recognition, bring into relief the heterogeneity and multiplicity of Japanese-language reading communities and the vast differences in resources those communities possessed.

The two works and the trajectories of their material instantiations are keys to disentangling the relationship of literature and the nation, particularly as those two have functioned in the case of modern Japan. By following the specific historical reading community for Japanese-language texts that existed in Brazil, we may clarify moments at which the nation was the appropriate frame of reference for the literary texts and—perhaps more importantly—moments at which it was not. This clarification reveals a more diverse history than is often imagined for "modern Japanese literature"; it also reveals a number of problematic assumptions that attend any analyses of individual literary texts within such a comprehensive rubric, particularly when the actual object of knowledge production either explicitly or implicitly shifts from the individual work or author to a "national literature."

The first of the two works was "The Emigrants" (蒼氓) by Ishikawa Tatsuzō (1905–85), which he originally composed and submitted to a literary prize competition held by Kaizō magazine in 1932; it was not selected for publication, but did receive honorable mention.[3] The following year he submitted a revised version to the Osaka literary coterie magazine Hata, but the journal ceased publication before the story appeared. It was not until April 1935 that the story finally made it into print, in the literary coterie magazine of the Shin Waseda Bungaku group, Seiza. It was this appearance in print that brought the story to the attention of the selection committee for the newly founded Akutagawa Prize for literature. Ishikawa's fame grew quickly after receipt of the award, particularly with the publication of Soldiers Alive (生きている兵隊) in 1938, and he remained an important figure in the Tokyo literary establishment until his death in 1985.

Ishikawa, who had attended Waseda University and was already a published author by the time he reached Brazil in 1930, remained in the country for just slightly longer than ten weeks, leading some (particularly in Brazil) to question the authenticity of his depiction. Upon his arrival, he traveled to Santa Rosa, in the state of Rio Grande do Sul, where he initially spent time in the home of another immigrant from Japan, Mera Isao; many of the depictions of life in Brazil that appeared in the later sections of his novel were drawn from what he observed there.[4] He then traveled to the city of São Paulo, where he remained until returning to Japan.

The other work, "An Age of Speculative Farming" (賭博農時代) by Sonobe Takeo (years unknown), won the Colonial Literary Short Fiction Award (植民文藝懸賞短編小説), which had been established in 1932 in São Paulo, Brazil, by the leading Japanese-language newspaper published in that country, on the opposite side of the globe. On 21 April 1932, the Burajiru jihō (伯剌西爾時報, Notícias do Brazil) announced that Sonobe had won the inaugural competition for his work, which then appeared in four installments between 21 April and 12 May. In his autobiographical note accompanying the announcement of the award, the author claimed to have only been in Brazil for seven months—a short time, but significantly longer than Ishikawa had spent.

In contrast to Ishikawa, the author Sonobe Takeo, whose real name seems to have been Inoue Tetsurō, is often considered to have possessed a more legitimate connection to Brazil.[5] Inoue, a graduate of Hokkaidō Imperial University's Department of Animal Science, arrived at the Instituto de Prática Agrícola de São Paulo as a leader of the first group of practicum agricultural students. He traveled to Brazil on or around 14 July 1931 and remained there until around 1939.⁶ By his own admission, when he wrote "An Age of Speculative Farming" he had not yet set foot on a coffee plantation; instead, he found himself in a situation "unsuited for someone of my age, fiddling around with tomatoes and potatoes, doing nothing more than playing farmer like some idiot son of a wealthy family who spends his days growing flowers."⁷ During the remainder of his stay in Brazil, Inoue did publish some additional pieces that we know about, such as "Shi to fukutsū to on'na" (誌と腹痛と女), which appeared in the fourth issue of the literary magazine *Nanteki* (南廸).⁸

Subsequently Inoue's life course diverged from Ishikawa's about as dramatically as one could imagine. He seems to have left Brazil around 1939, but apparently did not return to Japan—or, if he did, he did not stay long. In July 1950, he was arrested in the name of the commander of the army of Northern Sumatra, as he was (according to him) "working peacefully as an advisor to the Regular Army Farm and Construction Corps near Lake Tawar in (what was then) the Karo region."⁹ He had been there for perhaps as long as a decade at that point, having traveled to Sumatra after his return from Brazil. According to his own account, in Sumatra he had participated in the construction of an agricultural training camp and then led a group of individuals fighting for Indonesian independence. When the government demanded that they relinquish their arms, they fled into the jungle, where Inoue lived until he was arrested.¹⁰ It was not until 7 June 1952, two months after Ishikawa was appointed an officer (理事) of the Japan Writers' Association (Nihon Bungeika Kyōkai), that the Japanese government received word that Inoue (along with 170 other Japanese nationals) was still in Indonesia, had been arrested for political crimes, and was apparently known as the "Sumatran Tiger" (スマトラの虎).¹¹ Inoue Tetsurō went on to write about his experiences in an article in *Kingu* magazine and then in a book; it would seem that he did very little writing subsequent to these publications from 1953, so little is known about his later life.¹²

The different life trajectories of the two authors are stark, and perhaps not unrelated to the literary opportunities their different circumstances allowed. More instructive for our purposes, however, are the different trajectories their two stories have experienced since their initial publication. Though "The Emigrants" did initially appear in a small literary coterie magazine, that magazine was published in Tokyo and thus enjoyed a far higher likelihood of coming to the attention of the newly formed Akutagawa Prize selection committee. There it entered into the matrix of national literature or Japanese literature, a complex institutional structure comprising print capital, literary discourse, and academic reinforcement.

"An Age of Speculative Farming," for its part, entered into a different matrix, separate but not unrelated, which would go by many names over the subsequent decades: *shokumin bungei* (colonial literature), *koronia bungaku* (*colônia* literature), *Burajiru Nikkei bungaku* (Brazil Nikkei literature), and *Nikkei Burajiru imin bungaku* (Nikkei Brazil migrant literature), to name only a few. The differential material and discursive resources of these spheres undoubtedly affected the trajectories of these works in ways that cannot be attributed solely to inherent differences in literary value. To conclude that the differences in terms of reception are solely due to such intrinsic value and to the ongoing literary production of their authors would be to miss the consequential fact that the two works, despite their similarities (of topic, of language) have remained in two different literary spheres.

This study addresses not only the nature of the literary sphere within which "An Age of Speculative Farming" emerged, that is, the sphere of Japanese-language prose literary activity in Brazil prior to World War II, but also the ongoing relationship between marginalized literary texts such as this one and the dominant sphere of national "Japanese" literature in Japan. Though a powerful normative notion, the nature of this national literature is itself ambiguous (a fact that, counter-intuitively, contributes to its continuing influence.) Part of the ambiguity centers on what supposedly makes the literature "national" in the first place. Consider the oft-cited "National Literature Debate" (国民文学論争) begun by Takeuchi Yoshimi, which went on between roughly September 1951 and February 1954.[13] During that debate, the author Yamamoto Kenkichi wrote an article titled, "National Territory, National Language, the Nation: A Note on National Literature."[14] In it, he referred to a "holy trinity" (三位一体) made up of *kokudo* (national territory), *kokugo* (national language), and *kokumin* (the people of the nation). It was Yamamoto's belief that this holy trinity was the legitimate basis of "our" (われわれの) literature, despite the unfortunate form he felt it had come to assume (dominated by the elite literary establishment of the time.) For Yamamoto, the trinity was a self-evident and positive foundation for thinking about works of literature (and the individuals who read and write those works) collectively.

Subsequent thinkers have shown that this trinity is neither self-evident nor necessarily a salutary formation. Komori Yōichi addressed and slightly modified the metaphor in his 1998 book <*Yuragi*> *no Nihon bungaku* (＜ゆらぎ＞の日本文学). Komori describes how a reified notion of Japaneseness emerges as an amalgam of the notions of a "Japanese" ethnicity or race (民族), a sense of affiliation to the nation-state (国家) as a "Japanese" by means of citizenship, and the use of "Japanese" as one's language (言語). He then adds that a fourth element, "Japanese culture" (文化), results in a holy quadrinity, hypostatizing an imagined mode of being that is distinct from all other individual or social modes of being.[15] Komori acknowledges his debt to the work of Naoki Sakai in conceptualizing the problem in this way. Sakai's work reveals not only the arbitrary and constructed nature of this ambiguous national paradigm, but also its capacity for exclusion and discrimination.[16]

My own previous book, *Manufacturing Modern Japanese Literature*, examined certain aspects of the normative, national sphere, centered in Tokyo. In it, I contended that a combination of discursive and material mechanisms allowed for certain works to be valorized as "modern Japanese literature," and then to enter into an ever-expanding system of distribution and marketing that brought these texts to markets not only through the islands that now comprise the nation-state of Japan, but also to Japanese-reading populations throughout its colonies, the puppet state of Manchukuo, semicolonial spaces in China, emigrant communities, and beyond. Its ultimate argument, however, was that the texts were rarely available as the totality implied by the concept, and that, at least in terms of readership, the communities impacted by the works did not enjoy any of the homogeneity, consistency, or simultaneity suggested by the notion of a "national readership." Rather than specific texts, I proposed, what was most successfully propagated through this network was the concept of a modern national literature itself, which could then be activated through discursive and material mechanisms to valorize certain works and marginalize others. By winning the Akutagawa Prize for literature and thus being not only labeled as "pure" (putatively autonomous) "Japanese literature," but also backed by the economic power of the publishing company Bungei Shunjūsha, a story like "The Emigrants" (and its author) enjoyed a number of benefits that impacted its subsequent dissemination, reception, and preservation.

This book will examine the sphere that "An Age of Speculative Farming" entered, that of Japanese-language literary activity in Brazil. It should be noted at the outset that these spheres are being discussed as entities, and as separate entities, as a heuristic expedient; it would be a mistake to hypostatize these spheres, which are actually only metaphors for a series of related material institutions and discursive relationships. More importantly, as will be discussed in detail, these spheres were intimately connected, although often unilaterally. Seen from a different angle, this book examines related issues but moves the focus from the "center" to the "periphery" and also expands its purview to include the production of literature as well as its consumption.[17] While this change in perspective reinforces the argument of the first book, which challenged the notion of a modern national literature, it also begs the question of the function of normativity and the concomitant rise of notions of transgressive alterity with regard to "national literature."

The chapters that follow will be loosely organized around the metaphor of the holy quadrinity discussed above: state, culture, ethnos, and language. This is largely an organizational conceit, meant to help arrange different problematics and objects of research that are often quite distinct in terms of methodology; it should be noted in advance that many of the elements being examined have a place in other categories as well. Within each of these categories, the heuristic of alterity will be utilized, with various forms of othering presented depending on the case. In this, the study joins a growing body of scholarship that both highlights and problematizes assertions of alterity in modern Japan. Most importantly, though this book will focus exclusively on the particulars of this case, this should not be taken as an argument that this phenomenon in Japan is in any way unique. While the precise historical events and logical formations that lead to an assertion of categorical identity for literary texts revolving around the nation, however imagined, may differ, the phenomenon itself is not singular, and thus could be put into dialog with critiques of other national literatures and collective textual identities.

Issues related to the function of polities in thinking about literature will be addressed indirectly in the chapter on "The State." The combination of physical distance from the sovereign territory of the Japanese empire and the legal barrier of national (or, in the case of Japan at the time, imperial) borders significantly divided the Japanese-Brazilian marketplace from the one that existed within the formal Japanese empire (and Manchukuo). As a result, the marketplace did not benefit from state incentives to unify it (standardized shipping costs, for example) or industry incentives to expand and stabilize it (such as fixed retail prices); on the other hand, the marketplace did not suffer directly from state intervention, particular in the form of censorship (until intervention by the Brazilian state in 1941). This chapter will trace the development of the literary marketplace for Japanese-language texts in Brazil prior to World War II, with a focus on the bookstore that would become the most important during that period: Livraria Yendo, also known as Endō Shoten. This chapter will show the nature and scope of texts, primarily out of Tokyo, that were available for purchase in Brazil. What we see from this example is consistent with studies of other local markets for Japanese-language literature outside of Tokyo: that while the Tokyo-centered publishing industry was, unsurprisingly, the dominant force is producing the texts available for sale, the selection of texts actually available was both limited and locally determined. That is, it represented a locally-curated subset of "modern Japanese literature," one that did not always conform to the normative vision being advanced by academics and critics at the center of the Tokyo literary establishment.

The chapter on "Culture" will examine the dominant form of literary texts during this period: newspaper fiction. This chapter will draw from two sections of the newspaper that were literally separate: the "popular" fiction that almost always appeared on the first or last page, and the "pure" fiction that appeared on an inner page dedicated to literary activities in general. In examining the "popular" fiction, we will find texts that are (almost?) exclusively drawn from existing texts produced in Japan, but which are curated in a particularly extreme (and perhaps arbitrary) way. They are selected by the editors, and result in a very limited (and perhaps somewhat random, depending on the availability or affordability of sources) group of texts that do not come from the valorized sphere of "pure" literature and, particularly in the earlier years, were not originally produced in Tokyo. In examining the "pure" fiction, we will find a very conscious effort not only to print texts written locally that address local concerns, but also to cultivate the production of that sort of literature. While this goal surely had economic motivations of nurturing local writers and engaging more local readers, it was also motivated by the goal of community-building. The chapter will conclude by suggesting that perhaps this local reading community was less exceptional than it might appear; though it is beyond the scope of this study, it seems likely that the ideal of a normative national literature that dominates academic study of Japanese-language literature would have in fact been experienced at a local level in very individual and incomplete ways.

After this chapter come translations of ten works of fiction, all written in Brazil. By including these translations, I hope to allow the writers to speak for themselves, and in so doing somewhat redress the objectifying and instrumentalized gaze of this book. These texts do not represent an attempt by this author to provide either a representative sample of the literature produced within the rubric adopted by this book, nor a subjective (masquerading as disinterested) selection of the greatest works within the category. Rather, these ten works are ones that have enjoyed the benefits of the mechanisms of value ascription available in this sphere of literary activity: they have been selected by editors for publication, by judges for literary awards, and by scholars for their (allegedly) intrinsic merits. The totality implied by these texts, then, is (as with all such selections) a motivated one, curated by individuals who had agendas (whether laudable or not) of their own. If they are representative of anything, it is the story that has been told (by individuals with access to these mechanisms of valorization) about Japanese-language literary production in Brazil. That is not to say that these texts are unworthy of their reproduction, or that they share any culpability in the nature of their reproduction.

The chapter on "Ethnos" will look at these ten literary works produced in Brazil during this time, in order to see how an imagined ethnos functions within them. Contrary to what might be expected, these literary works, written by authors who had been immersed in a world of more obvious phenotypical, linguistic, and cultural diversity than they likely had ever experienced before, were not preoccupied by that form of alterity. Instead, the works show a preoccupation with two more complicated forms of alterity: acquired alterity, in which an individual once thought to be self-same comes to identify or be identified as an Other, and a postlapsarian alterity—a sense of ethnic betrayal—in which an individual recognized as nominally self-same betrays expectations thought to accompany that identity. Put simply, the writers are preoccupied with "fellow Japanese" as Other. The texts are riddled with moments of surprise, when expectations are subverted: either when the actions of a fellow Japanese fail to meet an ideal of ethnic solidarity, or when the actions of a non-Japanese fail to meet an expectation of racial animosity.[18] At the same time, the chapter will address an apparent discomfort with the specific ambiguity existing between a racial identity as Japanese and a political identity as Japanese, hinted at by a (perhaps unconscious) tendency to use terms indicating common descent (such as 同胞, which originally meant "of the same uterus,") or abstracted kinship as countrymen (such as 邦人), rather than as Japanese. The chapter shows that the ambiguous amalgam of state-culture-ethnos-language reveals its unsustainability under these moments *in extremis*, even as it fails to capture the historical diversity of experiences of individuals who self-identified as Japanese.

Finally, in the chapter on "Language," I will be focusing primarily on the ways in which the notion of a single, stable language as a completely transparent mode of communication with clear boundaries is undermined time and again both within the literary texts themselves, and in the metadiscourse about the texts. At the same time, the chapter will argue that language may still be the most reasonable logic by which to group texts, if such a need exists at all. In the course of the chapter, I will examine the phenomenon of *koronia-go*, the use of (primarily Portuguese) loanwords in Japanese-language discourse in Brazil and the issues of literary technique raised in the representation of a multilingual environment. Similarly, I will address the ways in which the dialogic portions of the stories discussed show a marked interest in linguistic diversity within "Japanese" in the form of dialectical difference. Differences within the notion of a single language are not only visible (audible) to that language's speakers, they are also key markers of alterity. The chapter will argue that while comprehensibility seems, at first glance, to be a clear standard for the linguistic grouping of texts, in fact this not only raises questions about degrees of linguistic intelligibility, it also raises question about the impossible notion of an ideal reader. The goal will be to call into question a normative relationship between a "native speaker" and a literary text, which renders all other readers to a subordinate, inferior, and artificial position.

The book concludes with a discussion of the conception of *Nihongo bungaku*, Japanese-language literature, and both its propriety and actual impact. While the legitimate motivations of its proponents must be acknowledged, the conclusion will argue that as long as the concept exists alongside a notion of *Nihon bungaku*, Japanese literature, it will almost inevitably connote a derivative, artificial, second-order form of literary activity in Japanese, and in so doing will reinforce a normative vision. The very act of seeing the Japanese-language literary production of Brazil as Other automatically reproduces an unproblematized norm of modern Japanese literature (written, presumably, by Japanese people in the Japanese language in Japan for Japanese people.) Rather than offer new terminology, the conclusion will urge its readers to consciously delink the elements of the amalgam, making certain that each time the term "Japanese" is employed it is done in full awareness of the assumptions and implications contained therein. Finally, the book will conclude with a discussion of possible outcomes for the Japanese-language literature of Brazil, discussing how economic realities likely demand that the works either be assimilated into a unified notion of Japanese literature or exoticized as an Other, all the more seductive for its proximity to an imagined Self.

For the sake of analysis, this study will posit an historical reading community determined geographically, temporally, and linguistically (acknowledging but not affirming a contemporary presumption that it would also contain an ethnic component) that is not the imagined nation. Instead, it is an imagined community of

Japanese-language literary readers in Brazil from the opening of mass migration in 1908 until the outlawing of the publication and circulation of Japanese-language texts in 1941. Since there is little evidence that these texts circulated outside of Brazil in any significant quantity during this period, the community is presumed to be limited to those national borders, and in the main to the borders of the state of São Paulo. Most of the readers will be assumed to have been first-generation immigrants to Brazil, either coming as adults (the issei 一世 immigrants) or as children (the jun-nisei 準二世), as there is limited evidence of a significant number of readers during this period who were born in Brazil.

This alternate notional community, however, is no more organic or inevitable than was that of a national readership. This is true both synchronically and diachronically. During the period in question, there is no way of knowing for certain how widely the texts circulated, or to how diverse an audience, how uniformly they reached this potential reading community, nor how consistently the members of such a community might have been affected. The uncertainty expands dramatically when we realize that the history of these texts' reception is not over. While their authors may never have dreamed this possible, the texts are now available to readers of extreme diversity, in terms of geographical location, personal experience, and national identification. If we presume that original texts can be experienced, at least to an extent, through translation, then the translations included in this volume allow the potential reading community to cross linguistic boundaries as well.

As Lisa Lowe writes, "the historical narrative not only disciplines the criteria for establishing evidence; it also identifies the proper units for the study of the past, whether the individual, family, polis, nation, or civilization. In short, the historical narrative . . . constitutes, organizes, and gives structure, meaning and finite contours to the historical past." This is more than just a problem of narrating the past. Lowe continues, "Since the very ability to conceptualize the contemporary predicament is shaped by the historical reconstructions of the past, we cannot conceive the present, or imagine its transformation, without this interrogation. Only by defamiliarizing both the object of the past and the established methods for apprehending that object do we make possible alternative forms of knowing, thinking, and being."[19] This study will have succeeded if it helps make the problem itself visible, and in so doing helps make clear the need to rethink the most fundamental concepts through which we read and understand Japanese-language texts—and perhaps all texts that are approached through a lens of national literature.

2

The State

Livraria Yendo and Japanese-Language Readers in Brazil

Governments—their laws, their policies, their borders, their sovereign territories—impacted the lives of Japanese emigrants to Brazil in countless ways, and as a result are visible not only in literary representations of those lives but also in emigrants' reading practices themselves. For that matter, governments played a pivotal role in those communities coming into existence in the first place. The population of Japanese-language readers in Brazil did not exist solely as a result of the individual choices of autonomous actors. Thanks to a variety of political and economic forces, the community of individuals capable of reading and writing Japanese in Brazil became an unexpectedly substantial one; during the decade spanning 1924–1933 in particular, Brazil became a primary destination, receiving 63 percent of the total emigration out of the Japanese empire.[1] Today, the largest population of persons of Japanese descent outside of Japan may not be in the United States, but in Brazil.[2] The origins of this population, and the reasons for its size, can be traced to the beginning of the twentieth century and the different immigration policies the two countries enacted.

As mentioned previously, the notion of a "national literature" revolves around an ambiguous notion of a community that is linked by some combination of factors, including the "holy quandrinity" of state (or sometimes territory), culture, ethnos, and language.[3] This chapter will address the first of these elements, which is also perhaps its most broad in possible interpretation. In addition to exploring the role of governmental forces on these immigrants and the history of this community's first decades, the chapter will also consider the spatial aspect of the concept (more visible in its formulation as "national territory" [国土])—that is, the impact of physical proximity, or lack thereof, on reading practices. Primarily, this will take the form of an attempt to reconstruct the marketplace for literary texts

11

in this community, focusing on the infrastructure through which readers would have gained access to Japanese-language books, magazines, and newspapers. In so doing, it will describe the nature and scope of the literary texts, mostly produced in Tokyo, that would have been available for consumption by this community. This will show us both the remarkable degree of continuity between the texts available to readers in Japan and in Brazil, and thus the importance of thinking about this literature in relation to a community bounded by a single state ("Japan"). At the same time, given that Brazil is a distinct, sovereign, and vastly distant territory from Japan, the chapter will show how this community was profoundly affected by, and bound by, multiple polities, each of which needs to be considered in thinking about these readers. The first factor in the notion of a "national literature"—state or territory—is thus revealed to be significant but not definitive; in fact, in thinking about spatial or legal boundaries of the reading community, those of the "nation" are by turns too small, too large, or inaccurately singular.

JAPANESE-LANGUAGE READERS OUTSIDE JAPAN

The arrival of the first group of immigrants from Japan to Brazil in 1908—and thus the creation of a community of readers there—occurred against a backdrop of both ongoing emigration from Japan to, and immigration into Brazil from, a variety of countries.[4] The migration of groups (rather than individuals), often organized and subsidized by the Japanese government, was motivated by a variety of "push" factors, among which was that government's strategy of "peaceful expansionism" (平和的膨張) intended to extend Japan's informal sphere of influence even as it expanded its formal empire through the acquisition of territories by force.[5] By 1908, the Japanese government had been supporting sanctioned group migration abroad for a quarter of a century, having lifted its ban on Japanese nationals emigrating abroad in 1883.[6] Unsanctioned group migration dated back earlier still, to the unauthorized transport of approximately two hundred individuals from Japan to Hawaii and Guam in 1868.[7]

As a result of these migration efforts, there were already communities of Japanese nationals in a number of countries around the world by the first decade of the twentieth century. The largest of these communities were in the United States and Hawaii, which the United States had annexed as a territory in 1898. Hawaii had received more than 50,000 immigrants from Japan (which opposed the annexation) by that time. Less than a decade later, in 1906, nearly 80,000 Japanese lived in the United States, roughly 60 percent of whom lived in California. With the so-called "Gentlemen's Agreement" (日米紳士協約) of 1907, however, migration to the United States declined dramatically, falling from 15,803 in 1907 to only 3,111 in 1908.[8] A similar agreement, negotiated in late 1907 and early 1908, established limitations on Japanese migration to Canada as well. With North

America growing increasing hostile to immigration from Japan, migrants to the Western Hemisphere were forced to find new destinations.

Contrary to the situation in the United States, Brazil continued to look favorably on immigration; in fact, migrants from Japan were initially subsidized not by the Japanese government, but by the state of São Paulo, a powerful "pull" factor. This was in keeping with practices that had existed in Brazil as early as 1851, when the government began subsidizing migration from Europe. With the full abolition of slavery looming—it was finally outlawed in 1888—the state government of São Paulo had begun subsidizing immigrants to work in the coffee industry from 1886, drawing primarily from Italy.[9] Migration from that country remained high from 1883 until 1902. That year, the Italian government issued the "Prinetti Decree," which banned agents from recruiting Italian laborers in response to complaints from *colonos* (contracted plantation workers) who had not received their wages, among other mistreatment.[10] As a result, the number of migrants from Italy dropped rapidly and the coffee plantation owners of São Paulo found themselves in need of a new labor force.

Planters were drawn to migrants from Japan not only as a potential source of labor, but also by a desire to increase their ties with that country, in the hope of cultivating the market there as another outlet for their coffee surplus.[11] In 1905, the owners formed the private São Paulo Immigration and Colonization Company (Companhia de Imigração e Colonização de São Paulo), to attract immigrants from Japan and bypass existing laws that might have impeded that process.[12] The following year, the state legislature of São Paulo changed the relevant laws, making it possible for individuals from Japan to receive subsidies as long as they met certain requirements.[13] The Paulista coffee plantation owners were so keen to attract laborers from Japan, in fact, that they had found ways to augment the legally limited state subsidies.[14] The initial agreement between Mizuno Ryō, as president of the Imperial Emigration Company (皇国殖民会社), and the São Paulo state government, signed in 1907, established a level of subvention that significantly reduced, but did not eliminate, the cost of migrating from Japan to Brazil.[15] Despite these remaining costs borne by the migrants, the company was able to attract a large first contingent (though not as many as had been requested.)

The reading community in this study, then, owes its very existence to large-scale forces, including the governments of Japan and Brazil. At the same time, however, in certain cases those governmental forces functioned in conjunction with private commercial interests; in other cases the polities were not national, but local, with the state government of São Paulo being the relevant actor, rather than the Republic of Brazil. Arguably, the community owes its existence to yet another government: that of the United States. As described above, it is not accidental that group migration from Japan to Brazil began in 1908, the year after the United States demanded the conclusion of the Gentleman's Agreement with Japan.

1908-24: THE EARLY YEARS OF THE JAPANESE IN BRAZIL

The first group of Japanese immigrants, nearly eight hundred in number, arrived at the port town of Santos aboard the *Kasato-maru* on 18 June 1908.[16] The composition of the group did not mirror the population from which it emerged. As with the migration from Japan to the United States that preceded it, the gender distribution skewed strongly towards males, with less than a quarter of the original group being female. The fact, then, that there were 165 families and only around fifty single immigrants among the 733 members of the first group requires some explanation. The São Paulo state government had contracted with the Imperial Emigration Company to bring migrants in family units, made up of at least three "adult" (over the age of twelve) members.[17] The goal was to produce social stability and increase the likelihood of long-term residence in the country, in the hopes of increasing both the populations and the productivity of areas of the interior that were deemed underutilized. As a result of these incentives, many migrants formed constructed families (構成家族) for the purpose of receiving the subsidies. Despite these steps to incentivize pre-formed bonds, this first group encountered many difficulties and did not meet many of the expectations of its patrons. Nonetheless, the *Kasato-maru* immigrants—who later become an important symbol for the community—formed a foundation that facilitated the explosive growth that would follow.[18] The group was also largely drawn from the island of Okinawa, with 325 of the individuals on board from that island.[19]

The years 1910–14 saw this initial community of immigrants grow dramatically. The second group of migrants arrived aboard the *Ryojun-maru* in 1910, having been brought by another of Mizuno's enterprises, the Takemura Emigration Company (竹村殖民商館). This time the group, consisting of 906 migrants and three regular passengers, fared somewhat better, partially due to more favorable harvests and partially to the presence of their predecessors. Although conditions remained difficult, three-quarters were still employed on their original *fazendas* one year after arrival, a key metric of success in the eyes of the São Paulo growers and government. After this positive experience, the state contracted with both the Takemura Emigration Company and with the Oriental Emigration Company (東洋移民合資会社) to continue bringing groups of migrants. The two companies transported more than 13,000 additional contract immigrants between 1912 and 1914, bringing the total of subsidized immigrants to nearly 15,000.[20] The First World War brought an end to this first burst of mass migration from Japan because it led to a brief resurgence of migration from Europe, which many in Brazil considered a more desirable source. This led to the state of São Paulo eliminating its support for Japanese migration, which accordingly dropped precipitously during 1915 and 1916.[21]

It was during these early years, in 1913, that Endō Tsunehachirō (1890–1961) traveled to Brazil for the first time. Endō was twenty-three years of age when he arrived, having sailed not as a subsidized immigrant, but as a relatively rare fare-paying "regular passenger."[22] Free of any labor contract, Endō worked as a doctor's assistant before going into business on his own; he was also able to reside in the city of São Paulo, rather than on a *fazenda* in the interior. Endō would go on to become the proprietor of what seems to have been the largest and most conse-quential prewar bookselling business: Endō Shoten, or Livraria Yendo.

Endō's home prefecture of Shimane, in western Japan, shared many of the characteristics that marked the hometowns of immigrants to Brazil: spatial, eco-nomic, and social remove from the seat of governmental power in Tokyo. A small number of prefectures provided the majority of migrants to Brazil; as many as half of them came from a handful of prefectures primarily in the southwest of Japan.[23] The most common prefectures of origin during the prewar period were Okinawa, Kumamoto, Fukuoka, Hokkaidō, Fukushima, Wakayama, and Kagoshima.[24] Though there is no consensus about why these prefectures were so heavily represented, some have speculated that it was due in part to deliberate strategies of the Japanese government to relocate individuals who posed threats to the new Meiji state.[25] More commonplace factors, such as migrant networks, also help explain these statistical tendencies, but it is unlikely that their origins are entirely benign; subsequent treatment of these migrants suggests the presence of less inno-cent biases.[26]

Foremost among the recipients of this discriminatory treatment were the pre-fectures of Kagoshima and Okinawa, which faced particular barriers during these early years. Emigration to Brazil from these prefectures was banned between 1913–16, nominally because of a higher degree of illegal documentation among their emigrants than among those from other prefectures. The ban on migration from Okinawa was reinstated between 1920–26; even after it was once again removed in 1926, the Japanese government applied special conditions to migrants from that prefecture. According to the new standards, Okinawans had to have finished their compulsory education, be under forty years of age, and be married for at least three years; they could not be adopted into their wives' families, could not (in the case of women) have tattoos on the backs of their hands (the Ryukyuan tradition of *hajichi*), and had to understand "standard Japanese."[27] The last of these is prob-ably the most salient for this study; while Okinawans would have had linguistic practices that deviated most dramatically from state-sanctioned Japanese, each of these prefectures-of-origin possessed a dialect that differed notably from the Tokyo dialect, which had only recently been elevated to the status of the official national dialect.

It is often thought that the common element among all of these source prefec-tures, and thus the sole driving force behind individuals' desire to migrate, was economic distress. Economics clearly played a role in many individuals' decisions to migrate, yet while it is often thought that Japanese emigrants to Brazil left out of desperation, this was not always the case. Apparently 86 percent of the migrants who arrived between 1908 and 1922 had belonged to the landed farmers' class in Japan. Moreover, whatever their stations had been in Japan, many were able to leave their *colono* status fairly quickly and become *sitiantes*, or landed farmers, in Brazil.[28] *Colonos* were paid for the work they did tending the plantations' coffee trees; they were also allowed to grow other crops between the rows of trees for their own use. Over time, some were able to amass sufficient capital to transition from working as a *colono* to sharecropping, contract farming, or lease farming, in the hope of eventually becoming owners of their own farms.[29] The first of these Japanese landowners in Brazil were the handful of families who settled the Brazilian-government-planned Monson Daiichi Shokuminchi, near the Cerqueira César station on the Sorocabana train line.[30]

That is not to say that prospective migrants were not motivated by the availability of subsidies. After having been suspended in 1914, subsidies from the state of São Paulo resumed again in 1917 (when European immigration dropped as a result of World War I) and remained generally available until around 1921, as well as available on a limited basis, funded by private plantation owners, until as late as 1925.[31] The subsidies provided financial incentives, but the actual recruitment, transportation, and other logistics of migration were still facilitated by private Japanese migration companies. These early years saw a number of companies form and disband; though they worked in close coordination with both governments, these companies were run by private individuals like Mizuno Ryō, who had founded the first two migration companies that brought groups to Brazil. After the Takemura Emigration Company was liquidated, Mizuno formed the South American Colonization Company (南米植民株式会社); he was also involved in the merger of the Oriental Emigration Company and the Morioka Emigration Company (盛岡移民合名会社) to form the Brazilian Emigration Society (ブラジル移民組合) in 1916.[32] This movement toward consolidation of the emigration companies continued until 1920, when all of them had been merged into the Overseas Development Company (海外興業株式会社, Kaigai Kōgyō Kabushiki Kaisha, also known as the KKKK).[33]

When the subsidies from Brazil resumed on 30 June 1917, some 18,259 Japanese (*honpōjin*, 本邦人) were in Brazil; the stark gender disparity continued to exist, with 16,805 men and only 1,454 women.[34] With migration more stably subsidized by the Overseas Development Company, the community grew dramatically: more than 12,000 new migrants arrived between 1917 and 1919. From 1920, however, migration to Brazil from Japan dropped again, and remained low (around one thousand per year) until 1924. It was in response to this drop in 1920 that the Japanese government began providing some financial assistance to migrants; it gradually increased its direct and indirect assistance until 1924, when a decision was made to attempt to cover the full cost of emigrants' passage to Brazil.[35] The historian Nobuya Tsuchida identifies three factors that led to this decision: the domestic instability produced by the Great Kantō Earthquake of 1923, the realization that the São Paulo government would likely no longer subsidize migration from Japan, and the more-or-less complete closing of the United States to Japanese migration with the Immigration Act of 1924 (which included the Asian Exclusion Act.)[36] As a result of these developments, the population of Japanese in Brazil had more than doubled by 1924. According to Japanese statistics, 41,774 individuals from the inner territories of Japan (内地人) were in Brazil as of 30 June 1924.[37] More specifically, the vast majority lived in the interior of the state of São Paulo, often together in communities of various sizes. This period saw the creation of a number of Japanese colonies, which provided environments that many immigrants from Japan found particularly desirable.[38]

Ethnic enclaves were not a new phenomenon in Brazil. *Núcleos coloniais* pre-dated Japanese migration to Brazil, beginning in the early- to mid-nineteenth century. One example was Nova Odessa, a community of Russian immigrants created in 1905 for agricultural laborers.[39] Plans began to be created for similar Japanese colonies as early as 1908, when a group of politicians, businessmen, and farmers created the Tokyo Syndicate (東京シンジケート) for that purpose. This led to the creation of the Katsura, Sete Barras, and Registro Colonies in Iguape, on the coast southwest of Santos.[40] The state government provided the land, created roads, subsidized passage, and exempted the Syndicate from taxes for a period of five years; in exchange, the Syndicate agreed to populate the colony.[41] Once the agreement was in place, the Brazilian Colonization Company (ブラジル拓殖株式会社) was founded in 1913 to oversee the actual creation of the colonies.[42] By 1916, Katsura and Registro were established and running successfully. The merger of the Brazilian Colonization Company and the KKKK in 1919 made the 1920 construction of Sete Barras even easier. Together, these three colonies, which were connected by newly constructed roads not only to one another but also to ports on the Ribeira river and to other nearby towns, came to be known jointly as the Iguape Colony. By the end of 1924, more than 2,500 individuals lived in these three colonies alone, which were focused more on the production of rice than of coffee.[43]

In the years that followed these early colonies did decline, but they had set the stage for similar experiments elsewhere in Brazil. From the mid-1920s, after the early experiments with the Iguape Colony, the Japanese government focused its energies on establishing similar colonies in other areas, primarily in the interior of the state of São Paulo. The Japanese colonies took five different forms: spontaneous colonies (such as the community in Mogi das Cruzes); interior colonies built on newly opened lands, with lots sold individually (such as the Hirano Colony); colonies created by private Japanese capital (such as Bastos); communities of cotton farmers who rented land along key train lines; and colonies set up by the federal or state governments (such as the Monson colonies).[44] Living in these colonies, Japanese emigrants came into less contact with non-Japanese than one might imagine, limited in some cases to day laborers, landowners, and merchants in neighboring towns.[45] This particular collective formation likely exacerbated existing anti-Japanese sentiment, which, though not as strong or as prevalent as in the United States, had existed for some time.[46] Other likely effects were the strengthening of ethnic identification and the inhibition of Portuguese language acquisition.

In both these formal enclaves and other communities, even of smaller size, civil organizations reinforced that identification by linking Japanese immigrants not only with one another but also with the Japanese government. Japanese Associations (日本人会), as well as Young Men's and Women's Associations (青年会), soon began to emerge wherever any significant number of families settled in the same area; these associations took on many of the functions of self-governance in these colonies.[47] Among the projects they undertook were community hygiene, road and bridge maintenance, youth education (including constructing schools), establishing communal facilities for different industries, and developing transportation systems. In some cases, the groups would handle the Japanese family registries (戸籍) for the area, and occasionally even the mail service. While not invested with any authority by the Brazilian government, these organizations did have some forms of internal power, up to and including the ability to "exile" individuals who did not adhere to their rules by posting notices of exclusion (除名広告) in the Japanese-language newspapers.

The Associations also played an important role in expanding the Japanese-language reading community in Brazil. Such groups would often not only operate evening and weekend schools, but also purchased magazines that would be circulated among their members.[48] While likely exaggerated, it is worth noting that an article from 1921 suggested that a given copy of a magazine might be read by dozens of, and in some cases as many as one hundred, different people.[49] This sort of sharing of texts speaks to the demand for Japanese-language reading material among the immigrants, who enjoyed a high level of literacy. Of the individuals who arrived aboard the *Kasato-maru* in 1908, 532 (68 percent) of the 781 were recorded as literate, and it has been estimated that fewer than 10 percent of the remaining 249 were completely illiterate.[50]

Needless to say, it was not only through the sort of associations described above that individuals gained access to print culture. In addition to all of the informal avenues that would have been available to them—bringing books and magazines from Japan, trading and lending them between friends and family, etc.—a commercial marketplace for Japanese-language print culture also emerged during these early years. As will be discussed in greater length in the next chapter, locally produced Japanese-language newspapers appeared with the launch of the *Nanbei shūhō* (南米週報) in 1915 and the *Nippaku shinbun* (日伯新聞) the following year.[51] The Japanese-language weekly *Burajiru jihō*, which would go on to be the central (though not always the largest) newspaper during the prewar period, was launched in 1917 on the Taishō emperor's birthday, August 31. Not only did these newspapers carry fiction themselves, as will be discussed, but they also carried advertisements for retailers; three of these that emerged during this early period—all general trading companies that dealt with printed matter—warrant specific mention.

One of the earliest ads that explicitly mentioned books, for a general store named Kidō Shōkai (木藤商会) located in the city of São Paulo, appeared in early 1918. The company had been founded by Kidō Isoemon, who had come to Brazil from the South Pacific. His company advertised in the pages of the *Burajiru jihō* from the time the newspaper was founded, describing how it changed money and sold Japanese non-prescription medicines, carpenter's tools, Tosa-style saws, and Japanese seeds, among other things. Those advertisements reveal that during these early years, along with these other essential items, books—and dictionaries in particular—were of great importance to the immigrants. On 1 February 1918, for example, Kidō advertised two English-Japanese dictionaries attributed to Inoue (Inouye) Jūkichi.

Some of the books listed had an obvious functional value for the new immigrants. Along with a book on Western cooking, the advertisement also listed the most popular Japanese-Portuguese reference available at the time, Kanazawa Ichirō's *Portuguese (Brazilian) Conversation* (*Conversação Portguez-Japoneza*, ぽるとがる（ぶらじる）語会話). At the same time, though, not all the books on offer were so practical. The advertisement also stated that the store had a stock of over five hundred *kōdan* (講談) titles; these were nominally transcriptions of orally performed storytelling. We might note that Kidō felt it was necessary to clarify that these *kōdan* were bound, suggesting that they may have been circulating in unbound form as well. Beyond *kōdan*, Kidō also apparently had more than five hundred titles in the genres of literary works (文芸作品) and self-improvement manuals (修養書), as well as a selection of songbooks (歌本). The quantity of the stock described suggests that while this might be the first time Kidō *advertised* books, it may have been *carrying* them for some time. One month later, on 8 March 1918, Kidō offered to buy used books and noted that books were available to be lent, again reminding us that books were already circulating through the community prior to the appearance of these advertisements. The 18 March advertisement also listed a complete set of the official primary school textbooks approved by the Japanese government.

A competitor appeared a year and a half later. Segi Yosoitsu announced the opening of his store at 49 Rua Conde de Sarzedas, Segi Shōten, on 31 August 1919; his stock included cosmetics, foodstuffs, medicines, seeds, tools, and books (書籍). On 5 December 1919, Segi listed the "new" October magazine issues that had arrived at the store (and their respective prices, here in *réis*, inclusive of shipping), including: *Taiyō* (2,500), *Chūō kōron* (3,500), *Waseda bungaku* (3,600), *Bungei kurabu* (2,300), and *Fujin no tomo* (1,500). By comparison, the October *Taiyō* had sold in Japan for 50 *sen*, *Chūō kōron* for 75 *sen*, *Waseda bungaku* for 80 *sen*, *Bungei kurabu* for 45 *sen*, and *Fujin no tomo* for 30 *sen*. It noted that supplies of each issue were limited.[52] The advertisement makes it clear that Segi had entered the distribution business of Japanese newspapers and magazines, but it was not exclusively a bookseller; the advertisement also listed the non-print goods the store continued to carry. A 16 April 1920 advertisement shows that Segi also stocked some newspapers, including the *Ōsaka Mainichi shinbun* (300 *réis*, shipping included), *Taishō nichinichi shinbun* (250 *réis*), *Yorozu chōhō* (200 *réis*), and *Hōchi shinbun* (200 *réis*). Looking at a related marketplace, Hibi Yoshitaka has written about advertisements that reveal that a vast selection of newspapers from throughout the Japanese empire was available to consumers living in California as early as 1913.[53] Just as in California, such newspapers were available to Brazilian retailers, including Segi, through the large central distributors in Tokyo, such as Tōkyōdō.

The last of the three retail competitors in the bookselling business was Nakaya Shōten, which began as Nippaku Bussan Benri-gumi. Despite advertising the opening of his store on 13 February 1920, Nakaya Kumatarō had already been in business for many years. At the time that the store opening was announced, the company did not list printed matter as one of the products it handled. But by at least 11 March 1921, the company was listing fiction (小説) alongside the other non-print goods it carried; by 15 April 1921, the number of literary genres offered had increased to include *kōdan*, popular song collections, and *Naniwa bushi* (a genre of sung narrative). The company announced its new name on 10 June 1921. Kidō, Nakaya, and Segi were in direct competition, and that competition could be fierce; in at least one case, the retailers even turned to the legal system for a resolution. On 5 August 1921, both Segi and Nakaya took out ads, which appeared side by side (and contained identical text), saying that a lawsuit had been brought against them by Kidō for carrying goods falsely labeled with counterfeit trademarks, but that the lawsuit had been thrown out as groundless by the Brazilian courts.

The company that produced the *Burajiru jihō* newspaper where the three retailers advertised also joined this emerging marketplace itself.[54] On 16 July 1920, Burajiru Jihōsha announced its entrance into the business with an appeal to the life of the mind:

> In the modern world, what is it that distinguishes human superiority from inferiority? Is it skin color? Is it physical strength? Is it eloquence? No! No! No! It is nothing less than a well-founded intellect.

The company then laid out the procedure by which customers could order magazines and books from Japan through them. Magazine prices would be 2.5 times the Japanese retail price, converted to *mil réis*; the example given was for a 25-sen magazine, which would be 1.25 *mil réis*. Customers would then pay for a full year in advance (the cost of special issues would be drawn from this prepayment and settled biannually.) Book prices would (in most cases) be calculated similarly; the example here was for a two-yen book, which would be 15 *mil réis*. The company would cover customs and shipping costs, including delivery to the customer. The resultant journal prices were slightly higher than those of its competitor, Segi; *Taiyō*, for example, would have sold for 3 *mil réis* (given the 60-sen price listed in Burajiru Jihōsha's 6 August 1920 advertisement), as compared to the 2.5 *mil réis* price at Segi.

As early as 20 December 1918, Burajiru Jihōsha also advertised one of the most important dictionaries in the Japanese-speaking community in Brazil prior to the Second World War: Ōtake Wasaburō's Portuguese-Japanese dictionary. Demand must have existed through the state, since the advertisements soon listed local agents to contact in the colonies of Iguape and Ribeirão. It sold well enough that on 13 October 1920, Burajiru Jihōsha ran an ad to inform potential buyers that the dictionary was currently sold out, but that it would run another notification as soon as a new shipment had arrived. By 13 May 1921, a new shipment of the "long-awaited" dictionaries is announced, though now at the price of 12 *mil réis* (plus 1 *mil réis* for shipping.)

During these early years, Endō Tsunehachirō ran a relatively small but ambitious operation. In 1917, his wife and (at that time) two children joined him in the city of São Paulo, where he seems to have been primarily focused on selling soy sauce. The first number of *Burajiru jihō*, dated 31 August 1917, contained two separate advertisements from Endō. One (on page 11) listed Endō as the retailer for "the cheapest and most delicious soy sauce made in Brazil," Marunishi; another (on page 5) notes that even as Endō was the "sole retailer" of Marunishi soy sauce, he was also engaged in the sale of sundries (雑貨). In this advertisement he mentioned that he had recently begun making sale trips to the city of Bauru and requested the patronage of the many fine individuals living along the railroad line(s). The small scale of his operation is suggested through his request that correspondence directed at him from Bauru be sent care of (a.c., *ao cuidado de*) the Hotel Japonez, at No. 8, Rua Batista de Carvalho. Finally, an announcement (also on page 5) from the newspaper listed Endō as being in charge of subscriptions for all readers outside of the city.

Things were developing rapidly for Endō, though. Two weeks later, in the 14 September 1917 issue of the newspaper, Endō advertised that he had relocated from No. 85, Conde Sarzedas, to No. 65 of the same street. He ran variants of these ads in nearly every issue of the newspaper (save for 26 October 1917) until 16 November

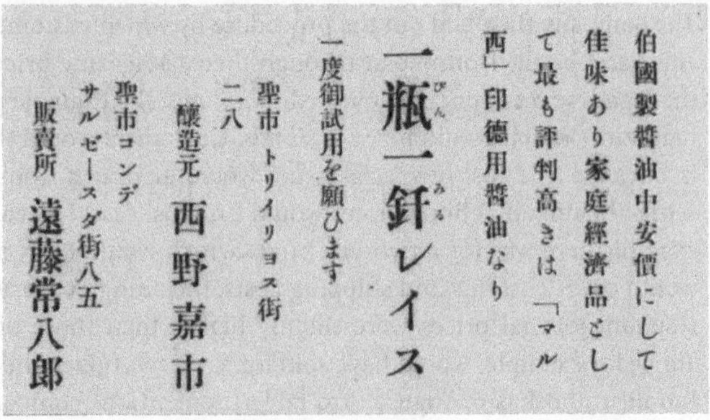

FIGURE 1. Advertisements for Endō Tsunehachirō, *Burajiru jihō*, 31 August 1917. Courtesy of the Hoji Shinbun Digital Collection

1917, when he announced that sales trips were now being made to Ribeirão Preto.[55] On 19 April 1918, Endō announced that his representative was now making sales trips along the Araraquara railway line, which ran into the interior in the northwest of the state. By 2 August 1918, Endō had extended his region along the Sorocabana line. By 7 September, he was covering the Mogiana line as well.

On 13 August 1920, Endō Shōten announced that it had opened a store in Birigui, roughly 500 kilometers from São Paulo.[56] The items advertised show the extent to which Endō's operation had grown: in addition to carrying candy and medicine, and to handling pesticide sprayers, mail, and official documents for the consulate and the Imin Kumiai (Cooperativa de Emigração para o Brasil), the store would lend books. We should note, however, that the address of the store was not given. Instead, the ad listed a *caixa postal* (post office box) at the Birigui train station. While it may well have been the case that Birigui was small enough at the time that one could find the store with little difficulty, the choice of address reveals that most of Endō's business would still be occurring via postal contact, followed by visits from traveling salemen (*viajantes*) representing Endō.

On 31 August 1923, Endō advertised as the owner of Endō Shōten, giving its address as Rua Bonita, 9, in Liberdade.[57] He explained that up until that point there had not been sufficient supply of "fancy goods" (小間物) to satisfy "the gentlewomen and young ladies in the countryside"; to remedy that, Endō had recently returned to Japan, where he had acquired a large stock. He encouraged individuals coming into the city and individuals who "wish to return briefly" (that is, to feel as though they have returned) to Japan to come visit his store. The store now had a large stock of books, including works by such authors as Kuroiwa Ruikō, Kagawa Toyohiko, Satō Kōroku, Kikuchi Yūhō, Nagata Mikihiko, Murakami Namiroku, and Tokutomi Kenjirō (Rōka). Needless to say, the store still carried a diverse range of products, including Italian-made pesticide sprayers (噴霧器).[58]

Endō did not stay at the Rua Bonita location for long; on 7 September 1923 he announced that Endō Shōten had moved to Rua Conde de Sarzedas, 23.[59] But the walk-in business in these storefronts in the city of São Paulo was likely

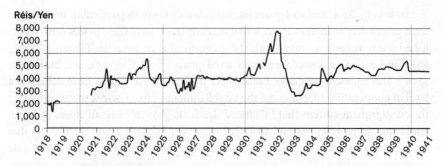

FIGURE 2. *Réis* per yen exchange rate, 1918–40.

not the center of the company's bookselling operation. At least as early as 13 June 1924, Endō Shōten began to list the titles and prices of books that it advertised as newly arrived, using the advertisement space as a form of catalog.[60] While this first catalog only listed fifteen titles, they soon grew in size. A 19 December 1924 advertisement, for example, listed over one hundred "newly arrived" titles; it also mentioned that the store had replenished its lending stock with new titles.[61] Prices in these advertisements (and those from the other companies mentioned above) often listed shipping costs or explicitly noted that prices included shipping, suggesting that the company did a lot of business by mail, sending printed matter out to the various colonies that were appearing in the interior of the state and beyond.

The prices in these advertisements show limited fluctuation, for the most part. One of the reasons for this is that the prewar period saw a reasonably stable exchange rate between the *real* and the yen, with one exception. The graph below shows the exchange rate from September 1917 through December 1940.[62] What is apparent is that between 1917 and 1921, the yen rose in relative value, from a starting level of 1900 *réis* to the level it would sustain for most of the period, between 4,000–5,000 *réis*. The most dramatic exception is the period beginning in the autumn of 1930, when the yen began a steady climb that peaked at 7753 in October 1931, only to then fall to 2579 a little more than a year later. This period of dramatic fluctuation coincided not only with the Great Depression, but also with Vargas's seizure of power in October 1930. The exchange rate returned to its previous stable level late in 1934 and remained there for the rest of the prewar period.

The marketplace for Japanese print in Brazil developed with such speed despite two of the factors that had been so pivotal for the rapid expansion of the retail market in Japan around the same time: fixed retail prices (定価) and the consignment (委託) system.[63] The fixed retail price system, established around 1920 in Japan by industry organizations such as the National League of Book Associations (全国書籍商組合連合会), minimized competition between bookstores and sustained price levels, allowing for more profitability. When shipping costs to markets in Asia, and to Japan's formal colonies there in particular, made these fixed prices detrimental to the colonial marketplaces, local fixed prices were established from as early as 1922 (with the creation of a set price in Taiwan [台湾売価]), and a general outer-territories fixed price (外地定価) was established in 1938.[64] The Japanese-language booksellers in Brazil seem not to have achieved a level of cooperation that allowed the establishment of fixed prices there. Similarly, the consignment system that facilitated dramatic growth in retail stores in Japan could not, in practice, extend to Brazil because of shipping and tariff costs that made returns impractical. As a result, the bookstores there remained under a de facto final purchase (買い切り) system. Despite the absence of these advantages, which had led to an increase from three thousand retail booksellers in Japan in 1912 to more than ten thousand by 1927, the marketplace in Brazil still saw significant growth.

Alongside this developing commercial market, there were also non-commercial efforts to disseminate Japanese-language texts throughout the various colonies in Brazil and beyond. One of the first and most visible of these efforts was led by the Rikkōkai (力行会), a group founded in Japan in 1897.[65] Nagata Shigeshi, the leader of the organization at the time, spent most of 1920 traveling through North and South America to see the conditions of Japanese emigrants to those countries. After his trip, he described his greatest source of distress as being the realization that there were so few Japanese-language books and magazines available to them.[66] He subsequently made a series of proposals for steps to improve the lives of fellow Japanese abroad using printed matter.[67]

His first plan was to establish overseas libraries, an idea he presented to the Foreign Ministry in February 1921.[68] The Ministry provided support from its private discretionary budget (機密費) and then donations were received from a variety of sources amounting to a total of 1000 yen. Moriya Hokichi, another Rikkōkai member, traveled around Japan collecting donations of books, and the organization's journal, *Rikkō sekai*, called for donations both of books and cash. In the end, Moriya had collected more than ten thousand volumes.[69] Roughly half of these he sent to countries including Mexico, Cuba, Panama, Peru, Chile, and Argentina. The other half he took to Brazil. An article in the *Burajiru jihō* in December 1921 announced that they had cleared customs.[70] Although the original plan was to send a box of books to migrant communities and then have representatives there circulate them, it was later decided to do otherwise. Instead, they were lent to Japanese Associations and youth groups (described earlier) for a term, with those groups making them available to people in their areas. The article reports that 110 requests were received from all over the country. Although the books were free to groups deemed suitable, shipping costs were to be covered by the recipient. Some of the recipients said that they had not held a book since arriving in Brazil years earlier; it was as if, the article states, they had been "starving for books."

1924-34: THE YEARS OF JAPANESE
STATE-SPONSORED MIGRATION

While the Japanese government had played a role in initiating and sustaining migration to Brazil from the beginning, in the early years the bulk of the administration was done by private emigration companies and most of the financial assistance came from Brazil. By no later than August 1922, however, the Japanese Home Ministry had already begun to work on measures by which it could more directly encourage migration to Brazil in order to prompt a significant increase in the number of people going abroad. In terms of direct support to migrants, one of the earliest forms this took was a 200-yen subvention per individual to those who had been affected by the Great Kantō Earthquake of 1923; the government began making this aid available in February 1924. By July of that year, funds had been allocated to cover the complete relocation expenses for some three thousand emigrants. The number of recipients was expanded to five thousand in 1926 and 7,750 in 1927. With steps such as these, the source of economic incentives shifted from the São Paulo state government to the Japanese government, and the period of (Japanese) state-sponsored migration (国策移民) had begun.

Various subsequent crises in the Japanese (and global) economies, beginning in 1927, incentivized the Japanese government to increase further its support for migration to Brazil, in the hopes of removing a portion of its excess labor force while providing other secondary economic benefits for Japan, including remittances from emigrants, trade with Brazil as a result of their presence, and stimulus for the shipping industry. In addition to direct financial subsidization, governmental support took other forms as well, including the creation of the Kobe Immigrants Assembly Center (国立移民収容所) in 1928. In June, 1929, the Japanese government created the Ministry of Overseas Affairs (拓務省) to oversee emigration and colonization beyond the main islands.[71] Governmental initiatives were not only occurring at the national level. The 1927 Overseas Emigration Cooperatives Act (or Emigration Cooperative Societies Law; 海外移住組合法) had enabled the creation of prefectural emigration cooperative societies to recruit and support emigrants to Brazil; by the mid-1930s, nearly every prefecture had such a society.[72]

These local activities were not operating in isolation. In 1927 the Overseas Emigration Cooperatives Federation (海外移住組合連合会) was formed to link these prefectural organizations together. By 1929, the Federation had purchased more than 500,000 acres of land in the states of São Paulo and Paraná. In March of that year it also established a subsidiary company in Brazil, the Sociedade Colonizadora do Brasil Limitada (ブラジル拓植組合 in Japanese, often shortened to "Bratac"), to oversee the founding of colonies, the managing of their lands, and the introduction of colonists. The company operated the Bastos, Tieté, Nova Aliança, and Três Barras (Paraná) colonies.[73] The company first acquired land, then sold it either to newly arrived immigrants or to immigrants already in Brazil (though the conditions of the sale changed depending on the category.) In the case of Bastos, ten-*alqueire* (roughly sixty-acre) lots cost 1,440 yen (or 7 *contos*, if bought by someone already in Brazil), though payment could be deferred until the fourth year of occupancy. They also needed to possess a significant amount of capital: 1,600 yen, if arriving from Japan. In 1930, one *conto*, or one-thousand *mil réis*, was worth 240 yen; at the time, a primary school teacher in Japan earned roughly 45 yen per month.[74] When fewer families than expected moved to Bastos, Bratac began providing incentives that proved quite successful in attracting families, not only from Japan, but also from within Brazil itself. Bratac also provided significant infrastructure for these colonies. In addition to experimental farms to grow crops other than coffee (including cotton, wheat, and tobacco), it built roads, offices, dormitories, hotels, stores, clinics, schools, power plants, mills, and other facilities that would be used in common by the colonists.[75]

While most Japanese immigrants lived in the states of São Paulo or Paraná, there were population clusters elsewhere as well. One example is the Acará Colony, with Tomé-Açu at its center, in the state of Pará in the far north of Brazil. This colony was run not by Bratac or the Overseas Development Company, but by the private South American Colonization Company (南米拓殖株式会社), founded in 1928, and its Brazilian subsidiary, the Companhia Nippônica de Plantação do Brazil S.A., founded in 1929. Some 1400 miles away from the city of São Paulo, this colony was built with facilities similar to those provided by Bratac to its colonies. This colony was not as successful in the prewar period as many of the other colonies, however, for a variety of reasons. First among these was the prevalence of malaria, which had largely been brought under control in the colonies farther to the south; this was compounded by other problems related to growing conditions, transportation, and nearby market demand.[76] In 1935 the company behind the colony turned over most of its operations to the colonists, the number of which steadily dwindled as people left for São Paulo or the nearby city of Belém.

While coffee production had driven migration from Japan, it proved to be an unstable foundation for building a sizable and enduring community in Brazil. Coffee prices fluctuated dramatically, leading the Japanese government to take dramatic steps in order to shore up the commodity price.[77] This price instability was particularly marked after the start of the Great Depression in 1929, when the price of a bag of unprocessed coffee beans dropped from 70 *mil réis* in 1928 to 8 *mil réis* in 1930. Needless to say, these devaluations were of great concern to the Brazilian government as well. In 1931, the new Vargas regime announced its plan to buy up and destroy excess coffee supplies in an effort to curb this commodity price collapse.[78] This was followed by a three-year ban on the planting of new coffee trees, announced in November 1932. The uncertainty that attended coffee prices led increasing numbers of immigrants to switch to other crops. One of the most important of these was cotton. In 1912, 92.6 percent of Japanese in Brazil were involved in coffee production, while only 1.2 percent were involved in cotton and 2.5 percent in rice; by 1937, cotton had surpassed coffee, with 32.1 percent of immigrants producing coffee, 39 percent growing cotton, and 6 percent cultivating rice.[79]

Notwithstanding this instability, immigration to Brazil from Japan increased dramatically over the decade of Japanese state-sponsored migration. 1924 saw more than four times as many immigrants from Japan as 1923 (from roughly eight hundred to roughly 3,700); this number continued to climb rapidly year after year until 1929, when more than fifteen thousand individuals undertook the journey. Many of these immigrants settled in or near the state of São Paulo.[80] In 1927, more than sixty-five thousand Japanese lived in and around the cities of São Paulo (21,303), Bauru (19,771), Riberão Preto (17,421), Santos (6,272), and Rio de Janeiro (314).[81] By October 1929, when the stock market crashed in the United States, the population of Japanese (邦人) in Brazil topped one hundred thousand.[82] Starting in 1932, the Japanese government offered ¥50 for each adult emigrant, further reducing economic barriers to migration.[83] In 1933, when Minister of Overseas Affairs Nagai Ryūtarō was asked in the House of Peers about the total amount of governmental support emigrants were receiving, he stated that each emigrant family was being subsidized (in various forms, both direct and indirect) on average ¥1,340.[84] The number of Japanese emigrating to Brazil rose to such an extent that Japan became the leading source of immigrants to Brazil during the years 1932–35.[85] According to statistics from the Japanese government, on 1 October 1935 a total of 116,502 Japanese (邦人) lived in Brazil; by this time the genders had come to be more equally represented, with 64,221 men and 52,281 women.[86] A full one-third of all the prewar immigrants from Japan arrived during the years 1930–35; in 1933, immigrants from Japan made up more than half of all those who came to Brazil.[87]

Even as the 1920s were a period of rapid and dramatic expansion of the immigrant communities from Japan, they were also a period in which a discourse emerged among the immigrants about the future of those communities. Was it appropriate for the presumption to be that the communities were transitory, with their members always looking toward a return to Japan (even if that return only happened for a small fraction of migrants), or should they begin thinking about settling permanently in Brazil? To give a sense of how powerful the expectation of eventually returning to Japan was (regardless of the reality), a 1937 survey of twelve thousand individuals living along the Noroeste line in São Paulo revealed that 85 percent intended to return to Japan eventually, 10 percent intended to stay permanently, and 5 percent were unsure.[88] This expectation often failed to be realized, as the circumstances in Brazil made it more difficult to amass any savings than it had been for earlier migrants to the United States; only around 10 percent of Japanese immigrants to Brazil ever did return.[89]

Central to this discussion (for individuals on both sides of the debate) was the education of the youngest members of the colony's population. For those who planned to return or who wanted to strengthen the linguistic competence (and thus coherence) of the ethnic population in Brazil, making sure the new generation was fluent in Japanese was essential. The first Japanese-language school, the Taishō Shōgakkō, was built in the Liberdade neighborhood of São Paulo in July 1915. By April 1932, there were a total of 187 such schools in the states of São Paulo, Paraná, and Mato Grosso, with over nine thousand students.[90] There were forces that worked against this process, however. In April 1933 new restrictions were promulgated by the Brazilian government that impacted this Japanese-language education. Not only did it become illegal to teach children ten years of age or younger a foreign language, but also teachers had to have passed Brazilian certification examinations, foreign language textbooks required approval by the Brazilian government, and textbooks that were deemed to impact negatively the development of Brazilian nationalist sentiment were banned. In 1938, the first of these rules was extended to include children fourteen and under.[91] On 25 December 1938, foreign language schools (primarily Japanese, Italian, and German) were all ordered closed.

These developments in language policy occurred against a backdrop of persistent (though not monolithic) concern about the relatively isolated colonies of Japanese immigrants, which some perceived as fundamentally unassimilable.[92] At the same time, there were moderate voices that rose in defense of the colonies: some argued for greater racial tolerance, and specifically cited the Japanese as "orderly, intelligent, and industrious." Surveys done in the mid-1920s of large plantations were cited to show that farm owners considered their Japanese employees to be "very sober, honest, orderly, and, above all, industrious without comparison." While the concerned parties never gained enough power to effect significant policy changes against these colonies, the fears persisted in many quarters. Despite the obvious contributions of these colonies to the Brazilian economy, by the mid-1930s their "social and physical isolation from the dominant society," compounded by "Japan's aggressive expansionist policy in Asia," led many to grow suspicious of them, and some to refer to them as "social cysts" (*quistos sociais*).[93]

This perception of the Japanese colonies as isolated was partially a result of their geographical remove, but was also due to their relative ethnic homogeneity, the involvement of the Japanese government in their development, and the extent of Japanese language use within them.[94] This was not merely a matter of perception within larger political struggles; it was also a source of various difficulties in daily life. The constant advertising of dictionaries and other language-learning texts speaks to these challenges. Significant language barriers existed between the first-generation immigrants and the Portuguese-speaking population, though this was somewhat mitigated not only as second-generation Portuguese-speaking children grew older, but also through interpreters who were often dispatched to the colonies. In May 1932, the Japanese Consulate General provided funds for the creation of an Agricultural Interpreters Association (耕地通訳協会, Associação dos Intérpretes), which originally had twenty-eight members but had grown to seventy-six by the end of that year.[95]

These problems aside, the intensive use of Japanese among so many of the individuals in this community caused the demand for Japanese-language texts to explode during these years of dramatic population growth. The growth led both to quantitative expansion of the market for texts, and qualitative changes in the nature of that market. For example, a 1926 advertisement for Endō suggests a number of ways in which its business was expanding. An announcement that Endō had formed a traveling reading group (巡回読書会) for its customers in the interior revealed that many of the company's customers remained far from its retail store.[96] The advertisement also mentioned that Endō carried back numbers (月遅れ) of magazines.[97] Many magazines from Japan were also available from at least 1919, when *Taiyō*, *Chūō kōron*, *Waseda bungaku*, *Shinshōsetsu*, *Bungei kurabu* and other titles were advertised.[98] Despite the distance separating the two countries, magazines arrived in Brazil not long after their cover publication date: according to one advertisement, July issues of magazines such as *Kingu* had arrived at member stores by July 10.[99] When newer issues arrived, the unsold stock from previous months was made available at reduced prices; the frequency of advertisements listing such titles reveals that demand remained high for periodicals even when their characteristic timeliness was diminished.

Another telling element of the April 1926 advertisement for Endō is its announcement of the "restocking" (再着) of a number of books, mostly concerning child-raising and hygiene, which presumably had attracted more interest than the original supply could meet. The booklists that appear in the advertisements of Endō and other booksellers do not reveal the quantities that were available; the possibility exists that in many cases only one copy of each book was purchased. It does seem, however, that the lists present newly arrived books, rather than the store's entire stock; a large, half-page advertisement on 4 April 1934, for example, listed titles specifically as "Newly Arrived Books."[100] Though the precise size of the market is unclear, what we do observe is Endō's increasing ability to sustain itself on that market alone. By 1928 Endō was representing itself as "specializing in books," despite its continuing to advertise other goods.[101] Although most of its sales likely continued to be made by mail, a series of moves suggests that the walk-in trade was also growing. On 30 August 1928, Endō Shōten announced that it was moving to a new location at Rua Conselheiro Furtado, 8.[102] Finally, in 1932, Endō changed the name of the company slightly but significantly from *shōten* (商店, general store) to *shoten* (書店, bookstore).[103]

We have some sense of the titles available in Brazil during these first decades, thanks to these advertisements that listed specific stock.[104] They suggest a dramatically increasing selection, as these mini-catalogs grow from lists of fifteen titles in

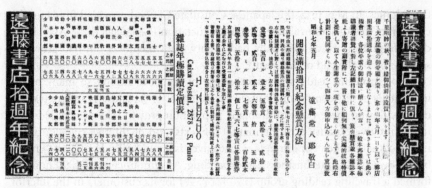

FIGURE 3. Endō Shoten, *Burajiru jihō*, 19 May 1932. Courtesy of the Museu Histórico Regional Saburo Yamanaka and the Kokusai Nihon Bunka Kenkyū Sentaa.

1924 to lists of nearly four hundred titles in 1935.[105] While this information verifies that a plentiful supply of printed matter from Japan was available, it still fails to illuminate the size of the audience. While limited, some additional data contributes to our understanding of the magnitude of the market for Japanese-language print. For example, two data points suggest the grossest of quantitative measures of that market: we know, for example, that 5,674 kilograms of books and magazines were imported into Brazil from Japan in 1928, and 7,147 kilograms in 1931.[106] Needless to say, such data provides us only the most general sense of the market's size. A small number of data points do exist, however, that illuminate details about the nature of this readership.

Analysis of a sample of newly arrived inventory advertised in the *Burajiru jihō*, for example, suggests that when consumers in Brazil bought books, they turned to authors who also enjoyed great popularity in Japan.[107] One of the most popular was Sasaki Kuni (1883–1964), who had himself lived in the Japanese colonial city of Busan, where he worked as a teacher and wrote his first work, 1909's *Itazura kozō nikki* (『いたづら小僧日記』). Between 1935 and 1940, at least twenty separate titles of Sasaki's appeared in bookstore advertisements. Kōdansha, which published many of Sasaki's works, was the source of many of the magazines and books in Brazil; the company, which regularly advertised its magazines in the Japanese-language papers, seems to have consciously cultivated the market. Books by Noma Seiji (1878–1938), the founder of Kōdansha, appeared at least fifteen times during the same period.

After Sasaki, the most popular authors were Noma, Tsurumi Yūsuke (1885–1974), Kikuchi Kan (1888–1948), and Naoki Sanjūgo (1891–1934), all of whom appeared at least thirteen times. The works of Tsurumi Yūsuke, who was both a politician and novelist, were the most diverse, with novels (*Haha* 『母』, *Ko* 『子』, *Chichi* 『父』), books on famous Westerners (Disraeli, Napoleon, Byron,

Bismarck), and treatises on Japanese expansion (『膨張の日本』). Works by Kikuchi Kan appeared over the longest span of time, from 1924 until 1940. By contrast, Naoki Sanjūgo's works appeared in a clump soon after his death on 24 February 1934. That is not to say that more unusual books did not appear as well. One example might be the work of the half-Russian, half-Japanese author Ōizumi Kokuseki (1894–1957), one of which appeared as early as 1924.

We also have some insight into one sample population and its consumption of print. In 1939, an almanac produced by the publisher of the *Nippaku shinbun* included a survey of reading habits of the approximately 11,500 households located in the Bauru region, along two major train lines (Noroeste and Paulista) in São Paulo. These households would have been almost exclusively rural and engaged in agriculture, as the region does not include the city of São Paulo. The survey found that of these households, 1,078 purchased "children's magazines," 1,908 purchased "women's magazines," 5,967 purchased "men's magazines," and 10,154 purchased newspapers.[108] Nearly every household, that is, purchased a newspaper. The survey notes, however, that it was very unusual for families to read newspapers from Japan; the vast majority were published in Brazil.

We have a little more detailed information about magazines. In 1935, when the total number of migrants to Brazil had surpassed 170,000, a single newspaper article gives us a glimpse into the magnitude of that market.[109] According to that article, August 1935 marked the first month in which more than ten thousand Japanese-language magazines were imported into Brazil. Of these, 35 percent were of one magazine: *Kingu* (the first Japanese magazine to have a circulation in excess of one million), with 3,500 copies. The next was *Shufu no tomo*, one of the most popular "women's magazines" in Japan, with 1,200 copies. By contrast, only eighty copies of *Kaizō* and seventy copies of *Chūō kōron* entered the country that month.

Although I have not found any evidence of a booksellers' association (書籍組合) of the sort that existed throughout Japan, its colonies, and even North America, an advertisement from 11 July 1929 reveals the existence of an importing collective, the São Paulo Motherland Products Import Association (サンパウロ母国品輸入組合), which possessed a book and magazine division (書籍雑誌部).[110] This particular advertisement announced the arrival of more than 250 newly published book titles (including prices, but not authors) to be offered for sale at stores that were members of the association. The advertisement lists twenty-one members in various cities.[111] Stores that specialized in books emerged, not just in the city of São Paulo, but in the interior as well. A few examples from the mid-1930s were Nippon Shoten in Lins, Chiyoda Shoten in Santos, Takahashi Yūmeidō (Livraria dos Amigos) in Araçatuba (with a branch store in Guararapes), Mikado Bunbōgu-ten in Bastos, and Mariria Shoten in Marília.[112]

There are indications that these competitors would work in concert when it suited their interests, even in the absence of a formal booksellers' association, as when increased costs necessitated across-the-board price hikes. For example, on 15 February 1932, Nakaya Shōten, Hase Shōten, and Endō Shoten published a joint announcement in the *Burajiru jihō*, in which they explained that they had intended to drop their magazine prices as a result of currency fluctuations, but that this had been rendered impossible by the recent changes in Brazilian postal law. In December 1931, the Departamento de Correios e Telégrafos (Department of Mail and Telegraphs) had been established within the Ministry of Industry, Transport, and Public Works. The three booksellers claimed that the new postal laws had resulted in a tripling of postal rates. On 15 May 1937, another notification explained that magazine prices had been raised due to a doubling of postage on materials sent overseas from Japan that went into effect on April 1.[113] The notification was sponsored by six stores carrying Japanese-language magazines in the city of São Paulo: Hase Shoten, Nakaya Shōten, Kunii Shōten, Sugayama Shōten, Endō Shoten, and Tōyō Shoten.

This increasingly large and mature marketplace for print seems to have come to the attention of Tokyo-based publishers from at least 1929, when they began running sizable advertisements in the local vernacular newspapers. For print capital based in Tokyo, these migrant communities presented a rich new market, an audience thought to have an insatiable desire for the cultural products of their home. Tokyo-based publishers and Brazil-based retailers launched significant newspaper advertising campaigns—more than the largely functional advertisements seen prior to this time—directed at these consumers. As one advertisement had it: "In a foreign land, without a doubt one of the greatest sources of consolation is a magazine from dear old Japan."[114]

Homesickness was not the only object of these advertisements: publishers and booksellers recognized that they could use a litany of fears that they presumed were shared by the community—of falling out of touch, of being insufficiently patriotic, of somehow becoming less-than-fully Japanese—to sell their products as the solution to this alienation of a diasporic existence.[115] Appeals to nationalism seemed to have been used to lend gravity to advertisements from early on:

> With the conclusion of the agreement to reduce military forces [the Five-Power Naval Limitation Treaty, signed 6 February 1922], the age of military might has ended and a new age of intellectual competition has begun. In order to stand at the forefront of society henceforth, the natural next step is for each and every individual to refine his intellect and expand his ken. To that end, our company has the ambitious plan to distribute broadly and rapidly an even greater range of newly published books and magazines from the homeland, which are the source of this intellectual strength.[116]

The companies also took advantage of concerns thought to be shared by many of the migrants, that they were being left behind as Japan moved forward without them:

> With each passing day, with each passing month, your motherland's culture is advancing. Is it not the case that all of you are falling behind? It is for this reason

in particular that we consider our work of importing new books and offering them to you to be a service to society.[117]

Companies based in Tokyo were also aware of the effectiveness of this rhetoric in stirring both nationalism and insecurity:

> To all of our readers in foreign countries!! Aren't you thrilled to hear news from the homeland when you are abroad? It is magazines from the homeland that allow you to forget the sadness of being all alone in this world and feel the ease and consolation you would enjoy if you were there!! Women's magazines in particular are the singular sustenance of the soul for all of you overseas!![118]

As Japanese militarism increased the rhetoric escalated commensurately, tapping nationalism, alienation, fear, and pride all at once:

> The nation's (国家) greatest blessing and its ultimate root is its unaffected and vigorous spirit. At this very moment the homeland, which is once again facing unprecedented adversities, has keenly committed itself to those virtues. Our homeland cultivated its national prestige through the efforts of the patriotic Japanese spirit and the national unity of seventy million brethren until it became the Japan that now shines brilliantly amid the countries of the world. This is not an autumn [n.b.: the ad appeared in late autumn, given the local season in Brazil] through which we, alone here in a foreign land, can remain uninvolved. We wish to draw on this new Japanese spirit, devise methods of spiritual cultivation, and display that spirit to people of other nations as men of the world. For some time now, our store has dedicated all of its energies to the advancement of the national (国民) spirit through its spirit of enterprise devoted to our nation. We believe that the regular reading of magazines from the homeland is the greatest means to cultivate the Japanese spirit here in this foreign land. With this in mind, we . . . have begun soliciting subscriptions for the coming year at prices that sacrifice our margin even as we offer valuable prizes for subscribers. We strongly hope that our loyal readers will continue to elevate Japan's national prestige.[119]

Print capitalism rapidly adapted to what it thought to be the specific psychology of its immigrant consumers in the hopes of marketing products as effectively as possible.

1934–41: A SIZABLE, STABILIZED MARKETPLACE

Despite this rapid expansion of immigration from Japan in the first part of the 1930s, some developments were already underway that would put an end to this rapid growth. With regard to the domestic situation within Brazil, one series of developments demands particular attention. In October 1930, Getúlio Vargas led a coup d'état that overthrew the existing government, and shortly thereafter declared a (limited) moratorium on immigration for the year 1931.[120] Because the moratorium explicitly exempted agricultural workers (under certain conditions), immigration from Japan did not cease; it did, however, fall during that year. The pressure from *fazendeiros* (plantation owners) in São Paulo against this ban was great; their desire for laborers from Japan, in fact, regularly exceeded the number that the KKKK could recruit.[121]

The pro-immigration position of the plantation owners in São Paulo, however, differed from the anti-immigration (particularly anti-Japanese immigration) position of certain racist intellectuals and politicians, particularly in the state of Rio de Janeiro. With the new Vargas regime, these groups found a political environment that was more receptive to their thinking, which saw Japanese immigrants as both unassimilable (and thus destabilizing to the nation) and possibly even agents of Japanese imperial expansion. This led to the addition of the "Miguel Couto Amendment" to the 1934 Constitution, which imposed a quota on subsequent immigration.[122] Modeled on the similar system in the United States, the quota limited annual immigration to 2 percent of the total number of immigrants from the source country over previous fifty years. The desired effect of this quota system was to significantly limit migration from Asia, and Japan in particular. The quota set for Japan, based on an extrapolated total drawn from migration between 1908–33, was 2,711 persons (as compared to 11,498 for Portugal, 3,838 for Italy, and 6,039 for Spain, for example).[123] Pressure from pro-Japanese immigration advocates resulted in adjustments and exemptions being made to this quota, thus diminishing its impact through 1937, when various factors (including the outbreak of war with China) led to an even more dramatic decline.[124]

On the other side of the Pacific, the focus of migration also shifted around this time. Although migration to Manchuria from Japan had been discussed by the Japanese government as early as 1906, the general attitude was that it was not as promising as migration to Korea, Taiwan, or even the Americas.[125] After the Japanese government established the puppet state of Manchukuo in 1932, however, this began to change quickly. By 1936, the Hirota cabinet had made emigration to, and colonization of, Manchuria a priority of state policy; the concomitant state support transformed what had been a local movement of minimal size into a phenomenon with national scope. Whereas an estimated 15,079 individuals had migrated to Manchuria between 1932 and 1936, 140,363 migrated there between 1937 and 1941.[126]

Despite this shift, the preceding decades had already resulted in a significant population of Japanese citizens in Brazil, and an even larger population of individuals who could comprehend the Japanese language to some extent. The precise size of that population, however, is not entirely clear. The 1940 Brazilian census gives us some information about the "Japanese" population in that country on the eve of the Second World War, the vast majority (87 percent) of whom were still involved in agriculture, though many of these had shifted to cultivating cotton after the weakening of the coffee market.[127] According to that source, 140,693 Japanese lived in Brazil. Of these, 77,200 were men and 63,493 were women. More than half of them were twenty-nine years of age or younger. 3,830 individuals born in Japan—2,292 men and 1,538 women—were naturalized Brazilian citizens.[128]

At first glance, these numbers seems to contradict the 1 October 1940 count of "countrymen" (邦人) performed by the Japanese government. According to this, 202,514 were living in Brazil.[129] In this case, "countrymen" seems to refer to individuals who, as in the *Nihon teikoku kokusei ippan* (日本帝国国勢一班) conducted by the Ministry of Home Affairs (内務省), had their permanent residence (本籍, the location of their family registry [戸籍]) in the "inner territories" of the Japanese empire.[130] That is, this number included both individuals with Japanese citizenship and individuals with dual citizenship (whom the Brazilian government would have excluded from their total); on the other hand, it would have excluded (for example) individuals with one or more parents who were either voluntarily or involuntarily (as Japanese citizenship required a Japanese father) excluded.

Brazilian-born citizens who possessed one or more parents with Japanese citizenship also make the total number of "Japanese" (in terms of heritage) hard to calculate. The principle of *jus soli* has been a part of Brazilian law since its inclusion in the 1824 Constitution; Japan, however, has followed the principle of *jus sanguinis* since its 1899 Nationality Law (国籍法). As a result, children born of Japanese fathers in Brazil were eligible for dual citizenship. After amendment of the Nationality Law in 1924, however, such children lost their Japanese citizenship two weeks after birth unless they expressly retained it; from 1924, individuals with dual citizenship gained the right to renounce their Japanese citizenship without permission from the Minister of the Interior.[131] It would seem, however, that most children born of Japanese fathers retained their Japanese as well as their Brazilian citizenship, and would have had little cause to renounce either; one source estimates that only around 2,600 children had opted out of their Japanese citizenship.[132] According to a 1937 survey of 23,549 births to Japanese in the vicinity of Bauru, 52.2 percent maintained dual citizenship, 45.2 percent took Brazilian citizenship only, and 2.6 percent took Japanese citizenship only. A full 35 percent of the 45,637 Japanese citizens living in Bauru in 1937 were second-generation.[133] It is possible that in 1940 the number of Nipo-Brasileiros, regardless of citizenship, was in excess of 100,000, making the total number of individuals who might be classified as "Japanese" (in one sense or another) between 200,000 and 250,000.[134]

What is perhaps more germane to this study is the language capacities of these individuals. According to the 1940 Brazilian census, 192,698 individuals stated that Japanese, rather than Portuguese, was the language they used at home; of this number, 70,476 were Brazilian-born, 2,887 were naturalized Brazilians, and 119,095 were foreign nationals.[135] That is to say, roughly 84 percent of male Japanese citizens and 86 percent of female Japanese citizens spoke Japanese at home, whereas 72 percent of male and 80 percent of female naturalized Brazilians of Japanese birth did. In terms of Brazilian-born descendants of foreign-national fathers,

104,355 listed their fathers as Japanese; of these, 69,304 (66 percent) declared that they did not usually speak Japanese at home.[136] Of the 3,830 naturalized Brazilians of Japanese birth, 1,425 (37 percent) were described as not speaking Portuguese "correctly" and 2,870 (67 percent) were described as not usually speaking Portuguese in the home.[137] Of the 140,693 Japanese citizens who lived in Brazil, 64,736 (46 percent) were described as not speaking Portuguese "correctly" and 119,499 (85 percent) were described as not usually speaking Portuguese at home.[138] When we consider this information in light of the fact that the practice of reading aloud (音読) still persisted in some settings, it seems clear that while most of the individuals consuming Japanese-language literary texts would have been first-generation migrants from Japan, there may have been many 1.5-generation and second-generation Nipo-Brasileiros who were exposed to the works in one form or another as well.

As discussed previously, a diverse array of sources for Japanese-language texts developed during the 1920s and 1930s, with many retailers participating in the marketplace. By the close of that period, however, two key players seemed to have emerged from among this varied competition. In its discussion of the state of the Japanese community in Brazil in 1939, the *Burajiru ni okeru Nihonjin hattenshi* (1953) named only two bookstores in its list of examples of businesses that grew quickly amid the boom in import/export business that year: Endō Shoten and Tōyō Shoten.[139] This suggests that people had begun to depend on these specialized bookstores, rather than the various general stores. Endō Shoten has already been discussed in detail throughout this chapter; the history of Tōyō Shoten, by contrast, is somewhat harder to reconstruct.

Part of this difficulty is that multiple concerns used variants of this common name. Between the late 1920s and the start of the Second World War, the city of São Paulo had at least three bookstores bearing names that might have been rendered in Portuguese as "Livraria Oriental": Tōyō Shobō (東洋書房), Tōyō Shoin (東洋書院), and Tōyō Shoten (東洋書店). The second and third of these were related operations; it is not clear that there is a link with the first. Tōyō Shobō, owned by Takeuchi Yosojirō, was active during at least 1928 and 1929.[140] Takeuchi passed away on 20 April 1928, but by July 27 the store was advertising once again and remained in business until at least the end of June, 1929.[141] While I have not yet discovered a link with the other two companies, it seems unlikely that such similarly named operations would have co-existed without any connection at all. Given the distressed nature of Tōyō Shobō's ownership in 1929, it is possible that the subsequent businesses took over the operation.

Tōyō Shoin, known in Portuguese as Livraria Oriental, was run by the author of a Portuguese conversation manual titled *Jitsuyō Burajiru-go*, Iwakami Saisuke, who had arrived in Brazil on 28 August 1931. While it is possible that Iwakami took over the business that had been operated by Takeuchi, it is also possible that the businesses merely shared a fairly intuitive name for such a bookstore. Tōyō Shoin seems to have specialized in the back issues of magazines that were discussed previously. For example, an advertisement from 6 July 1933 listed issues of popular magazines dating from February 1932 to March 1933, for anywhere from 2.1 *mil réis* to 4.1 *mil réis*. They did, however, also carry books. The company continued in this fashion until 11 April 1934, when it merged with the Goseikai (互生会).[142]

Not only was the Goseikai not a bookseller, it was not even primarily a commercial venture. The founder of the organization, the physician Takaoka Sentarō, had arrived in Brazil in June 1917 as the commissioned doctor for the Overseas Development Company, having previously worked at the Meiji Byōin in Fukushima.[143] In 1924, Takaoka was made director of the newly founded Dōjinkai, which engaged in medical research on key diseases such as malaria; the organization published a number of books on hygiene, prevention, and treatment. Traveling throughout the immigrant colonies in Brazil, Takaoka played a central role in addressing a variety of communicable diseases that were affecting those communities.

Takaoka established the Goseikai in 1933, chiefly in order to improve hygienic practices within immigrant households.[144] In addition to its section dedicated to hygiene, this "department store of social projects" had five additional divisions: publishing, information, education, consultation, and book retailing. The Goseikai considered the proliferation of Japanese-language magazines to be a worthy social project; to that end, it advertised that it was making magazines available nearly at cost.[145] The Goseikai argued that the magazines would help second-generation Japanese learn characters (漢字) and thus avoid what the organization believed was an inevitable weakening of their minds in Brazil. On 11 April 1934, the Goseikai announced that its book division would merge with Tōyō Shoin to form a new Goseikai retail book division.[146] On 18 April 1934, the new advertisements for the Goseikai Retail Book Division, also known as the Livraria Goseikai, appear within advertisements for the Goseikai itself.[147]

At the same time, the Goseikai reiterated its offer to other bookstores to provide distribution services to them, promising advantageous wholesale rates to any bookstore that became one of its special retail agents (特約店). This had been the relationship of Tōyō Shoin to the Goseikai since at least 14 April 1932. The Goseikai offered its services as a distributor of specially priced new books and *tsuki-okure* magazines to its special retail agents, which they limited to only one per community. As of 9 May 1934, the organization stated that it had already concluded agreements with agents in Lins, Cafelândia, Marília, Bastos, Registro, Santos, Campinas, Guararapes, Campo Grande, and Cambará.[148] They also began recruiting sales representatives; by 23 May 1934, they had people in Penápolis, Marília, Bela Cruz, Pompéia, Aliança, Cerqueira César, Agudos, Mato Grosso, and Tietê.[149] This number, and the regions they covered, increased over the subsequent weeks.

The Goseikai continued to function as a distributor of books and magazines from Japan, going on to develop the Goseikai Shōhi Kumiai (消費組合), which required that people become members in order to purchase from it.[150] On 8 August 1934, Goseikai Shoten relocated to Rua Conselheiro Furtado, 2-A; the same advertisement lists eight regional special sales agent stores (特約販売店), most of which were general stores (商店).[151] These were located in Lins, Cafelândia, Bastos, Jaboticabal, Birigui, Campo Grande, and Marília. On 16 October 1935, Livraria Goseikai (互生会書店) advertised a practical Portuguese conversation and composition (会話・作文実用ブラジル語) textbook, written by Iwakami.[152] An identical ad appears in the *Nippaku shinbun* as late as 25 July 1936.

At some point between June 1936 and May 1937, it seems likely that Iwakami changed the name of the Goseikai Shoten to Tōyō Shoten. That is not to say that the Goseikai did not continue in the publishing business. On 9 March 1937, for example, the Goseikai published a notification that the *Burajiru no katei isho* (医書) had been delayed by a printing problem but was now available and would be delivered to those who had pre-ordered.[153] No street address was given (only a postal box number), nor was the bookstore mentioned in the advertisement. It is also possible that the Goseikai continued to function as a book and magazine wholesaler. Its retail operation remained under the direction of Iwakami, but with a new name.[154] Whatever the relation between the two stores, Tōyō Shoten's operation was large: on 1 December 1939, the bookstore ran a massive, full-page catalog-style ad listing hundreds of titles.[155] This complex history might explain why the *Hattenshi* would have identified the operation alongside Endō Shoten, despite the fact that the former had only been in business under its current name for relatively short period.

This was the peak of the marketplace for books in prewar Brazil. In late 1939, with the creation of its Departamento de Imprensa e Propaganda, the Brazilian government began censoring Japanese-language newspapers and magazines. That year saw a net loss in immigration from Japan, with 1,314 new immigrants arriving, but 2,011 returning to Japan. In January 1940, the Brazilian government began a registry of foreign residents. The last boatload of prewar immigrants arrived in June 1941. From August 1941, publication of foreign-language newspapers was banned.[156] According to Mario Yendo, the son of Endō Tsunehachirō, Endō Shoten's retail sales were severely disrupted by the end of imports from Japan in November 1941, but the company remained in business after that, continuing to lend books out of a storage room even after the store was closed, until 1942, when the government truly cracked down and gathered up Japanese-language texts. Endō Shoten would not reopen until 1947.[157]

TERRITORIALIZATION AND JAPANESE LITERATURE

As the preceding overview shows, "Japan" as a polity had a central role in determining the scope and nature of the potential reading community and thus is a logical factor to bring into any consideration of these texts and their readers in the aggregate. To suggest, however, that this government's impact was the only one of significance would be mistaken. Not only was Japan not the only nation involved, but in addition other political formations (such as Brazilian states or Japanese prefectures) at different levels of locality had a similarly important impact. Similarly, spatial proximity or lack thereof had a noteworthy impact on the accessibility of texts, reminding us of one of the many ways that literature and territories are linked.

What does this partial snapshot of the marketplace for Japanese-language literary texts in São Paulo tell us? One thing is obvious: that the literary marketplace in Brazil was closely connected with the literary marketplace in Japan, itself concentrated almost entirely in Tokyo. Yet, as with regional markets there and throughout the empire, the selection was limited, idiosyncratic, and operating on an altered temporality from that of Tokyo (much less that of an idealized literary history), and the texts that dominated all of these markets were not the texts that dominate our critical attention. Having said that, attention to polities, and borders in particular, is important: sheer geographical distance, shipping costs (and lack of unified shipping costs within a given political territory), taxation, the persistence of a de facto final sales system rather than the adoption of a consignment system, and the altered impact of censorship regimes all speak to the salience of political boundaries and unified territories. In these aspects and more, the function of the national polity in thinking about texts in the aggregate is essential, but the nature of that function is not self-evident.

3

Culture

Samurai, Spies, and Serialized Fiction

The notion of a national literature may be invoked in a variety of situations, in conjunction with a number of distinct claims. One such claim, be it explicit or implicit, is that the texts are related to a distinct, singular culture. In this case, the claim may invoke the notion of culture itself in a productively ambiguous way, referring both to a broad definition of culture—all the shared daily practices that are presumed to make one community of individuals different from another—and to a narrow definition of culture: the shared creative (in this case literary) products that (putatively) both reveal and reproduce the particular genius of that community. In many cases, the latter notion is treated as so self-evident as to require neither evidence nor a clear explication of what sort of relationships are supposed to obtain between the nation on the one hand and the works, the authors, and the readers on the other.

Frequently the focus is on the production side of texts, considering commonalities in authors' identification, experience, or environment to justify grouping their works together. In many cases a homology is then presumed between this production side and the consumption side, at least with a text's "original" readers, implying that they would have shared these commonalities as well. In the case of Japanese-language literature there seems often to be an operative assumption that the readers are "Japanese" in the same way the writers are "Japanese"; when the focus is on high-brow literary texts, there is an implication that the texts participate in a dialogue of a similar sort, together forming a literary culture (narrowly defined) and portraying a national culture (broadly defined). The shared literary culture then somehow simultaneously reflects a given community's particularities and, in the case of its literary canon, its most profound insights. As a result, the function of such a canon is alternatively imagined as both performative (reflecting

41

the national character) and pedagogical (molding national subjects to come into alignment with this national ideal.)[1]

When we consider actual experiences of readers, however, we realize that reading does not adhere to an idealized canon as defined by a prescriptive winnowing of texts produced. A descriptive record of actual consumption reveals a far less disciplined model. Readers are exposed to a wide diversity of texts and may not interpret the texts they read through the lens—generic or national, for example— foregrounded by the literary historian. As one example, we might consider the case of Kiyotani Masuji (1916–2012). Born in Hiroshima, Kiyotani migrated to Brazil in 1926 at the age of ten. In his 1985 memoir he describes the reading he did as a young man in prewar Brazil, presumably during the 1920s and 1930s. He writes:

> How many hundreds, thousands, of novels did I read? Starting with the *kōdan* in the Tachikawa Library series (if these can be called novels) and other juvenilia, magazines of all types, newspaper fiction, novels. In terms of types, I read lowbrow works, pure literature, and translations. There was practically never a day that went by without me reading some fiction of one type or another.[2]

Kiyotani's adult self retroactively applies the categories of literary analysis— particularly the pure/lowbrow divide that functions as a primary mechanism of canonization—but what characterizes the reading experiences of his youth is the inability of these categories to effectively discipline his consumption. It is likely that Kiyotani's experience, while perhaps exceptional in terms of the quantity of his reading, is not so in terms of its diversity.

In considering the Japanese-language literary activities of prewar Brazil, then, we must note important ways in which the production and consumption sides are asymmetrical. While the authors of (nearly all) the texts this chapter examines— the long-form "popular" literature serialized in locally produced newspapers— had no direct relation (or perhaps even awareness) of the community in Brazil, their texts were likely the most widely read Japanese-language fiction in that community. From the perspective of readers, it is inarguable that they played a central role in the Japanese literary activities of prewar Brazil, if we grant reading the same amount of attention as we do writing. Moreover, a preliminary analysis of the texts suggests that they do, in fact, seem to tell us something about the production side as well, and that they cannot be seen as simply the borrowed cultural objects of another, putatively central, monolithic community in Japan.

BACKGROUND

As noted in the last chapter, a 1939 survey of reading habits of the approximately 11,500 households located in the Bauru region found that nearly every household purchased a newspaper and that the vast majority were Japanese-language newspapers published in Brazil.[3] What these statistics suggest is that if a reader of Japanese in Brazil prior to the Second World War were to have access to prose fiction, rather than the books and magazines from Japan that were circulating throughout the marketplace described in the previous chapter, it would likely be in the form of the serialized novels carried in the locally produced Japanese-language newspapers.

The first Japanese-language newspapers produced in Brazil appeared less than a decade after the first immigrants arrived from Japan in 1908. As the historian (and emigrant to Brazil) Handa Tomoo (1906–96) wrote, not only did these newspapers provide news more promptly than imported journals, they also became a forum for immigrant intellectuals and opinion makers; as a result, they contributed to a growing consciousness among immigrants of themselves as "(Japanese) countrymen in Brazil" (在伯同胞).[4] One major component of these newspapers was prose fiction, the diverse forms of which made up a literary ecosystem in their pages, though that metaphor suggests a greater level of organicity and interrelation than necessarily existed. Perhaps rather than an ecosystem, it would be better described as a cultivated field, with genres and works selected consciously (though with varying levels of care) to speak to different expectations and desires.

The forms of fiction these papers carried included realistic pieces set in Brazil, tales of swordsmen set in the past, stories of detectives and "poison women" set in the present, translated works from Portuguese and English (and perhaps other languages as well), comedic anecdotes, and accounts of the mysterious, just to name the most prominent. The few studies that thus far have been undertaken of Japanese-language fiction in Brazil have understandably focused on the first of these categories, perhaps assuming that the other categories were generic products of a cultural industry based in Japan.[5] Such an assumption would be justified, at least to a certain extent. As will be discussed in detail below, most of these works were produced in Japan and ended up in Brazil after passing through a system of literary production and distribution that might be characterized as semi-industrial.

At the same time, however, ignoring these works means ignoring the vast majority of the fiction that would have been available to the readers in Brazil at the time. A closer look at these serialized works gives us a more complete understanding of the Japanese-language literary landscape of Brazil prior to World War II. Moreover, changes over the period examined reveal that this "industrial" system of literary production and distribution, while centered in Japan, likely did not result in a uniform literary culture throughout Japan itself, much less the Japanese-reading community abroad. Instead, it seems likely to have created particular local literary environments emerging from a concentrated (and thus perhaps somewhat homogenized) creative source. If this is in fact the case, it further problematizes the notion of a singular aggregate "Japanese literature" usually implied within the logic of national literatures.

By examining the literary texts most readily available to Japanese-language readers in Brazil, we find one example of a community possessing a potential shared literary culture related, but not identical, to those in similar communities within Japan. What is perhaps more significant is the fact that this would not have made this reading community exceptional, despite the radical difference in historical circumstances from other intra-national (and intra-imperial) Japanese-language reading communities. Instead, it is likely that the reading community formed by this concrete medium of text circulation bore a close structural resemblance to local readerships outside of the largest metropolitan areas in Japan. Though some regional newspapers in Japan had begun to affiliate with the large, national newspapers prior to the Second World War—and thus often share works of serialized fiction with other newspapers within those networks—unaffiliated newspapers filled their pages using many of the same mechanisms that were used in Brazil at this time.

We can see in newspaper fiction both of the distinct mechanisms that Benedict Anderson describes: namely, the effect of simultaneity, as readers consume texts synchronously through the medium of the newspaper, and the effect of interpellation, as texts hail readers to a common national identity.[6] The time-sensitive nature of these texts (readers wanting to know what happens next, as soon as possible, and in many cases doing so essentially simultaneously with one another) largely conforms to the synchronicity stressed by Anderson, even if there were also cases of asynchronous consumption. At the same time, these texts raise serious questions about the interpellative mechanism described by Anderson, in which there seems to be a tacit assumption that readers will respond affirmatively to (and recognize uniformly) forms of national identity-interpellation present in a given text. While it is impossible to know with precision how individual readers responded to identities implied by texts, it is possible to imagine alternate forms of identification (beside one associated with the nation) that would have been available to all readers, and perhaps these deterritorialized readers more than most.

With these questions in mind, this chapter considers one subsection of the literary ecosystem of Japanese-language newspapers in Brazil: the lengthy serializations, located in high-profile positions within the newspapers, which would conventionally be categorized as "popular fiction." The focus will be on the *Burajiru jihō*, which both enjoyed the widest circulation over the period studied and provided the most literary content. While the resulting picture is incomplete, even for this one community, it nonetheless presents us with a sense of what may have been the widest read Japanese-language fiction in Brazil between 1917 and 1941.

JAPANESE-LANGUAGE NEWSPAPERS IN BRAZIL

The first newspaper produced in Brazil was the *Shūkan Nanbei*, a weekly mimeograph established in early 1916 by Hoshina Ken'ichirō. At the time there were roughly fifteen thousand immigrants from Japan in Brazil, most of whom (as described in the previous chapter) were working as agricultural laborers in the countryside, spread throughout the state of São Paulo; by contrast, only around two or three hundred Japanese immigrants lived in the city of São Paulo. This was not the first newspaper that Hoshina had worked on, and Brazil was not his first home in the Western Hemisphere; he was a serial migrant, having originally emigrated to Hawaii, where he had run a Japanese-language newspaper, and then to Texas, where for many years he had been involved in large-scale rice farming. Nor was Brazil his first destination in South America: in 1909, prior to relocating to Brazil, he had moved to Argentina. Hoshina's *Shūkan Nanbei* ran for slightly longer than two years before folding.[7] According to Kōyama Rokurō, the newspaper carried a variety of material, including a column dedicated to local literary production.[8]

The second major newspaper produced and the one that came to be the primary rival of the *Burajiru jihō* during the prewar was the *Nippaku shinbun* (日伯新聞), originally conceived of by Kaneko Yasusaburō and Wako Shungorō in April 1914. Their project was delayed as the two became involved with Hoshina and his paper, but ultimately they did launch on 31 August 1916 as an eight-page weekly. Feeling that a mimeographed paper such as the *Shūkan Nanbei* lacked authority, the two decided to use lithography for the *Nippaku shinbun*. It rapidly outstripped the *Shūkan Nanbei* in popularity, with a circulation of seven to eight hundred. In early 1917 Kaneko and Wako had a falling out, and Wako—who had been doing all of the editing—left for Mato Grosso. When Kaneko fell ill in 1919 he sold the paper to Miura Saku (also known as Sack.) Unlike the emigration company-funded *Burajiru jihō*, which was perceived as supporting the positions of the emigration companies and the Japanese consulate (more about this below), the *Nippaku* came to be seen as the popular, critical, unorthodox alternative.[9] On 20 October 1931, *Nippaku* switched to a twice-weekly schedule. By 1933, the paper's circulation was estimated at over seven thousand.[10] On 27 March 1936, it began publishing thrice-weekly, and then on 26 August 1937 it shifted to a daily printing schedule. The paper continued publication until 25 July 1939 (when Miura was driven out of the country), at which point its circulation was roughly 19,500.[11]

The third major newspaper to appear was the *Burajiru jihō* (伯剌西爾時報), which was established in July 1917 as the official organ of the Kaigai Kōgyō Kabushiki Kaisha (KKKK) emigration company. Originally a weekly paper produced in São Paulo city, the paper launched on 31 August 1917; from the beginning it was printed with movable type in runs of 1,500, an ambitious quantity made possible by the support of the emigration companies. Kuroishi Seisaku was invited from the United States to run the operation; in 1922 he purchased the paper outright. The paper shifted to a twice-weekly schedule in October 1931, then to thrice-weekly in March 1936, and finally to a "daily" schedule (actually six days a week, taking Mondays off) in August 1937.[12] Its circulation in 1933 was 8,200; by 1941 it had climbed to 18,000.[13]

The *Seishū shinpō* (聖州新報) was the first Japanese-language newspaper published outside of the city of São Paulo. It was launched by Kōyama Rokurō on 7 September 1921 in the city of Bauru. At the time, it took more than ten days for the

São Paulo papers to reach readers in the most distant *colônias*, and their content was overwhelmingly focused on events of interest in the city. The *Seishū shinpō* provided a welcome contrast through its attention to rural affairs. Originally the paper was printed using hand-etched zinc plates, but movable type was adopted from 1925.[14] The paper shifted to a twice-weekly schedule in September 1931, then to thrice-weekly in September 1935, and finally became a daily in August 1937.[15] In the meantime, it had relocated to the city of São Paulo.[16] Where it had begun with a circulation of 350, it rose to 5,300 by 1931 and 9,000 by 1941.[17]

While there were a few other papers, such as the *Nanbei shinpō* (南米新報), the *Ariansa jihō* (アリアンサ時報), and a wide variety of community and organization bulletins, the *Burajiru jihō*, *Nippaku shinbun*, and *Seishū shinpō* were the largest papers during the prewar period and are the newspapers we still possess in reasonable quantity (if not complete runs) today.

DUELS IN THE PRESENCE OF THE SHOGUN IEMITSU

Although fiction played a role in most, if not all, of these locally produced newspapers, it was most prevalent and conspicuous in the *Burajiru jihō*. As mentioned above, the newspaper launched on 31 August 1917, and fiction played a central part in the newspaper from the beginning.[18] The inaugural issue included the first installment of the *kōdan Duels in the Presence of the Shogun Iemitsu* (寛永御前試合). The serialization continued for a little more than a year, until its conclusion on 13 September 1918. A close look at this work tells us a great deal about the processes by which serialization occurred in the newspaper; it also challenges any implicit beliefs that a national literature might be made up of texts that are themselves static and authoritative.

The basic tale in question was a famous one, based on a competition that was supposedly held during the Kan'ei period (1624–44) in the presence of the Shogun Tokugawa Iemitsu. The competition brought together legendary warriors from throughout the realm, who competed against one another to show the relative strengths of their special martial abilities. The story was not created for serialization in the *Burajiru jihō*; it was regularly performed by storytellers in Japan and had already appeared in print there. The version printed in the *Burajiru jihō*, originally performed by Takarai Bakin the fourth (1853–1928) and transcribed by Imamura Jirō (1868–1937)[19], was one that had previously been published in two volumes of the Yachiyo Bunko (八千代文庫)—volume 32, *Kan'ei gozen jiai* (寛永御前試合), and volume 33, *Kan'ei yūshi bujustsu no homare* (寛永勇士武術誉)—both of which first appeared earlier in 1917.

This was not the only published version of the story in circulation at the time. One earlier version, told by Tanabe Dairyū, was published by Kyūkōkaku (求光閣) in 1895. The version used by the *Burajiru jihō* was not even the first version published by Shūeidō Ōkawaya Shoten (聚栄堂大川屋書店), the publisher

FIGURE 4. *Kan'ei gozen jiai*, *Burajiru jihō*, 31 August 1917. Courtesy of the Hoji Shinbun Digital Collection.

of the Yachiyo Bunko; in fact, it was not even the first version told and transcribed by Takarai Bakin and Imamura Jirō for that publisher. Ōkawaya Shoten had previously published a different version of the story, also told by Takarai and transcribed by Imamura, in 1899.[20] An extant copy of the fourth printing (1906) of this version contains very similar language but is in a different sequence and contains different illustrations. The serialization as it appears in the *Burajiru jihō* is nearly identical to the later 1917 Yachiyo Bunko version.

The work stands out on the page. The illustrated title image (題字飾りカット) for *Duels* contains the title of the work, the name of the original storyteller, and the name of the transcriber, in addition to an eye-catching illustration. Elements such as these help not only identify the source of the text, but also provide clues about the means by which it was reproduced. The title image used at the beginning of each installment of the story is a reproduction of the illustration that appears on the first page of the Yachiyo volume. It is unclear which of the available technologies was used for this reproduction; it is possible that a mechanical process was used, but the slightly deteriorated quality of the reproduction suggests that it may have been traced and re-etched by hand. Given considerations of economy, one might speculate that this was done locally, in Brazil.

What we can determine was done locally was the setting of the type. While the reproduction is nearly word-for-word, the page composition, script choices, and distribution of phonetic glosses are not identical. A few examples from the first installments illustrate this. The different page composition is immediately obvious; the beginning and ending of these installments does not match that in the book, and is accompanied by an installment title that does not appear in it either.[21] Script modifications range from the substitution of *kanji* for *kana* (or the reverse) to the use of *hentaigana*, or alternate forms of *kana*, that are not used in the book version, but which were regularly used in the *Burajiru jihō*. Finally, phonetic glosses are added, removed, or differently positioned vis-à-vis the words they gloss.

What all of these changes indicate is that the type for the story was set as part of the composition of the newspaper as a whole. This also suggests that the more substantive changes present in the newspaper serialization would have been introduced locally. These changes primarily occur at the beginnings and endings of installments, where sentences are removed, divided, or (on rare occasion) expanded in order to allow breaks that are not present in the book version. This differs from the United States, where syndication services would often provide a complete stereotype of the story (and, in many cases, the remainder of the newspaper page, including advertisements) to the newspapers that carried it.

The *Burajiru jihō* serialization did not carry the complete contents of both of the Yachiyo Bunko volumes. The installments from 31 August 1917 through 21 June 1918 covered the first volume; the 21 June 1918 installment then moved on to the second volume. When the serialization of the work in the newspaper concluded, however, it had only reached page 50 of the second volume. On 7 September 1918, it was announced that because *Duels* "would soon reach a point at which the story could be paused," the newspaper would begin serializing *Kume no Heinai* (粂平内) in its place.

In the absence of direct data concerning readers' responses, one can only speculate about what such a work might have meant to them. Perhaps the tale of honor, strength, justice, cleverness, and achievement, depicting a Japan in its past glory days, dominated by its most powerful Shogun, would have been of great consolation to readers arriving in Brazil to find themselves not only in an unfamiliar landscape, but also in a marginalized position of material and psychological hardship. Such a generalization, however, is of limited usefulness given the fact that individual readers respond to literary works differently, and often in ways that cannot be predicted simply through textual analysis. What we can say about the reception of *Duels in the Presence of the Shogun Iemitsu*, though, is that it was perceived to have been a success, at least by one of *Burajiru jihō*'s primary competitors.

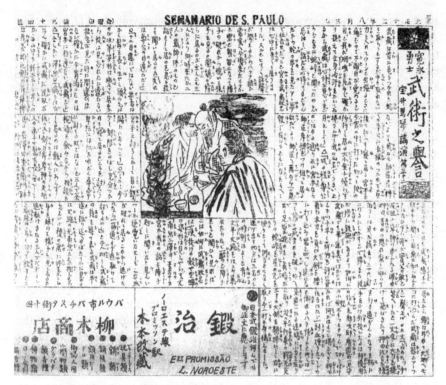

FIGURE 5. *Kan'ei bujutsu no homare*, *Seishū shinpō*, 3 August 1923. Courtesy of the Museu Histórico da Imigração Japonesa no Brasil and the Kokusai Nihon Bunka Kenkyū Sentaa.

When the *Seishū shinpō* was launched three years later, that newspaper serialized the same version of the story once again.[22] The earliest extant issue of that weekly, number 71 (dated 23 February 1923), contains installment eight; the serialization continued until the end of that year, stopping midway through the volume.[23] At first, the newspaper made an attempt to match the divisions established in the Yachiyo Bunko version precisely, even if it involved simplifications or elisions in the course of the installment. By installment sixteen, however, it ceased to adhere to the book version's breaks.[24] As with the *Burajiru jihō* version, in the *Seishū shinpō* version we see editorial intervention: altering the transcription system, adding or (more commonly) removing glosses, and sometimes even rephrasing, particularly when sections are especially detailed or use obscure terminology. It is particularly clear that the text was being reproduced in Brazil: as mentioned previously, unlike the *Burajiru jihō*, the *Seishū shinpō* did not yet use movable type, so each page had to be etched by hand. Despite all of these alterations, the majority of the text remains identical to the Yachiyo Bunko version.

Five years later, in 1928, the *Seishū shinpō* returned to the story, continuing more or less where it had left off. From September until January, the paper reproduced another roughly forty pages of the Yachiyo Bunko version, volume 32 (*Kan'ei gozen jiai*).[25] As with previous serializations, the newspaper showed little concern with the divisions present in the original version, breaking off mid-section when necessary (in all but two of the thirteen installments), eliminating section divisions altogether when an installment bridged two sections, and adding or altering text as necessary to provide clarity or coherence.

Just as we speculated about the attraction of this story for readers, we might speculate now about its attraction to editors: namely, that the collection of relatively autonomous sections— and perhaps flexible reader expectations about fidelity to a precise text—was useful. It would have provided a plasticity that allowed editors to adjust to the newspaper's shifting needs, rather than being forced to adhere to the story's precise structure. It allowed them to start, stop, and jump as they needed, filling available space with content that they knew would draw readers back for the next installment.

Clearly, the editors felt enough license over the text to intervene in ways they found necessary. This reminds us that we must consider at least two possible motivations for the ubiquity of fiction in the pages of these newspapers: its importance to readers and its convenience to editors for its dependable and malleable content. Undoubtedly the stories were carried partially because of the literary or entertainment value of their content; at the same time, however, we should acknowledge that for the newspaper's editors the texts had other forms of value that had little to do with that content. In this way, the *Burajiru jihō*'s and the *Seishū shinpō*'s use of *Duels in the Presence of the Shogun Iemitsu* functions as an introduction to the ways in which the newspapers utilized existing texts during these early years.

THE EARLY YEARS: HISTORICAL FICTION, 1917–33

Duels in the Presence of the Shogun Iemitsu was the first of six such works of historical fiction that ran steadily in the *Burajiru jihō* for the first fifteen and a half years of its existence. *Duels* was followed by *Kume no Heinai*, which ran for 116 installments over two and a half years, from September 1918 until January 1921.[26] The story—of a masterless samurai, or *rōnin*, from Kyūshū who, after having killed many men, becomes a monk in Asakusa in order to pray for their repose and expiate his sins—had appeared in print many times before, and in a variety of versions. Stories about the historical figure, who lived during the seventeenth century, had been produced since at least 1808, when Kyokutei Bakin wrote about him.[27] It had been serialized in a newspaper before (as early as 1904), had been published in book form (as early as 1905), and had been made into films (starting in 1911).[28] The version used for the serialization here, told by Koganei Roshū, originally appeared in book form from Hakubunkan in 1918.[29]

As with *Duels*, the *Burajiru jihō* version replicated not only the text of this version, but also the illustrations. Unlike *Duels*, however, this serialization covered the full length of, and was almost identical to, the original, roughly three-hundred-page Hakubunkan text. The *Burajiru jihō* version changed phonetic glosses, *okurigana*, and other minor elements throughout the text, as well as made more substantial changes at the beginning and end of installments in order to clarify transitions. Beyond that, however, the text is functionally identical to the one it reproduces, which had been published five months earlier in Tokyo.[30]

On 28 January 1921, along with the last installment of *Kume no Heinai*, the newspaper ran an announcement advertising its next serialized work, *Ōishi Kuranosuke* (大石内蔵助) as told by Nakarai Tōsui. In his history of newspaper fiction in Japan, Takagi Takeo describes Nakarai as one of the premier writers of historical fiction in the first decade of the twentieth century.[31] The first installment appeared on 4 February 1921. This work ran longer than any other, continuing for 383 installments—nearly eight years—until 22 November 1928. The story revolves around Ōishi Kuranosuke Yoshio (Yoshitaka) (大石良雄), the leader of the forty-seven *rōnin* in *Chūshingura*. Nakarai's version of the story was originally serialized in the *Tōkyō Asahi shinbun*, from 29 August 1913 until 21 April 1915; as such, it ran concurrently with such works as Natsume Sōseki's *Kokoro*.[32] After this serialization in Japan was completed, the Tokyo publisher Hakuaikan published it in four volumes between 1916–17. The *Burajiru jihō* version followed the original text precisely, dividing the story into sections based on the installments.

The three works that followed *Ōishi* were period pieces, but not explicitly *kōdan*. The first was *Ōkubo Hikozaemon* (大久保彦左衛門), which began on 29 November 1928 and continued for a year and a half.[33] Ōkubo (1560–1639) was a Tokugawa retainer who became an archetype of the rough but frank warrior. The *Burajiru jihō* serialization, which is unattributed, is clearly related to the version published by Tachikawa Bunko in 1911.[34] That version was attributed to Sekka San-jin (雪花散人), one of the pen names used to indicate not an individual, but rather the group of writers/transcribers employed by the company. The *Burajiru jihō* seri-alization follows the specific phrasing of the Tachikawa edition closely but is far more aggressive in eliminating and condensing text than was the case with any of the earlier stories. This may reflect a shifting editorial posture, but it might also be the case that the serialization and the Tachikawa edition share an earlier source text; scholars have theorized that the earlier Tachikawa volumes (of which this was one) may have drawn from existing published *kōdan*.[35] If the Tachikawa Bunko version is the original, however, that will come as little surprise; it was widely avail-able, already in its fourteenth edition by 1913.[36]

It is important to note that while *Ōkubo* was the first story serialized by the *Burajiru jihō* that ran without attribution to an author, storyteller, or transcriber, it was not the last. The story that followed it, *Nihon jūdai kenkaku-den* (日本十

大劍客傳), was published without attribution either. The serialization, however, replicates the text of a volume by the same name written by Shimota Norimitsu, published in 1926 by Seibundō Shoten (誠文堂書店) in Tokyo; why it is unattributed is unclear.[37] The *Burajiru jihō* version, which was serialized from 5 June 1930 until 18 December 1931, hews even more closely to its source text than did previous reproductions. Although the newspaper was unable to reprint the long sections of the original book in single installments, it nonetheless maintained those divisions and made no modifications to address newly added breaks.[38] The only changes that I have found between the serialization and the source text involves the phonetic gloss.[39] The *Burajiru jihō* serialization reproduced the entirety of the body of the book version, eliminating only a preface, a short series of adages concerning swordfighting, and a chronology that appeared in the book version.

Starting on 20 October 1931, the *Burajiru jihō* shifted from its weekly print schedule to a biweekly schedule. At first, the serialization schedule continued unchanged, with installments of *Nihon jūdai kenkaku-den* appearing on the final page of each number. From Friday, 13 November 1931, the paper began running a "Literary Arts" (文芸) column in addition to *Swordsmen*, which continued to appear on the final page. The column was not limited to fiction; as early as 21 November 1931, a work of criticism titled "Nōmin bungaku no koto" (農民文学の事) began running there. From Friday, 4 December 1931, however, the column stopped appearing in Friday issues, and instead ran only in Tuesday issues; *Nihon jūdai kenkaku-den* continued to run in every number. This continues to be the case until what appears to have been the last number of 1931, which appeared on December 22 and contained no works of fiction in either conventional location.

The last of the six historical pieces that ran during this first fourteen years was *Kataki-uchi yari morotomo* (敵討鎗諸共), which ran for fifty-five installments from 1 January 1932 until 2 February 1933. Unlike the previous two works, this story was attributed to Hasegawa Shin. The work had originally been serialized in the *Sandee mainichi* between 8 November 1925 and 14 February 1926 and printed in book form by Shun'yōdō later that year.[40] The story was also the lead work in volume eight of the Heibonsha *enpon* anthology, *Gendai taishū bungaku zenshū* (現代大衆文學全集), which was published in 1928. The *Burajiru jihō* version ends with the phrase, "I don't know if that was the case. . . ." (さうであらうか知らん), which did not appear in the *Sandee mainichi* edition but does appear in the *zenshū* version, suggesting that the newspaper may have used the latter as its source.

One of these six works appeared in practically every number of the newspaper for the first fifteen years of its existence, appearing on the back page with only rare exceptions. Even the shortest ran for over a year. All of them were works of period fiction involving warriors and their exploits. Not only were the subjects of the stories characters with which many of the readers would have had familiarity, but also the versions themselves were relatively high-profile, often produced by well-known publishers (including Hakubunkan, the Asahi Shinbunsha, and Tachikawa

Bunko.) Despite the size of these publishers and their presumable interest in protecting their intellectual property, it seems likely that these works were reproduced illegally; although that is a difficult claim to prove definitively, anecdotes about the time in Brazil treat it as a given.

ILLEGAL PRINTING

We know that some newspapers in the Americas did engage in this sort of illegal reproduction, thanks to well-documented incidents such as the one that follows, concerning a story that ran in Los Angeles at the same time that the *Burajiru jihō* was serializing *Ōishi Kuranosuke*. On 13 February 1925, the *Nichibei shinbun* began running the novel *Naraku* (奈落) by Masuda Hajime.[41] In the pages of the *Nichibei*, the serialization seems unexceptional; a brief note on February 12 announced that the story would be starting the following day, and the serialization itself does not differ in any obvious way from those that preceded or succeeded it.

On 3 June 1925, Saburi Sadao, then head of the Bureau of Commercial Affairs of the Ministry of Foreign Affairs, received a letter from Masuda regarding this reproduction of his novel, which had originally appeared in the *Miyako shinbun* between 8 December 1924 and 3 May 1925.[42] Apparently an acquaintance of Masuda's who had been traveling in the United States had contacted the author upon his return and informed him that he had seen the story running there. Masuda contacted Saburi, he explained, because he had not given permission for the reproduction, and hoped that Saburi would intervene on his behalf, as the *Nichibei* had not responded to the author's queries. In order to further highlight the seriousness of the situation, Masuda mentioned that it was his understanding that the paper had also illegally serialized Nakazato Kaizan's *Daibosatsu tōge* (大菩薩峠).[43]

While it has not been possible thus far to verify Masuda's claim that the reproduction was not approved by Nakazato, the *Nichibei shinbun* had indeed been reproducing *Daibosatsu tōge*. The multivolume novel ran in the newspaper for years. In the earliest number of *Nichibei* that I was able to check, 1 January 1919, installment 255 (from *Ai no yama*, volume [巻] 6 of the novel) appears.[44] This would suggest not only that the story had been running for some time, but also that *Nichibei* was reproducing installments fairly soon after they appeared in the *Miyako shinbun*. On the day Masuda wrote his letter in June 1925, *Nichibei* printed an installment of the *Mumyō* volume (21), which had begun publication in January of the same year in both the *Tokyo Nichinichi* and the *Ōsaka Mainichi* newspapers.

In his letter, Masuda asked Saburi to take three concrete steps: first, to declare this an infringement of his copyright and to order the newspaper to cease publication of the work immediately; second, to demand that the two newspapers (*Nichibei* and *Rafu*) pay twenty yen each for each day of serialization; and third, to convey that if the newspapers wished to complete the serialization, that they contact the author's representative and enter into formal negotiations. The demand may have achieved some or all of the desired effect; *Nichibei*'s serialization of *Naraku* concluded on 25 June 1925 with installment 132, prior to the conclusion of the original work (which had spanned 147 installments). Masuda's claim may have impacted the serialization of *Daibosatsu tōge* as well, which seems to have been suspended with the close of the *Mumyō* chapter less than a month later, on 18 July 1925.

Though much remains unknown about this incident, it does tell us a few things: first, that illegal reproductions seem to have existed in the Americas, even when the original texts were quite well-known and produced by high-profile publishers; second, that information about serialization overseas was sufficiently scarce that a coincidence of this sort was required for the original author to become aware that it was happening (and that authors either assumed their rights were being protected, or were unaware that these extranational markets existed in the first place); and third, that these markets were sufficiently meaningful for these authors that once the illegal printings became known, they felt compelled to respond. Finally, the incident grants some credence to the oral history that suggests that early serializations in the Brazil newspapers were reproduced illegally.

EXPERIMENTATION AND TRANSITION, 1932–34

The year 1932 saw a number of changes in the *Burajiru jihō*'s literary offerings, even as it continued to run the last of the six long historical pieces. Though no fiction appeared on 18 January 1932, in the following number (January 21) an announcement appeared on "the expansion of the Literary Arts column." In it, the paper revealed its plans to "open the column and make it available as a stage for the activities of literature lovers," presumably among "the society of fellow countrymen" (邦人社会) that desired that access. Over the following numbers, Monday issues lacked any fiction, but Thursday numbers contained both a newly expanded literary section (on page 5 of 8) and the most recent *Kataki-uchi* installment. This schedule—fiction on both pages 5 and 8 on Thursdays, but no fiction appearing on Mondays, when the paper was four pages rather than eight—continued for some time, with only occasional adjustments. This lasted until 22 August 1932, when the paper began experimenting with mid-length pieces about war and other nonfiction topics. Throughout this time, the final long historical piece of this first period, *Kataki-uchi yari morotomo*, continued running, concluding on 2 February 1933.

Between 9 February 1933 and 6 April 1933, the newspaper serialized "Kuni-iri Sankichi" (國入り三吉) by Shirai Kyōji. Far shorter than the previous works, this story was explicitly marked as being short-form fiction. It had originally been published in the July 1931 special summer issue of *Shūkan asahi*.[45] For the remainder of 1933, the newspaper ran a series of short works, many based on *rakugo*. On 12 August 1933, the newspaper switched its publication schedule yet again, to a Wednesday/Saturday schedule. After the initial transition issue on that day, the

Saturday numbers became the shorter four-page format, containing no literary texts, and the Wednesday numbers became the longer eight-page format with literary texts both on an inner page (usually page four) and on the final page. The serialized fiction that appears on the final page of the newspaper during this year bore little resemblance to what readers would have grown accustomed to in previous years.

It is unclear what prompted this period of experimentation during the years 1932 and 1933, but one wonders if the pressures to acquire texts legally led the newspaper first to try to avoid purchasing long pieces. In addition to choosing shorter works, many only single installments, the newspaper experimented with a wide variety of genres and directed more attention to locally produced fiction, which it could acquire for free or for minimal expense. Given the brevity of the period, however, it would seem that demand for extended serializations was greater than the editors had realized. So great, in fact, that the newspaper then turned to lengthy pieces that they were likely not able to reproduce without proper compensation to their authors. This would help explain the new types of fiction serializations that emerged after this year of transition.

A NEW ORDER, 1934–41

Beginning on 17 January 1934, the distribution and nature of fiction in the newspaper changed noticeably. Page four of the Wednesday edition remained dedicated (primarily) to local literary production of various forms, but the amount of fiction on the last page was once again reduced. Unlike most serializations since the institution of the twice-weekly printing schedule, the novel that began appearing there, *Kinpatsu-ma* (金髪魔), ran initially in both the Wednesday and Saturday editions. Unlike the stories that had preceded it, this novel was set in the present day. It also brought even more visual appeal to the page, with a new large illustration accompanying Wednesday installments and the standardized illustrated masthead accompanying the work both days.

From this time forward, *rakugo* and other short, popular pieces were less common, often only appearing in special (longer) numbers, such as the New Year's Day issue. *Kinpatsu-ma* ran for 135 installments over one and a half years, from January 1934 until July 1935, followed by Ichiryūsai Teikyō's historical piece *Sanza shigure* (さんざ時雨), which ran for a similar duration, from July 1935 until January 1937.[46]

When the newspaper went to its new thrice-weekly schedule on 27 March 1936, it began running an extended work of contemporary fiction on the front page of each number even as it continued to run a separate, historical work on its last page. This is the format—two pieces running simultaneously, one set in present day, one in the past—that the paper would eventually maintain until it was shut down in 1941.

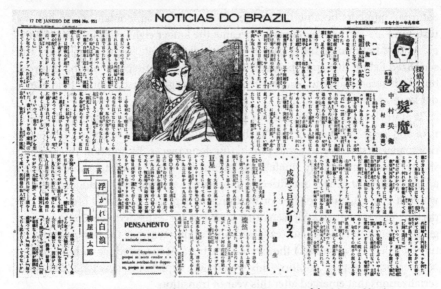

FIGURE 6. *Kinpatsu-ma, Burajiru jihō*, 17 January 1934. Courtesy of the Museu Histórico Regional Saburo Yamanaka and the Kokusai Nihon Bunka Kenkyū Sentaa.

On 23 August 1937, *Burajiru jihō* became a "daily" paper, running Mondays through Saturdays. With each issue shorter, at four pages each, the literary column began appearing on Saturdays, sharing the back page with an installment of the contemporary work *Reijin aika* (麗人哀歌). In the closing months of 1937, fiction went on almost total hiatus in the newspaper, with only the occasional literary section or installment of *Reijin aika*. This continued until the New Year's Day issue in 1938, which contained a *rakugo* piece, a *kōdan* piece, and a literary section, among other things. The first regular issue of the year, 5 January 1938, contained the next installment of *Reijin aika*, which appeared on the front page until January 26, when it was once again placed on the last page.

By 30 May 1938, historical fiction had returned to the front page with the tale that was then being serialized, the famous *Chūshingura* (忠臣蔵). At the same time, a new contemporary work was launched on the fourth (last) page: *Tōge on josei* (峠の女性), a work of contemporary fiction by Yamanaka Minetarō, which began on 27 May 1938.[47] Though the newspaper changed its "daily" schedule to a Tuesday through Sunday printing schedule on 5 June 1938, the distribution of fiction was not significantly altered. When *Chūshingura* concluded on 3 February 1939, its front-page spot was taken over the next day by another historical novel, *Shigure hakkō* (時雨八荒) by Hiki Takeshi. When *Tōge on josei* finished on 14 May 1939, its back-page spot was taken over the next day by Kikuchi Kan's *Nishizumi senshachō-den* (西住戦車長伝). When *Shigure hakkō* ended its run on 3 December 1939, another period piece did not take its place; instead, *Moyuru seiza* (燃ゆる星座), which had been running on the back page, moved to

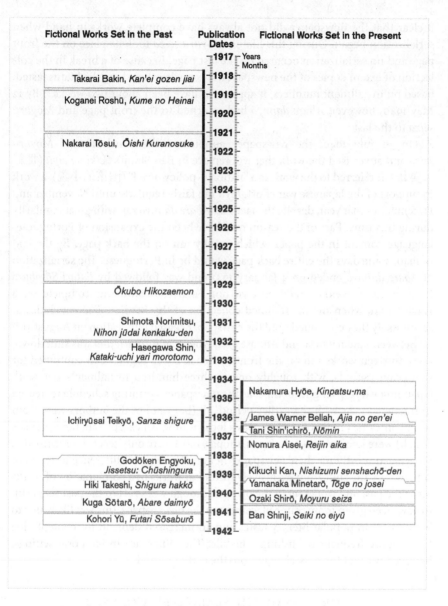

FIGURE 7. Extended serializations in the *Burajiru jihō*, 1917–1941.

the front page from 5 December 1939. No serialization took its place, presumably because it was so close to the end of the year. When the period piece *Abare daimyō* (あばれ大名) began serialization on 7 January 1940, however, *Moyuru seiza* returned to the back page. On 23 April 1940, *Burajiru jihō* announced that *Abare daimyō* would pause because the manuscript had not yet arrived, making it clear that the newspaper did not always have complete works in hand when serialization began. During this hiatus, *Moyuru seiza* took its place on the front page and no serialization occured on the last page. Because of a break in the collection of extant copies of the newspaper, it is unclear how long the hiatus lasted; based on installment numbers, it appears to have been about two weeks.[48] By 12 May 1940, however, *Abare daimyō* had returned to the front page and *Moyuru seiza* to the last.

On 30 July 1940, the newspaper announced the conclusion of *Moyuru seiza* and advertised the work that will replace it, Ban Shinji's *Seiki no eiyū* (世紀 の英雄). It referred to the work as a "national-policy novel" (国策的小説), a work in support of the Japanese war effort. *Eiyū* ran fairly regularly until November and December of that year, despite the fact that *Abare daimyō* ran with great regularity during this time. Part of the reason may have been the expansion of Portuguese-language content in the paper, which usually ran on the back page. By the end of 1940, some days the entire back page would be in Portuguese. The serialization of *Abare daimyō* ended on 4 January 1941 and was followed by *Futari Sōsaburō* (二人草三郎). Neither *Seiki no eiyū* nor *Futari Sōsaburō* was complete on 8 August 1941, when the microfilmed collection of the *Burajiru jihō* concludes; it seems likely they continued until the newspaper ceased publication on August 31.[49]

Between January 1934 and August 1941, when the *Burajiru jihō* was shut down, these thirteen works ran on the front and back cover pages. Each continued for significant periods, with roughly one to three hundred installments per work (spanning varying lengths of time, as the newspaper's printing schedule increased in frequency). As with the earlier period, all (but one) of the authors were from Japan; only one (Tani Shin'ichirō) was a local author. All except Tani (and perhaps Bellah) were known writers in Japan, though most were only second- or third-tier, recognized mostly for their newspaper fiction. The biggest difference in terms of content was the shift from exclusively historical works to a combination of works set in the past and works set in the present (though works set in the past seem still to have been given more prime placement in the newspaper.) This was likely due to both a shift in popular literary tastes and an increased demand for content, due to the more frequent publishing schedule. This difference in temporal settings, however, was not the only change from the earlier period.

ORIGINS OF THE SERIALIZED WORKS

Unlike works that appeared during the first period, which had been drawn from texts already published in Japan, I have not yet discovered any evidence that these later works (with the notable exception of Kikuchi Kan's *Nishizumi senshachō-den*) had been previously published in Japan.[50] In many cases, they seem not to have been republished there subsequently either.

This is not to say that the works appeared exclusively in the *Burajiru jihō*. First, the works may have appeared in regional newspapers that have not yet been catalogued. Second, the works may be known, but under different titles, perhaps with some changes. Third, the works may not be by the authors they are attributed to at all, perhaps with the author's knowledge and direction or perhaps not. We know in the case of the author Tokuda Shūsei, for example, that such practices did occur. Richard Torrance describes cosmetic rewrites that were given new titles and resold by Shūsei, and of translations of foreign novels that Shūsei presented as his own, both at the turn of the twentieth century.[51] Similarly, Asaoka Kunio describes a case from 1910 in which it seems likely that the *Kyūshū nichinichi shinbun* borrowed both Tokuda Shūsei's name and title (slightly) modified for a work that he likely had nothing to do with whatsoever.[52]

In the case of works that only appeared in the *Burajiru jihō*, it is possible that they were acquired by agents who offered such works to newspapers throughout Japan and the global Japanese-language community, and who did not hesitate to sell the same work to multiple outlets. Though few have researched this system, Asaoka has discussed the phenomenon in which a given work by a famous author would appear in different regional newspapers, either simultaneously or at different times.[53] While his research uses the specific case of Yamada Bimyō (1868–1910), he notes work done by two other scholars on the cases of Izumi Kyōka (1873–1939) and Tokuda Shūsei (1871–1943); in the case of Kyōka, Okazaki Hajime has shown that in one case the same work appeared simultaneously in multiple regional papers.[54]

One of the details that emerges from this research is the fact that, at least at the end of the nineteenth century, newspapers and agents utilized the texts they purchased with great flexibility. Asaoka notes that from around 1887–1895, a side industry emerged that purchased previously published woodblock illustrations from the various illustrated newspapers in Tokyo, had unknown authors write new stories to accompany them, and then sold them to regional newspapers; later, the same industry began selling original works solicited from famous Tokyo authors and then selling them to multiple newspapers throughout the country.[55] Some of the authors that participated in this system were Hirotsu Ryūryō (1861–1928), Emi Suiin (1869–1934), Tayama Katai (1871–1930), and Oguri Fūyō (1875–1926).

The system grew more formalized in the first decades of the twentieth century. Asaoka cites a 1909 article that names a number of companies involved in this sort of work, including the Teikoku Shinbun Yōtatsu-sha (帝国新聞用達社) and the Genjikan (元治館), both based in Tokyo.[56] In 1910, Teikoku Shinbun Yōtatsu-sha, Genjikan, and Zuga Tsūshin (図画通信) merged to form the Tokyo-based Tōyō Bungei Kabushiki Kaisha (東洋文芸株式会社). An advertisement from the new company, published in 1911, claimed that the company provided fiction to more than three hundred newspapers throughout the country.[57] Kawai

Sumio writes about the company Gakugei Tsūshinsha (学芸通信社), founded in 1929, which was also involved in this system. The company was started by a former employee of Nihon Denpō Tsūshinsha (日本電報通信社), Kawai Yasushi (1900–63), as Shinbun Bungeisha (新聞文芸社). Kawai Yasushi later also launched the Nihon Gakugei Shinbunsha (日本学芸新聞社).[58] There certainly was a growing market for such a system; Ozaki Hotsuki describes how by the 1950s newspaper fiction was so popular that it was common for a newspaper to run three works each day, one appearing in the morning edition and two appearing in the evening edition.[59]

In the early years of this system, authors were paid between one and two yen per installment, which the companies would then arrange to have illustrated.[60] The companies would approach larger regional newspapers, offering to sell them the finished blocks at a similar rate on the condition that the newspaper return the blocks after they had finished the printing process. These companies would then offer these works in a catalog sent to other newspapers throughout the country (and likely beyond as well.) For these subsequent printings, newspapers were only charged 25–35 *sen* per installment (or less, in the case of *kōdan*), again under the condition that they return the blocks.) In some cases, they sold these under the oxymoronic name of "New Works the Second Time Around" (二度目の新作). Yamada Bimyō discusses his dealings with Genjikan in his diary, and it is these entries that Asaoka draws on to understand how this business operated. The regional newspapers apparently had little or no direct contact with the authors, and in many cases the works appeared in the newspapers without the original authors even being aware that they had.[61]

A study conducted by the Asahi Shinbunsha in 1949 reveals opinions about the functioning of this system that can probably be considered representative. One critic, writing about the situation in Yamagata Prefecture under a pen name taken from a famous local bandit, Gando Tarō, described the basic logic of this system through which the newspapers acquired the stories they carried:

> Most works of fiction carried in regional newspapers are ones written by the author completely unaware of what newspaper will eventually purchase it. Newspapers select and purchase works they like from a group of stories for sale, reproduced in printed form and sold to the highest bidder. The author's fame and influence act as the brand informing the exchange, and no one questions the literary value of the [particular] work.[62]

In much scholarship to this day, there is a faith in the economic rationality of this system, which would render works of lower literary quality less valuable, and thus cause these works to flow away from the center as their merit declines. In the 1949 study, a critic identified as Yokota Yūji wrote the following about newspaper fiction in Aomori:

> Originally regional newspapers would inherit the poor imitators of the center, using a combination of contemporary and period fiction to fill in gaps and provide some

variety among the headlines. If one were to climb on a train, go to a neighboring prefecture, and buy a newspaper, for example, one would find the same story from some
discount news service, with the same illustrations, totally bereft of either originality
or sincerity of intent. Even if the regional newspapers would occasionally open their
pages to local 'authors' in the hopes of introducing local color, the resulting works
would be utterly devoid of vitality; at the very least, it left the pages covered with the
most provincial of content. This is how things were prior to the War.[63]

Commenting on this issue of local authors, Gando Tarō offered the following
opinion:

> I don't think that newspaper novels are so easy to produce that an unknown au-
> thor could just knock one out. Still, compared to the stupidity of relying on works
> dumped by central authors on regional newspapers, it would be better for those [re-
> gional] papers to midwife the births of new literature and authors, even if they are
> unable to acquire great works in the process.[64]

We know that local newspapers did in fact attempt to cultivate local writers; at
the same time, on occasion they appear to have been able to bypass the system
described above and contact famous authors through direct connections. Yokota
(quoted above) acknowledged that at times the newspapers would shrewdly
importune a famous author originally from the region, or catch one in the area on
holiday, and ask him or her to write something for them.[65]

Based on what appeared in the newspaper, one might suspect this to have
been the case at least once with the *Burajiru jihō* as well: an advertisement
that announced the upcoming serialization of Ozaki Shirō's *Moyuru seiza* in
1939 indicated just such an arrangement.[66] The advertisement claimed that the
Burajiru Jihōsha had contacted the author directly to request that he write for
the newspaper, and that he had readily agreed. The advertisement goes on to
say that the newspaper had received the manuscript that he sent upon its comple-
tion. This was the first time that the newspaper printed a statement about the process
by which it had obtained a work of fiction from Japan. While the fact that this
is the only time that the newspaper makes such a claim seems to bolster its
believability, the fact that the "author's words" included in a later advertisement
did not mention the (presumably noteworthy) detail that it would be serialized in
Brazil might have introduced some doubt in readers' minds.[67] They would have
been right to be skeptical: the work had in fact been serialized two years earlier in
three separate newspapers in North America, at least one of them with the same
author's note.[68]

At the beginning of this section, I noted that works from these later periods
do not seem to have appeared elsewhere in Japan. The same cannot be said of the
Americas. Ban Shinji's *Seiki no eiyū* followed the serialization of *Moyuru seiza* in
Seattle's *Taihoku nippō* from 24 May 1940, just as it did in the *Burajiru jihō* on 1
August 1940; it also ran in Los Angeles's *Kashū mainichi shinbun* from 20 February
1941. *Reijin aikai*, which appeareded in Brazil beginning on New Year's Day 1937,

had earlier run in the *Nippū jiji* newspaper in Honolulu, Hawaii, from 8 October 1932. *Abare daimyō* by Kuga Sōtarō was serialized in Seattle's *Taihoku nippō* in 1940, at the same time (or nearly the same time) it was being serialized in Brazil. *Futari Sōsaburō*, which began serialization in Brazil in January 1941, ran in Seattle's *Taihoku nippō* from 3 July 1940. It is not clear what business links existed between most of these newspapers, if there were any at all. Rather, this evidence seems to suggest the existence of agents like those described earlier, who specialized in selling works in multiple diasporic communities.

PERIODIZATION OF PREWAR SERIALIZATIONS

Although it is unclear how the *Burajiru jihō* acquired the long works by non-local authors that it serialized on the front and back pages of the newspaper, it seems possible that the works that appeared in the first period (1917–33) were reproduced locally and without legal permission, working from existing printed versions of the texts that the newspaper could have acquired through any number of channels. By contrast, it seems likely that after the brief window of experimentation and transition (1932–34), the works that appeared in the later period (1934–41) were acquired legally. To begin with, the authors and works printed in the second period are notably less famous than those in the first period; had all works been "free" for the newspaper, why not choose more proven works to reproduce? It seems unlikely that these lower-profile choices were made to avoid legal action, for though the authors and works were not as famous, neither were they unknown. The serializations also came with various forms of advertising paratext (words from the authors, as well as their photographs), which were standard advertising material that accompanied the stories rather than something created in or for São Paulo.

As noted above, the other transition—which seems more likely to have resulted from changes in tastes than economic motivations—was from exclusively historical works to a combination of works set in the past and works set in the present. Similar to the first period, all but one of the long works that appeared in these key positions in the newspaper were composed by authors who were not local. Finally, it seems likely that the authors (again with the exception of Tani) were not aware that their works would appear in Brazil. Statements by the authors included in the advertisements for the pieces, all of which are addressed explicitly to the readers, never mention the exceptional nature of the readership. Instead, they are entirely generic, even in cases that one might expect an author to draw a connection—as with *Reijin aika*, which involves migration to North America, or with *Seiki no eiyū*, which involves migration to Manchuria. This would have allowed each audience—in Honolulu, Seattle, Los Angeles, and São Paulo—to think it was the one being addressed, even when the works were being published in multiple venues throughout the Western Hemisphere.

NOTABLE EXCEPTIONS

Despite these clear patterns, three stories did deviate from them in some notable way. The first was Kikuchi Kan's *Nishizumi senshachō-den*, which ran from 16 May 1939 until 2 November 1939. Unlike any of the other works serialized during the second period, *Nishizumi senshachō-den* was serialized in the *Tōkyō Nichinichi shinbun* and the *Ōsaka Mainichi shinbun* from 7 March 1939 until 6 August 1939; this means that the serialization in the *Burajiru jihō* began while the serialization in the other papers was still ongoing. It also used, with proper attribution, the illustrations from the original version by Ihara Usaburō; the first installment shows the recognizable figure of Kikuchi reading on a train.

It seems unlikely that the *Burajiru jihō* would risk unauthorized reproduction of a work published in such a prominent venue, by such a powerful author. It is interesting to note, however, that this is the only work of this prominence that was published during this second period.

The second exceptional story was the work by Tani Shin'ichirō entitled "Nōmin," which appeared from 18 May 1936 until 12 October 1936. Tani, a writer based in São Paulo, also contributed to the local literary magazine *Chiheisen*.[69] This is one of only two serialized works of length by writers in Brazil that appeared in the newspaper during the prewar (the other being *Kyōhakushaku* [狂伯爵]), and the only one that appeared in the highly visible slots on the front and rear pages. This fact would be sufficient to make the work exceptional, but the content of the work is similarly singular. In addition to focusing on life in Brazil, rather than in Japan, this is one of the few works written in Japanese in Brazil prior to World War II that focuses on non-Japanese characters. In fact, aside from a passing reference to a Japanese in the third installment (of fifty), none of the characters are Japanese. This introduces the possibility that the story is a translation from a work originally written in Portuguese.

The third exception requires greater elaboration. On 27 March 1936, on the front page of the first Friday issue of the newspaper's new thrice-weekly schedule, readers of the *Burajiru jihō* encountered a new serialization, "Ajia no gen'ei" (亜細亜の幻影), attributed to James Warner Bellah (1899–1976). The serialization was marked by no particular fanfare, nor did it receive any special treatment; it is not marked as a translation, and the only thing that would have set it apart was the author's clearly "foreign" (non-Japanese) name (ジェームス・ワーナー・ベラー). The graphics that accompany this first installment are a map of Northeast Asia with the flags of Japan and Manchukuo and a picture of the exterior of Frank Lloyd Wright's Tokyo Imperial Hotel.

James Warner Bellah is now known as the American author whose works became the bases for such films as "She Wore a Yellow Ribbon" (1949), "Rio Grande" (1950), and "The Man Who Shot Liberty Valance" (1962). In 1936 he was publishing popular fiction in such venues as *Collier's*, *Redbook*, *Argosy*, and the

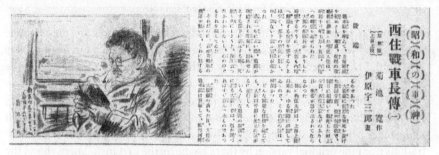

FIGURE 8. *Nishizumi senshachō-den*, *Burajiru jihō*, 16 May 1939. Courtesy of the Museu Histórico Regional Saburo Yamanaka and the Kokusai Nihon Bunka Kenkyū Sentaa.

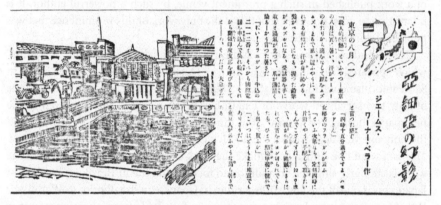

FIGURE 9. "Ajia no gen'ei," *Burajiru jihō*, 27 March 1936. Courtesy of the Museu Histórico Regional Saburo Yamanaka and the Kokusai Nihon Bunka Kenkyū Sentaa.

Saturday Evening Post. It is not clear how Bellah could have come to write a story for a newspaper in Japan, let alone a Japanese-language newspaper in Brazil; even more surprising is the fact that no English version of the story seems to have been published. For this reason, and because of the content of the story, it seems possible that the story was written (in English, with the understanding that it would then be translated) for publication in Japanese.

Bellah himself served in the Canadian Royal Flying Corps in World War I, and then on the staff of Admiral Lord Louis Mountbatten in World War II. It was in this capacity that he traveled to Southeast Asia. In his autobiography, *Irregular Gentleman*, he describes his time in Manchuria and his interactions there with George Hanson, who served as American consul general in Harbin.[70] Hanson, who was known as "Mr. Manchuria," knew many in the expat community there, including the spy Amieto Vespa.[71] Bellah describes one night on the town with Hanson during which they met two Russian girls at a club called the Fantasie. Bellah describes one's aristocratic manner, and how Hanson told him, "No one in

Harbin has ever failed to fall in love with Nahta . . . nor will you fail, my friend."
Nahta met a gruesome end, however, with Hanson and Bellah discovering her
body in the gutter, having "jumped or fallen or . . . [been] thrown from the car."[72]

These details from Bellah's life match many of those from the fictional "Ajia no
gen'ei," which depicts a newspaper reporter based in Tokyo who travels to Manchuria, where he interacts with American consular officials, an Italian consular
official, an aviatrix-turned-spy, a wheelchair-bound criminal mastermind, and
a captivatingly beautiful Russian woman named Nahta. Although the story has
some scenes set in Japan, they are limited to superficial descriptions of Ginza, the
Imperial Hotel, and Tokyo Station—places that an American author might very
well gain a passing familiarity with during even the shortest of stays in Tokyo.
Although Bellah's autobiography does not describe any travels to Japan, it is not
unlikely that he would have passed through Tokyo at some point in his journey;
he certainly encountered many Japanese during his time in Manchuria. It is hard
to know how the arrangements would have been made for him to write a piece for
a Japanese newspaper, let alone who would have translated it for him. There is no
evidence that it was published anywhere beyond the *Burajiru jihō*, but it would
come as no surprise to discover that it had.

TRANSLATIONS

Although the Bellah work was not marked as being a translation, works marked
clearly as such appeared with some frequency in the newspaper, though usually not in the key positions on the first and last pages. One of the earliest and
longest was a partial translation of the novel *A Escrava Isaura* (1875) by the Brazilian writer Bernardo Guimarães. *Dorei no musume* (奴隷の娘), translated by
Sugiyama Hokage, ran for 117 installments from 19 January 1922 through 11 July
1924. The translation was not complete when it ended, though the translation did
cover three-quarters of the more than fifty-three-thousand-word novel. In the
postwar, another attempt was made to translate it into Japanese, in the pages of
Koronia shibungaku.[73] Although the work is little known in English, it is a very
famous work in Brazil and was the inspiration for a 1976–77 telenovela of the same
name, which became a global hit broadcast in some eighty countries. There were
also instances of summaries of works in other languages, such as that of Graciliano
Ramos's *Vidas Secas* (1938), written by Tani Kiyoshi.[74]

JAPANESE LITERATURES

Returning to the idea of a singular Japanese literary ecosystem, we can see a substantial difference between the early and later serializations in the *Burajiru jihō*. In
the early period, we see characters and stories—though not necessarily singular
versions—that would have been broadly shared throughout the islands of Japan.

We note here, though, that this differs significantly from the implicit logic of modern literary studies, which usually presumes a (relatively) stable text by a single author; it is this logic that justifies close, stylistic analyses that are then linked to an historical creator. Depending on how we employ the terms, then, the argument for a shared culture might be more persuasive than one for a shared literature, narrowly defined. In the later period, we see the serialization of texts that are likely more stable (singular), but less common; most likely these texts would have only appeared in a few (and not the same few) regional newspapers, if not this newspaper alone. The literature that emerges, then, is one that cannot be generalized in terms of reception, even if there may be some homogeneity among the producers. In this sense among others, these serialized works in Brazil not only tell us about the interest in popular fiction that existed in that far-flung community, but also remind us of the Japanese-language *literatures*—in the sense of aggregations of texts that would have been available to given historical reading communities—that are elided each time a singular (national) *literature* is invoked.

Ten Stories from Brazil

THE TWO PREVIOUS CHAPTERS CAN BE SEEN AS PRIMARILY FOCUSED on the consumption, in the sense of both purchasing and reading, of Japanese-language texts produced almost exclusively in Japan by readers in Brazil. While an awareness of the consumption of such texts is necessary to understanding Japanese-language literary activity in Brazil prior to the Second World War, it is by no means sufficient. Individuals were also emerging from that community who were engaged in the production of literary works—in the creation of original works of literature—that were subsequently published and circulated within this reading population. As none of these texts currently exists in English translation, ten stories are presented here as samples of that local literary production.

It is uncertain whether these texts should be considered "representative" of that production, just as any sample of texts cannot but fail to represent the entirety of a larger body of literary production. At the same time, the texts do contain themes that were common among stories produced during that period and are, for the most part, written in a literary form (Naturalism) that was predominant. While it would therefore be inevitably problematic to claim that these texts *do* represent the entirety of literary production by this community, it is a less problematic historical fact that these ten texts *have* represented that entirety for the last half-century, precisely because these are the texts that have enjoyed reproduction and dissemination, with either a tacit or explicit claim that they were representative thereof.

The history of that reproduction is largely known. The ten stories presented here were chosen by the anthropologist Maeyama Takashi for inclusion in the first volume of the *Koronia shōsetsu senshū*, published in 1975 by the Koronia Bungaku-kai (Grêmio Literário Colônia). As Maeyama notes in his epilogue to that volume, despite the fact that he had contacted many individuals asking for recommendations, he received no responses. This, compounded by the lack of information about and access to primary materials from the period, led Maeyama to choose the works to be included himself, from the roughly 150 works to which he had access.

The ten included here, which appear at the beginning of the collection and appear here in the order they are presented there, are the only works from before the Second World War. The result was that these works, which Maeyama felt were the best representatives (or perhaps highest literary achievements) of the period, became, as a result of their reproduction, the de facto representatives of the period. The collection of selected stories, which was the first of what has now grown to a four-volume series, was the continuation of an undertaking by the Koronia Bungakukai to preserve literary texts produced in Brazil. That undertaking had begun in 1965 with the formation of the association and the reproduction of individual works in the association's journal, *Koronia bungaku*, between 1966–68. The first volume of stories, published in 1975, expanded the number of works available from the prewar to ten and preserved them in the more durable book form. The collection was reproduced as part of a DVD-ROM in 2008 by the Burajiru Imin 100 Shūnen Kinen Kyōkai as part of the commemoration of the Centenário, the celebration of the centennial anniversary of Japanese migration to Brazil, and later its contents were made available online.[75] Over the last half-century, then, were anyone to have wanted to read Japanese-language fiction written in Brazil prior the Second World War, it is likely these would have been the only stories to which they would have had relatively easy access.

This is not to say that Maeyama's decisions were not based on prior acts of selection by other individuals. Of the ten stories, four had been selected to either receive or be a runner-up for the Colonial Literary Short Fiction Award competition held by the *Burajiru jihō* newspaper: "An Age of Speculative Farming," which won the first competition in 1932; "The Death of a Certain Settler," which had come in second; "Natsuyo," which won the second competition in 1933; and "Vortices," which had tied for second (no first-place award was given) in the third competition in 1935. That is, these were works that had already enjoyed the imprimatur of an authoritative source as being exceptional and/or representative; at the very least, they had been chosen with the explicit goal of cultivating among the Japanese-language writers in Brazil not only literary production in general, but a specific type of literary production deemed worthy by the newspaper's literary editors. Maeyama then selected six additional works, which had been published in either the *Burajiru jihō* or one of two additional venues: *Chiheisen*, a literary journal, and *Shin-Burajiru*, about which I have found no record. The ten works were written by a total of eight authors (two authors each had two works included), who will be briefly introduced below, with the exception of Sonobe Takeo, who is discussed in the introduction.

These eight authors and their ten works, then, while inevitably not able to fully represent Japanese-language literary production in prewar Brazil, are certainly not marginal either. These seven men and one woman (a gender disparity that reflects the times and perhaps Maeyama's tastes) were published in central literary venues, and thus received the implicit imprimatur of being published in those sites, even if the publications were not also accompanied by the explicit imprimatur of a literary competition.

A note on the translations: the original stories contain a number of terms transliterated from the Portuguese. In some cases, these transliterations are accompanied in the original texts by semantic glosses of one form or another, providing in Japanese the meanings of the Portuguese terms. In such cases, the English translation provides the term in Portuguese and the gloss in English. In other cases, the transliterations lack a semantic gloss in the original; the English translation of these terms will similarly lack a gloss. Ideally this will approximate the reading experience of the original texts lingustically. That is, if one knows the Portuguese terms, the absence of gloss will not be a problem; if one does not, the word will remain incomprehensible. This possibility of incomprehensibility, in fact, led the editors of the 1975 anthology to provide a glossary of common Portuguese terms in the back of the volume, though that glossary also cautioned readers that the usage of the terms might not perfectly coincide with their normative usages in Portuguese. Similarly, this volume contains a glossary of relevant terms in its backmatter.

"An Age of Speculative Farming"

Sonobe Takeo

This could be nothing more than a reverie during a sleepless night in the colonies. . . .

1

The *vagabundo*[1] would often notice these things.

"Hey, look, a whore (*puta*)!"

Hanaoka Ruriko, with her fake beauty spot, ignored the gobs spat onto the road by the Conde gang[2] (I didn't make that name up) as she strutted through the warm, sticky breeze of the rainy season. It was the time of day when the Martinelli building's advertisements[3] were illuminated, a half-eaten scoop of ice cream sat in the shadow of the palm trees in the Praça João Mendes, and the woman's pure white legs, bound with garters covered in crimson roses, overflowed with a fresh energy. Unconnected to the half-breed girl, Ruriko, Conrad Nagel[4] was wooing movie-crazy *señoritas* from the screen of the Odeon Theatre. . . .

These were the many symbols of modern life in São Paulo, which has long indulged in dreams of peace enveloped by the sounds of the *caboclo*'s *bandolim* and the bells of the *tropeiro*'s horses. The two busy streets that emerged at a forty-five-degree angle from the Praça da Sé heading toward the Mosteiro de São Bento and the Teatro Municipal, respectively, formed a triangle when capped by the Rua São Bento on the final side.[5] Within this triangle (*triângulo*) the lack of idealism of the colonial-era Portuguese was laid bare.

Buildings, stores, cafés, women's calves, beggars. Alongside these, at every corner the sight of *loteria* tickets being loudly hawked by crippled men. . . .

Hanaoka Ruriko. . . . Her hobbies were men, *sorvete*, cinema, smelling the soiled flesh of farmers, perverted sex, collecting cheap jewelry.

She always weaved through the dizzying triangle (*triângulo*) as a single seductive Oriental insect. She moved endlessly as a point along the edges of that triangle,

---

"An Age of Speculative Farming" first appeared in 1932 in the April 21, April 29, May 5, and May 12 issues of the *Burajiru jihō*.

as she passed through the entangled races, through the city of flesh mixed with that of the Portuguese—Italian, French, Spanish, German, Russian, and black—in her single-cut dress and snake-skin shoes, the perfumed secret of her flesh, visible through her gauzy wrap.

Then, just as the night wind from the coastal mountain range blew a handbill up to this beggar woman's feet, a new-model Ford stopped right before Hanaoka Ruriko, filling her field of vision as she looked up; it was the man indicated on her dance card[6] for that evening. The tomato parvenu Ōmura.[7] She was embraced in the filthy farmer's flesh she loved.

"Ohmura.[8] I might be too tired tonight. If only I could sleep behind rose-colored curtains, where there's a bath, a powder room, and a toilet, my heart pounding at the scent of someone's cigar (charuto). . . ."

"Ruriko, are you trying to say that you want to marry me?" the tomato parvenu said, dyeing his obscene breath with his gigantic heart.

While popping out her stylish, inside-out socks, Ruriko replied, "Idiot! Who would want to marry someone like you?"

Ōmura was speechless.

"Ohmura, don't take it so seriously. Kiss me."

The car sped off in the direction of the Odeon, where Conrad Nagel was playing.

2

Five kilometers from X station on the Central line[9]—the Ōmura farm.

The farm, made up of two hundred thousand tomato plants on a five-degree slope, included a ferocious guard dog, a farm manager from Tieté, and many agricultural laborers. Were the hands of its agricultural laborers on the front line of the tomato wars perpetually stained by the tomato juice, despite its being the off-season, because the morning activities of the market are about to be disrupted by the decreased supply and dramatically increased prices bearing down on greater São Paulo?

Hawks flew overhead. It was a bleak scene of tank after tank, with the sapé[10] huts of the natives huddled in the distance, palm trees here and there with a mountain range far in the background. The slope with the squirming burros and the temptation of the mamão fruit.

Near a well on the tomato farm, operated by the clever Nipponico who encamped here and took advantage of the meat-loving races, a number of laborers in torn clothing battled the stifling heat of latitude 23.5 degrees south, encircling a large vat used in the making of a Bordeaux solution.[11]

One of the laborers dissolved quicklime into the solution, choking all the while on the cloud of dust in the air. He then combined the dissolved lime with just the right amount of copper sulfate. The color of the Bordeaux solution that resulted from the combination became an extremely faint blue, like that of the autumn

sky in the laborer's hometown, making him sentimental. The greedy history of
the immigrant pioneers became an opaque precipitate; the endless exploitative
competition swirls in the mixture, dissolving into the Bordeaux solution.

Over the course of three months the solution was dusted on the plants by the
laborers, who bore the sprayers upon their backs like debt; the resulting tomatoes,
produced after these repeated attacks against the macrosporum bacillus[12]—the
red tomatoes that had previously caused such fear in Japan that they had been
nicknamed "poison eggplants"—did not even stir the appetites of the already
exhausted farm workers.

The sprawling farm was one with no history to be proud of; it was merely one
upon which chemical fertilizers were recklessly dumped. Nonetheless, its production during the previous period had been:

A: The initial planting of 20,000 had been such a success that it was immediately increased to 120,000.

B: Even considering the average price per crate to be 15 *mil réis*, the average
daily shipment was between seventy and eighty crates, for a grand total of roughly
ten thousand. The proceeds from this were 150 *contos*.

The upshot of this was that even though Ōmura stealthily skimmed off the
majority of the profits at market, requests to sharecrop came in one after another
from thickheaded Brazilieros who had been astonished by the sales, only to be followed by a swarm of heroic *Nipponicos*, enslaved by their gambling "savvy." One
from Itaquaquecetuba, one from Itaquera, one from Mogi, others from Suzano,
Romanópolis, São Miguel. . . .

Their speculative spirits were aroused as though struck by a hammer; as the
mountains of *mamona* dregs[13], powdered bone, saltpeter, and potassium chloride
(among others) that had been resting in the storehouses of the ambitious fertilizer entrepreneur began to crumble away, operations expanded willy-nilly. Anyone who did not move quickly to seize his portion of the wealth by producing
tomatoes soon became the object of derision, as one ignorant of the ways of the
world. No one paid any thought to diversification[14] or producing quality goods.
The tomato-farming families—even those poor families that had just set foot on
Brazilian soil—responded to the call, swaying on their horse-drawn carts as they
moved to the farm, filled with anticipation.

Of course every day there were other migrants who marched down the Santos
wharf toward the frightening customs office, hearing the sound of gunfire behind
them in Manchuria. Indeed, the so-called migrants were gradually being replaced
by individuals filled with new ideas and novel schemes. The Ōmura farm was
oblivious to this, completely absorbed in tracking down its next big take.

3

Even the hot sidewalks of São Paulo cooled late at night, under the rows of sycamore trees.[15]

Hanaoka Ruriko walked the road to her apartment, treading on the pollen-covered ground and feeling a fleeting romanticism (*romantismo*) as she looked upon the slightly blurred night scene in the direction of Bras, until she entered the heavy door, which the black woman had opened for her.

In those rooms was Hanaoka Ruriko's deviant playground: a double bed hidden behind a floral-patterned curtain of Indian silk.

She kept a youth in those rooms.

This was her so-called stray dog, a preoccupied young man who had just come to Brazil. Having just been awoken with a smack, he stared at her lewd figure as she sat cross-legged atop her bed, after merely unhooking the waist of her skirt. Then he spoke.

"Did something happen to you? Or was it the stinky farmer?"

For a moment Ruriko was caught off guard, then she suddenly grabbed his hair and while shaking him responded, "You think you'd be able to live without me?"

"Let's not make empty threats."

"I'm serious, damn it!"

"Then where should I go?"

The stray dog, pale, rolled on the carpet looking sad.

The springs of the mattress groaned beneath her as she looked down on him pityingly.

"Forgive me. I am going to get married."

"What do you mean by that?"

"Oh my stray dog, do even you still have the capacity for chagrin?"

"So rather than smacking me around, you want to be cradled in a farmer's strong arms when you sleep. Is that it?"

"Would you begrudge me some rest?"

"No, but. . . ."

So saying he crawled toward Ruriko to give her feet an imploring kiss.

With this, their pathetic deviant play finally began.

The stray dog's cries; Ruriko's mad laughter; kicking, collapsing; sound, sweat.

"I don't want to leave. After all—I live not in Brazil, but in you, Ruriko."

"Idiot, idiot, idiot. Ha, ha, ha. . . ."

4

Tomato prices were far lower than expected. Ōmura, though, continued to carry himself as if he were full of confidence.

He thought he could still snatch a profit despite the bleakness of the situation.

The entire area in and around the Mercado Central[16] was spotted with the footprints of the *kuronbō*[17] workers whose feet tread on the rotted fruits and vegetables. When the tomato parvenu Ōmura arrived at the offices of the *comprador* Kurose on Rua 25 de Março the next morning, he passed through the throng of sallow vegetable growers on his way to the meeting room on the second floor. There he met Kurose.

"Ōmura, why don't you just play along? You know, on that matter I mentioned earlier. . . ."

"What? You know, that growers' association already has an advance contract with the Colombo[18] canning company for two thousand crates—at 200 *reis* per kilo, no less. . . . No matter how *misturado*[19] it might be, it is not very good news for you. It would be safer for you to leave things to me. Hehehe. . . ."

Afterwards Ōmura spat onto the wall of the *mercado*—the central nerve of life in São Paulo—and then raced his new-model Ford toward the Hotel Noroeste, the lively building that stood facing the Largo da Sé, the muscles in his face twitching all the way. "That upstart Kurose. He just got started recently but now he is acting like a big *comprador*. Damn him. It would be one thing if I were just another tomato grower. This is the great Ōmura he is dealing with. . . ."

"So I take it that there is no way that I can convince you. . . ." The thought of Kurose's scheming face as he said this stuck in his craw.

Hanaoka Ruriko, already at the entrance in her daytime makeup, was being chased off by the black doorman because of her palpable eroticism, visible through the emerald green georgette fabric.

Ōmura arrived just as she was about to kick him with those snakeskin shoes of hers, yelling, "I'm not a prostitute, *kuronbō-me!*" A record of jazzy Carnaval music could be heard in the distance.

After blowing the bubbles off of a bottle of champagne in one of the rooms at the Hotel Noroeste, the two married in a very unconventional way.

Why did Hanaoka Ruriko marry?

If Ōmura were asked, he would say that it was nothing more than the fulfillment of a casual desire using Ruriko's body, as one feels hungry for *terceiro*[20] tomatoes at times, cracks and all.

Even a monstrous love requires certain appurtenances. The tomato parvenu Ōmura addressed his bride in the full light of day.

"We are leaving tonight on the express train to Rio for our honeymoon."

"Are you planning on selling me on Rio's bride *mercado*, Ohmura?"

"I am not such a brute as to sell my own bride."

To this, the woman—still disheveled from her wedding—continued.

"Ohmura, I have a request."

"Are you going to ask me to quit growing tomatoes?"

"No! I want you to buy me some jewels!"

5

A thrilling rain squall passed from *rua* to *rua*, pelting the pure white legs. Drops of water sparkled as they fell from the eaves of the *sorveteria*.

Hanaoka Ruriko and Ōmura were strolling the sidewalk of Rua Direita, which was invigorated by the recent rain. Along the street wax *señoritas* were trailing *amarelo* afternoon dresses in the display windows. Weaving their way through the elegant crowds, the newly married couple visited the Jewish precious metal dealer at Casa Esplendor and browsed the collection of magnificent jewels. The collection enslaved the hearts of *señoritas* from throughout the world.

"My, how amazing. Diamonds. Rubies. Pyropes. Uvarovites. Carnelians. Turquoises. Moonstones. Cat's Eyes . . . etc., etc."

There was no doubt that he would buy one for her, but even for Ruriko, whose eyes were confronted with the radiance of every imaginable luster, the luminescence of the andalusite, the queen of noctilucent stones, possessed a rare austere brilliance. What was one to do under the thrall of such a prodigious intoxication?

"Oh, Ohmura, they're all just so beautiful!"

"Don't cry, now."

Ruriko swung her handbag around wildly.

"I am going to cry, I am. . . . Ohmura, I love you."

Ōmura chewed on his cigar (*charuto*), smiling.

Meanwhile, in the heart of the city of São Paulo. . . .

A line of *caminhões* packed with tomatoes were being sucked into the red brick fortress, preparing to open the market for the day. After the five hundred crates of tomatoes were stacked up, the *caminhões* made their retreat outside of the red bricks. With that, the chaotic and uncontrolled clamor made by this band of crooks—*compradores*, tomato growers, and retailers—rose to an unparalleled din, as though a beehive had been struck. The foreman of the Ōmura farm himself, his eyes darting around the room, had two hundred cases of his own. For a variety of complex reasons, today's market would necessarily foretell the fate of the tomato producers this season; yet because it was here in Brazil—which in all ways treaded the very tip of the world's tail—it lacked anything like brokers, overseers, bookkeepers, clerks, or traders. It was nothing more than buyers and sellers pushed into a pen, only to have each in his own way—man to man, hand to hand—battle out the sales.

There were many *compradores*—let's call them A, B, C, D, E—but this day something strange happened. The tomato producers, who are living under constant fear of malnutrition and for that reason tend to accede on matters of price, demanded the exorbitant sum of 25 *mil réis*. The buyers, however, shouted out from all over, as if an answering echo, a price of 10 mil reis. A did, as did B, C, D. . . . Normally the price would then settle, like the air bubble in a level, on a price of 14 or 15 *mil réis*. Today's air bubble, however, did not budge. Ten minutes . . . twenty . . . thirty . . . The buying price remained firm at 10 *mil réis*. This unexpected turn caused the air in the room to dye a peculiar tint.

"Why 10 *mil réis*?"

The cries of the already hungry producers raced through the room. In response, A, B, C, D, etc. forced smiles as they met the gazes of the farmers. Men who were in some cases too cowardly even to smell the raw tomatoes when on the farms in the mountains became drunk and aroused on the air of the *mercado*. The farmers had no idea what was going on, and instead just milled around blindly.

"Could the *compradores* be conspiring together?"

"No, Kurose bought them all off as a challenge to Ōmura."

These thoughts were whispered by some, shouted by others. The farmers marched on, their sleep-deprived eyes remained fixed on that price of 10 *mil réis*, a price too shocking to even elicit tears. When the comprador Kurose determined that price as part of his strategy, he had been so caught up in idle excitement that he had lost even the ability to imagine how this would affect them, as they plunged into the hardship of a livelihood dependent on the tomato. . . . Ōmura heard of this crash in the price of tomatoes on the São Paulo market moments after returning to the Hotel Noroeste with Hanaoka Ruriko.

When Ōmura realized that this artificial drop had been due to disruptions in the market caused by the *comprador* Kurose, he was overwhelmed with fury. It was an unimaginable price. For Ōmura, who had come through any number of fusillades in these tomato speculation wars, the fate of his own farm was all too clear.

"I have to do something . . . but can anything be done? Damn it! Damn it all!"

Ōmura paced around the room like a tiger in a cage. No matter how he writhed about, all he could see was the scornful expression of the fertilizer salesman, the resentful glares of the laborers, and the storehouses filled with tomatoes despite the bad harvest, held in waiting for the perfect moment. The sound that filled his ears, coming back from his memory, was the strained roars of the *caminhões* rushing toward him, bearing mountains of artificial fertilizer!

Ōmura groaned.

Hanaoka Ruriko, caressing the Burmese ruby she bought at the Jew's shop and eating a *manga*, smiled ironically and perversely mused, "My groom, I feel so wonderful. . . . Will I ever have another evening this fortunate?"

Ōmura was dumbfounded.

"Ohmura, why aren't you saying anything?"

"Ohmura, you promised, you know. To take me to Rio. . . ."

Ōmura suddenly struck the table and shouted, "Are you kidding, you slut!"

The fruit plate overturned and a *manga* fell lethargically from the table.

"Well, thank you very much (*muita obrigada*)! You're calling me a prostitute? I suppose that's true, Mr. Former-Tomato Bigshot. . . . I feel like I finally understand, now hearing your groaning. Idiot . . . idiot. For what reason are you the *japoneses'* boss man? You have no idea why the migrants are suffering these days. . . . They want a goal, like the one the *alemães* have. How hard are you working to establish such a goal? To make matters worse, you don't really do any work at all.

... All of you ... all of you. .... The world would be better off if people like you just died in the gutter. Perhaps then you could at least become fertilizer for *milho*. Listen, Ohmura. I am going home and then I am going to tell my stray dog that the time has come! The time to take up the *enxada* and cultivate a new world. .... Needless to say, today marks the beginning and end of our marriage. A curse on you! Goodbye."

That Japanese blood circulated in Hanaoka Ruriko's corrupted flesh was nothing short of a miracle. Rather, it was as if some invisible power had inhabited Ruriko's painted lips to say those words. In place of Ōmura's bride, who disappeared from his life after this spectacle, a waiter from the hotel stood firm in front of him, carrying a prodigious bill. .... Throughout the world there are places that are paralyzed, but this simply means that they lack an objective.

Regardless of this sort of airing of dirty laundry, the more exhausted the agricultural laborers became, the more the juice of the tomatoes permeated their flesh. With the drop in price resulting from the *compradores'* machinations, the rampancy of the macrosporum bacteria, and the indignation of the soil, there was only one way that this last page of the history of the fall of Ōmura farm could be written: with a boy picking diseased leaves from what tomato plants had grown. ...

Aah ... these precious pages of the history of migration had finally sunk into corruption, having been committed to Ōmura, Kurose, Hanaoka Ruriko, and the stray dog. .... The bodies of agricultural laborers, bent by exhaustion! Sunset. ... A solitary laborer stood tall atop the soil, impoverished from the immoderate application of artificial fertilizers, staring at the distant mountain range. ... In its shadow were plains, hills, and mountains, across this vast land called Brazil ...

Those who roam about, unable to recognize that objective, perpetually entranced by the intermittent glory of speculative farming were merely ants ... ants. ...

When would the day finally come that those desultory ants gather and erect a towering anthill?

Even now a new migrant ship approached from across the Atlantic—in order to establish a brilliant objective for the Japanese migrants.

Damn it!

The laborer drew in a deep breath and then screamed. ...

9 March 1932

"The Death of a Certain Settler"

Nishioka Kunio

1.THE BLACK *CAMARADA*

"What? You want a job?"

Daisuke shouted in his deep voice, in an attempt to intimidate him. A man who seemed to be *baiano*, with a face that gleamed black, and a woman who was presumably his wife, with her belly hugely swollen, stood with their shoulders shrugged in front of his home. On the ground to their side was one *arroz saco* jammed with all of their worldly possessions and a large child, with a thin, monkey-like face and wide eyes, who sat staring uneasily at Daisuke.

"If you'll work hard for me I can give you something. Let's start off with two or three days and see how it goes. Leave your sack over here and come with me."

So saying, the diminutive Daisuke started walking briskly toward the back of the house. Just as the black family was about to reach the *milho* shed out back, Daisuke once again barked out in his gruff voice, "Hurry up. We are going to the *cafèzal.*"

The black man, who was nearly six feet tall, trailed behind Daisuke as he climbed the mountain behind Daisuke's home with his *enxada* over his shoulder. The afternoon sun in the cloudless sky hurt his eyes as it shone down on them.

The sun had already disappeared over the horizon. The small group of four *camaradas* came down from the plantation dragging their heavy, exhausted legs with each step. For these brave warriors who have spent the whole day battling the blazing heat, as it baked their bodies and souls, nighttime was paradise, from which they could hope for nothing more than full bellies and deep sleep. They, however, were happy enough with satisfying these two desires. Each of the four men had returned from the fields gulping down the saliva that filled his mouth every time he imagined the supper that would fill his empty stomach.

The four men, the three young Japanese and the black man who had come that day, shivered as they washed their faces at the well, wiping them with their sweat-stained *camisas*, and then one by one entered the dining room, which was dimly

"Aru kaitakusha no shi" appeared in 1932 in the 19 May, 2 June, 9 June, 16 June, 23 June, and 30 June issues of the *Burajiru jihō*.

lit by the light of a lantern.[21] Their long-awaited supper was about to begin. Seven people sat at the table: the four *camaradas*, Daisuke, his small-framed wife who bore a striking resemblance to him, and a boy of around ten. The black woman who had come that day looked in from the window, with only her eyes showing any life. Suddenly Daisuke's gruff voice ripped through the silence.

"Get the hell out of here, you beggar! Is there any law that says that someone who doesn't work should eat?"

The light from the lantern started to swing wildly as the commotion in the dining room burst out. The black man, who had leapt up with a fierce expression on his face, glared at the diminutive Daisuke and emitted a growl that sounded as though it had been squeezed out from the depths of his gut. The other *camaradas*, tense in the face of what seemed about to happen, readied themselves. In this situation, however, it was the black *camarada* who was the weaker party. It was this weakness that caused him to slowly release his clenched fists, showing how even someone like him, with the growing rage that consumed him, apparently must lower his head before his master. His wife had fled back to the shed sobbing. Sadly, she would not eat at all today. Where would they go if they left here now? *Let me bring my wife, heavy with child, and ask, plead, for food*, the black man had thought; but now he collapsed back into his chair. Seeing this, the others present felt some relief, but there was no way they could go back to eating. They had known all along that the landowner was a strict man, but they had not realized he was this sort of devil. Thinking *surely no other person in the world is as evil as this*, the black man addressed the landowner with his face downturned, as though he had just been castigated.

"*Patrão*, she didn't eat anything today either, a-and she's in her last month of pregnancy so she can't work, she's in a tough spot. I-i-is there any way you could let her have *um plato*[22] of food? I will gratefully put in an extra hard day of work tomorrow in return."

"Absolutely not. In my home, we follow my rules: those who do not work are not fed."[23]

Saying this, Daisuke pinched a few silver coins out of his *bolso* and tossed them onto the *mesa*. The black man, who rose with a look of pained sadness on his face and did not even look at the coins, picked up the torn *chapéu* that he had been sitting upon and quietly went out of the home. For a time they could hear him returning to the shack out back, but before long the pathetic *baiano* family had disappeared into the darkness, with the *saco* over his shoulder and the child in her arms.

2.SELLING *LARANJA*

The following day—with beautiful weather both dry and sunny, wiping away the events of the previous evening as though they were but a dream of the distant past—after the *camaradas* had gone out *carpir*, Daisuke was stacking, one-by-one, the bricks from the *terreiro* extension near the main house.

"Idiot. . . . Who can survive in this world with as womanly a sentiment as compassion. I despise people who tell sob stories. Who does that big ox think he is? Young people today really are cheeky. Then last night to leave without even eating after working that whole day. . . . What a goddamn bore."

Clearly it was bothering him, because he went over and over the events of the previous evening in his mind.

The home of this man, who with 150 *alqueires* was the largest landowner in this colony, was an extremely crude affair of red clay; behind it was a banana grove while the front of the home was surrounded by overgrown *laranja* trees. Overgrown with weeds, it was the kind of estate that children feared. A slender stream of smoke rose from the *cozinha*; likely his small wife was preparing *almôço*.

Three or four small, blue-eyed children—of the sort one can see in the *colônia* on the other side of the mountain—emerged from a path cut through the thicket.

"*Bom dia.*"

The boys greeted Daisuke as they approached him.

"May we have this many *laranjas?*"

The tallest of the boys held out a one-*mil* coin.

Daisuke stood lethargically, handed the boys a pole, and had the children knock them down.

After a few minutes, Daisuke, who was watching the golden *laranjas* plunk down on the undergrowth one after another, stopped them.

"Ok, ok. That's enough."

They've knocked too many down. *Um, dois, três* . . . he counted loudly as he dropped them into the *saco* the children had brought.

3.WANDERING

Kaneko Daisuke—a man of such small stature that the other people in the colony would ridicule him behind his back, saying that while the name 'Kaneko' was fitting with its reference to gold, "It's funny that they named that little guy 'Daisuke,'" meaning 'Big man'—had settled in this K colony in the *noroeste* interior fourteen years earlier.

While working as a carpenter for around three years after arriving in the city of São Paulo, Daisuke had squirreled away his pennies until he had saved up the eight *contos* necessary to buy a 150-*alqueire* plot of the highest-quality land here in this colony before coming as one of its early settlers.

With a little bit of *pinga* in him, Daisuke was more than happy to speak of his struggles during those early years, which he remembered as a period of great personal triumph, to anyone who would listen. As he did, his face would transform completely, taking on a handsome, relaxed expression.

One day after supper he began telling a number of young *camaradas* of his past.

"I am no one special. I was born in Hokkaidō. If anyone asked about his origins, my father would say that his family had been retainers of the Aizu domain; the reality, though, was that he was a cowardly samurai who had dashed off to southern Ezo just before Aizu castle fell in the Meiji Restoration. There he was forced to farm as a peasant, growing millet and barely getting by. . . . I was his third son. What? Why was I given the name Daisuke? Give me a break. Ha! Because my dad, like me, was made fun of for being a small guy. I guess he wanted me to become a "big man." In the autumn of 1884 I was apprenticed to a carpenter in Muroran but, how should I say it, I fell for his daughter . . . my "first love" . . . When my master found out, he was furious. I got out of there that very night. . . . Let's see, I was twenty when that happened, so it's been about twenty-eight years since I set foot in my hometown. I fooled around for two years in Tokyo, before I had the simple idea to see another country as I kept up my playing and went over to Manchuria. . . . I sure did have a good time there, too. . . ."

4.WANDERING

"Next I decided to go someplace really far away and came to South America mixed in with a group of migrants headed to Peru. In Lima, I passed myself off as an apprentice to a barber, cutting the hair of a one hairy foreigner after another. . . . When I was young I was really useless, so I couldn't settle down in Lima, either. From there I went to Chile, where I made a living as a laborer in a nitratine mine. Because I was born this sort of small man, wherever I have gone people have taken a shine to me, calling me pipsqueak and the like; as a result, I have never had any trouble earning a livelihood. From Chile I went to Argentina, where I must have lived for something like two years on the outskirts of Buenos Aires. It was there where I heard that Brazil was good to Japanese and felt compelled to head to São Paulo. Now that I think about it, that was already seventeen years ago. By that time I was already over thirty and had begun to realize that I couldn't keep wandering forever. I decided it was time to call it quits with all the fooling around. That marked the end of the first half of my life . . . haha!"

Daisuke took a break from the story to have a drink of *pinga*.

The lantern swayed slightly from the cool breeze coming in the window.

The young men breathed deep sighs of relief at this break in the story, which they had been listening to as they leaned on the *mesa* and stared at Daisuke's small, red-black face.

Daisuke continued.

"Humans too, once enlightened, can do great things. Even a good-for-nothing like me, who had lived a life of dissipation right up until that moment, was able to become a serious man. Fortunately, there was decent work for carpenters in São Paulo, so I could really throw myself into my work. Here too my boss was fond of me, and I was able to put away a good amount of money. The other guys had the attitude of most artisans, who go through money as though it were water, thinking, "No need to hold back at night what I can earn the next day." One look at them convinced me to get my house in order. I wasn't completely lonely. . . . I even had enough of a *Look at me now!* attitude that I could have a laugh at their expense. . . . What? My wife? The old lady, you mean? Around that time she was on her allotted land with her first husband, who was sick. He went to the Santa Casa hospital, but he died while she was working as a maid in my boss's house. She sobbed herself to sleep every night, alone now as she was in the world. My boss acted as go-between and got the two of us together. Then one day a guy I know asks me whether I want to buy some land. Since I knew a lot of people who had made money buying land in Hokkaidō, I had been thinking that if nothing else, I had to own land someday. So I was interested in the idea right away. . . . The guy went on and on about places where the land was supposed to good, talking about the Pau-d'alho are like this and the Perobom are like that. When I asked, 'What about the title to the land?', the man assured me that it was land the government of Doutor Pedro had sold off, so it was legitimate. I was hooked. . . . When I think about it now, I should have been more nervous . . . I mean, I was buying land knowing nothing about it; I had just glanced at *a mapa*. This is how I paid the full 8 *contos* or so that I had saved up and purchased those 150 *alqueires* of land."

As he said this, Daisuke's face grew increasingly radiant with pleasure. The lantern cast a flickering light as though its oil could run out at any moment.

Daisuke stood and blew it out—"wow, the moon sure is pretty tonight"—and gazed out the window as he beckoned the others over.

The pale blue moonlight of a foreign moon illuminated all of their bronzed faces.

One of the men was nodding off, his head bobbing up and down.

One enthusiastic young man asked a question, to once again spur the conversation.

"You sure had a good eye for the land you chose."

"No more than any other Tom, Dick, or Harry; it was completely chance."

Daisuke then smiled and continued.

"When that guy I knew spread out the *mapa* and asked me which parcel I wanted to buy, I said, 'Any is fine. I have no idea. I suppose the one closest to the seller's land would be good.' That's all I said and it was decided. It was just this and some good luck. Now that I think about it, that was fourteen years ago, when I finally decided to become a settler. At that time Masabō, who is now in

São Paulo, had just been born. . . . When the three of us, me, my old lady, and my son, were on the train heading out on the Sorocabana Line, I guess even I—who had bounced all over South America—was a little scared. All day the train passed through nothing but barren *campo*; it felt as though we were being carried off to some circle of hell. . . . Two days later, in the evening, we reached ○ ○ town. Now that area had been completely cleared, but at that time the train only went as far as ○ ○ town. The previous landowner's home was in ○ ○ town, so that night we stayed in his storage shed. We had the little money that was left, and what rice and beans we could carry on our backs; once we had purchased salt and matches, we decided to head to our settlement the next day. It was forty kilometers away from ○ ○ town, but because what little road there was overgrown from both sides by thicket, even a *carroça* could not pass easily. The forty kilometers of so-called road was all through forest so thick that it was like a dim tunnel. Through this tunnel I walked ahead, carrying a heavy load of provisions on my shoulders, and gripping a *foice*, a *machado*, and an *enxada* in my hand. Behind me followed my wife, with Masabō on her back and a bag filled with a pot, salt, and matches in her hands. I'm not proud of it, but I have to admit I wept with joy when, thirty kilometers in, I came across an Italian who was letting his pigs forage there and let us stay the night. I had never been so happy to see another human being as I was that day. I was as happy as one who had discovered a savior in hell.[24] He even gave us our fill in pork. It was truly as they say: deep in the mountains, any man you encounter is a brother. Anyway, so the route I walked in to my property is the valley that the train line runs through; that line was just a road then. I could not believe that I had become the owner of 150 *alqueires*; I kept saying to myself, "This really is a lot of land." At the same time, I was at a total loss, thinking, "What have I gotten myself into?," but it was too late for that sort of thing. I mean, there wasn't even a way to ship crops out once I grew them. With no other options, my old lady and I decided to forget about the outside world and just wait for the train line to come through, making do by slowly clearing land and raising pigs and chickens. We made a hut from split palm wood and the three of us began our lives as mountain hermits."

It had gotten quite late, but Daisuke showed no sign whatsoever of finishing.

"When I think about it, the human body seems weak but is actually quite strong. The whole reason that I can work as hard as any young guy today is because of what I went through then. My old lady worked hard too. There were many nights she went to bed without even taking off her straw sandals. Our faces looked just like those of a Hokkaidō bear. Nowadays a person will *perde* a package of matches in a month; the pack we carried in with us lasted three years—until the train line opened. By lighting a *tôco* that I had stuck into the ground in the middle of the hut, I could keep it burning for six or seven days. That way we didn't need a drop of oil and could save our matches. Since we settled there in September, it wasn't until December that we could harvest any *milho*, beans, or *batata*; in the meantime, all we had to eat was rice, beans, salt, and vegetables. We were heartened to see that chickens we had gotten from the Italian were increasing in number despite constantly losing some to *bichos*, and to know that in the new year the pigs we had gotten would give birth to a litter. It didn't particularly feel like we were waiting for the train line to arrive, but we also felt that if we didn't seed at least a few coffee plants we really couldn't be called pioneers, because it would make us no different from all of the people who would come in so easily later. The cries of the wild-cats were only bothersome at first; before too long I would miss them if I didn't hear them. I was fortunate to have made it this far without getting sick even once, but the other settlers all say I succeeded because of luck. It definitely wasn't luck. Men make themselves through work. If one just sticks to it, even a good-for-nothing like me can make quite a success of himself. Well, we've had a good, long talk, but it's time we get to sleep. Tomorrow I am going to have you weeding out at S."

Daisuke stood, stretched both arms out, and yawned deeply. Then he trotted off into the bedroom to his right.

6 (SIC). NOSTALGIA

From time to time during the twenty-eight years since he had fled his hometown, Daisuke would count the years on his fingers, bending one after another. . . .

"Forty-eight? I too have become an old man. I wonder what has become of my father? I guess he would be over eighty now, and my mother seventy-eight. My older brother must be fifty-seven, and I bet as poor as ever. . . . My first love . . . she was seventeen, three years younger than me. She too must be gray-haired by now, someone's old lady, no, perhaps an old spinster somewhere. All of my primary school friends are all older now, but I bet none has made much of a success of himself. I suppose I am the *yokozuna* of the group. . . ."

Daisuke planned to return to his hometown soon, wearing the proverbial golden brocade,[25] and as such had lately found himself slipping deeply into this sort of reverie.

The *camaradas*, having already been out to the fields on this beautiful day, had retreated to the shade of a tree in the garden, where they were nodding off as they enjoyed the cool, morning breeze.

"I had them make the best clothes, shoes, and *chapéu* this town has ever seen by far, and am going to wear them back to Japan. I am just going to go third-class on the ship, but as for the train once there, I am going to ride in second-class like the *yokozuna* I am. Everyone back home will be so surprised. 'Kaneko's third son has come back home a big success—they say he owns 370 hectares of land in Brazil.' I can't wait. No matter how the people here in the colony vilify me and call me a brute, in the end money makes the world go around. What is it they say? 'What use is a cherry blossom if you don't have money?'[26] My ability to make my aged parents happy now, in the midst of this downturn, is a reward for my tenacity. . . . All of these idiots who go on and on about compassion this and compassion that—what use is compassion if one can't take proper care of one's parents? I have no memory of having done even the smallest wrong thing; the path I have walked has been completely proper. . . . Sure, maybe I have pushed back a repayment or two, but have I ever not paid my debts? What about those guys in the colony? Who was it who drove Yamamoto's store in town out of business, all along wearing faces filled with compassion? Incompetent people are just resentful, backbiting whomever they please. They love to prattle on about luck this, luck that, shamelessly ignoring their own incompetence. Look at what we pioneers went through! Look at my house! Is this the mansion of a great landowner, with 150 *alquieres* and 160,000 coffee plants? If all I had were pretension and luck, I wouldn't have a penny to my name. Those guys in the colony will call me a violent and greedy demon behind my back, but to my face it is nothing but flattery, with their heads pressed to the ground. My chairmanship of the Japan Association is the same way. This is my fifth year in a row in that position, but not because I want to do it or anything. Every time the election comes around they push me into it and then say 'Kaneko monopolizes the chairmanship!' I am sick of the whole business."

He couldn't but grow discontented as he looked back on the hardships of his life thus far and the baseless rumors that were spread about him nowadays in the colony. As he remembered it, the path his life had taken was anything but a commonplace one; all along it had been a grueling climb bordered by precipitous cliffs. But he had reached the summit, achieved his goal: success. It is natural that this should be met with the roaring applause of the crowds. When in place of such applause he overheard the cold scorn that ran through the colony, it naturally left him agitated.

"What are you thinking over there?"

Daisuke addressed the question to his wife, who seemed uncharacteristically lost in thought, having returned from the hills out back with her empty lunch box clattering at her side.

"Nothing. I was just thinking about back home."

For a moment Daisuke smiled slightly before restoring his serious expression and continuing.

"You have really aged too, haven't you. It is because you have worked really hard as well. I owe as much to you for that success. People say that we resemble one another; I wonder if any couple resembles one another as much in both body and spirit as we do. Poor, dim-witted people would be going on and on about new clothes, fine food, a grand house . . . but you, you let me wear this patched *camisa*. You're something. That boy of ours, Masabō, now he's another story. At sixteen, when he should be hard at work, he runs off to São Paulo saying he needs to study. But what is a *vagabundo* like him going to do with that learning? He should learn something from his father. I told him I would happily hire him if he got a degree in agriculture or graduated from a vocational school. When I told him, though, that rather than becoming a person with learning who is used, he should become a person who himself does the using, he up and ran off. Eldest son or not, there is no way I can make him my successor. Shinbō is only eleven, but we have to be careful not to let him grow up into a *vagabundo* too."

Daisuke grumbled as he stood.

7. CALAMITY

The day of his return home approached quickly. Today was his last tour of the coffee plantation. The arable land stretched over five kilometers long, and in the various intervening valleys were four *colônias*, with four-year contract laborers and *colonos* from twenty-four families. Straddling a packhorse, Daisuke rode up and down the hills, peaceful and content atop his mount. The thickly grown coffee trees shone in the afternoon sun, looking like distant, undulating waves. Daisuke gripped the reins with his chest pressed out proudly and his eyes sparkling with satisfaction. As he approached the third elevation, Daisuke remembered how half a year earlier an Italian *colono* had drawn a knife and chased after him at that very spot. He clicked his tongue in annoyance and thought to himself, "That was a close call. When I was just the slightest bit strict with him about the *carpi* and yelled at him, the next thing I knew my eyes opened wide and I began to scream when I saw something metal flash. He had already drawn his *faca* and was coming at me. I rounded my back and then ran, if I remember correctly. Fortunately there was a horse nearby, so I leapt on to it and took off at full speed. That's the only reason I escaped. That's why I can't stand hairy foreigners. You say the slightest thing and suddenly they pull a knife. With Japanese you don't have that worry, but they drive you crazy with all of their quibbling. I suppose *baianos* are the best; they can be dangerous, but they are the easiest to trick into doing what you want. When I get back, I am only going to have *baianos* for *colonos*." As the slight breeze that slipped between the coffee trees cooled his sweat-soaked body, Daisuke visited the homes of the *colonos*, which were scatted here and there. He let them know that he was going back to Japan temporarily, and asked the four-year contract worker Harada if he would kindly look after things while he was gone. Having finished his rounds, Daisuke returned home.

The day of his departure had finally arrived. Because it was the chairman of the Japan Association returning home, around ten members of the leadership of the Association and then the *colonos* each made an appearance and gave him a rousing send-off.

For Daisuke it was a day full of a sort of anticipation he had never experienced before. In his newly made suit he served everyone *pinga* and spent the day smiling heartily.

His plan was to spend the night in town and then leave for São Paulo on the first train in the morning, so around dusk he mounted his horse and set off from home alone.

To Daisuke, riding alone down paths by himself like this, lost in thought, felt far more pleasurable than exchanging boorish small talk, so he quite strenuously refused the people who offered to ride in with him.

As the light breeze brushed his cheeks, which were flushed from the bit of drink he had had, he finally took a moment to dwell on the sense of well-being that swelled up in his chest, threatening to burst out.

As he approached the town, he saw some rustling in the dark undergrowth that pressed in on the road from the side. At the moment he turned to look, he saw the eyes of a man who was staring directly at him.

Something flashed like lightning amid Daisuke's crowded memories.

"Ah! That *ku*. . . ."[27]

The pistol the man held erased the remainder of that scream as it rang out in the twilight, *bang, bang, bang.*

"Uhhh. . . ."

Daisuke groaned faintly as he rolled off the horse and fell to the ground.

The returnee, dressed in gold brocade covered with flesh and blood, lay on the ground, his feet twitching slightly until the darkness slipped over him and the curtain of night fell.

It was some days later.

Not far from the town, in the communal graveyard, a single new cross was discovered standing, upon which was written in clear Japanese characters, "Here lies Kaneko Daisuke, Pioneer of K Colony."

NISHIOKA KUNIO is the penname of Tanabe Shigeyuki (1908–?).[28] Nishioka was born in Hokkaidō in 1908 and studied agriculture at a vocational upper school there (despite claiming to have only finished primary school) before migrating to Brazil in 1928. He originally lived in Santo Anastácio in São Paulo State, but in 1930 moved to the Cocuera Colony in Mogi das Cruzes.[29] As with most all Japanese-language writers active in Brazil, Nishioka was engaged in non-literary activities as well. In April 1938, for example, he helped form the KTK Association in the Caxingui neighborhood of São Paulo City, which distributed newly hatched chicks that had been born using a new ten-thousand-egg incubator that had been imported from Japan.[30] As of 1975, he was still participating in literary activities in Brazil as a member of the Koronia Bungakukai.[31]

"Natsuyo"

Katayama Yōko

Natsuyo, a truly good-natured and clever woman whom we never referred to as anything but Natsu, was our maid for a full ten years. I have never again met such a good maid, and it is unlikely that I ever will. No, I take that back: it is a mistake to refer to her as just a maid; Natsu is someone who would have made a splendid wife and mother, regardless of the station of the household she entered. As a result of these qualities, her reputation was excellent throughout the neighborhood as well, and marriage proposals came on a regular basis from all quarters. Natsu never displayed any inclination to accept any, however, during her decade with us. In the end, she had no choice but to return to her parents after they expressed their displeasure with the situation.

Natsu, who is originally from Hokkaidō, came to our household when she was just a child of fifteen.[32] My husband arranged to have her come through the good offices of the inn where he stayed during his frequent travels there for work. Having been born to a poor family with many siblings, Natsu had been apprenticed at a young age; despite this, however, she remained an innocent who worked with great care, whether supervised or not, and as such quickly became indispensible and trusted by my husband and his first wife.

The event that made her truly essential to this family, however, was when my husband's wife, who was by all accounts normally quite hale, passed away suddenly from pneumonia at the young age of twenty-five, leaving behind children of only two and three. The pneumonia had been a byproduct of the highly contagious influenza that was so prevalent at that time, now many years past. How distraught my husband must have been, having suddenly lost someone he loved, leaving two small children motherless. Even now when he thinks back to those events, he is overcome with countless emotions; at the time, he must found himself utterly at a loss. To make matters worse, apparently the love that the two had held for each other for many years had only borne fruit in marriage three or four years prior; one can presume that my husband's anguish must have been profound.

"Natsuyo" appeared in 1933, in the June 29, July 6, and July 13 issues of the *Burajiru jihō*.

One can hardly imagine, given all this, Natsu's shock and bewilderment. Despite this, she rallied bravely, supporting my grieving and suffering husband and the motherless children; for two long years she bore this heavy responsibility. It was at that point that I met him.

Out of sheer coincidence, I learned that my husband's family home neighbored that of my elder brother's wife, and on the grounds of that connection he came to visit us with some frequency.

I was raised in a family of military men, with my deceased father and uncle having served and my two elder brothers serving currently serving. As one might imagine, then, I tended to come in contact with individuals almost entirely drawn from that world. When the man who became my husband began visiting this sort of household on a regular basis, my interest in him—given his different background— began as curiosity but at some point became a deep affection. My mother was taken by his charm and appearance, which belied his youth, while my brothers, for their part, at least displayed respect for the intelligence and experience he possessed in a wide variety of areas, compared to their own, which was limited to military matters. Needless to say, my sister-in-law approved of the match. An environment as conducive as this greatly facilitated our coming together. I should add that around this time my husband was operating a concern dealing in woolen goods, based in Yokohama.

I have veered far from my story of Natsu. I too had heard constantly about her, and how grateful he was to her. "I owe Natsu my life. Whatever else may happen, I must repay my debt to her somehow. . . ."

All of the family had heard these words of my husband's countless times. One day, as our wedding date was approaching, my husband once again raised the issue with me. "Keiko, I have you to thank for the happiness which this marriage will bring me. Please consider Natsu's circumstances. Once you have joined my household and settled in, I would very much like to give Natsu some leave to rest. I hope that you will understand my feelings on this matter." Why would I have had any objection? I was happy to give my approval.

Eventually Natsu and I came to live under the same roof. Once the initial days of morning-to-night work finally ended and a measure of calm had been restored to the home in Ushigome, Natsu welcomed me there with great joy.

"Madam, welcome to the household. Since you have arrived, the master has been in the highest of spirits, and I too share his great joy," Natsu said, with tears running down her cheeks. I imagined that she must have been overwhelmed by a sudden rush of emotions that she had born for so long. For my part, I was at a loss at how to express the feelings that filled my breast.

With the passage of time, Natsu and I became truly close. As a result, I never did carry through on the plan to give Natsu a holiday soon after I arrived, nor did Natsu seem to have the slightest interest in it either. The matter was simply forgotten. Of course, I helped Natsu with many of the tasks around the house, and as a result, despite the fact that my mother had expressed her concern multiple times to me when I left to join the new household that Natsu, having been there longer than I, would be difficult to control, I did not share that fear in the slightest, and instead grew as close to her as a sister or close friend. Natsu was also around my age, which allowed me to talk with her about things I otherwise might not have. Despite our similar ages, though, Natsu had not been raised as casually as I had, so even though she was twenty, one year younger than I, she also took the role of the senior in our conversations, providing me advice and counsel. I may have enjoyed far more of an education, but that learning did me no good at all. She was particularly good in dealing with the children. For example, when the children were getting a little carried away with their mischief, while I would not be able to scold them firmly no matter how hard I tried, Natsu would put a quick end to it, saying, "Young master, that simply will not do." That is not to say that Natsu was cold with the children. Being boys, they are prone to being quite rough and making trouble, but Natsu never once displayed a cross expression. Rather, she always maintained an air one would expect of a loving mother toward her beloved children.

It only occurred to me later, but it seemed as though Natsu might have been in love with my husband.

While there is nothing specific that I can put my finger on, Natsu was fond of always saying "The master this, the master that" and telling stories about him from before we met, and she always carried out any job that was for him with great care. Things like this just made me suspect. Another time, after she had just taken the children out to play, they remained out for an unusually long time; come evening, I was quite worried until I heard the sounds of my husband walking up to the front gate, mixed with the sounds of the children. When I hurried to the front door, I found them holding his hands and smiling, with Natsu right behind them, unable to conceal her pleasure. Then, presumably feeling guilty upon seeing me, Natsu's face reddened and she said, "The young masters said they wished to go to meet their father, and would not hear a word to the contrary. . . ." The encounter left me with an unpleasant feeling, that had I just not come to this household, Natsu would be living this sort of blissful life.

Moreover, it seemed clear that despite everything I did for her, Natsu preferred my husband to me. Things that she was not willing to reveal to me, she would freely speak to my husband about. Once, when my husband was in the bath, I happened to pass by the bathroom. I could hear the voices of my husband and Natsu, who would always go to check the temperature of the water. I was unable to make out Natsu's voice clearly due to the closed door and the sound of the water, but I did hear my husband say, "Don't worry. Leave everything to me." For a time I trembled with insecurity over what this might mean, but it gave me some comfort when I decided it must have been over the matter of the multiple requests Natsu had received recently from her parents asking for money. Still, this sort of attitude of Natsu's left me feeling vaguely discomfited and betrayed.

Despite that, there was no reason for me to lash out at Natsu, or to chastise her for secretly loving my husband. No, to the contrary, it was precisely because she loved him that she had been willing to do so much for him. If anything, it even caused me to feel pity toward her.

Though we wished she would stay with us indefinitely, of course that could not be, and it was at the end of March, when the cherry blossoms had finally begun to swell, that her time with us came to an end. She announced that she would leave this house in which she had lived for a full decade and the children that she had raised from their infancy. She returned home in tears. We too all cried as we saw her off, as though we were saying goodbye to a close relative.

We all went to the station with her. I will never forget her face, swollen and red from all of the tears, as she receded into the distance, her head bowing all the while.

The wall calendar had been replaced three times since that day. Not a single letter had arrived with news from Natsu. I hoped that no news was good news. In my case, much had changed, starting with that earthquake.[33] Because both the business and our home were severely damaged, I had developed a distaste for heading into the city.[34] I had also miscarried twice, which had taken a profound toll on my health. For these reasons, I had remained here, at our new home, since. It was located close to Kamakura, so my husband was able to go into Tokyo in only two hours, which allowed him to commute daily. I, however, became a complete provincial. I rarely went to Tokyo, and instead had most of my daily necessities provided by my husband. It was only in the most special of circumstances that I would need to go into the city, and even then my husband would come to Tokyo Station to meet me when I arrived. As a result, it had been three years since I had walked the streets of Tokyo. It seemed that my husband had deep misgivings about letting me head out on my own, given that my health had not yet been fully restored.

The day before yesterday, though, my cousin came to visit for the first time in quite a while. Succumbing to her encouragement, I decided to accompany her to Tokyo. I was not very inclined to do so, and I had never before gone out without telling my husband, so I agonized over the decision for some time, but I had not seen my cousin since my brothers were transferred away and I was loathe to say goodbye. In the end, I chose to go with her.

It being so long since I had been jostled by the thronging crowds, I soon grew tired of swimming against the current of people. We had gone into M department store and had finally finished the shopping my cousin had hoped to do when, upon entering the third-floor toy department, we found ourselves amid the countless parents with their children one would expect to encounter given the season. As I was thinking that I might try to find some Christmas presents for the children, ahead of me I caught sight of a man's profile that I thought I recognized, even though four or five people stood between us. Thinking, *could it be?*, I took a closer look, upon which I discovered that it was indeed my husband, whom I had seen off to work that very morning. His gaze was cast downward, and he was saying something to the three- or four-year-old boy who was with him. On the verge of being trampled, the boy clung to my husband, who quickly scooped him up into his arms and then fixed the boy's cap, which was about to fall off.

But wait, what's this? That boy's face was the spitting image of my husband's when he was still a child, in that photograph in which his nursemaid was holding him. Nor was that all. As I approached, I noticed that my husband had a young woman with him. As the two were about to pass me, walking side-by-side, something caused them both to look in my direction, even as I was realizing with a start what was happening. By chance, their eyes met mine. Without thinking, I blurted out, "Natsu!" She responded, "Mistress. . . ." but I have no recollection not only of what she said after that, or even of how I returned home after the encounter. All I remember is the blanched face of my cousin, saying over and over again, "Be strong, Keiko, be strong."

My husband visited my bedside again today, seemingly wanting to tell me something, but it was too painful for me even to look at him. All I wanted was to be done with it all.

These events are starting to seem to me to be a tale of the distant past. I now pass my days happily here, in the colony, surrounded by my adorable students.

Mine is a quiet, if monotonous, existence. From time to time, despite my best efforts not to, I experience deep homesickness. My elder brothers are always telling me to come back whenever I wish.

These events, however, forced me to abandon the notion of living a normal life. I am now searching for a new way, looking at things differently in the hopes of finding something true.

Until such time as I find that, however, I intend to maintain this happy life that I enjoy here.

KATAYAMA YŌKO is the penname for Hayashi Ise (1899–1994), the younger sister of Tanizaki Jun'ichirō.[35] Born in Tokyo, Katayama had migrated to Brazil in 1926 alone after divorcing her husband.[36] Presumably she paid her own fare when she came, which would have provided her more flexibility upon her arrival as she would not have been contracted to work on a farm.[37] Instead, she supported herself working at a hotel and at a newspaper, and continued writing until her death in 1994. According to Arata Sumu, Katayama's relation to Tanizaki was a secret when she began first writing in Brazil.[38] In addition to a 1978 work about her family, *Ani Jun'ichirō to Tanizaki-ke no hitobito* (兄潤一郎と谷崎家の人々), she also wrote the story "Senchū yobanashi" (船中夜話) about her voyage from Japan to Brazil.[39]

"Placement"

Furuno Kikuo

The ocean had grown gradually more muddied. The whine of the engine dropped suddenly and before them the opening of the Mekong Delta traced a wide arc in the direction the ship was headed.

As the speed of the ship dropped, the warm air in the sealed infirmary on the aft upper deck became unbearable.

Time and again Shinkichi, who was sick to his stomach from the smells of new paint and carbolic acid mixing with the musk of the patients' feverish bodies, fled the room with the urge to vomit.

When he jammed his finger down his throat in an attempt to throw up as he clung to the rail, however, all that came up from his retching stomach was sticky bile. Staring at the incredible tumult of white froth caused by the screw, Shinkichi's exhausted mind began to reel.

Over the last two or three days, Shinkichi's almost-two-year-old son had grown emaciated, like some sort of dried persimmon, from his stubborn fever that refused to drop even a degree below 104. The doctor had said there was a likelihood he would develop diarrhea, but so far there had been no sign of it; the only symptom was this lingering fever.

The bell signaling lunch rang. The migrants, weakened by the heat of the South China Sea, however, had no appetites whatsoever. They wearily left their bunks,[40] and then plodded over to the mess tables, where they gathered. Atop the insufficiently salted potatoes had been quietly placed two strangely pungent dried fish. For a moment, a look of disgust seized the migrants' faces—"not again!"—but soon they returned to their state of utter resignation and cast down their eyes as they picked up the chopsticks covered with peeling red paint.

"Food, food, no matter how many times I say that, it always makes me feel better. Let's eat!" One of the boys, with his hands cupped around his mouth to make a megaphone, went around shouting into each bunk to get everyone going.

"Haikō" appeared in 1934 in the 17 January, 24 January, 7 February, and 21 February issues of the *Burajiru jihō*. The title, *Haikō* (配耕), refers to the process by which migrants would be placed as contract laborers in settlements by migration companies. See Hosokawa, *Nikkei Burajiru imin bungaku*, II:309–13.

Whenever he was met by some complaint or other, the boy would give the person a scolding in a cold, sharp voice as he played with the acne on his chin.

"If you have some gripe, take it up with the purser. Do you want to go to Mogiana or not?"

Shinkichi's wife was balled up in the corner of her bunk, gritting her teeth and trying to endure her nausea and headache, which felt like a rake being dragged across the surface of her brain. *If the boy, with his pale, oily face, finds me, I am sure he will curse at me again.* The woman pulled the blanket, marked with the symbol of the shipping line, up over her face. Things swirled into a blur as they raced through her throbbing head, which felt as though it would split: Her son, who lacked even the energy to speak, with his inexplicable fever and his gauntness, which resulted from the heat of the sealed cabin; the constant pulsing of the ship's engines; the small, drenched body of her aged mother, who had come to the Kobe processing facility[41] to meet her; the expressionless Chinamen in Hong Kong who had lacked eyebrows; the chilly Shinshū train station; bells, bells, and potatoes; these. She sobbed as she thought of her husband, Shinkichi, with his visibly emaciated neck, who had forced himself to go to the infirmary this morning to look after their son despite being sick himself, and was now confined there.

The whole ship shuddered, the bass whistle blew long, and commotion burst out suddenly on deck.

The port of Saigon. . . .

Night fell early, perhaps because of the rain.

Water oxen gathered in the paddies, which seemed to blur into the muddy river, and white cranes flew about in the twilight like slips of paper.

Light escaped from the natives' huts near the shore, and glowed dully as it reflected on the river.

On order of the ship's doctor, all portals on the ship were sealed in order to avoid the malaria-carrying insects.

Hot air, filled with humidity from the rain, enveloped the ship. The cabins reeked like a garbage can, as they grew increasingly steamy.

The migrants passed the sleepless night in the depths of the ship, feeling the lapping of the jaundiced, murky flow of the Mekong river lap though their sweaty and oily skin.

The next day. . . .

This ship will depart for Singapore today at noon. Ship's captain.

Despite this posted announcement, the greedy immigrant ship's tentacle-like cranes continued moving freight long after the designated time. After all, the shipping company would not reap its great profits on the transport of migrants alone.

It was slightly after the ship had set sail that Shinkichi and his wife staggered out from the medical room—little more than a doghouse at the stern of the ship—with dazed, haunted expressions.

Even as they wiped sweat from his gaunt, shrunken face, their son had breathed his last.

Late at night on the South China Sea, the stars glowed red and the wind sounded on the mast and the antenna. With a single blast of the whistle, which rang out like a howl, their son's little casket, wrapped in a burlap sack, fell straight down into the white ripples on the surface and was swallowed up by the sea.

Shinkichi's wife collapsed into a heap, feeling as though her heart had been seized by a giant black hand and smashed down onto the deck.

The various migrants who had gathered into a semi-circle around them—more out of curiosity about their first burial at sea than out of sympathy—felt a chill race down their backs and then all together withdrew to their bunks.

Now Shinkichi's wife was bedridden in the same room where her son had laid.

Singapore, Colombo, and the Indian Ocean—"England's Lake"—the immigration ship continued sailing south, moving away from Japan at the rate of 13 knots.[42] Shinkichi's wife, however, was moving at an even faster rate away from her aging mother back amid the mountains of Shinshū, from Shinkichi, and from everything else in this world in her race toward death.

Once their placement was determined, the migrants' feelings changed; the "familial" feelings that had pervaded right up until the previous day were now gone. At the very least, they were not the same feelings that had lashed them one to the other atop the summer rollers of the South Pacific a few days earlier.

Brazil was a vast, elusive expanse of a new world, against which they themselves were miniscule, pathetically indistinct beings on the far edge of that wilderness. What good will come from all their struggles? This mood—despair mixed with a self-defensive posture that bordered on the primal, a feeling like sand being rubbed against sand—wafted from the immigrant ship like methane gas.

Shinkichi's placement was on a parcel behind C Station on the Noroeste line. The next day, after the trachoma exam, they were scheduled to leave for their allotted parcel.

Shinkichi's wife's condition had grown serious; she had been bordering on unconsciousness since the day before they reached Rio de Janeiro.

Rain came and went. They emerged on deck to find a day as depressing as any late-autumn day in Japan. The range of mountains along the coast lay silent, like a sprawled-out farm animal, beyond the low-hanging evening sky.

The young men and women of the bible study group gathered in a circle near the infirmary and sang "Till We Meet Again" in saccharine voices.[43]

The head of the study group, who was despised by both young women and all those who had children because he had purchased all of the starch at the ship's store and had washed his undergarments in the women's sink, spoke in a strained voice like that of a squawking crow, saying, "The kingdom of heaven approaches."

With this he concluded his tedious sermon. A youth on his second crossing, who was sitting in one of the chairs at the ship's store, smiled ironically and muttered, "I don't know if it is heaven or hell, but you sure will find out when you reach your plot tomorrow. By that time it won't help to say, "*Eloi Eloi lama sabachthani* (My God, why have You forsaken me?)"

Shinkichi had to walk between the infirmary and the cabin many times, each time passing by these "puritans."[44]

The ship's doctor and nurses were busy preparing for the next day's eye exams, and paid little attention to either Shinkichi's wife or the other patients in the infirmary.

Shinkichi's wife had to be hospitalized at Santa Casa, but Shinkichi had to depart with everyone else for his parcel the next day.[45]

According to the people who had been to Brazil before, the parcel to which he was headed was known as "a Japanese farm—more like a prison cell—that was famous for sucking all of the marrow out of immigrants' bones by means of the most devious of mechanisms."

The thing these old, crafty Japanese were referring to when they spoke of this "mechanism" was a tightly run system. One old Kumamoto man who was returning to Brazil added a strangely abstract explanation to this: "While there may be any number of vines stretching out in different directions, they all lead back to one great tree. It's an old tree with really thick bark; quite a *garganta*." If you want to see this great tree, the man said, you should go tonight to the first-class dining hall, where he will be having a drink; just be prepared for his thundering voice.

For Shinkichi at this moment, however, it did not matter what sort of parcel he was headed for in the *noroeste*, or what sort of "system" was exploiting the immigrants. He did not have the luxury of worrying about it. He had to confer with the cabin representative and try to arrange *something*.

His wife would enter Santa Casa, while he would go to the *noroeste* interior, hundreds of kilometers away. He felt as though he were being frantically chased by some sort of ball of flame; as though immediately in front of him a pitch-black abyss was stretching open its rapacious maw.

The rain, now falling in earnest, frantically pummeled the starboard side of the ship, which was turned toward the open sea. Onto the deck, surrounded by darkness, dashed a group of men, moving as a single mass. They seemed just like prisoners mid-escape.

Agitated and hurling epithets, the men raced away noisily to the migrant quarters. The group, which included Shinkichi, was made up of the quarters' representative and various officers.

The men were returning from the first-class dining hall, where they had been split right down the middle by the thundering voice of the "great tree," just as the old returnee from Kumamoto had predicted.

However, the touchiness and sense of camaraderie among the immigrants in the cabin, with their departure for their designated farms set for the very next day, were now completely gone; amid that environment, the excitement of the men cooled and oxidized like sensitive litmus paper. Even if there was a modicum of pleasant sentimentality on this last night of communal life in this dark, unpleasant, unsanitary hole in the ground they called the migrants' cabin, the pervading sense was of a vacuum, in which people would not even try to muster sympathy for the tragedy of their neighbor. Look, Shōda-san, it's all fate. You might as well resign yourself to it. It's unlikely that Akio will be able to change your land assignment. It's sad about your wife, but. . . .

The room representative avoided Shinkichi's face and said,

"It's not that it's impossible. The boss will go on and on about how he can't do anything about it, but don't listen to that. If you tell him you will find him a lively girl for the night, and then slip some of this in his pocket. . . ."

The man from Kumamoto rubbed his thumb and pointer finger right in front of Shinkichi's nose, making it clear that a bribe would do the trick. Shinkichi, for his part, sat on the edge of his bunk as if stunned, clutching his hair, which was still wet from the rain, with both hands.

Cold, lifeless eyes—as though belonging to mere spectators—encircled him, gazing from every bunk.

Dear K: That poor young couple whom I mentioned in a postscript to my last letter—that's right, Shōda Shinkichi from Wakayama—as I expected, they were eventually processed as migrants. As migrants, that is, and definitely not as people. The next morning his wife was sent in the rain to Santa Casa in Santos and Shōda went with the other migrants to the *noroeste*.

I suspect his kind wife probably died alone among those foreigners at Santa Casa. In that serious a condition, alone like that—I don't believe in god's miracles.

I have no doubt that you will think that there must have been some other way. Even I, who have just arrived at my assigned land, think that to some extent. But when I look at myself objectively—as a person, no, as a single migrant who was taken from the processing facility in Kobe and placed on my assigned land—Shōda's situation does not seem the least unusual; to the contrary, it even seems like the usual way for the emigration company to treat someone. I am not being facetious.

I have heard of countless cases like Shōda's even just here in this area; in fact, some were more brutal and inhumane.

I believe that the source of all of this tragedy lies not merely in the corruption of a single person in charge of the emigrants, but in the fundamental irrationality of the migration companies.

These for-profit emigration companies remain in business because of the commercial and postal shipping companies that are their primary shareholders. In their frantic desire to produce profits, the resulting pressure is applied at the point least capable of resisting it: the migrants. It is a completely natural phenomenon.

Shōda's case was no more than a tiny sliver of that natural phenomenon.

The ultimate failure, the most fundamental part of our tragedy as migrants, however, is of course in the indifference and inattention of the Japanese government to those migrants (shall I refrain from saying migrants to South America?). In Brazil, we have a word for it: *kimin* (棄民), or "discarded people." It hits the nail right on the head.

If I were to tell you that all of the people who fled Japan because they had grown sick of it were already filled with resentment and anger, despite having only recently arrived in South America, I think that you would probably be unable to keep that characteristic sarcastic grin of yours from slipping.

With that in mind, I add my brief apologies for having been out of touch for so long. Tomorrow I will finally put these skinny arms to work weeding in the coffee fields. With that, I bid you goodbye.

The writer has been unable to learn anything more about what became of the Shōda couple after that, though I suspect I could hazard a reasonable guess. By chance, a close friend of the author added his thoughts on this matter to a letter he was writing to someone in Japan; I have borrowed that text for use here.

The End

"Tumbleweeds"

Furuno Kikuo

Peeking out the door that he had half-opened, João exclaimed, "*Neve* (snow)! The ocean and the deck are both covered! Snow! Come quickly, Akita-san!"

"Akita-san, *sorvete* (ice cream), eh?" João's eight-year-old sister Luísa, with her white-rabbit-fur collar, came up and hung from Akita's arm.

"I'll lift you up, Lui!"

Clumped together, the three of them went out on the aft deck. It was just as João had described it. Everything was covered with snow. The twilight, which seemed not quite dawn nor dusk, was eerily silent, as the white nights at the poles must be.

The gentle snow falling in the twilight made it hard to believe that they were at sea. *This afternoon it might snow; the barometric pressure is dropping. Snow—that's another thing I haven't seen in a while.* When the second mate he met in the wireless operator's office had said this in the morning, Akita had felt a slight ache in his chest.

When he was a student and was boarding near Uguisudani in Shitaya, he would often stand on the bridge over the railroad tracks there and watch the trains that passed beneath him on their way into Tokyo from the Northeast, with their roofs covered with snow that had not yet reached the city.

How many years had it been since he had stopped experiencing the anticipation that came with the change of seasons?

... *Oh, neve, como a saudade,*
   Caes leve, caes leve,...
   (The snow falls, like a memory
   so lightly, so lightly ...)[46]
"Do you know the poem, João?" muttered Akita, staring intently into the snow with his head tilted horizontally.

"*Eu não sei* (I don't know it)."

Maeyama states that the first appearance of "Tenpō" was in the July 1940 issue of the journal *Shin Burajiru*. Unable to find that journal, I have based this translation on the version that appeared in *Bungei shuto* 27, no. 6 (June 1958): 31–40.

With this, Luísa, silent and being held by Akita, pulled on his hair.

"What is *saudade* (nostalgia)?"

"That's a pretty hard one. João, explain it to your sister."

"*Saudade* is, let's see, ok. . . . When we were in Brazil, every evening we would give *milho* (corn) to the pigs in the *chiqueiro* (pig pen), right? So now every evening I think of the pig pen. *Aquele mesmo, não* (It's like that, isn't it), Akita-san?"

Without intending to, Akita let out a sardonic smile. "Close enough. Do you get it, Luísa?"

Luísa shrugged her shoulders, raised her eyebrows as foreigners do, and answered *não*.

"*Que boba!* (What a dummy!)" João said, smiling.

The tips of the siblings' fingers grew red with the cold, as they ran around on the deck, kicked the snow as they went, pressed snowballs to their cheeks, and even tried taking bites of them; all the while they joked with each other in some sort of eccentric Portuguese.

Luísa, this small, precocious "Brazilian girl," had once been told by her father that snow is a little like ice cream, so she must have been disillusioned when she first tasted it and discovered that it was merely cold, and not the least bit sweet. Perhaps seventeen-year-old João felt the same way.

"*Que fria! Merda!*" João went to throw the snowball he had in his hand down on the deck.

Luísa snatched it away, saying, "I am going to show it to *mamãe*," and then ran off in the direction of the passengers' quarters.

It was only quiet for a brief time. Apparently the ship had entered deep into a low pressure zone. The ship ran against the Japan Current, just south of the Aleutian Islands, shuddering incessantly and emitting creaking sounds that sounded just like screams as it steamed at full speed into the blizzard.

That night Akita had fragmentary dreams. All were of Brazil. One seemed to be of a country road along the Sorocabana. The blue of the sky, so deep that it seemed to overwhelm his optic nerve, was above him like a great, round lid. There were large *pinholas* (silk cotton trees) whose flowers were beginning to open, and beneath them Akita sat with his mother. It resembled the day he left the farm and went to Rio de Janeiro.

Akita looked up at the sky and thought of the verse from the bible: "Let there be a firmament in the midst of the waters." His mother had her shoes off and her legs extended on the grass. Buttercups were mixed in among the grasses. Let me look for chiggers (*bicho*), he said in a Kyūshū dialect, as Akita reached out his hand toward his mother's legs. As he did, the area suddenly grew red, as though it were sunrise. The *pinhola* (silk cotton tree) flowers had opened and the petals begun to fall. When Akita looked up, mixed-blood girls from the farm were high in the treetops like bunches of unripe fruit, calling something down toward Akita.

This is where the dream broke off and Akita awoke. He got up from his bed and staggered over to the porthole. Opening the two steel covers, he peered out through the glass. Waves were striking the window and the snow was still falling. The cry of a petrel could be heard amid the creaking of the hull of the ship, which sounded as though it could break apart at any moment.

Akita returned to bed and, pulling the blanket redolent of seawater and mold over his face, uttered the words, Brazil! Brazil!

Twice there was a loud sound as though someone had struck the surface of the water with a plank or something of that sort. *There's no need for that—I will just apologize . . .* a thick Osaka accent followed the resonant strikes, swirling around the kiosk near the third-class dining hall.

Despite the fact that many people skip lunch due to seasickness, there were still fifteen or sixteen passengers in the hall. They turned in unison, casting their questioning gazes in the direction of the sound. Before them appeared Akita, who was being calmed by another man of similar age named Wakabayashi. Visible following along behind him, as though trying to hide in his shadow, was Luísa, who wore a deep red coat and reeled with the swaying of the ship.

The young men who always sat with Akita during meals asked him, "What happened?" They were unable even to wait for him, with his ashen face, to sit down.

"The first-class cabin boy—I hit him." Akita had sat at the table and slowly poured some tea into a cup, but his hand as he lifted it still shook from excitement.

"Why didn't you tell *me, mister* Akita? I haven't had any exercise in ten days! Ha ha ha. . . ." Tani, the college student from California who was sitting next to him, interrupted in his awkward combination of Japanese and English.

"Luísa came back down from upstairs crying. When I asked her why, she said that the boy had taken her to a group of first-class passengers in the lounge upstairs."

"The guy's a jerk. His complexion is always the color of asparagus. *Mucho bien!*" A young man who had worked as a laundryman in Buenos Aires added, in a supportive tone, as he sat with his arms crossed.

"He may not have intended to do it at first, but when Luísa brought the snowball in apparently he told her *This is a cold ball, but if you take good care of it you can take it with you to Japan, so you should keep it in your pocket. . . .*"

All any of them could do was smile wryly.

". . . then he said, come over here and stand near the stove. Apparently she was happy at first. At some point, though, water started dripping down out of her pocket. The ball was gone. According to her, the foreigners and Japanese who were there found it so funny that they burst out laughing, seeing the girl who had been so happy up until now start crying."

"So the brown-noser probably figured that he had really scored some points. *Che! Puta merda!*"[47]

At the other side of the table, glaring at Akita with wide, blood-shot eyes as though Akita himself were that cabin boy, was a man who had been the gardener on a wealthy estate in Rio de Janeiro. This was a man who every night played cards by himself, guzzled *pinga* (a hard liquor), and on top of that would force his way into Akita's cabin, regardless of the time and for as long as he cared to stay, to ask him ridiculous questions such as, "Akita-kun, how do you interpret the true intentions of American Minister Valkenburgh's advocacy for neutrality in 1868?"[48]

Akita, wiping his thick glasses, spoke to Wakabayashi, who had been sitting silently. "If you think about it, there was no reason for me to go so far as to hit him. It's just that I was out of my mind with anger. To be honest, perhaps it was because I myself have some sort of inferiority complex as a migrant or something, but I felt as though all of us immigrants to Brazil were being ridiculed."

Having heard about this from Luísa, Akita had called the first-class cabin boy down to the lower decks and slapped both checks of his face with an open hand, as they do in the army. He hit him hard enough to leave palm imprints on the cabin boy's fine, feminine cheeks. For his part, the cabin boy did not even try to fight back, and instead just maintained a smile despite his tears. This enflamed Akita all the more. The third-class cabin boys had had to calm him down.

"Akita, why don't you come by my cabin later?" Wakabayashi said, as he stood, patted Akita lightly on the shoulder, and left. Akita had fallen silent and was sipping his tea.

"Anyway, it wasn't adult behavior," Akita muttered, having finally regained his composure. Glancing to his side, he noticed that João, who was sitting three or four people over, was handling his chopsticks with difficulty and concealing his cutlery with his right hand as though afraid of what others would think. The voyage on this Japanese ship was the first time in his life that he had ever held chopsticks.

The bridge to his life in Brazil had crumbled when he boarded the Japanese ship. Around him was in all ways Japan. To the individuals whose eyes pored over this dual-citizenship-holding youth of seventeen, he bore not the slightest handicap. Little did they know that the ceaseless, severe training that this child of nature, of that vast continent, would receive in Japan had already begun during this sea crossing, which otherwise should have been fun. *He cannot use chopsticks. He doesn't even know conversational Japanese. Halfwit!* The cold glares that poured over João made him feel frightened of the table, as though he were some sort of thief, and led him to speak the language of his parents' homeland timidly and with a lisp, further muddying his thick accent. Luísa was in the very same situation.

"Thrust your chests out with pride, João and Luísa! Throw away those chopsticks and eat proudly with your forks. Speak to any you encounter loudly in the language of your birthplace, Brazil. If you shrink before them like that, once in Japan you will have people convincing you to put snowballs in your pockets every day!"

Drinking old tea from the kettle with the shipping company's logo on it, Akita stared through the ship's portal, steamed up by the perspiration of all the passengers, at the undulating horizon of the North Pacific in winter as it rose and fell in the distance.

Congratulations on your safe return home. Koyama Hotel.

Telegrams had already begun to arrive from random hotels in Yokohama for various passengers aboard ship.

"It's unforgiving, Japan. I feel as though I can't let down my guard somehow, even though I am returning to the country of my birth," Wakabayashi's wife Makiko muttered, as she peeked at the telegram that Akita was reading.

"Makiko, don't be so grumpy. Why don't you get us some Sunkist oranges or something?" Throwing the guitar he had been playing down on the bed, Wakabayashi sat down alongside Akita.

When Makiko deftly sank a knife into the Sunkist orange she had taken from the crate, a sweet scent filled the small cabin as though a bouquet of flowers had been scattered about. The color and scent of the fruit, raised on that fertile continent, had the exuberance of youth.

Tasting the slice of fruit, it had a sweet but mild flavor, with a freshness that pierced the tongue. It was similar to the flavor of a Brazilian *laranja*, though the sweetness of the *laranja* was less reliable. Akita recalled reading an article on economics that said that when introduced to the French consumer market, it had not been well received, having been deemed to lack sufficient citrus flavor. Is it only the fruit in Brazil that is lacking in flavor?

"I suppose that even on Californian orchards Japanese are encountering all sorts of difficulties," Wakabayashi said, to no one in particular, as he held one Sunkist up at eye level, resting on the palm of his hand. Just then there was a knock at the door and Tani came in, bending his tall frame as he entered. He was wearing a loud green jacket.

Akita looked up and said, "Look at that, it's gotten to the point where he is dressed as though he were performing the role of the madman in the Life of Christ."

"Sure! Green is the color of hope. Dream a green dream! That's what they say."[49]

"Have a seat, Tani-san."

"Sit down, young man of California, enjoy a nostalgic Sunkist and tell us tales of your romances." Wakabayashi had a little fun at Tani's expense, even as he made room for him on the chair.

With exaggerated gestures, Tani responded, "Romances? Me?"

"Sure!" Maiko mimicked Tani's way of speaking, which made everyone, including Tani, burst out laughing.

Soon Tani calmed down again, relaxing his expression and falling silent for a moment before suddenly erupting once again, apparently having remembered something suddenly. "Goddamn! I forgot to pass on some important information. I am supposed to tell you that there will be a movie tonight in the special third-class cafeteria. It will begin at seven on the dot. Anyway, I'll be back. The work of a messenger boy is never done! Bye-bye!" Having said all that in one burst, Tani threw a kiss as though he were some sort of acrobat and then ran off down the corridor.

"Kids raised among Yankees sure are loud," Wakabayashi said while looking at Akita and Makiko. The three of them smiled wryly.

"Every time I look at that Tani-san, I think to myself how very gloomy Brazilian kids are. Do you think it is because they have to grow up so quickly, Akita-san?"

"I read this in a book once. According to it, a world traveler once said he had traveled all the world and found that nowhere were children more melancholic than in Brazil. The book's author, who was Brazilian, wrote that he agreed with the traveler's impression and added that the main reason for the melancholia was because Brazilian children were mobilized to the front lines of life earlier than those in any other country in the world. Once they turned twelve, they already carried the responsibility of providing important 'supplementary income' for their family; by the time they were eighteen, they played an essential role in the economic life of the family."

"The interior is harsh, isn't it. Even at such an early age they are made to play such an important role."

"The first thing that surprised me when I arrived at the Japanese colony was how early the children matured when it came to daily life. Sometimes I even caught myself wondering why an adult was speaking in a child's voice."

"It's true. Even more so for girls. Parents are more exacting on them than they are for kids from the outskirts of Tokyo."

The ship pitched slowly from side to side, and the steam whistle blew. Before the sound that slipped through the narrow gap between the low-hanging snow clouds and the hide-colored surface of the ocean had reached the horizon, the whistle that followed it flew off in fast pursuit.

Makiko got up, went to the portal, and gazed through it at the ocean.

"A ship?" Wakabayashi, still sitting, asked of Makiko, who had her back to him.

"No."

"Birds?"

"Today as yesterday, just waves and clouds? It is just like the log from the voyage of the Santa Maria."

Wakabayashi reached out, grabbed his guitar, and plucked a few notes before saying, "There are times when crossing this sort of interminable ocean just makes me want scream out with all my might. Akita-kun, didn't you ever feel that sort of impulse in Brazil?"

"I did."

Akita thought of evenings on the coffee plantation near the state border with Paraná. The phrase "sea of trees" would be an apt description for the grand undulations of the coffee plantation, which stretched as far as one could see and then beyond the horizon for dozens of kilometers. Leaning his tired body against the fence surrounding the ranch on his walk home from the plantation and taking in the view of that sea of trees had been one of the best parts of Akita's daily routine. The angled rays of the setting sun cast Akita's shadow long over the fragrant *grossura* grasses. Wild tomatoes, resembling *hōzuki* groundcherries, ripened amid the grasses. As far as he could see, his was the only shadow. Frequently, amid this sea of trees into which he himself was vanishing, Akita would be seized with the desire to scream so loudly that his throat would split open. Likely even that scream, though, would be swallowed up by the infinite silence, and not even one blade of grass would waver in response to the single human's pathos and outcry.

Akita recalled this sea of trees as the ship passed through the tropics. The ocean never stops forming perfect ellipses. With the various forms it created around the ship, the waves' colors sometimes perfectly resembled those of the coffee plantations just before the flowers bloomed. The squalls that came at the ship from the distant horizon were just like those that crossed the plantation from the Paraná border. The clouds would begin to visibly darken around the border and then, in half an hour, the showers would form a number of silver screens that enveloped the plantation where Akita and the others were working.

The half-blacks[50] and the women of Iberian blood, with burlap bags over their heads, were on the verge of racing the rain down the wet, clay street, leaping forward on their doe-like chestnut- and barley-colored legs. At that moment, from the stand of coffee bushes right behind him, he heard a low, suppressed laughing voice quietly slip out. It was the women teasing him, saying *"Venha cá*, Akita! (Come here, Akita!)."

"I think it was Irving who said something to the effect that a sea crossing is a blank in one's life; these words strike me as being completely apposite. In Akita-kun's case, for example, it is a powerful hyphen that connects his life in Brazil to that in Japan,"[51] Wakabayashi said, as he wiped his glasses, which he had taken off, with his handkerchief.

"In something I read by Anatole France recently there was a passage to the following effect: All change, even that which we have every reason to consider a blessing, also possesses an element of melancholy. This is because that which we are attempting to leave behind is a part of ourselves. In order to enter into one life, man must die to another.[52] It might be rude of me, but I wonder if you do have some sense of defeat after having to leave Brazil, Wakabayashi-kun. I wonder if that might be nothing more than the melancholy of having to die to another life, as France said. Be that as it may, you and Makiko gave it your best. Think of this as a home leave."[53]

"This is certainly a poor state in which to be heading for home," Makiko said, stopping her knitting. All three chuckled lightly.

Wakabayashi and his wife had spent five and a half years in Brazil, living in a *colônia* in the interior. Wakabayashi's health, however, did not allow him even to pick up a hoe. Makiko had given birth to a child while he was sick with malaria.

Brazil was in the midst of one of the many revolutions it had experienced in its history.[54] Soldiers from the neighboring state had crossed the river that comprised the border, and were attacking with the newest and most powerful machine guns. . . . This sort of gossip spread, leading strong young men to cast aside their hoes and flee into the primordial forests[55] despite the rattlesnakes that inhabited them. It was amid this tumult that their infant son died of acute pneumonia.

It was nighttime. In the darkness, a fire that was set to clear a mountain traced a crimson arc at one point on the distant horizon. Both Wakabayashi and Makiko felt that they would never forget this scene as long as they lived.

They buried their dead child in a communal graveyard on a hillside where lush green alfalfa flourished. They placed a Japanese-style grave marker that they had carved from Paraná pine alongside the many crosses. Black, white, and half-black[56] children of the *colônia* brought flowers, leaving the small marker covered in *copo-de-leite* and other wild blossoms.

On their way down the hillside, Wakabayashi spoke to Makiko as though making an oath both to her and to himself: "We will be buried in Brazil."[57]

For three successive years they grew cotton, but they were beset by hardships, from insects to plummeting prices. Wakabayashi's body, which had not fully recovered from the malaria, was put through one difficulty after another until his health was damaged to an extreme.

Around that time, a letter arrived from Wakabayashi's older brother in Hokkaidō saying that it would be a great help if he could come and help with the store. He read this letter while confined to bed in his house with a thatched roof that leaked in the rain.

That night the frogs that lived in the swamp behind the house croaked louder than they normally did. He thought well into the night, until nearly dawn, about returning to Japan. His thoughts swung like a pendulum between the small grave on the hillside and that bow-shaped archipelago to the east of the Asian continent.

"Let's return to Japan and try to start life over again."

Wakabayashi blew out the flame in the lantern with a deep breath drawn from the depths of his lungs. For a moment, the scent of the smoking wick was strong in the darkness.

The rolling of the ship continued unabated into the night. The film in the third-class cafeteria began. There is little doubt that seasickness had left many unable to leave their beds, yet the cafeteria was full.

There were two sorts of films. The first of these was a typical film of fourteen or fifteen years earlier. It was an exceedingly banal comedy, but after a previous break in the film a few hundred of its frames had been reversed or inverted or just rearranged with no concern for the development of the plot, perhaps because it was so nonsensical to begin with. The outcome was a reel that seemed like some bizarre nightmare and left everyone confusing the strange resulting sensation with seasickness.

"Ah, you made it, Akita-san!"

Turning in the direction of the *pinga* liquor breath near his collar, Akita saw the face of João's father. Despite his skin the color of *terra roxa* (purplish-brown soil) that was also flushed from alcohol and a torso like a camouflaged tank, he appeared to be in high spirits.

"Good evening. Is your wife here?"

"She's out of commission because she can't take boats well. I left her to watch over our things."

João and Luísa's mother, despite being more than ten years younger than her husband, had the appearance of a woman old enough to be his mother. There are housewives who work from dawn until late into the night with their dry, matted hair up, their bare feet caked in mud, and their toothless mouths hidden by their sealed lips; these women have worked continuously for decades, like draft animals, having lost any trace of sentiment, knowing only the world of primordial forests, cotton fields, and thatched huts. She was one of these women.

As for the men, every harvest they come out of the primordial forest, cross the cotton fields, and race their trucks to town, where alcohol, prostitutes, and dice await. The towns, which pop up near the Japanese collectives, are filled with cheap restaurants catering to Japanese. They resemble suppurations on filthy flesh.

The men join their voices with those of the barmaids, with their large, bony hands burned by insecticides, and sing songs that were popular in Japan more than a decade earlier. João and Luísa's father was one of these men.

When night falls, after Luísa's mother lights the wick of the lantern and puts the children to sleep in their handmade beds, she goes to the kitchen and makes beans for the next day. Many large fireflies with their bodies glowing come in through the open window. It has been a very long time since seeing them made her recollect those of her village in Japan. She has neither memories nor hopes. She has only a mountain of work that must be done, which looms over her. A woman who does not even look up at the sky, let alone think back to her hometown—that is their mother.

Japanese women in farming villages in Brazil do not experience middle age. The men, however, remain forever youthful and vibrant.

If one could call returning to Japan with some money in hand, even if only a small amount, "fortunate," then João's mother was "fortunate." However, nowhere in João's mother's facial expression—as she lay in her third-class "silkworm shelf" wracked with seasickness already even as the lights of the port of Santos were still visible like a string of pearls on the horizon—could one see even a hint of the happiness or satisfaction of a person on their way home after having survived more than a decade of struggle overseas. It was just as if she were lying in her thatched hut with her feet—which she was only able to wash on the rarest occasion—bare.

For João and perhaps for Luísa as well, the ship was just confined, constricting, and inconvenient. Japan, to which they were returning, was an unknown country. Luísa even threw tantrums in the middle of the Pacific Ocean about wanting to return to Brazil in the morning after having dreamt of it the previous night. How much more fun had it seemed the first time they had taken her by truck to the station to see the train. . . . Only their father was excited. His genteel hometown of the first years of Taishō (1912–26), when he had left Japan, was waiting for him. His vow to return with money in his pocket had been, at least to some extent, achieved. Sure, his children might be a bit "easy going" when compared with children in Japan, but he had money. Money! And if things didn't go well in Japan, he could always return to Brazil. He swigged his *pinga* and carried himself in the third-class quarters as though he were a great success.

That money, though only a pittance, was being guarded by the children's mother, who watched over the sack with the greatest care. Rumors even started that the seasickness was only a pretense, and that her husband had in fact ordered her not to leave her bed so that she could guard their treasure.

Whatever the case may be, their father was the only one of the four who was enjoying himself.

The second film began. This too was a typical film over a decade old. It was the story of an American Indian youth from a farming community who is inspired to go to the big city and through hard work graduates from college and becomes a writer. He falls in love with a young white woman, but he is ridiculed by society for being an Indian and returns to his Indian community in despair after having written one novel. Akita found it not only dull, but also filmed in an excessive, old-fashioned style, and did not have the wherewithal to watch it through to the end.

Coming out of the stuffy viewing room, he realized that the rolling of the ship had calmed completely. He casually opened the door to the afterdeck, which allowed the light of the moon to cascade in like a waterfall. The deck was covered with white snow. As he was about to walk around to the side of the ship, he stopped in his tracks. Just to the side of one of the nearby ventilator ducts an old man, one of the third-class passengers, was frozen in place, staring at the moonlit snow in the palm of his hand as if it were gold dust.

"Hello, Mister Akita! Wake up, wake up! You can see cherry blossoms and Japanese girls on the horizon." The Californian university student came around knocking energetically on the door and calling out his announcement.

Morning clouds stretched the width of the sea's horizon. The clouds were the light purple color of wisteria flowers. Behind those wisteria blossoms, the nearest reaches of the Japanese islands may already be outstretching their hands to us.

He remembered having heard that people returning from Europe are often overcome by homesickness and throw themselves to their deaths in the ocean when they finally come in sight of the Japanese islands. But what was this dispassionate sensation he is experiencing? Is it because he had already decided in his heart to die in Brazil? Or is it from the dulling of emotions that results from even a few years of living on the South American continent?

Akita looked absentmindedly at the round sky visible through the portal. It was the pale blue of early spring, which he thought would have the feel of a ceramic vessel if he were to touch it. It was the sky of Japan, which he had grown accustomed to from birth but which he had been unable to gaze up at once during these past years. This country has four seasons, but the place he had decided in his heart to live out his remaining years was a country that had no seasons. It was a land just like that which Su Shi (蘇軾, 1037–1101) wrote about when he composed the verse, "The four seasons are all like summer, but when it rains it suddenly becomes autumn" after having been exiled to Hainan Island.

He opened the portal. The sound of the waves crashed into the cabin. Sticking out his head, Akita caught the strong scent of seawater. The breeze and the spray felt pleasant on his skin. A flock of gulls reminded him how close they were to land.

"Good morning," said Wakabayashi in his usual calm manner. He too was sticking his head out of the portal of the neighboring room. He was smiling at Akita.

"I have decided to settled down in Brazil after all. It will take a month to finish my business in Japan and then I will return to Brazil, Wakabayashi-kun." Akita spoke loudly and with an artificially cheerful tone.

"So you have decided." Wakabayashi nodded a number of times as he looked at Akita. The morning exercise broadcast began on the radio.

"I went back and forth about it in my head during the weeks we have spent onboard ship, but I was unable to decide. It's strange, but now that I have finally gotten close enough to catch the scent of Japanese soil, I suddenly want to settle in Brazil permanently. . . ."

"So you will go into the interior, along the Sorocabana?"

"Yes, along the Paraná River. On the other side is Mato Grosso. It brings me great relief to have decided to become a cowherd," Akita said, wiping the spray off his cheeks with his right hand. "At the same time, it may be that I am just unwilling to admit defeat."

"I am envious of you, Akita-kun. For the two of us, it really is a case of *vae victis* (Woe to the vanquished!) It is hard to imagine that we will actually find happiness by going to Hokkaidō."

"But you know, Wakabayashi-kun, my decision to live in Brazil permanently— no, not just me, sometimes I think every *issei*'s decision to live in Brazil permanently—represents the sad final stop on the journey of an individual who has tired of the search for a meaningful life. I think that it is impossible to choose permanent residence abroad without some tragic resignation. . . ."

The two continued looking down at the waterline of the ship without raising their faces. The ship slowed. It had entered Japanese territorial waters.

FURUNO KIKUO (1907–1989?), the author of both "Placement" and "Tumbleweeds," was born in 1907 in Fukuoka Prefecture and graduated from Waseda University, where he studied French literature.[58] He arrived in Brazil in 1932, returned to Japan in 1935, and then returned to Brazil once again in 1936.[59] After his arrival, he worked at the *Burajiru jihō* (where he was in charge of the literary arts column) and at the Burajiru Takushoku Kumiai.[60] He participated as one of the judges for the *Burajiru jihō's* fiction award, beginning from the second competition in 1933.[61] In 1970 or 1971, he returned to Japan and worked as a lecturer of Portuguese at Kyoto Gaikokugo Daigaku until 1988.[62] During his time in Brazil, Furuno was a central figure in the Japanese-language literary world there; unlike many of the other authors, he produced a number of both fiction and non-fiction writings.[63]

"After We Had Settled"

Sakurada Takeo

[1]

For Shunsaku, who had such difficulty with ships that he felt sick just from looking at one, the forty-nine-day sea crossing had left him as haggard as a young girl experiencing all of the physiological changes that lead to womanhood. It had seemed as though a mere phantasm or dream. With the hurried change of circumstances and his planning for the future, his mind seemed to be absorbing things with an unprecedented voraciousness; the night before arriving in Santos, however, when he realized that his field of vision was absent of waves, that his cabin lacked the sound of the engines, and that his bed no longer rocked, he could not but feel as though he had been granted a new life, as though he had been returned to his earliest years in a cradle. That too, though, lasted for only a day; the next morning he had to board the train on the Santos-Juquiá Line.

He had a strange disposition: it was often the case that the view of things around him and his emotions could suddenly create an effect similar to that of the two poles of an electrical current; conversely, he also often became so dazed that he would seem to have lost track of the world before his eyes—or even his very own existence.

Perhaps it was because the ride aboard the steam train on the Juquiá Line coincided with one of those frigid states, so the half-day-long trip was an attenuated passage that left little more than fragments in his memory.

He had to ride on a riverboat the next day as well. It was a new grueling undertaking, causing him to feel like a long-distance swimmer encountering a sudden tidal surge during the last two hundred meters of a race. The night before the ship was to set off, when he had looked at his own face reflected in the mirror, illuminated by the reddish-black light from a *cantera* that he had turned on its side, he felt the large, piercing eyes filled with resentment, wretchedness, and sorrow. It was as if he were gazing upon a scorned woman. When he pulled his hair up he

---

"Nyūshoku kara" first appeared in 1934 in the 7 February, 14 February, 21 February, 28 February, 7 March, and 14 March issues of the *Burajiru jihō*.

thought he noticed a strange glint come off some shiny object; when he touched the ring on his finger in an attempt to look at it, it slid smoothly off his finger.

The water wheel at the stern of the river steamer, which hardly seemed a product of the twentieth century, made his head throb with its din; mixed with the other sounds—the pistons, the conversations of the passengers, and the loud footfalls— it all seemed to him to be a greater cacophony than he would have experienced had he stuck his head inside a ringing bell. It caused his mood to grow ever darker. Somewhere amid this clamor he overheard that the river's name was Ribeira.

The rain that fell steadily from the morning showed no signs of abating even at noon, and the sky in the distance was a leaden color that seemed just like the snow clouds he knew from Japan. With the bushes on both shores, covered with parasitic plants in a way so distinctive of the tropics, the jungle behind them, the occasional native's home, and the vast ranches in the background, the streaks of rain seemed like grey lines drawn vertically, side by side. On the river, which was not only the color of drainage water but also gave off a stench as a result of the long rainy season, the patterned rain seemed to form a mist as the drops bounced off the surface.

When the wind, which one could hardly imagine was a gas and not a liquid, came, the rain whipped up the surface as though marine plants were engaged in some sort of commotion, causing the sound of the water wheel at the stern to be obscured at times, to blend into the background at others.

From far away, over 12,000 nautical miles,
To the end of the earth,
By ship—by river steamer I travel,
No, I *must* travel,
Is the river steamer traveling upstream?
Or down?
The leaden rain—skies boding snowfall,
Tropical trees, the horse neighing in the rain,
Nothing more than the smoke of harsh tobacco.

He, who had never composed one before, recited the poem aloud.

As he thrust his arm into his coat, countless drops of rain streaked his face, from his eyebrows down his cheeks.

At his feet, four or five skeletal chickens that had been put in a box were clucking.

"The boat will soon arrive in the Sete Barras colony."

[2]

In fact, this river steamer was not just transporting them; it was ferrying them all to their fates. Here in Brazil, on the opposite side of the world from Japan—

and not just Brazil, but well up the Ribeira river—their futures would be determined.

We will soon reach our destination, the Sete Barras colony, said the guide from Kaikō, as he stood facing into the wind at the bow and pointed, expressionlessly, into the distance upstream. At the same moment, the whistle blew for a duration that seemed appropriately long for the ridiculously tall smoke stack; it was as though the ship were mooing like a cow as it glided over the surface of the river. The eight families of settlers all jumped up, as if operated by springs, and looked toward the bow.

Their new fates were gradually appearing before their eyes. The settlers stared, unintentionally, at the very spot toward which the guide was pointing, their gazes both silent and searing. They were like cats fixed on their prey, but at the same time they were brimming with anxiety. They had grown hushed at the guide's hortatory explanation, and without realizing it were rising up on the balls of their feet. The reeds whistled and bent in the wind, while the waves divided in two at the bow, leaving smaller wakes to stretch out to either side. It was as if the current were flowing perpetually against them. River birds that resembled herons skimmed the surface of the river again and again, catching their prey.

All of the settlers had been expecting that the port they would enter in Brazil would at the very least be comparable to that of Saigon. As such, they felt like sparring swordsmen who had been struck by unexpected blows when they caught sight of the row of small houses lining the coast, which itself was being borne down upon by heavy skies barely withholding their rain. All enthusiasm drained from them as they gathered their belongings.

Despite the guide's reference to this place as a "town," besides the small, solitary, white-walled church that loomed over everything else from a slightly elevated vantage, nearly all of the homes' walls were crumbling, with their skeletal frames exposed, and only a few had tiled roofs. The sight could not but cause them to feel the sort of demoralization they would have experienced facing a completely failed crop. Some thirty or so of these houses lined the coast, terraced along it like steps.

When the boat docked, the native children of the town, their skin a mixture of black and white, flocked to the ship emitting strange squeals of the sort that often signal terror, but with their muddied eyes, the color of the river, brimming with curiosity. As though it had been prearranged, they all wore crumpled adult hats and pants held up by suspenders so twisted they could have been mistaken for twine. While some had dirty bandages covering abscesses below their knees, others had exposed wounds that resembled pomegranates. Gathering on these were swarms of flies so dense that it appeared the wounds had been coated with charcoal. Their toes were bent like sickles, and the feet themselves were just like those of hairless monkeys. First thinking in shock, *these are Brazilian children?*, Shunsaku then reconsidered, realizing how suitable these creatures were for living among poisonous snakes. Among the fourteen or fifteen children, four or five of them were apparently Japanese, though their movement and behavior were so assimilated as to make this nigh-impossible to discern. This, and the fact that they spoke Portuguese fluently, only reinforced his initial impression.

These were Japanese settlers who had arrived four or five years earlier, so even though a large number of foreigners from the "town" had gathered as well, they all merely looked like grown versions of those children.

The adults of the full complement of eight families were fully occupied in getting their women and children off the ship and transporting their bags despite each being consumed with his various thoughts as they reconsidered Sete Barras, where they were now to settle. A clash of relief and despondency filled their hearts.

This scene of Japanese engaged in bustling activity was surely one that this wharf had not seen for five years.

"The goal was just to get away from Japan, so. . . ."

Shunsaku had undoubtedly achieved that goal, but as he exposed his body to the wind that blew from the far reaches of the vast plains, over the surface of the river, carrying along with it the moisture that follows the rain, there was nothing he could do about the pain he always bore in his sentimental breast.

[3]

Five or six horse-drawn wagons were waiting to meet them in the square over-grown with colchão next to the school. The wagon wheels were caked with red soil, and large, black horseflies gathered on the ears and bellies of the horses.

Pale afternoon shadows began to spill out of the low skies, and the white sand under the soles of the settlers' shoes was unusually rough beneath them.

"Yukimori-san, which carriage is mine? Should I ask the horses?" called out blue gaiters, a jocular man from Osaka, to the guide. "I hear that not only are Brazilian cars fast, with their four legs and all, but they throw in long ears for good measure!"

The man from Osaka's family burst out laughing.

Kichibei, Shunsaku's uncle, was up in the carriage, gathering the baggage that his eldest son Kichitarō, Kichitarō's wife Misao, Haruko, Kichiji, and Kichisaburō had brought with them, when he suddenly, as if recalling something, called out to Haruko.

"Where is Shunsaku? Off somewhere when we are so busy . . . "

Haruko, who was Shunsaku's wife for the purposes of the family registry, responded nonchalantly to these indirect but barbed words about Shunsaku, her on-paper husband.

"Masuda-san is passed out drunk on the boat; Shunsaku is looking after him."

Blue veins stood out on Kichibei's face, and he appeared on the verge of kicking the carriage.

"Kichiji! Bring him here now, whether he wants to come or not. Tell him his father is calling him. It is not like he is Masuda's servant or anything."

Running to the wharf, Kichiji came across Shunsaku, carrying Masuda Gengo over his shoulder. Miyo, Takuji, and two others walked beside them. A large group of children from the town followed behind, curious. Shunsaku cared for and looked after the drunk Gengo, being careful not to hurt anyone, just as one would treat one's own parent. Shunsaku got involved with this drunk for precisely this reason, because he reminded him of his parent. As he felt the weight of Gengo, reeking of alcohol, on his boney shoulder, he began to recall his failed father—his father who spent his later years bankrupt and melancholic. Here was just the same sort of fifty-year-old man, drunk and all. . . .

Despite having angrily called for him, when Kichibei saw the beauty of Shunsaku carrying the drunk Gengo his face contorted as though he had bitten down on some sand.

"Hey! Everyone, Kichiji, Haruko are already on the carriage. We have to get going. The facility is a long way off." Fidgeting nervously in the carriage, Kichibei yelled as he pulled his wife Yone up by the hand.

"Yukimori-san, which is Masuda's carriage?" Shunsaku asked.

"Yeah, let's see . . . everyone has already filled up all the other carriages, so those are out. Why don't you go with Yoshikawa-san." Then, turning his face up to Kichibei in the carriage, Yukimori asked, "How about it, Yoshikawa-san?"

"No, I'm sorry, but we can't take him drunk like that. Anyway, we already have all of our family and our things."

In response not only to the coldness, but also to this hostility of Yoshikawa's rejection of Masuda, Yukimori thought that there was something between them that was a little strange; as a man who had seen his fair share of this world, though, he realized this without letting on.

"Uncle, the other carriages are full, so we can't just turn him away. Please let him ride in the carriage. In order to make space, I can walk."

"I didn't say that in order to get you to walk."

Shunsaku was driven mad by his uncle's constant spiteful remarks.

[4]

Even now, as he looked back on his life, a life that had certainly had its share of problems, and wondered what it all had meant, as he stood on this wharf, which bridged from this old life in Japan to the settlement that would mark the start of his new life, even now the fight with his uncle cast a pall of depression over him. Having disobeyed him like that, or rather, having stuck up for Masuda Gengo like that, Shunsaku had to go with Masuda. Still, for someone as timid as Shunsaku, it was a difficult position to be in with a blood relative.

Yukimori arranged for them to go in a carriage that happened to pass by just then, from a Japanese-owned lumber mill.

Shunsaku, who returned to his senses when the whip cracked and the rig began to move, looked at the driver. Though a large Japanese man of around thirty, with sunken cheeks and dark skin, he was distant and unapproachable in a way that one would not expect from a countryman. Shunsaku's carriage, which had gotten started well after the others had already left, clattered down the narrow road through the expansive *campo*. The horses were already fatigued from having brought lumber to the wharf, pulling the cart down a road studded here and there with large rocks, projecting like boulders from the surface, into which the wheels would collide and over which they would have to be pulled, falling with heavy thuds each time. Though the horses would occasionally stop lethargically, with each crack of the whip they would cringe and then break into a fast trot. As they ran, lather formed on their legs, like oil bubbling up from a well. Gengo leaned innocently against the edge of the cart and snored.

Miyo, downcast with her chin drawn in, stared at a single spot, her eyes moist and seemingly ready to drop full tears. Again and again her younger brother Takuji and her thirteen-year-old sister would look at their father and then look fondly at Shunsaku. Though he had only met them aboard the ship, Shunsaku already felt a familial warmth in their eyes, and it was when he was with them that he finally thought of himself.

As the white road went on, as they distanced themselves from the wharf, the color of the road grew increasingly reddish and the jostling of the carriage grew increasingly rough. At the seven-kilometer marker, the road forked and entered into the old-growth forest.

Red- and blue-colored birds flitted deftly and vigorously through the fragrant gloom, making the primordial forest such a peaceful place, making one feel as though one was hearing the amicable, nostalgic, still, silent words calling out to the present from centuries past. This was characteristic of these woods, which were imbued with the fragrance of the canopy, the bark, and the fallen leaves below. Thinking that they themselves would have to fell these trees, which battle one another in their race to the heavens and whose trunks not even two men could wrap their arms about, with their own hands, made them feel as weak as flowing water down there upon the narrow road where the sky is only visible as a thin band above and the trees seemed to grow rapidly before their eyes.

The road increasingly worsened, and the horses' stomachs were coated with mud and looked like earthen walls. Each time they pulled their hooves from the deep mud with an off-putting *thunk*, the spray would fly up to the carriage.

Some time later, where the road forked again, the carriages were unable to ascend the slope, and everyone but Gengo was forced to get down and push.

When at long last they reached the top of the slope, the horses breathed long and deeply, as though they had just escaped the slaughterhouse. With each breath, the carriage rocked forward and back as though floating.

As the darkness pressed in upon them, the deep night came as if a settling fog. When he asked how much longer it would take, the driver, scratching his head, answered that once they had come around this mountain the schoolhouse would come into sight, and that the facility would be down the hill from there. The reddish-yellow light of the lamp projected a point into the dark, occasionally flashing in reflection off something metallic. The camp was floating in the darkness somewhere close by.

[5]

This "camp" was merely a mud-plaster shanty with no proper foundation. Toadstools grew on the columns, and weeds like dyed strings grew out of the earthen floor. Every part of the building, which apparently had been a night school with some fifteen pupils, suggested that people had just wanted to find some use for it. At the same time, though, there was something nostalgic about this ten-meter-long building here in the depths of the mountains, from which poured the writhing light of lanterns and voices of people. It was like encountering another ship far out at sea.

A six-mat room was allocated to Gengo's family, though getting to it was a bit confusing as it was already nighttime. From the entrance at the center of the building, they went to the rear, then turned left, then returned back in the direction of the entrance. The room was located at the end of that hall.

The others, who had arrived earlier, were already building simple stoves from bricks, preparing dinner, and unpacking their things. Realizing how hungry he was when he smelled the food, Shunsaku brought from the carriage the rice, *bacalhau*, dried meat (*carne sêca*), salt, sugar, and other provisions they had been given by the company. Gathering up bricks he found lying about, he dug out a rudimentary stove in the embankment in front of the room's window. Once this was complete, he and Miyo went together to the small river out back to get water. The river ran along the boundary between the forest, which towered behind them like a folding screen, and the *campo*. The water emerged in the shadow of this screen, cut through the grasses of the plain, and then turned into the forest, as though being sucked in by the trees. The sounds of owls whooting and frogs croaking *oi, oi*—as though calling out to people—seemed to well up from the ground and then rise to the tops of the trees, even as the darkness itself seemed to moan deeply. Shunsaku suddenly felt depressed and exhausted.

As he went around to the right side of the building to get firewood, he could hear the mingled sounds of water and laughing voices; when he finally could see what was happening, he realized that there were people in a large metal half-cylinder. The shadows cast by the lantern, the color of flesh, and the glow on the water made it all seem somehow supernatural.

"Even a Kaikō company old-timer wouldn't have thought to use this truck as a bath, . . ."[64] Two or three of the laughing ghouls seemed to have senses of humor.

As Shunsaku returned carrying firewood in his arms, Miyo was lighting newspaper in the makeshift stove. The smoke that rose when they added the wood blew sideways, crawling out into the darkness like fog. Just as the fire started to ignite in earnest, Shunsaku's uncle Kichibei came and dragged him off.

Though Miyo felt terrible about the position she had put Shunsaku in, it was absolutely impossible for her, a woman—moreover, a young woman—to handle the settling of her whole family herself, given that her mother had died at sea and her father was in the state he was in. She had no choice but to enlist the aid of Shunsaku and his male strength, though it was all she could do to withhold her tears when she wondered what could possibly be done about the rift this had created between Shunsaku and his uncle.

"What shall I make for dinner? What was it again, *baca, baca* . . . oh, I have forgotten the name of that fish."

"It's called *carne sêca*, it's the one that smells like soap."

Fifteen-year-old Takuji, who had spoken, and Ruriko seemed like orphans abandoned in the woods.

"Miyo, are you crying?" Ruriko, whose head Miyo was stroking, looked up at Miyo with her big eyes and her cheeks glowing red like an apple from the flames. All was silent for a moment.

"It was a long way from the wharf, wasn't it. If I remember correctly, we left at three, so three, four, five, six, seven, . . ." Miyo counted on her fingers, starting with her thumb. As she bent her middle finger, Shunsaku came in with some sort of document, like a letter, in his right hand.

Everyone stared silently at him.

Miyo felt a swirling pain in her forehead.

"It was nothing."

The three of them could not miss the contrast between his words and his demeanor. Shunsaku squatted down between Miyo and Ruriko and spoke to Ruriko.

"Open wide. I am going to give you some chocolate from Santos."

Ruriko stared hard at the silver paper, shining with the light from the fire, and innocently opened her mouth.

[6]

The mountain range running parallel to the coast in southern São Paulo stopped the dense, moist air of the Atlantic that blows in from the south, causing it to rain nearly non-stop throughout the year. Even as the interior entered into its dry season, this area was still threatened with floods. The second buds sprouted even as the first crops still stood, the harvest not yet complete. With the exception of the banks of the river, the rice yield in this colony was half that of colonies in the interior. The bean and potato crops were lost, including seeds that had only just been planted. There was no way to plant a second crop.

After their second year of planting, there was nothing for them to do but to look for other land to use as a *capoeira*. As the area of the *capoeira* increased, they all deflated at their ill-fortune with nature, and began to lose what fight they had had, as though they had been knocked to the ground.

Some even began to forget the dawn. And night as well. Those who live without being conscious of, and aware of the significance of, their lives are prisoners of and addicts to those lives. These prisoners, these addicts, inevitably work as slaves to the basest of human principles: that if one does not work—if one does not work even a little—one does not eat. As a reaction, they sought after carnal stimuli when night fell, warming their chests with strong spirits (*pinga*) until they were intoxicated and then sleeping on the earthen floor like stones.

These were lives of neither healthy joys nor healthy sorrows. Then there were pioneers, living corpses who were now so divorced from the hopes and passions that had filled them when they first settled. It was natural that the exuberant spirits of the new settlers, whose breasts burned with ambition, would collide emotionally with the decadent and desperate attitudes of the older settlers.

The new young settlers, however, handled it deftly. While it was emotionally galling to be obsequious to the elders, they enjoyed a good laugh when it suited them. On the other hand, if there was ever a risk of disadvantage, they would stand and fight without the slightest hesitancy. "10 *mil réis* for a dozen daikon? You have to be kidding. That's two and a half yen![65] We might be new settlers, but we know about the *palmito* growing in the forest."

The new settlers looked upon the old settlers with scorn, thinking to themselves, "How could someone fail even to secure their livelihoods after living in the same place for five years?" Thinking that they would not make the same blunders, they began selecting their plots as if in a dream, dressed in their new, khaki-colored clothing. They settled on an area centered on a blue-black, pyramid-shaped mountain named "Laranjeira." They began building our homes here, surrounded by small rivers and with the mountain at their backs.

———For many years after that, there was not even enough time to look at the situation coolly and to wonder whether those homes would succeed or fail. Whether good or bad, the camp sent out increasing numbers of families. Shunsaku could not but be irritated by this. Because he was young and had been raised in the city, each time he thought about settlement as an ideal, he would make himself return to the concrete reality. *At this moment, can I build a house with my own hands? Can I wield a* machado *as well as someone who came here after first clearing land in Hokkaidō?*

Time and time again, he could not but get carried away with these unnecessary thoughts as he looked upon the all-too-obvious impossibilities that lay before him.

Hope. Inevitabilities. Impossibilities. Outcomes. These things that are composed organically of cellular structures must be left to the fates of the world of impermanence.

Masuda began spitting up blood the day after they arrived at the camp. The doctor who saw him was a veterinarian who had just finished castrating a horse.

(End of first part.)

From the author: Though I am concluding "After We Had Settled" at a point better described as being "up until settlement," this is only the first part of the work; I intend to publish the second half in the near future.[66]

SAKURADA TAKEO, the author of "After We Had Settled," was born in Yamaguchi Prefecture and migrated to Brazil in 1927.[67] He worked as an editor for *Nōgyō no Burajiru* and the *Burajiru jihō*, but returned to Japan prior to the war after having fallen ill.[68] Although I have been unable to discover the nature and extent of his schooling, the fact that he worked as an editor suggests that he had completed a substantial education prior to coming to Brazil. Furuno Kikuo suggests that "After We Had Settled" is an autobiographical depiction of Sakurada's experience in Registro.[69]

"Revenge"

Sugi Takeo

At the end of September, farming families get a bit of rest and so are able to do things like go fishing on Sundays. Because the river is small, there are no real fish to be caught. If you are lucky you might be able to catch a five-centimeter or at most ten-centimeter *taraíra*; still, it seems to be enough for those who like fishing. On Sundays one sees lots of people out by the river.

Maekawa is one of those who likes fishing; on Sundays he cannot wait to grab his pole and head out.

That day was a rare clear one. The September sun sparkled in the bright, cloudless blue sky, and a gentle breeze rustled the leaves in the trees. It was an absolutely perfect day for fishing.

As always, when Maekawa passed in front of Sachiko's house he whistled to her. Sachiko, with her round, white face, quickly emerged.

"You are already off to go fish?" Sachiko feigned surprise and looked up at the sky. "What a nice day it is turning into. *Papai* and everyone are still sleeping." Sachiko's black eyes smiled at Maekawa, and then she turned her head to peek into the house. Maekawa felt aroused by Sachiko's slender neck and, without realizing, gripped the pole tighter.

"It being Sunday, please let them sleep. Instead, won't you walk with me for a bit?"

"All right."

Sachiko looked to see if anyone was around before walking beside Maekawa.

"I am going into town next Sunday. Do you want to go with me, Sachi-chan? It's been three months since I last went in."

"Hmmm . . . Maybe I can. I have to buy books for my little brother, and I have some other errands to do. . . ." Sachiko's eyes, which seemed lost in a dream, encouraged Maekawa and drew him, too, into pleasant reveries.

At some point the two had stopped. They were enveloped in the strong scent of the pure white coffee flowers that surrounded them.

"Fukushū" first appeared in 1938 in the eighth issue of *Chiheisen*.

"Oh, Sachiko!" It was her *mamai*'s voice.

"So you are going with me next Sunday?"

"All right." After Sachiko disappeared, Maekawa walked down toward the river alone, whistling as he went.

"Where have you been wandering off to? Really. Aida has been waiting for some time." Her mother stared at her while Sachiko put up her hair, which she had yet to comb.

For some reason Sachiko was not pleased to hear her mother talking about "Aida, Aida." When Sachiko thought about how her mother had her eye on him because he was rich, she felt a distaste at the mere sound of his name.

"Where have you been, Sachiko? I am going into town by *caminhão* today, if you have something you need, I would be happy to do it for you. Please don't hesitate to ask." Aida was wearing a black *casimira*, was cleanly shaven, and seemed ready for some assignation; his affectations made Sachiko feeling nothing but dislike for him.

"Sachiko, why don't you ask him for that comb you said you wanted the other day? Aida-san, we have spoiled her, as our only daughter, and as a result she is quite stubborn. So, Sachiko, was the comb the only thing you wanted?" Her mother realized that Sachiko was simply standing there and had not yet greeted him, so she quickly scrutinized Aida's expression.

"I am going into town next *domingo*, and will buy it then, so I am fine." Sachiko could not take any more of her mother's transparent obsequiousness.

"Sachiko, Aida-san has been kind enough to offer, so why don't you take him up on it?"

"Aida-san, I will buy it myself next Sunday, so please don't bother. I can wait." With that, Sachiko dashed off into the house.

The two of them just stood there for a moment, at a loss.

"Auntie, Sachiko is in a really bad mood today, isn't she?"

Sachiko's mother continued to look toward the door for a bit longer and then turned to face Aida, sighing slightly. "I'm so sorry. She didn't use to be this way, but lately Maekawa and his son just won't leave her alone. I bet they said something to her. I am sure that's what it is."

"Maekawa's son? Seriously? But wasn't he born here and can only barely read any Japanese?" In so saying, Aida both flaunted his own social status and casually dismissed Maekawa's son; nonetheless, he was unable to conceal his agitation. His red-black face was tense. "Well, I'll be going. I will bring you something." He tried to cover his shock by smiling casually, but it seemed forced and thus made his feelings all that much more obvious.

During the *semana* every household was busy with work. There had been good weather for some time, but on Thursday and Friday it rained and the rural streets were quickly washed out. What was left was pathetic, pitted everywhere and with large pools of water here and there.

They decided to do the annual roadwork a little on the early side.

Normally the Japanese Association did the work, but this year the Young Men's Association took it on, sending all the money set aside for it to Japan as a donation for national defense.

That decision was arrived at as a result of Aida's encouragement, in his position as group leader in the association. All the newspapers carried articles about the donations for national defense. In addition, the constant articles about the war stirred up the blood of all fellow countrymen in Brazil. It goes without saying that the unsolicited offer by the Young Men's Association was met with great praise.

Maekawa had gone into town on the *jardineira* at half-past six, and returned at six that evening. It was at that point that he first heard that the youth group had done road repairs that day. He thought to himself that the roads had been better on his return, but he had not given it much more attention than that because he had assumed that the heads of household that made up the Japanese Association had done the work as they did every year. Apparently his neighbor Yamada had come by right after he left to let him know there had been an *aviso* about the road repair project. As a member of the Young Men's Association, Maekawa naturally felt guilty for not fulfilling his responsibility despite realizing that there was nothing he could have done, since he had not known. Moreover, the fact that he had gone into town with Sachiko, despite being irrelevant to the matter, nonetheless added to his feelings of guilt.

That night there was a plenary session of the youth group.

Maekawa had really rushed to get there, but by the time he reached the school the anthem had already begun. When he heard this, his legs slowed down of their own accord, now dragging along heavily. One after the other, the black face of Aida, the group leader, and then that of Sachiko rose up in his mind. Despite not having known about it, the fact that he had gone into town today and not participated in the work on behalf of national security made it seem as though he had done something wrong; this, in turn, caused Maekawa's feet to grow even heavier with each step.

He once again began to rush when he realized that he might be able to sneak in without drawing any attention to himself if he made it before the anthem ended.

The door of the poorly built classroom squeaked loudly, despite Maekawa's attempts to open it quietly. It seemed as though none of the members noticed, but he could see a sparkle in the eyes of Aida, who was facing the door.

Maekawa nodded his head slightly, stood behind the last desks to hide himself, and began singing. Despite all this, he could not but feel agitated.

"Gentlemen! Our homeland is in a state of emergency. Since war broke out with China, our nation's citizens in Japan have been working tirelessly, as one, to collect donations for national defense, to send off and welcome back troops dispatched to the front lines, and to console bereaved families. Gentlemen, what is it that allows those of us here in Brazil to live in safety and security? Needless to say, it is the existence of our homeland of Japan. The tragic circumstances of a people without a state are obvious when one looks at the persecution of the Jews. And what of the misery of the Chinese people, constantly engaged in civil war because while they might possess a state, they lack a polity like that of Japan, enjoying an imperial line, unbroken since time immemorial, such as the world has never seen? Gentlemen, when we ponder this, we realize how great our homeland is and how fortunate we are to have been born a member of that nation. However, this homeland of ours now faces an unprecedented crisis. This autumn, what shall we do to help? The people of our homeland, one and all, have rallied to its defense. We youths residing in Brazil, is it really a time for us to remain silent, consumed by our own individual pleasure, profit, and good fortune?"

Aida paused momentarily, leaned back triumphantly, and looked around the room. Maekawa shifted his gaze away from the group leader's face, bathed in lamplight.

"Japan is in a state of crisis . . . crisis."

That voice grew entangled with the image of Sachiko hidden deep in his heart until the group leader's words ceased affecting him.

All Japanese are anxious about this. Was I this morning? I did cast aside my work and meet with Sachiko, after all. No, that was not how it was. I didn't know anything about it. The *aviso* came late. That was how Maekawa reassured himself in his mind. Before he knew it, though, Maekawa found himself standing up when he heard what Aida said next.

"Gentlemen, I was truly dismayed to learn that while all of the members of our group, deeply concerned about this situation as we are, were engaged in the road-work project so that we might contribute to the designated funds to the national defense, one of our number had casually gone into town for his amusement. To make matters worse, he had gone with a woman. At a time like this, when all members of our nation are working as one, in the greatest awareness of the current state of crisis, there is no greater dishonor for our group than to have such a member among us."

"Who are you talking about, group leader?" Maekawa's loud voice rang out suddenly and everyone turned around to face him. At that moment, they were certain whom the group leader had been speaking of.

When group leader Aida's face, utterly calm and displaying a cold smile, and the combined gazes of all the members turned to Maekawa, he sat down onto the desk behind him in spite of himself.

"If that person says he wants to know, I will go ahead and say. That person is none other than *you*. You alone were absent from the work detail today."

"But I did not receive an *aviso*. And to say that I took a woman. It was mere coincidence that she was with me. For you to say such a thing. . . ." Maekawa could take no more and so he stood and fled out the door.

Going out into the pitch black, the tears he had been suppressing with all his might now streamed down his face.

"That bastard. Making a fool of me. I will give him a beating he won't soon forget." He was so riled up that he could feel nothing but hatred for his antagonizer and could think of nothing to do to help his own situation.

"Hey, Maekawa! I know what really happened. Don't be mad. That bastard is up to something. He is mistaken. Don't get so worked up." Upon hearing these words of consolation from his closest friend, Gondō, Maekawa gradually calmed down. "He puts on a good show, but do you think he is a real patriot? He is a good self-promoter. Let's go home and sleep this off. You will forget this whole thing by tomorrow."

Maekawa nodded silently, though Gondō's words had not entirely satisfied him.

Revenge—Maekawa remembered what he had heard about Aida from Sachiko today, and realized that this was Aida's revenge for Sachiko having rejected him. The coward. But there was nothing he could do. More than anything, he felt sad that even Gondō, who knew him so well, could not figure out what was happening.

"Am I unpatriotic?" Maekawa had intended to say that Aida had behaved the way he did in retaliation for being rejected by Sachiko, but in the end these were the words that came out.

"Are you kidding? How could missing road work because you didn't know about it make you unpatriotic?" Gondō said, laughing loudly.

The night was pitch black, without a star in the sky.

As the men walked, insects cried incessantly from both sides of the road.

SUGI TAKEO is the penname of Takei Makoto (1909–2011). Sugi was born in Hokkaidō. In 1931, he graduated from the Hosei University Special Division (法政大学専門部), where he studied to be a teacher. The following year he migrated under the auspices of the Rikkōkai to Brazil, where he worked as a teacher in Japanese-language schools.[70] In 1937, a fellow writer, Ikeda Shigeji, described him as already being an established writer of fiction and a sound thinker on issues related to "the education of our countrymen [in Brazil]."[71] Sugi, like Furuno, was a central voice both as an author and critic in prewar Brazil, leaving a number of published writings, some of which will be addressed in the conclusion to this volume.[72]

"Vortices"

Takemoto Yoshio

(1)

After the morning glories in the small beds framing the entrance began to open, heavy with dew, and the white morning sun illuminated the stains on the curtain, bringing them into relief, the early autumn skies at long last cleared.

"Fall has come early this year. These last two or three days my neuralgia has begun acting up, just as I have been starting to think that the mornings were cold." Her mother, Tatsuyo, winced in pain as she clung to the kitchen door with one hand and rubbed her knee with the other. Michiyo, who was cleaning the room, peacefully gazed out the window to the *grama* that spread out behind the houses with steam rising from their roofs.

The *grama* only continued briefly before reaching a red dirt road; beyond that was the neighbor's coffee orchard. Following the perfect rows of coffee trees, the ground sloped up slowly until one's field of vision opened suddenly and, in the distance, one could make out a hazy swath of virgin forest.

One *paineira* standing alongside the road with its broad branches had lost its leaves early, and blossoms on the lower branches on the north side of the tree had begun to open and tint the tree. Two or three small birds with colorful plumage alighted on its branches.

Without fail, every Sunday children carrying slingshots came early in the morning to shoot at the birds.

Today as well mischievous kids were here, with their glowing cheeks, shooting incessantly at them, but the birds merely flitted casually from one branch to another. This scene, framed by the window, caused Michiyo to smile.

"Mom, the kids are here again."

"They're early. Poor birds. As soon as the kids have any free time, they are straight to their slingshots."

"It's true. Oh, by the way, Matsuda-san said he would leave the school at the end of March."

"Really? But he was so committed to it."

"Uzu" first appeared in 1935 in the 3 July, 10 July, 17 July, and 24 July issues of the *Burajiru jihō*.

"That school is always suffering some sort of *fecha*; with him leaving I feel even more sorry for the children."

"It's strange. I wonder what happened."

"A change of heart, he said."

"A change of heart? With the parents' association such a mess and the educational laws so strict, I imagine one gets tired of it. He's young, so it's not hard to understand."

Her mother headed toward the kitchen with an expression that seemed to say, *it stands to reason.*[73]

"I submitted my resignation."

"But why?"

"I am going to continue my studies in São Paulo."

"But we will all miss you."

She was truly shocked when Matsuda, who always said that he would spend his life as a simple teacher to these children in the colony, suddenly out of the blue said he was going to São Paulo. When Michiyo raised a few possible superficial reasons for his decision, Matsuda's pale face clouded over and then grew pained, as he struggled with words that he could not say directly.

Her chest constricted as she watched his expression and she recalled the previous day, when she had felt a dull pain arising in a place she could not pinpoint, caused by something that she could not clearly identify.

From the other side of the newspaper he had spread on the *mesa*, Shinshuke said, "Matsuda is leaving?"

"Yes, that's what he said. I suppose you're going to lose your conversation partner."

"More than me, you will."

"Yes." When she casually gave this reply and turned to look at Shinsuke, his staring eyes and cold smile communicated more to Michiyo than his words. She startled, at a loss.

Tatsuyo scraped a pot on the edge of the well to remove charring from it, resulting in a noise that almost seemed intended to disrupt the strange silence between them.

Worrying that she had to say something, but also that if she did whatever she said might come out sounding unnatural, Michiyo grew more and more uncomfortable. She felt the probing gaze of her husband on her cheek so she extended her gaze, which had settled on the window frame, out into the garden.

(2)

Michiyo, whose condition had taken a dramatic turn for the worse, was passing a Sunday with nothing in particular to do.

The evening sun, which until only a short time ago had been reflecting off an *enxada* left lying on the *grama*, had begun to set, like a flower wilting behind the jagged, light-indigo forest in the distance. The green hills that formed a series of arcs stretching out into the distance gradually grew indistinct as visibility fell. Eventually only a few bands of golden rays stretched into a radial pattern against the dark-blue sky, and three or four thin, amber-trimmed clouds strode off pompously in the same direction. While this was the view she was used to seeing, it nonetheless remained invigorating, filled with happiness and charm.

While drinking tea after dinner, her mother stopped picking her teeth and glanced at Shinsuke's face. "So, Kimura-san came this morning?"

"Oh, that. It was the debts as usual." Ending any chance of conversation, Shinsuke fell silent again.

This was the standard atmosphere in the household of late. Although it seemed normal to her that sadness filled the household, given the recent loss of her father, Michiyo still wondered at what point this friction between them had started.

Suddenly it felt as though shards of glass began racing around in her head.

"Cut it for me. I can't take it. Cut off my leg with the *machado*."

Having received the urgent message, Tatsuyo and Michiyo raced in horror to where her husband was, only to find him screaming, his body drenched in sweat and exhausted from struggling, and his face contorted in agony.

The people who had gone logging with Shinsuke, their faces hard like Noh masks, sawed away the tree that had fallen on her husband's leg.

Nonetheless, by now Shinsuke had gotten to the point where he could get around by dragging his incapacitated leg. However, the depression that developed even as the wound healed was warping Shinsuke into an increasingly intolerant man.

Clear to her that Shinsuke's despairing demeanor was what was tearing the three of them apart, Michiyo was frightened for herself, given her tendency to be pulled into her husband's emotional states.

Be that as it may, no one could really be blamed. Even as Shinsuke, who had been a happy, vigorous man, endured this serious blow to his spirit, which little by little ate away like a writhing *bicheira* at that inherent will to fight against society that every man possesses, his practical nature prevented him from entering into the particular state of self-reflection that emerges from grief and resignation in the face of a grave personal setback. Knowing Shinsuke as well as she did, Michiyo could say nothing to him.

Her mother, despite commonplace gestures of affection that she would show Shinsuke even as a dark, painful shadow crept over him, could not keep from expressing her womanly complaints, filled with disappointment over his attitude. Time and time again she would say to Michiyo, "I've given up. If you just resign yourself, it's actually easier, you know?" Still, Michiyo was saddened every time she saw the desolate envy that appeared in her mother's face each time she heard of a celebratory occasion, or even simple good fortune, befalling the household of one of the people with whom she had come from Japan, migrating to the ten-*alquiere lotes* each had acquired.

"Debts?"

"We settle debts in April, so he asked me to try to get the money by then."

"What did you say?"

"To let me settle it with him another way."

"With the *lote*? He didn't need to make you say it; he is fully aware of the situation. People really can be unbelievable."

My mother could not forget our favorable circumstances when we first settled here. Director Maeda of the Shinano Overseas Association showed us the land, saying things like, "Look at this. These huge trees are proof that that this area doesn't get frost," or he would look up at some large trees and say, "They are this dense because the soil is good." He built up our fathers, who had no background knowledge on the subject, convincing them to clear the mountain and invest all they had in growing coffee. As it turns out, the soil was good and crops grew well. The market was strong and the settlers waited for the four years to pass until they could harvest their coffee, all the while indulging their outrageous fantasies.

But the future they had waited for arrived in a miserable state. The market had dropped precipitously and then came the frost, which they had not even considered a possibility.

In Michiyo's household, that was not all: her father also died suddenly and unexpectedly.

In the face of these unavoidable events, these people who had invested all they had were torn up like sheets left out hanging in a storm. By contrast, the people who had lacked the capital to buy land and had been making do under them, have today, ten years later, ended up in the exact opposite position.

Her mother, who watched these developments of the colony over the past decade, cried bitter tears every time a reminder comes to pay their debt from Ōmura, whom she had looked after when he was a contract worker.

She could not bear seeing her mother's lips, on that frail face of hers, begin to quiver as she lost her composure, so Michiyo changed the topic.

"Did I hear that Tami came today?"

"That's right. She wondered if we had any purple embroidery thread."

"It's too bad we didn't have any for her. Ah, embroidery. It has been so long since I have been able to even think about embroidering anything."

"She was wearing a new pink outfit. With her modest figure and pale skin, it really suited her." Her mother stared straight at Michiyo, as though she wanted to tell her that she naturally deserved even greater fortune than Tami, but that circumstances had allowed that to be stolen away from her. Instead, she merely blinked.

Each time Michiyo felt this sort of pure affection so directly from her mother, who knew no other way than to confront everything in her life directly, she felt joy well up in her chest.

(3)

We must *colhêr* the berries, because they will fall from the trees. Today Michiyo, like the others, did not get a sense of reality from those words. They just worked in the fields as though chasing desultory shadows until the whistle sounded and they returned home.

"Tami said that they will be showing a moving picture in the central area and asked me if we wanted to come."

"They've been coming a lot lately, haven't they?"

When Michiyo came in the rear door with the setting sun at her back, her mother, who was frying *bacalhau* on a screen grill, passed on what Tamiko had said, squinting her eyes as the smoke from the fish poured past them.

When they finished their unexceptional dinner, Michiyo decided to invite her husband to go see the movie. The thought occurred to her that perhaps by doing something as simple (for women) as going to see a movie, they might be able to untangle themselves from their emotions as easily as unraveling a knot by pulling gently on the end of the string. Her hope was that they could escape the awkward sensation that had come to dominate their daily lives, which felt something like reading a mistake-laden letter, or the unpleasant chill of fear that seizes one's body as one tries to peek at something through a tiny crack.

"Shall the two of us go tonight?"

"Hmm. . . ."

"I want to see it. Take me? It's been such a long time."

She tried inviting him in a sweet voice she had long left unused, her eyes sparkling seductively. As she leaned her whole body toward him, grasping his arm, she felt as though her words, which had passed her lips more easily than she had feared they might, had drawn closer to his heart than she had been in some time, piercing the mysterious web-like fog that her husband usually wrapped himself in; while that fog normally caused her to heart to lose its way, this time she felt it had reached through to his.

At that moment, however, she glanced at her husband's profile and saw his expression, which resembled nothing more than that of a patient at the moment he swallows bitter medicine: his brow furrowed, as though drawn together by the minute twitches of his lips.

Her profound disappointment triggered a hatred that she had unconsciously suppressed until that moment.

Recently the traveling sections of such film companies as Baieisha and X Cinema had begun showing films from the old country once every three of four months even here in the northwest interior.

Left behind by entertainment media that use modern technology and instead focusing exclusively on growing accustomed to this new land, the settlers, both young and old, packed themselves in before the movie screen, despite the exorbitant price, as though they were possessed, as though they were rice plants wilted from a long drought that were preparing to drink in a passing shower.

The village, which lacked an auditorium despite ten years having passed already since they settled there, instead held it in the primary school. Michiyo walked the more than two kilometers to the school, still dressed in her everyday clothes.

Broad-shouldered young men, women who exchanged excessively chatty and Japanese-y greetings with insincere smiles on their faces, and young girls raised in Brazil with their chests pushed out, their flat faces covered in cheap powder, and their skirts fluttering every time they laughed; groups of these people would form and then disappear like moths at the flickering light of the entrance, which this night only was illuminated using power produced by car engines.

With the film apparently not yet having begun, the clamor inside melted into one, until it sounded like a single deep roar.

Michiyo hid herself behind Tamiko and Tamiko's brother, Ken'ichi, as they moved their bodies, chilled from the winter winds, into the auditorium, which in turn was stuffy and rank and filled with a cacophony of sounds from which there was no avenue for escape.

Before them, near the white screen at the front of the room, the *benshi* carefully wound the insufficiently oiled phonograph and put on the record; the only ones listening, however, were the dozen or so persons near him. In this corner a man whistled impatiently, while in that corner a squinting woman gabbed on and on, her back to the screen. In the rear, precocious youths grabbed at the young girls, making lewd gestures unthinkable for unmarried people; everyone was shocked at their impudence.

Michiyo thought of herself, sitting there silently under the vast ceiling, tobacco smoke and dust swirling in the air, and wondered why in the world she was there.

As she thought about how cowardly she must appear, having fled all the way here out of fear that she might lash out, she grew increasingly unhappy.

What if she had taken the next step, as she had looked upon her husband's heartless face. . . . What if she had actually entered into this emotional battle between the two sexes. . . . But such a decision represents the ultimate challenge for any woman. She had to consider her self, unable to deny the existence in her of feelings for Matsuda and yet all-too-lacking in sophistication to admit them either.

At some point the lights had been extinguished and the story had begun unfolding on the surface of the screen in front.

As people passed in front of Michiyo and Tamiko and poured out the exit, their faces filled with unconcealed and organic excitement, a deep bass voice said, "Oh, so you were here?" Turning in the direction of the speaker, Michiyo saw Matsuda standing there. Taller than most, his gentlemanly face was illuminated by the light.

"What timing. With it being just me, Tami, and her brother, we were feeling a bit lonely and wondering if anyone else we knew had come."

The moment Tamiko turned around she showed the shyness one would expect from a proper young woman, instinctively lowering her face to the point that she almost did a full bow. Using that as a pretext, Michiyo stepped closer to Matsuda.

When they left the empty hall, now scattered with discarded paper, it was colder than they expected. The nighttime winds whistled through the tops of the Paraná pines that had been planted around the primary school.

A moon hung in the clear night sky, looking for all the world like a piece of fresh fruit that had been washed and then cast into the air. The women's shadows were cast starkly onto the parched road.

Michiyo thought of how she had recently had many occasions to speak with Matsuda.

Nothing is nicer than when two strangers come together by chance, but then come across some shared ideas or interests as they explore topics to discuss. Nothing makes one feel a deeper sense of friendship. As they continue having conversations, they draw increasingly close to one another, until eventually they are even revealing problems they are experiencing both at home and in the community.

It would be impossible to describe how much consolation Matsuda's wise, humble words, filled with friendship, had brought to Michiyo when they discussed her troubles with her husband. However, the way he had been looking at her recently had been filled with a different sort of intensity, and, when she took a closer look, she noticed that his fine cheekbones possessed an intensity that made them seem aflame, crackling like a conflagration. Even before her husband made that comment, she had felt a dangerous premonition about her relationship with Matsuda.

Against her better judgment, she allowed the conversations to grow even more intense, beginning to speak about topics that they shared in common. It was as though her will were constrained, silencing the voice that said she must not.

"Well then, goodnight," Tamiko said mechanically as they reached her house, and then turned on her heel sadly as she pulled her brother along by the hand.

"Matsuda-san, what do you think of Tami-chan?"

"She seems like a nice girl, if that is what you mean."

"That's all? She is in love with you, you know."

" . . . ."

Michiyo, suddenly feeling guilty as she realized that they were now walking alone on the road, consciously began to tease Matsuda as a way to deflect that sensation. She stared down at their shadows, cast side-by-side on the road that wound through the empty coffee fields. The caws of the crows, sounding like babies' cries, interrupted their now-awkward conversation time and again. Suddenly Matsuda's strong shoulders and arms, visible amid the ominous silence, began to frighten her.

"Before I go to São Paulo, I. . . ."

"No, you mustn't say it!"

Matsuda, who had been silently clutching his hair in his hands, seized her shoulder like a fierce beast that lives deep in the recesses of the forest. Because of her sudden fear and dismay, she was not able to catch the words he quickly whispered to her as if in a delirium. Directly confronted with this danger, however, Michiyo merely shook her head no, as though pleading with him, and instinctively evaded him by continuing to walk on, not even glancing at him for a moment.

As soon as the light was turned off, her husband rolled over slowly in bed, until he faced the wall. His scent and his body heat, which she had grown accustomed to over the years, permeated the bedding, gently enveloping Michiyo's body, which was still faintly quivering from the excitement, and gradually helped calm her breathing.

In her heart, where the concentric ripples were fading from the outside in until all that was left was quiet, still water, an animalistic fear that resides hidden somewhere in the hearts of all people, overrun as they are by chance encounters, could be deeply felt.

The emotions that Matsuda, who was so cerebral, had developed over time as he closely observed her suffering shifted from warm feelings of friendship to idolization and then finally had become an intense, single-minded love.

As one would upon discovering a single stain on an otherwise pristine sheet of white paper, she both fixated on and despised the momentary sense of stark and rough male desire pressing in on her, overwhelming her. It did not leave her even a moment to resist it. The powerful and vigorous touch of his hand, even through her layers of clothes, drove her toward her own instinctive feelings of ecstasy, filled with sensual secrets. In an attempt to rid herself of the self-hatred that was increasingly bearing down on her as she scrutinized herself, she fervently tried repeating the words, "I am right." However, no matter how many times these words raced around in her mind, and no matter how she tried to tell herself that she had no reason to feel guilty about anything, right there beside her was her husband, whose suspicious gaze kept her so anxious that she felt as though she were being pierced by needles. Regardless of how well she might compose herself now, come morning, the moment their eyes meet there in bed, he will give her a look that says, "You did something last night that you are keeping from me, didn't you? I know because

I can see last night's quivers lingering in your face." At these thoughts, disconsolate tears poured down Michiyo's cheeks.

I am not bad. It is all my husband's fault. There is no way for a woman to live when her husband has taken such an attitude. Particularly when I am a young, healthy woman.

Michiyo felt physical pain from the loss of naturalness in their relationship as husband and wife, resulting from the towering wall that had begun to arise between them. She began to fear that she might explode from within, just as the fruit of a pomegranate bursts open. She grew forlorn whenever she thought of how she had to hate the vitality in her breast, and the primitive desire that burned within her, a woman in her prime. She came to find that whenever she suppressed her feelings in one spot, tears seemed on the verge of pouring out of another, as with a sponge saturated with water.

"Ashes"

Takemoto Yoshio

The *caminhão* Haruta was riding in gradually disappeared into the distance. It was about a decade ago. All too easily he receded, wearing high on his waist the snugly fitting, light brown pants with thin, black stripes that Ushichi had bought for him when the immigration ship called into port in Hong Kong. His blank face was flushed red from the *pinga* and his pores were wide open, the skin of his neck resting lightly on his tight, soiled collar. He was holding his sweat-stained straw boater in one hand. He didn't say anything, not even "Well then" or "Where am I headed?" After Haruta disappeared from sight, the sun, looking like a rotten *mamão*, lingered eerily at the point at which the main road, bleached white and baked dry after days of clear weather, reached the horizon.

Ushichi headed back, stepping firmly on his own doddering, emaciated shadow, which had been following him around now for four decades. A mean-spirited relief tickled the back of his throat. Aboard the truck, which had been only two or three feet away from him, Haruta's face had distorted and blurred for an extended moment, as a drop or two of affection for his kin dampened Ushichi's desiccated eyelids, and a sense of distress like an unexpected backflow of blood struck him, undercutting his willpower and making him avert his eyes guiltily. As the truck started off, its engine revving and its chassis shuddering, a profound brazenness raced up Ushichi's spine, quickly allowing him to restore the expression on his face, which seemed to say, "It's ok. This will make everything better."

The plot that he had resolved to see through was quite a strange one, and seemed an increasingly dim-witted strategy the more definitive, the more concrete, it became. Ushichi had planned time and again over the past two or three years to toss Haruta out, but no matter how reasonable the plan, as it came time to implement it he began to be tormented by a fear that it would not come to fruition.

Now, when the clear realization that he had so easily been able to send Haruta off was sinking in, an anti-climactic feeling, as when the rush of adrenaline recedes, caused him to shake his head again and again in disbelief.

"Shihai" first appeared in 1937 in the third issue of *Chiheisen*.

138

What rose up so clearly in this empty space in his mind—and then solidified there, like a lump of lead—was the image of the unsalvageable, corrupted, filthy friction among himself, Oshin, and Haruta.

The petroleum lamp sputtered and snapped. Stains speckled the rough earthen walls where cockroaches have been smashed; in the darkness, the room stifling with the stench of garlic, Oshin rustled through some old rags. Ushichi lay sprawled out on his *cama*, a futon left out year-round whose cotton has been almost entirely pressed out, rolling handmade cigarettes with his palm. He wrapped the tobacco in newspaper and spit on the floor as he smoked one after another. In the ravine out back, a frog fell again and again with an irritating thud on the bottom of a *lata*. Ushichi was discussing with Oshin the fact the plantation manager had slipped a comment about next year's wages into a conversation during *almoça* that day. The manager had smiled even as he feigned regret at the indiscretion, as though to say, *oops, did I let that slip?*

"Ōno-san said that he would pay 35 *mil* more than this year."

"Really? Does this mean you promised to stay put next year?"

"Wh-what do you mean? It's too early for that. Why would I be in such a rush to decide?"

With Oshin's growing indignation at his evasions, Ushichi grew flustered.

In truth, after having been called into the plantation manager's home for a drink on his way home from the fields that evening, Ushichi had given him the responses he had wanted to hear. The very same manager who had exploited everything he could from the *colonos* up until this point was now suddenly all smiles, telling them everything they wanted to hear: "I will be paying 275 *mil* per thousand coffee *covas*" and "I will throw in 5 or 6 piglets as well." It was clear to Ushichi that this was just a strategy to persuade the *colonos*, who had clearly become restless hearing the call of the cotton market, to stay, given the labor shortage bound to result from the passage of the two percent rule. Yet Ushichi gave him the servile response he did—"In that case, I guess I may be imposing on you next year as well. . . ."—partially because he thought that with those conditions he might be able to relax a bit, but more so because of the self-defeating thoughts that carried his mind to a place of peace and a filled belly. At this point those things were all he could think of, having for such a long time suffered from and struggled against unavoidable events amid inopportune circumstances. At some point his ambition and connection with society had eroded completely away and he was left unable to confront his life seriously or imagine any bright prospects for the future.

"That's right. You were taken in by a fast talker, all while chuckling like a fool. And then you lied about what happened. . . ."

" . . . ."

"You are useless! Who was it who said he would buy land in Nova Aliança next year and grow cotton. . . ."

" . . . "

The way the blue veins at Oshin's temples throbbed intimidated Ushichi, leaving him speechless.

Ever since February, when their only child was torn away from them, Oshin had been unable to find even a day of peace. The child had suffered from trachoma that left his eyes swollen and itchy, but still the cause of the fever that took him was something even the best doctor in the colony could not wrap his bald head around. Oshin had long been asking Ushichi to buy some virgin land where they could live in their own home—it didn't matter where. She had come to think that the reason their son had died and they had no place to call home was because of her husband's uselessness. This was why she would lash out at him, regardless of how trivial the issue. When he handled these conversations poorly they soon became fights. In the end, Ushichi would quickly change the subject, realizing that the only possible outcome would be for him to be crushed pathetically beneath Oshin's frenzy of thunderous insults.

"Haruta's late again."

"I'm sure he's at the *boteco* again."

"I'm not worried about him drinking, but lately he's really been hitting it hard, hasn't he?"

"He's earning his own money, and choosing to drink his pay, so no one says anything about it."

"That's why I don't mention it. I don't say anything, but. . . ."

"You still think you can count on Haruta?"

"That's not . . . let me worry about that. . . ."

"If that's how you feel."

" . . . "

Ushichi threw his cigarette on the earthen floor, crawled straight into his bed, and closed his eyes.

Ushichi thought about Haruta. The one who had made Haruta crazy—Haruta, who was so gentle when they arrived in Brazil—was Oshin. Oshin is really the one to blame. That woman is evil. Ushichi superimposed Oshin's face over Haruta's in his mind.

Oshin was the one who set her mind on using the exceptionally strong and totally idiotic Haruta.

Oshin would coddle and coax him, and even on occasion manipulate him through a provocative fawning that she would flaunt before Ushichi, and which he despised. In the course of being manipulated by Oshin's persistent devices, Haruta had grown increasingly stubborn, avaricious, and inclined to drink. As a result, over the last year or two, Oshin had been forced time and again to grit her teeth, thinking that her plan had been foiled. Since the time he got wildly drunk and violent at their son's funeral, Oshin would jump at any pretense at all. She would scream at Ushichi in a voice simultaneously suspicious and hysterical, "Get rid of Haruta!"; Ushichi would respond reflexively, "Yeah, I'll get rid of him all right. I'll throw the bastard out." Each time, though, a feeling of resistance to Oshin's vile nature would quickly rise up, and the anger Ushichi felt toward Haruta would fail to materialize as words, but instead remain a mere withered emotion. Inevitably Ushichi would then fall into a fierce sense of self-hatred.

Whenever he closed his eyes, an intense loathing would begin to torment Ushichi's body.

Ah, everything I have done has been a mistake.

He had come to Brazil filled with empty bravado, muttering to himself—as though talking nonsense in his sleep—about *freedom, truth, love,* all the while forgetting his own uncontrollable foolishness. On top of that, he had brought along his utterly idiotic brother with him. When he thought of these decisions that led to his life today, he realized that the flames that currently torment him had been smoldering for quite some time.

"That's it. I give up."

Ushichi tossed and turned under the heaviness of these thoughts, mumbling to himself.

The sound of Oshin rinsing the following day's rice could be heard from the kitchen. *I have an early start tomorrow. I have to get to sleep.* Impending reality forced slumber upon Ushichi.

"Ishida-san, wake up!"

Just as he realized that the calls were coming from outside the house, a fist began pounding on the front door. Ushichi grabbed hold of the hem of his bedshirt and jumped toward the door. When he quickly opened it, a voice crashed in upon him. Startled, Ushichi looked into the eyes of the man there, who was clearly alarmed.

"Booze—Haruta—Foreigner—*faca*—pistol!" The words made no sense; merely holding this string of fragmentary information in his ears, Ushichi grabbed a jacket and ran toward the *botequim.*

"I-Idiot. Did someone finally do you in, Haruta!?"

Not even waiting for the lamps of his neighbors, who were coming out behind him in an uproar, Ushichi ran the two kilometers down the pitch-black road, choking with tears as he screamed, "Goddamn it, Haruta!"

A purplish straight line split the air above his head and then dug deep into Haruta's torso. His final moments were brutish and cruel. As a dark spray of blood flew from his body, he collapsed with a thud onto the ground.

Ushichi was driven on by this image, which had burst into his mind the instant that the man's trembling voice bore into his chest. The actual scene at the store that greeted Ushichi, filling his bloodshot eyes as he leapt in and let out a deep sigh, however, was a completely ordinary one: cans, bottles, soaps, and household utensils packed the shelves in the gloomy room. He cast his eyes downward in confusion, feeling just like a rubber band that, having been stretched too far, had finally snapped. Shards from *copinhos* that had been smashed were scattered everywhere, and a cold, eerie *faca* lay on the floor with its blade facing upwards. From the moment his gaze, turned upside down, landed directly upon that blade, the feeling that he had been walking on some sort of unbalanced chain, a feeling he had had up until this point, mixed with the bloody gore that covered the blade, dragged Ushichi down into a natural terror.

Sensing that someone was in the back, Ushichi called out. From behind the various goods for sale, a squat, round-faced, older man emerged and smiled, exposing his white teeth. When the man saw Ushichi's troubled expression, his own grew somewhat bewildered.

"Oh, you've come. For Haru? Sorry to put you out like this."

"I figured as much. . . . Is he. . . ."

"What? No, he's just drunk."

As Ushichi was being led out back, he compared the vast gap between the older man's attitude with the conclusion that his imagination had raced to and marveled at the difference.

Haruta, who was nearly blacked-out drunk, was lying in the back of the yard with his head stuck in a *capoeira*. In a hoarse voice that sounded on the verge of tears, he was moaning and thrashing his legs.

"He-y! Kill me! You can't kill me? Goddammit. You, my brother, can't kill me either?"

When Ushichi heard Haruta's voice, which sounded more as though his throat was squeezing out sounds of its own accord, he experienced a simple and honest relief: "Oh, thank goodness." Ushichi lifted Haruta onto his back as one would a child. Slumped over Ushichi's shoulder, Haruta's warm, acrid breath stood out from the bitter cold of the night wind as it passed over Ushichi's neck.

Later, by the time the people from the village had crowded in noisily around him with *enxadas* and hunting rifles over their shoulders, Ushichi had calmed down completely. He conveyed to them everything the old man from the *botequim* had told him, going around and apologizing to each and every one for his brother's extreme indiscretion while offering them *copinhos* of the *pinga* he had bought for that purpose.

The incident had been a foolish one. Haruta, who had drunk himself into such a stupor that he could not tell one person from another, had gotten mixed up with a *kuronbo* who had just stopped in for a drink. The argument eventually got ugly enough that knives were drawn, but Haruta was too drunk for it to get really serious.

It was the threats and the shouting, however, that upset the onlookers sufficiently to alert Ushichi.

After his morning coffee, Ushichi dragged a reluctant Haruta around the neighborhood to apologize once again to everyone for the previous night.

Haruta, bandaging the arm that he himself had apparently cut while brandishing his *faca*, suddenly muttered something, as if to himself, in a serious tone that Ushichi had never seen in him before.

"Brother, I . . . want to go. I want to try living someplace else."

"Where? Where do you want to go?"

"No where particular. . . ."

"Are you kidding? Where can you go with no money? Heck, you can't even get *agua* to drink if you don't have any money."

"I might not have any money, but I'm strong. . . ."

"*'I'm strong?'*"

Repeating Haruta's last words, Ushichi cast his eyes down at his own arms. His skin, its elasticity lost under a layer of fur singed by the blazing sun, was rough and old. His lower body, every part of it, moaned of the hardship of a wanderer who had suffered over many long years under the cruel power of this world. Ushichi let out a deep sigh. He could not care less for fame or for character, neither of which could even replace a *tamanco*, but he wanted money and power to his core. Day and night he deceived himself, saying "luck is hard to come by," as if chanting some sort of mantra; at this point he had completely lost hope of getting his hands on any money. He could not even rely on his body: touching his arms, which unlike Haruta's had completely lost any significant strength of any kind, he sank into a deep despair.

Suddenly the whistle signaling *almoço* sounded at the lumber mill, surprisingly loud as it emanated out across the clear sky. Haruta, who had been staring obliviously into the distance after having at some point finished bandaging his arm, turned his head at the sounding of the whistle. It was as if he had remembered something.

"When is it that that bus comes by here?"

"So, you're going to Araçatuba? That's not a bad idea."

"Yeah. . . ."

"Since it's *almoço* now, the next time the bus comes by should be at four."

Twelve o'clock, one, two. . . . Haruta walked out unsteadily, bending his fingers as he counted. Just as Ushichi was stifling a yawn and squeezing his eyes shut, Oshin came rushing out of the *cozinha*. Hearing Oshin's shrill, high-pitched voice and thinking that it was time to eat, the events of the previous evening jumbled in Ushichi's mind. No matter how he tried, he could not get up.

TAKEMOTO YOSHIO (1911–83), who wrote both "Vortices" and "Ashes," was born in 1911 in Okayama Prefecture, and then migrated alone to Brazil in 1930 after having graduated from Shizutani Middle School (閑谷中学校). After farming on the (Dai-ichi) Aliança Colony for six years, Takemoto moved to the city of São Paulo where he worked as a Japanese-language teacher and a newspaper reporter.[74] He was a founding coterie member of the literary journals *Chiheisen* (地平線), *Yashiju* (椰子樹), *Koronia bungaku* (コロニア文学), and *Koronia shibungaku* (コロニア詩文学).[75] Takemoto, who died in 1983, became a central figure in the Japanese-language literary world; today, perhaps the most prestigious Japanese-language literary award in Brazil is named after him, the Concurso Literário Yoshio Takemoto (Takemoto Yoshio Literary Prize).[76]

"A Certain Ghetto"

Akino Shū

Paulo Senda truly could not bear it. Now, when it was too late, he regretted having visited the woman.

Not only had she excused herself the moment he arrived, leaving the room and then not returning, but also he had grown even more edgy as a result of the groaning—it sounded as though someone were ill—coming from the next room.

The room was unbearable, both from the stifling air and from the oppressive feeling produced by the eerie silence.

As though an afterthought, the strangely chilled breeze carried in a slight odor, making him feel as though his brain itself might be affected.

He felt it was because of his own negligence that he did not know that one of her family members was sick.

It must have been her younger sister who was indisposed.

He left, spat out the saliva that he had been accumulating in his mouth, and began walking up the hill in front of him.

Sickly weeds bearing some white berries had pressed unsteadily up from between the cobblestones. Climbing the steep hill as far as the N newspaper offices, he looked toward Rua Tomas de Lima. Spotting Okamoto, who was walking quickly in his direction, his mood brightened. When he whistled and waved, stretching his hand high, Okamoto waved back.

At this corner of Conde and Tomas de Lima the residence of the Count of Sarzedas towered, surrounded by an imposing wall of red brick.

That centuries-old structure enjoyed the protection of a sturdy iron fence and thick flagstones. Across the street from it, in the direction from which he had just come, stretched out the ghetto where his countrymen lived.

Senda, with his pale, nervous face, cast his gaze at a third-floor window of this home, which resembled an old castle. The windows were never open.

Beneath the windows a single thin vine of over two feet in length stretched parasitically on its host, this Elizabethan building.

"Aru uramachi" first appeared in 1937 in the second issue of *Chiheisen*.

Senda's eyes then travelled from the windows of the Count's home to the old trees that filled its garden.

Ancient secrets were hidden in the moss-covered branches of the trees. The rust-covered, eerie building, its old trees, and the gate that seemed unlikely to ever be opened again—these things thrust themselves into his field of vision.

Despite this, for some reason there seemed to be no need for a second-generation Japanese like Senda to investigate the matter any further. It was enough merely to observe, gathering what he could from just looking.

Whenever he thought, "What is that for?" the answer "It's not *for* anything; it just *is*" popped quickly into his head. Just this caused him to grow listless and weary. This was not because he felt he must not think too hard about this or anything else, but rather because he just did not really *want* to think about it.

He knew all too well that even if he were to investigate further, the results would not be worth even *um tostão*.

Instead, what occured to him first was how he ought to go bet on some *bicho*. People like him, people who were raised in an environment and by parents that considered the material to be all that mattered, had a frightening paucity of both the spirit of inquiry and powers of deduction.

Senda, fortunately, did not try to understand this, nor was there any need for him to do so. These momentary feelings, conjured to kill time, had been nothing more than a half-conscious attempt to find a diversion.

"Paulo, are you going home already?"

Miho approached with her eyes filled with resentment, but Senda merely pretended to listen quietly to the sound of the wind blowing through the treetops around the old-fashioned home. For his part, he was angry just to have been kept waiting despite having gone out of his way to visit.

"Paulo, why don't you stay longer this time."

"No, I have things to do."

Miho looked away despite being on pins and needles, while Senda lit a cigarette.

Miho had wrapped her pale torso, with her narrow shoulders and supple limbs, in deep red clothes, into which the *cinta* she wore around her slim waist seemed to bite. Nearly every night she had to go out to the shop done up in this pitiful way in order to please the customers.

The place she worked was T restaurant, a quite popular place. Even aware of that issue, some sort of fragile, pale, morbid charm aroused Senda's emotions and drew him to her. Senda and Miho did not hate one another.

Miho had only just turned nineteen, but with her malnourished and fatigued face, she looked two or three years older.

Senda remembered clearly her expression when she had smiled sadly as she told him that none of the customers ever took her for younger than twenty.

For his part, Senda too had matured quite early, with a stature that made it hard to believe that he was only twenty. A handsome youth, he had been taken for an adult from a young age.

"Let's forget about today. You have work anyway, right?" He said this kindly, without unpleasantness, and then saw her off as she walked down the hill.

"Hey!" At some point, Okamoto had come up behind him and now was standing there beaming, filled with vigor.

"Of course, . . ." Miho responded to Senda. "You're right."

Okamoto patted Senda on the back and started walking.

"What?" Senda more or less understood, but asked anyway. Okamoto mimed taking a drink.

Senda forced a smile in response to Okamoto, who was as easygoing as always, and went into the nearby Japanese people's restaurant, K.

Okamoto ordered *cerveja* and sausage without consulting Senda, then sat down next to him before looking around the place.

The *cerveja* took a long time to arrive. The shop was quiet at this hour, right before *janta*.

In the seats next to them, two men were making a ruckus, their voices echoing through the empty restaurant.

One, a red-faced man of around fifty, was wearing unbecoming gold-framed glasses. The other had a wrinkled face and was yammering on with his large mouth opened wide.

The bottles of *cerveja* were lined up before the two men, who were completely absorbed in a conversation about the *loteria*.

The red-faced man, whose mouth was ringed with foam, listened to the wrinkled-face man bluster vigorously, but was lamenting having missed winning by only one number. It appeared that he was drinking as a form of consolation.

When their agitation about the *loteria* subsided, the two men left the restaurant. Once they had left, the place grew quiet, with only the hum of the *sorvete* maker audible.

Senda and Okamoto drank, their expressions dull, fully absorbed in their own thoughts.

Watching the waitress named Shizuko pass in front of them four or five times, the two men were struck with different, but equally unexpected, feelings.

When Senda, who had awoken to sexuality early, gazed upon Shizuko's sensuous figure, he experienced an instinctive aversion.

By contrast, that voluptuousness aroused Okamoto's passions. Assisted by the alcohol, he stared at Shizuko, unconcerned with Senda's displeasure. Senda, being Senda, thought less of Okamoto for being taken with such a woman.

It was eight o'clock by the time the two of them left the K restaurant, but the pleasures of the city at night were already being arrayed before them, darting around like a bouncing rubber ball.

"A walk." Senda's eyes were bloodshot from the alcohol. When the foreign women around them heard his raised voice, they turned around to look.

Okamoto followed behind him, smiling nonchalantly.

When they arrived in front of the Cinema Santa Helena, having passed in front of the oppressive edifice that housed the court, Senda entered the adjacent building as though he had been sucked into it.

The white structure had become a gambling house that was filled with the stuffy smell of tobacco and the displeasing odor of its inhabitants.

This basement room was the pleasure center for the morbid amusements of the city.

It was a place where, when one's bets went well, they returned twenty or thirty times over; when they did not, fifty or one hundred *mil* would vanish before one knew it.

The betting men (and here there were only men) watched intently a ball being hit by something resembling a racquet. One woman struck the number ten, and then it was the next woman's turn.[77] She hit the number twenty-five.

This continued until there were only two numbers left. When the number thirty-five came up as the winning number, the winner ran off to claim his money.

The losers gazed ruefully upon the posted total winnings, their expressions sour. The payout was forty *mil*. The man with bloodshot eyes in front of Okamoto tore his tickets into bits and then threw them down onto the floor.

All Okamoto could do was stare at the man, smiling all the while.

"Look who's here."

The man whose shoulder Okamoto had tapped turned around and grinned broadly. As Senda was thinking that this man with sharp eyes was named Murai, if he remembered correctly, Okamoto glanced at Senda and then took the tickets that Murai had been holding.

Murai, who was not at all happy about this, quietly clicked his tongue.

"This guy never picks 'em," Okamoto said, and then returned the tickets.

After the ringing bell stopped and the whistle blew, one woman on roller skates came racing over to them.

For a while now, Okamoto had been paying closer attention to Senda's movements than to the competition. Thinking to himself, "He placed a bet," Okamoto focused on Senda's pained expression, and did not take his eyes off of him.

As the competition progressed, Senda leaned his body farther and farther forward.

Okamoto overheard the four or five Brazilians in front of him calling out, "Lola! Lola!" They must have their money on that woman.

Okamoto was not concerned with the suspicious-looking man with the fidgety hands who was behind those men either.

Just as Okamoto started thinking something was strange about him, though, he realized the man was no longer there.

Senda, lost in the competition, just stared forward. Okamoto found Senda comical looking this way. He remained silent, having decided to come up behind Senda and surprise him.

Senda had never been the sort to give any credence to Okamoto's cautions, so Okamoto had quit offering them, concluding that Senda was quite the inveterate gambler. Okamoto thought to himself, though, *keep at it like this, and you will always lose.*

At that moment Senda was panicking.

Having won 20 *mil* right off the bat, his calculations had all been thrown off. He went so far as to buy a fiver, but lost it.

He thought that he was hot that night, so there was no way he was going to stop before he had at least won back the money he had lost.

Whenever Senda thought about how helpless he was to change himself, and not become so perversely stubborn, he would begin to feel an oppressiveness that he could not contain. He thought that the fact that he could not even overcome as meager an opponent as himself was linked to his pathological nerves.

"Damn it."

His last hopes dashed, he tore his tickets into shreds and threw them down in front of him.

The floor, upon which the tracked-in mud and scraps of paper resembled a decorative pattern, exposed the chaotic, grubby undersides of lives on the verge of tears.

"Damn it," he muttered once again, scratching his head. Senda steeled the expression on his pale face and tried to smile for Okamoto, who had approached him, but the despair in his face was only revealed that much more clearly.

Okamoto recalled the name "Lola" from a moment earlier, and in his mind tried to see that woman and the dark-skinned Iracema as one.[78] He then whispered in Senda's ear, *this one will win.*

"I'm going to bet on sixteen."

Senda lifted his pale face and looked into Okamoto's eyes, which were filled with confidence, and then left to place his bet, but not before cracking a wan smile that twitched sickly into place. As Senda went, Okamoto purchased forty-six, the least-bet number. Even if it misses, it is still worth two *mil.* His mood brightened when he thought to himself, *if it hits, I will give it all to Senda.*

Amid the cacophony of voices and the cigarette smoke, the man standing on the dais was blowing a whistle.

The surrounding clamor went completely silent almost instantly. The first woman came racing up along with the sound of her wheels; there within the steel cage the expression on her face, with its high cheekbones, was anxious.

The ball fell into number twenty-two with a thud.

The room, which had been silent to that moment, suddenly emitted a sound like that of the wind blowing through trees.

Soon the next woman appeared, strangely composed given the uproar. She was quite beautiful, particularly for a woman of her sort, with fine features.

If this did not go in, then the ticket Senda was holding would be bust.

"It's Lola," Senda said, as though groaning.

His eyes were bloodshot.

Okamoto was not smiling anymore, either. He darkened his serious expression slightly and tightened his right hand into a fist.

The woman, who had gone around once, let out a high-pitched squeal as she did, but no one laughed even when she hit the enclosure.

When she came around again to take another shot, what gave off the thudding noise was the number five.

The woman spun around once, ducking her head, and then spun again, ending up facing backwards.

The man who had been next to them clicked his tongue, threw his tickets onto the floor, and stormed out.

When Okamoto looked back at Senda, he noticed that Senda's eyes had a strange sparkle to them despite his pale expression. They were the particular sort of passionate eyes that the people who come to this sort of place have.

A lot of people around here have larger-than-average eyes and protruding foreheads.

Senda was standing next to Okamoto with a face that suggested a degree of despair.

At that moment, the final result was determined: the number forty-six remained.

"I won."

Okamoto pressed his ticket into Senda's hand and quickly walked out by himself.

After Senda, who was in shocked disbelief, got his forty-five *mil*, he went outside, and walked over to Okamoto, who was standing in front of the cinema next door.

"Haha. . . . Consider it my way of saying thank you." Having said this, he smiled and added, "If you take that money and head back in there, you will lose it as well. Just take it and go home."

With that, Okamoto took his leave from Senda. By the time he reached the Y. pension, where he lived, it would surely be midnight already.

"You have a guest," said the maid at the pension, who looked as though she had been waiting to say that.

"Thanks."

"*Não.*" The woman smiled and looked up at Okamoto's eyes as though seeking something, but Okamoto got stuck on the word *guest*. Moreover, he felt that for someone to come to his place at this late an hour, it must be some important matter.

He walked past the maid and pushed open his door. At the desk beside where his fellow lodgers were sleeping, Senda sat looking despondent.

Cigarette butts were piled high on his desk. Words written in some Western language squirmed in horizontal lines on the paper before him.

"What is it, this late at night?"

Staring at the deep wrinkles carved into Senda's face, Okamoto thought, *he sure has aged, given how young he is.*

"Come out with me."

Senda stood, silently, and then said, "I came by because there was something I definitely want to talk with you about today. The minute I saw your face, though, I changed my mind. I had wanted to get your advice about something I was planning, but it's not necessary. At any rate, I want to thank you. From now on, if there is something wrong with me, I want you to tell me. I realize that I have made a lot of mistakes in the past, and I feel bad about that.

"I was going to meet Mihoko tonight, but I have decided not to. I have invested too much in her. I am sorry for worrying you."

"I am serious about this. I will not cause you any more concern in the future. Even now, if I were to give up this desperate, crazy way of living it would help a lot of people. My father, my mother, it would help everyone. It would allow my illness to heal. I am ashamed to say it, but I had thought to take the money you gave me and go drink. But when I remembered what you said when you gave it to me—*if you take that money and head back in there, you will lose it as well*—I went home with it after all. I can't tell you how happy my dad and mom were about that forty-five *mil*. You know, filial piety is a good thing. I feel like going to Japan, entering normal school, and starting again from the beginning. Tonight really is a good night."

While listening to Senda, Okamoto felt a feeling spreading throughout his chest. Partly he was angry because he felt as though his good deed had been snatched away from him, and partly he felt a blandness as though he were chewing on sand.

He was seized by a sense of regret, thinking, "I shouldn't have given him that money."

· On the other hand, mixed in was a sense of relief, a satisfaction with how things turned out.

AKINO SHŪ is the penname of Sumiyoshi Mitsuo (1916–?). Akino was born in Tokushima Prefecture. He migrated to Brazil in 1932, after having graduated from the Tokyo Imperial College of Sericulture (蚕糸学校). Once in Brazil, he studied writing under the guidance of Furuno Kikuo; in the mid-1970s, he was still living in São Paulo and working at a bank.[79]

An author of both prose and verse, in addition to "Ghetto" he published at least two other stories in *Chiheisen*, including "Kagami" (鏡) in issue 4 and "Shin'en" (深淵) in issue 9. It might be worth noting that while Maeyama chose "A Certain Ghetto" to appear in the short story anthology, Furuno seems to have thought "Shin'en" to be the superior work, commenting on its "extremely masterful technique."[80]

4

Ethnos

Tacit Promises

Stories such as the ones just presented became a medium through which first-generation immigrants from Japan in Brazil worked through the ramifications of their dramatically altered circumstances.[1] Again, though one must not take given literary representations as simple reproductions of historical individuals, let alone communities, it is worth noting how many individuals from Japan were experiencing similar situations. Japan's expansion resulted in a large-scale population shift that placed Japanese citizens in direct contact with heterogeneity of various sorts, which is reflected in these literary texts. That is not to say that these texts were solely concerned with typical manifestations of difference. These works not only represented individuals marked as other—primarily, but not solely, through the lens of race—but also reappraised what could be expected from relationships with individuals thought to be racially identical. What these representations reveal, unsurprisingly, is that "race" is a central concern; perhaps counter-intuitively, however, the writers seem to be even more preoccupied with intraracial, rather than interracial, alterity.[2] This, I suggest, is prompted not merely by a fear of the instability of identity itself, but also by a recognition that the implied solidarity of racial identity did not, in fact, vouchsafe preferential treatment.

Three of the stories show a particular sensitivity to racial, gender, and linguistic alterity: "The Death of a Certain Settler," "An Age of Speculative Farming," and "Tumbleweeds."[3] In addition, they display an awareness of economic alterity that exceeds simple disparity, as the writers describe exceptional degrees of privation and hardship. What perhaps is unexpected is that perceived difference between racial categories and between languages plays a far less significant role in the stories than does perceived intraracial and intralingual difference.[4] As such, the stories show far greater concern with what I will call "acquired" alterity, and with betrayals of bonds thought to be implied by racial filiation, than they do with threats posed by conventional racial alterity. An examination of these moments of representations of alterity, which are often marked by a negative affective valence and an increased affective intensity, reveals a powerful sense of racial betrayal that stands in relief from any normative evaluations of racial others that appear in the stories. In addition, an examination of edits made to the stories over time reveals the shifting sensibilities and sensitivities of the community.

RACIAL OTHER AS INSTRUMENT OF JUSTICE

"The Death of a Certain Settler" by Nishioka Kunio most closely conforms (at least at first glance) with a stereotypical narrative of the racial other as both abject and threatening. A settler, having just begun his triumphant return to Japan after achieving financial success in Brazil, is murdered, presumably by a non-Japanese laborer. Rather than portraying the murdered settler sympathetically, however, the story depicts him in an unflattering light, even implying that the settler's brutal end was deserved; to the extent that the non-Japanese assailant is developed as a character, he is presented as being hard-working, honorable, and worthy of the reader's sympathies.

The story begins with a confrontation between the races: a Japanese landowner, Kaneko Daisuke, is facing a man with "gleaming black" skin:[5]

> A man who seemed to be *baiano*, with a face that gleamed black, and a woman who was presumably his wife, with her belly hugely swollen, stood with their shoulders shrugged in front of his [Daisuke's] home. On the ground to their side was one *arroz saco* jammed with all of their worldly possessions and a large child, with a thin, monkey-like face and wide eyes, who sat staring uneasily at Daisuke.[6]

Although we discover later that the "nearly six-foot-tall" black man would be towering over Daisuke, this is not a case of the threatening Other; rather, it is actually Daisuke who is attempting to intimidate the visitor verbally. The man has come to Daisuke's home to ask for work, so that he and his impoverished family might eat; Daisuke responds with aggression and condescension but in the end agrees to hire the man.

After Daisuke returns from the day working on his *cafezal* (coffee plantation) with the man and three young Japanese laborers, they all sit down at a table with Daisuke's wife and son to share a meal. When Daisuke sees the man's wife staring in through the window, however, he calls out abusively, referring to her as a "beggar" (乞食奴) and shouting at her to get lost, asking if there is "any law that says that someone who doesn't work should eat?"[7] This prompts another confrontation with the man, who leaps up from his chair, glaring down at the diminutive Daisuke with his fists clenched. The man, quickly recognizing that there is nothing he can do under the circumstances but defer to his "master" (支配者), unclenches his fists, collapses back into his chair, and appeals to the charity of the "*patrão*" (パ

トロ ン, boss). His wife, he pleads, has not eaten all day and cannot work because she is in the last month of her pregnancy. The man assures Daisuke that were he to feed her, in return the man would work even harder the next day. Daisuke remains firm, but eventually fishes some coins from his purse and casts them onto the table. The man, wearing a saddened expression, stands up and leaves with his family, refusing to acknowledge the coins.

It is interesting to note that in reflecting on these events the next day, Daisuke does not attribute the "unreasonable" demands of the man and his wife to their race; instead, he disparages the man's "womanly" sentimentality and the "impertinence" he believes the man shares with other young people. To the contrary, later in the story Daisuke states that in the future he intends to hire only *baiano* laborers, who, while potentially dangerous, are perfect for "taking advantage of"; simultaneously, he differentiates them from "hairy foreigners" (毛唐人), who will pull out a knife without the least provocation, and Japanese, who are not dangerous but are constantly quibbling.

This confrontation is followed by a second, briefer interaction with racial alterity, which in its positioning is implicitly contrasted with the first. Three or four blue-eyed children, "the sort one sees in the *colônia* on the other side of the mountain," come asking to buy oranges from the trees on Daisuke's property.[8] When they produce a one-*mil* coin, Daisuke stands up and gets them a stick, which the tallest uses to knock down the fruit. Chiding them for knocking so many down, Daisuke counts the fruit off one by one as he puts them into the children's bag. The scene reinforces the idea that Daisuke is motivated not by racial animosity, but instead by imperiousness, greed, and parsimony. While the blue eyes mark the children as likely either white or *mestiço* (multiracial) children, producing the option of reading this as differential racial treatment, the story does not explore this further.

After these interactions, the story devotes itself to Daisuke's drunken recounting of his life to an audience of young Japanese men, as he prepares for his first trip back to his hometown in Japan in twenty-eight years. Throughout the narrative, Daisuke goes to great lengths to establish that his success is the result of his own labors, often explicitly rebutting assertions by other Japanese that it was the result of luck. We learn that Daisuke, born in Hokkaidō in the early 1880s (the narrative never exactly establishes the years) to a former samurai turned millet farmer, left home at the age of twenty. After two years in Tokyo, he began a process of serial migration: first to Manchuria, then to Lima, Peru (where he was a barber to "hairy foreigners"), Chile (where he worked mining nitratine for fertilizer), and Buenos Aires before finally moving to Brazil because he had heard that it was "friendly to Japanese." After a dramatic change of attitude when he realized he needed to think about the future, he began to save his carpenter's pay diligently and eventually bought land.

Having purchased the land sight-unseen, he, his wife, and his young son headed inland to begin their new lives. At that time, the train line did not yet reach all the way to the property, so the three of them were forced to hike forty kilometers through dense growth while carrying their supplies. Daisuke acknowledges the relief he felt when they encountered the home of "an Italian" thirty kilometers in and describes the generosity he and his family received from him. As Daisuke points out to his audience (unaware of the irony), "deep in the mountains, any man you encounter is a brother."[9] Thanks to the chickens and pigs he purchased from the Italian, he and his family were able to survive until the train line was extended. Despite this fact, he concludes his story by telling the young men that although people in their *colônia* believe he succeeded through luck, he, like all men, was made through his own efforts. Although it is not a central component of this story, we should note here that the young Japanese laborers to whom he is speaking are explicitly described as "copper-colored"; Daisuke's own face is described as "reddish black," the result of both intoxication and sun exposure. Though this skin color would be a natural effect of prolonged exposure to the sun in the course of agricultural labor, the fact that it warrants mention is our first indication of the importance of a discourse of acquired alterity, which is present in all of the stories under consideration here and to which we will turn later.

On his last day before setting off on his trip to Japan—a trip in which he will achieve the clichéd goal attributed to many migrants to Brazil, that of eventually returning home "wearing a gold brocade" (錦を着て)—Daisuke visits the twenty-four families, including both *colonos* and four-year contract workers, living on his property.[10] It is at this point that Daisuke decides to contract only *baianos* upon his return, as he recalls an incident from the previous year in which an Italian *colono* had come after him with a knife after Daisuke had berated him. The night before his journey back to Japan he sets off for town, where he plans to stay so as to be able to catch his early morning train the next day. On the way, however, he is confronted by a man who steps out from the dense growth on the side of the road. The narrative describes how something "flashed like lightning" amid his "crowded memories" as Daisuke sees the man's face. In the 2008 version of this story, it is not clear which of the many wronged men from Daisuke's past it might be. A shot is fired, Daisuke falls to the ground with a groan, and after a few slight shudders, his body lies still. The story closes a few days later, with a brief description of a new grave marker dedicated to Daisuke in the communal cemetery.

As mentioned, "The Death of a Certain Settler" superficially conforms to a narrative of the racial other as both abject and threatening: the destitute black laborer, his desperate wife, and his silent child are placed in a position of abjection and supplication vis-à-vis the Japanese landowner; when the laborer is refused food for his wife, the men nearly come to blows. Later in the story, the racial other—be he *baiano*, Italian, or some other "hairy foreigner"—is characterized as inclined to violence, and one (unclear in the 2008 version, though much clearer in the original, as I will argue) finally carries through on this implied threat of violence. Despite this basic narrative, however, the story functions not to demonize the racial other, but rather to vilify the miserly, arrogant, and cruel Daisuke, who despite receiving kindness from others in his time of need—most notably the Italian—refuses to acknowledge any ethical debt to anyone in a similar situation. The violence visited upon Daisuke is implicitly presented as a form of retribution for his vanity—in the end, his body lies on the ground clothed portentously in a "gold brocade covered with fresh blood"—and for the economic violence to which he has subjected both Japanese and non-Japanese alike.

The editorial staff of the 1975 anthology made a number of changes to the original text of "The Death of a Certain Settler," though most were attempts to make superficial corrections. Further—and more noteworthy—changes were introduced when the anthology was reproduced for inclusion on the DVD-ROM in 2008. One specific bowdlerization, which was introduced in the 2008 version, should be given particular attention: the removal of the adjective "black" as a descriptor of skin color. Sufficient information remains—the "gleaming black" face, the "black family," and the reference to the worker as a *baiano*—that the racial marking is preserved. The elimination, rather, seems to be a response to shifting normative attitudes about the propriety of terms denoting blackness, with the editors choosing in most cases to avoid them.[11]

In one way, however, the 2008 edition's concern with discriminatory language actually undermines the apparent intentions of its editors. In the final confrontation, when the figure emerges from the dense growth on the side of the road and is described (in the original and revised versions) as merely a "man," the sudden absence of the modifier "black" is very noticeable in the early versions; in the 2008 version, where nearly all references lack it, the absence is less conspicuous. Furthermore, when Daisuke sees the face of the man and experiences the shock of recognition, his original response is "Aah! That *ku. . . .*"; the "*ku*" is removed from the revised version. In discussing this scene previously, I stated that it was ambiguous (in the 2008 version) who the shooter was; in earlier versions, however, something more complex is happening. The "*ku*," I would argue, would likely be interpreted by readers as the first syllable of the racial slur for blacks, *kuronbō* (黒坊), that appears in a number of the stories; the fact that it was removed by the 2008 editors suggests they may have interpreted it similarly. This fragment, then, marks the shooter as being black, which when combined with the demonstrative "that," creates a strong likelihood that the assailant is the *baiano* who was wronged in the initial scenes of the story. This makes the idiosyncratic and conspicuous usage of "man" (rather than "black man") all the more interesting; while it is possible that it was an oversight on the part of the author, it is also possible to read the character as having become a stand-in for all of the individuals wronged by Daisuke, an instrument of justice who at that moment has transcended his individual race. The racial other becomes a faceless (or, more accurately, nameless) instrument of a cosmic order that punishes transgressions against an ethic that transcends the racial self-same.

INTRARACIAL BETRAYAL

While "The Death of a Certain Settler" clearly establishes a narratorial perspective of limited sympathy for its protagonist, it lacks the sustained affective intensity in response not only to alterity but also to intraracial betrayal that is present in Sonobe Takeo's "An Age of Speculative Farming." This story was selected as the first-place recipient in the first Colonial Literary Short Fiction Award competition, which had explicitly sought works that grappled with "the society of Japanese in Brazil today," which possessed "conditions that were completely different from those in Japan."[12] The story certainly addresses contemporary society; it also dwells extensively on two of the same concerns that we have already seen: acquired alterity and intraracial betrayal. To this story is added a preoccupation with female sexuality, and the ways in which it is seen as integrally tied to the other dangers lurking in this new, overtly heterogeneous space.

Unlike the preceding story, "An Age of Speculative Farming" is set in the city (not the state) of São Paulo. The narrative focuses on a "mixed-blood" (混血児, glossed as アーイノコ [sic]) prostitute named Hanaoka Ruriko, but also involves her wealthy patron, the tomato parvenu Ōmura; his rival, the trader Kurose; and a young Japanese man, newly arrived in Brazil, who is kept by Hanaoka. The story opens with an unnamed *vagabundo*—a "vagabond," which was a common term for young Japanese men who had abandoned the life of an agricultural laborer in the countryside for the lures of the city—observing Hanaoka, as she ignores a group of young thugs who yell out an epithet at her ("whore" [売笑婦], glossed as *puta* [プータ]). It is a sight, the text tells us, he sees often. The story first tells us a little about her tastes; we are told she likes "men, *sorvete*, cinema, smelling the soiled flesh of farmers, perverted sexual desire, collecting cheap jewelry."[13] We are then shown Hanaoka plying her trade in the center of São Paulo:

> She always weaves through the dizzying triangle (*triângulo*) as a single seductive Oriental insect. She moves endlessly as a point along the edges of that triangle, as she passes through the entangled races, through the city of flesh mixed with that of the Portuguese—Italian, French, Spanish, German, Russian, and black—in her single-cut dress and snake-skin shoes, the perfumed secret of her flesh, visible through her gauzy wrap.[14]

As she walks through this entertainment district, a new-model Ford suddenly pulls up in front of her. It is her lover, Ōmura, who (the text tells us, again) embraces her "with his soiled, farmer's flesh, which she loves."

The disgust in the narrative is palpable, and its objects are many. Even as the text disdains the proximity to (not to mention participation in) manual agricultural labor that is suggested by Ōmura's "soiled flesh," it is also repulsed by his immodest displays of wealth, visible in its repeated mention of the parvenu's new-model Ford. It evinces discomfort not only at the presence of multiple races, but also by the potentially deleterious "entangling" (錯綜) of them. The text is also critical of the abusive urban youth who form the "Conde" gang, the beggars it describes populating the streets, and the "movie-crazy *señoritas*" Conrad Nagel woos from the screen of the Odeon Theater.

More than anyone else, though, the story's disgust seems directed at Hanaoka. She has placed her chastity up for sale, the text laments, offering herself to a filthy farmer and perhaps even to the men of assorted and blended races who fill São Paulo's streets; worse yet, she seems to desire them sexually. She indulges in other vices as well, be it ice cream or the jewels that we later learn are her main reason for being with Ōmura; after all, the text reminds us, "even a monstrous love requires certain appurtenances."[15] All the while, she abuses (emotionally, verbally, and physically) the "stray dog"—a youth who has recently immigrated from Japan— who waits for her pathetically in her rooms (her "deviant playground") and lusts for her "lewd figure" even as (or perhaps precisely because) he knows that she has just been with other men. Most fundamentally, the text registers both derision and disbelief toward Hanaoka's body itself: when she finally takes a stand against Ōmura, the narrator opines that the fact (sic) "that Japanese blood circulated in Hanaoka Ruriko's rotting flesh was nothing short of a miracle."[16] As a multiracial subject, Hanaoka becomes an extreme embodiment of acquired alterity, in which the ethnic compatriot is only momentarily recognizable as such, before its acquired alterity renders that racial affiliation irretrievable.

The text is at its most intense and experimental in the passages that describe Hanaoka and her overt sexuality; yet after the powerful opening section of the story, the narrative's attention is drawn to another object of disgust: the quest for profit at any cost, and the concomitant exploitation of Japanese by Japanese. This obsession with profit explains the somewhat-awkward title of the story. As Arata Sumu points out, "speculative farming" refers to the growing of crops (including tomatoes, potatoes, and onions) with an eye towards commodity speculation.[17] Contemporary Brazilian society, the title seems to be suggesting, has entered into a period in which agricultural capitalists engage in a form of farming that speculates—literally, "gambles" (賭博)—on the market, rather than (one presumes) engaging in sustainable practices determined by organic demand. All of the people involved, the text tells us, make up a "band of crooks" (インチキの 群); this is exemplified by Ōmura, who owns a vast tomato farm. Employing all manner of techniques—some of dubious ethicality—Ōmura has produced a large, out-of-season crop that he hopes to sell at market for a great profit. It is also a crop that is of little interest, as a food, to the Japanese laborers; instead, this is a tomato farm "operated by the clever *Nipponico* who encamped here and took advantage of the tastes of the meat-loving races."

In its criticisms of Ōmura's strategies, the text shows a nascent environmental conscience, seemingly concerned with practices that do not allow for sustained cultivation by men and women (particularly Japanese men and women) in such a way as to provide them with dignified livelihoods. The story signals this early on through a scene in which laborers encircle a large vat as they make a pesticide known as Bordeaux solution:

> One of the laborers dissolved quicklime into the solution, choking all the while on the cloud of dust in the air. He then combined the dissolved lime with just the right amount of copper sulfate. The Bordeaux solution that resulted from the combination became an extremely faint blue, like that of the autumn sky in the laborer's hometown, making him sentimental. The greedy history of the immigrants who preceded him became an opaque precipitate; the endless exploitative competition swirled in the mixture, disappearing into the Bordeaux solution.[18]

The text describes the tomatoes as unable to excite the appetites of the exhausted workers who "bore the insecticide sprayers on their backs like debt" as they dusted the plants for three straight months. It describes the sprawling farm as one made possible by the "reckless dumping of chemical fertilizers" such as nitratine and potassium chloride. Ōmura's greed has left the soil "impoverished from the immoderate application of artificial fertilizers." In fact, "the rampancy of the macrosporum bacteria" and "the indignation of the soil" are explicitly given as two of the factors that eventually come to determine the fate of the Ōmura farm.

Ōmura's plans are foiled, however, by the machinations of the *comprador* Kurose, who arranges an unusually low price for tomatoes on the day Ōmura brings in his crop. Kurose has conspired with the other buyers at the Mercado Central—the giant wholesale market in São Paulo, now called the Mercado Municipal—to hold their offered price at 10 *mil réis* per crate, a price so low that its announcement leaves all of the farmers dazed. This is not simply a matter of collusion; the story informs us that Kurose has paid the buyers in order to secure their compliance, all with the goal of snubbing Ōmura in revenge for his refusal to accede to a deal Kurose had earlier offered him. Ōmura had been offended at Kurose's attempt to manipulate him, an attempt which insulted Ōmura's pride: "It would be one thing if I were one of those wretched tomato farmers, but he needs to think about who he is talking to!"[19] The battle between these two egoists not only exacts a cost from each of them, but also wreaks havoc on the subsistence tomato farmers caught up in the price manipulations.

The only group not subjected to the narrative's unadulterated disdain—the agricultural laborers who had migrated from Japan, choosing the "frightening customs officers" over the "sounds of gunfire in Manchuria"—is instead subjected to its pity and condescension. These include workers with hands "perpetually stained by tomato juice" and farmers who "live under fear of malnutrition." At one point the narrator laments spontaneously: "The bodies of agricultural laborers, bent by exhaustion!"[20] Some are themselves caught up in greed, including the "swarm of heroic *Nipponicos*" who vie with one another, "enslaved by their gambling 'savvy'"—an imaginary savvy they begin to believe they too might possess when they see Ōmura's profit. The story explains how "anyone who did not move quickly to seize his portion of the wealth by producing tomatoes soon became the object of derision, as one ignorant of the ways of the world."[21] Despite this disdain toward their greed, the narrative voice finally sees all of these migrants as "merely ants," and thus pathetic rather than villainous. What is missing, the narrator suggests, is common purpose and unity of action: "When will the day finally come that those desultory ants gather and erect a towering anthill?"[22] In despair that to wait for such a day would be in vain, despite the steady flow of shiploads of migrants from Japan, the narrative ends with a laborer (perhaps the *vagabundo* from the story's opening) taking in a deep breath and letting out a scream.

As the quotes above suggests, language in the story is marked throughout with value judgments and affective intensity. It is also filled with problematic terminology, almost all of which is maintained through to the DVD-ROM version. What is removed is unsurprising, given the examples from the previous story: while a reference to a "black woman" remains unchanged, the color of a "black doorman" is removed, as is Hanaoka's epithetic reference to him as a *kuronbō-me* when he tries to drive her off. Left unchanged are terms such as "mixed-blood child" (混血児)—though now without its similarly problematic gloss of "love child" (愛の子)—"beggars" (乞食), and "natives" (土人); a derogatory reference to physically impaired movement (ちんば、ちんばして) is removed, but not a reference to "slow" (鈍重な) Brazilians. We also have the term *caboclo* (カボクロ), which appears here without any apparent derogatory intent (at one point, the sounds of a *caboclo*'s *bandolim* can be heard in the background), but which had a complex function in Brazilian racial discourse at this time.[23] Finally, we have a non-Japanese gendered epithet, *puta*, which is left unchanged. Perhaps the editors felt that the term lost expressive potency as it crossed language barriers.

The overwhelming sense conveyed by the story is one of disgust and despair: over migrants who are weak of spirit and solidarity, over female bodies that are deviant through both their desires and their descent, and over the willingness of Japanese to exploit other Japanese, in ways that can transcend simple greed and enter into the realm of viciousness, with no concern for collateral damage. Since the implied, fictional interiority experiencing the emotional state that leads to this affective intensity is unclear—perhaps it is that of the *vagabundo* and worker character/s that frame the story—the disgust and despair cannot be confined to a single character; there is no point of detachment made available by the narrative. The result is a sense that the story itself is some sort of *cri de coeur*.

VALORIZING HETEROGENEITY

Furuno Kikuo's "Tumbleweeds" may be the only story written during the prewar period in Brazil that ever reached a significant reading audience in Japan.[24] After having been published in July 1940 in the journal *Shin Burajiru*, it was subsequently republished in the June 1958 issue of the Tokyo literary journal *Bungei shuto*. The story takes place aboard a ship sailing westward from the Americas and focuses on a group of Japanese emigrants who are returning to Japan, most from Brazil but some from other countries, including Argentina and the United States. The story begins as the ship passes south of the Aleutian Islands and concludes just as it enters Japan's territorial waters. In this depiction of bodies in transit, we see the complexity of the process we know as "migration": in addition to the serial migration described in "The Death of a Certain Settler," we see diverse destinations of migration, multiple migration involving trips to and from Japan, and the ill-named "return migration" of people of Japanese descent who may never have set foot in the country before.

As with earlier stories, while "Tumbleweeds" does present some instances of racial alterity—we know that there are non-Japanese in the first-class spaces above, and we hear about non-Japanese living alongside Japanese in the *colônia* back in Brazil—the story is almost entirely dedicated to the Japanese passengers and crew in the third-class sections of the ship. As with the previous works, the story's attention is firmly focused on acquired alterity and intraracial interactions. Unlike the earlier works, however, "Tumbleweeds" explicitly asserts a positive valence to acquired alterity, and valorizes respectful coexistence.[25] There are limits to this, however; while the focal figures valorize alterity produced by familiar exogenous elements, variant acquired alterity resulting from unfamiliar exogenous elements is met with less enthusiasm. That is, while individuals altered by their connection to Brazil are encouraged to embrace that difference, individuals altered by their connection to the United States, for example, are met with critique that, while not particularly hostile, is negative. The story's strongest criticisms, however, seem to be reserved for Japan.

In the course of the story, we meet a number of characters: the siblings João (age seventeen) and Luísa (age eight); Wakabayashi and his wife, Makiko; Tani, a college student from California; an unnamed former gardener for a rich family in Buenos Aires; and Akita, the character who acts as the focal figure for most of the story. While the information we are given about each of the characters is incomplete, the recounting of fragments from their pasts comprises much of the story, which depicts the coincidental gathering of these diverse individuals as they are about to enter a space of symbolic importance to all of them.

We learn that Akita was born in Japan and lived there long enough to receive his education but has since lived in Brazil for years. We know from references to her accent that his mother, who emigrated with Akita, is from Kyūshū. We are told that they lived together in rural Paraná before he moved to the city of São Paulo. Finally, during the course of the voyage back to Japan we learn that Akita has decided to spend one month settling some affairs before returning permanently to Brazil to raise cattle in Sorocobana. Of the Wakabayashi couple, we learn that they spent more than five years in a *colônia* in the interior of the state of São Paulo, where malaria and pneumonia took their young son's life and the husband's capacity to work. Despite wishing to remain in Brazil, where their child is buried, they have no choice but to accept their relative's offer of work in Hokkaidō. We learn little about the origins, destinations, or circumstances of the other characters.

The descriptions of João and Luísa's parents come from Akita's perspective. The mother is described as one of the many housewives "who work from dawn until late into the night with their dry, matted hair up, their bare feet caked in mud, and their toothless mouths hidden by their sealed lips."[26] In this regard, she resembles women Akita saw frequently in the *colônia:* one of those women "who has worked continuously for decades, like a draft animal, having lost any trace of sentiment, knowing only the world of virgin jungle, cotton fields, and thatched huts."[27] The description of the children's father differs dramatically: when we see him (through Akita's eyes), he is described as having "skin the color of *terra roxa* (purplish-brown soil) that was also flushed from alcohol and a torso like a camouflaged tank."[28] The difference between the husband and wife is then generalized, with men described as enjoying far different lives than women: "As for the men, every harvest they come out of the primordial forest, cross the cotton fields, and race their trucks to town, where alcohol, prostitutes, and dice await. The towns, which pop up near the Japanese collectives, are filled with cheap restaurants catering to Japanese. They resemble suppurations on filthy flesh."[29]

Akita treats the couple as representatives of their genders, in a society with distinct roles that are profoundly unfair to women. Here we have a female body that is not the site of desires that lead to transgressions that in turn threaten the racial community, but rather one that is the worn vessel of a pitiable victim who has consigned herself to suffering through her own virtue; by contrast, the male body is the vehicle of a corrupt agency, which indulges itself regardless of collateral damage. The male's unwillingness to consider the well-being or desires of his family continues even as they leave Brazil: we discover that the family is only going to Tokyo because of the father; neither the children nor their mother wishes to go.

Despite not providing us much concrete information about their background, the text does spend significant time on the siblings João and Luísa and the ways in which they differ from the Japanese around them. The children are native Portuguese speakers but have some Japanese competency. They have acquired gestures that mark them as other: Luísa raises her eyebrows "like a foreigner" and is described by the narrator as a "young Brazilian woman." This latter description appears in quotes in the text itself, problematizing (or denaturalizing) the relation of the descriptor to the descriptee. The country of their birth has left an imprint on Luísa and João that differentiates them from their peers in Japan: Akita, Makiko, and Wakabayashi find the children raised in Brazil to "all be melancholic to the core" and attribute that to the adult responsibilities children are given in the *colônia*. Makiko adds that girls have it even worse than boys, with upbringings stricter than those of children on the outskirts of Tokyo.

At another point in the story, Luísa and João's father also addresses the fundamental differences in character that he sees in his children as compared to the way he remembers children in Japan; in his case, however, he considers his own children to be more "easy going" (鷹揚). This word, attributed to the father, is also in quotes, again suggesting some dissatisfaction with the word's precision. The siblings are not the only individuals raised outside of Japan to have this sort of acquired alterity. Tani, the university student from California, is frequently judged (from Akita's perspective, primarily) as behaving differently. Wakabayashi sums it up when he says, "Kids raised among Yankees sure are flashy (派手), aren't they?" In Tani's case, this excessiveness extends not only to his clothing (he is earlier described as wearing a flashy green jacket) but also to his physical size (he has to bend down his "tall frame" to enter the room they are in).

The one dramatic event in the story, a confrontation between Akita and a (presumably Japanese) waiter, occurs because of the treatment that Luísa receives from the people around her, who see her as a suitable target for ridicule. The waiter convinces Luísa, who is seeing snow for the first time in her life, that if she puts a snowball in her pocket and is careful with it, she will be able to take it to Japan. He then coaxes her over to the stove, in front of the first-class passengers. When she touches her pocket and discovers that the snowball has melted, she breaks into tears; the waiter and the passengers, both Japanese and non-Japanese, laugh at her ignorance. Upon hearing of this, Akita tracks down the waiter, brings him down to the third-class rooms, and slaps him hard across the face. Once he recovers his composure, Akita is angry about his reaction, which he considers to have been childish and excessive. This eruption of affect—a moment in which an emotional response prompts the body to act—is then interpreted by Akita himself, as he speculates about the source of the sentiment that had welled up in him: "Perhaps it was because I myself have some sort of inferiority complex as a migrant or something, but I felt as though all of us immigrants to Brazil were being ridiculed."[30] It is clear that Akita feels protective of Luísa and João, but this is more than mere sympathy; there is some process of identification occurring as well. The identification, I would argue, is not as "Japanese Brazilians"; Akita is clear about the difference he perceives between himself and these children. Instead, the identification seems to be between subjects who have been similarly thrust into specific peripheral, hardship positions vis-à-vis a normative center.

When we learn that João has never used chopsticks before, the narrator speculates on what awaits him (and his sister) in Japan:

> The bridge to his life in Brazil had crumbled when he boarded the Japanese ship. Around him was in all ways Japan. To the individuals whose eyes pored over this dual-citizenship-holding youth of seventeen, he bore not the slightest handicap. Little did they know that the ceaseless, severe training that this child of nature, of that vast continent, would receive in Japan had already begun during this sea crossing, which

otherwise should have been fun. *He cannot use chopsticks. He doesn't even know con-versational Japanese. Halfwit!* The cold glares that poured over João made him feel frightened of the table, as though he were some sort of thief, and led him to speak the language of his parents' homeland timidly and with a lisp, further muddying his thick accent. Luísa was in the very same situation.[31]

Akita rejects the position of abjection that he feels they are forced into vis-à-vis a normative notion of what it is to be Japanese. The action he urges upon them bears some similarity to the one he took in response to the waiter: an aggressive asser-tion of the value of their non-normative positionality. Akita urges the children to feel pride in their history, and to resist the self-hatred that this normative vision would cultivate within them:

Thrust your chests out with pride, João and Luísa! Throw away those chopsticks and eat proudly with your forks. Speak to any you encounter loudly in the language of your birthplace, Brazil. If you shrink before them like that, once in Japan you will have people convincing you to put snowballs in your pockets every day!

The story presents Japan, in fact, as a difficult place for more than just these chil-dren. Makiko, Wakabayashi's wife, describes her birthplace of Japan as an "unfor-giving" country where she feels that she "can't let down my guard somehow."

Wakabayashi envies Akita's decision to return to Brazil and settle there perma-nently. By contrast he describes his and his wife's situation using the Latin phrase "*va* (sic) *victus*" (*vae victus*, Woe to the vanquished!); he doubts that happiness awaits them in Sapporo. Akita reminds him, though, that Brazil is not necessarily a solution, either:

My decision to live in Brazil permanently—no, not just me, sometimes I think every *issei*'s decision to live in Brazil permanently—represents the sad final stop on the journey of an individual who has tired of the search for a meaningful life. I think that it is impossible to choose permanent residence abroad without some tragic resignation.[32]

Despite the critical attitude held by the key characters toward Japan, it is not the case that Brazil is held up as an ideal solution to an alienated existence either.

As with the earlier stories, a few changes have been made over the history of the text's reproduction. The editor's primary concern again seems to have been with terms involving blackness.[33] The fairly strong Portuguese epithet *puta merda* (プータ・メルダ) remains in the text, whereas "half-black" (半黒) women become "mulatta" (ムラト, mulatto) in one spot in the 2008 version and "mixed-bloods" (混血) in another. It is interesting to note the different value judgments conveyed by the terms in this story as compared to those conveyed in "An Age of Specula-tive Farming." Akita describes the legs of the mulatto women and those of women with "the blood of the people of the Iberian Peninsula" as being the more literally descriptive colors of chestnut and barley, respectively. While noting difference, his gaze seems positive, desiring; more importantly, those individuals are not mere objects, but subjects who interact with him in a way he describes as playful (perhaps flirtatious). In "Tumbleweeds," racial others are not merely potential romantic partners; they are also members of a functioning, heterogeneous community. At the funeral for Wakabayashi and Makiko's child, "black, white, and mixed children of the *colônia* brought flowers" that ended up covering the grave. While we might wonder what category Japanese would join here, it is more important to note the image of a compassionate (though certainly not utopian) multiracial community, mourning the tragic loss of a child.

EXTREMES OF ALTERITY AND IDENTITY

Before drawing conclusions about these portrayals of acquired alterity and intraracial betrayal, it is worth noting two additional forms of alterity and identity: the imagined extreme alterity of the "uncivilized human" and the presumed organic identity of kinship.[34]

The term *dojin* (土人, meaning "native," "aborigine," or "indigenous person,") was often used prior to the Second World War in Brazil to represent the presumed indigeneity of an observed individual. It was often used with a derogatory (though perhaps not fully conscious) connotation, implying not only racial difference but a lack of civilization. This relates to the term *caboclo* (カボクロ), meaning an individual of mixed background including part indigenous Brazilian, which was borrowed from Portuguese into the vocabulary of Japanese-speakers in the colonies and often implied potential loss of civilization through miscegenation. The glossary in the 1975 anthology defines the term *caboclo* as "lower class natives in farming villages (racially speaking, primarily *mestiço*); ignorant hicks" and does not define *dojin*, which had a long history of use in Japanese discourse of racial and civilizational alterity.[35]

Of the stories presented here, we see the term *dojin* appear in at least three: "An Age of Speculative Farming," "Placement," and "After We Had Settled." In the first and second of those stories, it is used in passing to refer to the thatched huts of the poor workers; in the third, it is used to describe the children who come to meet the new group of immigrants from Japan. When "After We Had Settled" was reproduced, that reference to "native" children was changed to children of "mixed black and white" racial origin, presumably to eliminate a term now thought inappropriate. Additionally, in that story it is later revealed that four or five of the children are actually of Japanese descent, suggesting the ways acquired alterity can render these children of a civilized country, like Japan, indistinguishable from the poor, "native" children.

On the other end of the spectrum, however, is a form of identity that is presumably more intimate (and innate) than ethnonational identity: kinship. As ethnonationality is based in some imagined degree of consanguinity, it is also a form of imagined kinship, though more diluted than that imagined to obtain between members of both nuclear and extended families. As was mentioned previously, Brazil encouraged migration from Japan by families, rather than individual laborers. The result of this was that kinship relations among Japanese-identifying sub-. jects, and kinship relations that had originated in Japan rather than being formed in the destination country, were perhaps more common as immediate elements of daily life (as opposed to absent objects of nostalgia or desire) in Brazil than they were in other destinations of the Japanese diaspora. Such relations are depicted throughout the stories presented here.

There is a particular form of familial (or kinship) relationship that emerged in the context of migration to Brazil that is worthy of note, however: that of the "constructed family." A paradigmatic (though not necessarily historically precise) representation of the phenomenon comes at the beginning of Ishikawa Tatsuzō's "The Emigrants," as groups are gathering at the Immigrants Assembly Center in Kobe in preparation for their journey to Brazil.[36] In one early scene, the prospective emigrants are being subjected to a number of administrative processes, including the trachoma test the Brazilian government demanded of all emigrants in an attempt to prevent the spread of this infectious disease. As they await their exams in the facility, a clerk calls out their names, one-by-one but grouped by family:

"*Sato Katsuji. . . . His wife Natsu.*" The clerk had called them in a loud voice. That was the first time O-Natsu had been called wife in the presence of her younger brother and strangers. [. . .] "*Sato Katsuji's mother, Kadoma Kura. His younger brother, Kadoma Yoshizo. His wife's younger brother, Sato Magoichi.*" [. . .] His elder sister O-Natsu and Katsuji were only nominally man and wife. Katsuji, Magoichi's friend, had had his name entered in the Sato family register as O-Natsu's husband. They had nominally married to receive the allowance to cover the cost of a family's emigrating to Brazil. A family that included a married couple each of whom was younger than fifty years of age and another member who was at least twelve years of age were eligible for the allowance. The Kadoma family had comprised Katsuji, his old mother, and his younger brother, while the Sato family comprised Magoichi and his elder sister, Natsu. The nominal marriage joined the two families together temporarily to form a larger family eligible for the allowance.[37]Mago-san himself had not conceived of the idea of the nominal marriage: the idea had been suggested by Yamada-san, a member of the emigration agency. The officials concerned, who were accustomed to such cases, would probably praise rather than criticize the nominal marriage. The marriage offered a number of pluses: an increase in the number of emigrants and a concomitant easing of population pressure in Japan; the contribution of the increase in emigrants to the business of the emigration agency; and for Yamada-san an increase in his commission proportional to the increase in the number of emigrants he processed. Katsuta-san, a man of worldly wisdom, was even cleverer than Magoichi. He had sent 5,000 yen to Brazil through the emigration agency and now had 3,000 yen in his bosom. A wealthy man like him was ineligible for the allowance. Traveling expenses were estimated at 200 yen per capita, and there were eight in the Katsuta family. So if he were to take his family to Brazil at his own expense, it would cost him 1,600 yen. But it had occurred to him to nominally marry his sixteen-year-old daughter to a young relative. The young man, who had yet to undergo the conscription examination, became the head of the family.[38] Since he was penniless, he was, of course, eligible to emigrate. And Katsuta-san was now his father-in-law. The nominal marriage brought him 1,600 yen—the passage for the Katsuta family, who were now the family of the emigrant man. Thus Katsuta had been clever enough to hoodwink the Emigration Ministry.[39]

While exact numbers are understandably hard to determine, constructed families were not uncommon in prewar Brazil. As described previously, in order to receive financial assistance individuals had to migrate in family units that included three people of working age (between twelve and fifty), two of whom had to be married. As a result, individuals often misrepresented their relations in order to receive these subsidies. While this rule was nominally enforced by government officials, it is clear from this quote that they were familiar with the phenomenon of constructed families and did not overexert themselves to discover the misrepresentation.[40] The semi-governmental emigration agencies that were economically motivated to facilitate migration did not even bother with this sort of plausible deniability; in the story, for example, it was an employee of such an agency who recommended it to them in the first place.

Here, Natsu's "fictive" marriage to Katsuji has prevented a "real" marriage, though perhaps only temporarily; before leaving Japan, the foreman at her mill had proposed to Natsu and she imagines returning to Japan to be with him once her obligatory one-year labor contract has been fulfilled.[41] One might read the decision to form a constructed family as a form of fraud, undertaken to take advantage of governmental resources, creating an artificial family unit that led to problematic bonds resulting in difficulties not present in "natural" family units. Subsequent scholars have gone so far as to claim that the colonies saw more marital problems than in Japan, partially because of the constructed families.[42]

Given the centrality of this arrangement to "The Emigrants," the way these arrangements are portrayed in works written in Brazil around the same time (including the ten stories presented here) come as a surprise. To be sure, such arrangements are present and can be represented as obstructions to "real" bonds based on love. "After We Had Settled," for example, in depicting a group of recent immigrants arriving at a staging facility at the Sete Barras colony as they settle in to their new lives, centers on a young man who has come to Brazil with his uncle's family, nominally married to a young woman for the purpose of the stipend, but who is drawn to a young woman he meets during the journey. The stage is set for a conflict, with the young man torn between the arrangement and his true feelings, but as the story's planned second part was never written, that conflict remains unrealized.

A very different outcome, however, is presented in a story not translated here: "Wakareta hito e: futatabi kokoku no K-ko ni," by Takahashi Saburō-sei.[43] The narrator, responding to a letter he has received from his beloved in Japan, expresses sadness about how circumstances a year earlier had forced them to separate, as she stayed home with her aging mother and he emigrated to Brazil. In the letter that forms the vignette, he describes how he sometimes finds himself imagining her face, only to have the red, jowly face of his now-wife superimpose itself on her image. Addressing the desire to come to Brazil that his sweetheart had apparently expressed in her most recent letter, the narrator dissuades her, reminding her of the obligations that kept her in Japan in the first place, and urges her to construct a new life without him. For his part, the narrator seems to imagine himself building a life with his now-wife, even if that thought does not seem to fill him with any joy. Here we have a constructed family—the marriage of convenience seems to have been treated as essential to migrating, whether for the subsidies alone or not—but this depiction raises the possibility that a constructed family based on convenience and circumstance might not be so different from the other practical decisions to marry that determine so many individuals' choice of partners—particularly but not exclusively women's choices.

Other representations remind us that constructed families often involved not entirely fictive relationships, but rather existing kinship relations that were represented as different in nature. Takemoto Yoshio's "Ashes" seems to present just such a constructed family; the relations are not entirely fictive (a man, his legitimate wife, and his brother) but they have been pressed into a particular arrangement due to the stipulations that required them to migrate as one family, resulting in stresses in the family.[44] In the story, the brother is physically intimidating but mentally limited, while the wife is shrewd and manipulative. The husband tries to balance his love and sense of responsibility toward his brother not only with the frustrations that his brother's ill-conceived actions cause him, but also with the regular criticisms from his wife, who now wants the brother out of their lives. The resolution of the story is uninspired—the brother finally takes the initiative and leaves the family, relieving the husband of a difficult decision—but the story is nonetheless significant to us both in that it reminds us of the impact of the family policy on interpersonal dynamics and in the reminder that the kinship bonds in constructed families were often not fictive. The anthropologist Maeyama Takashi describes the ways in which these constructed families were assembled not necessarily of complete strangers, but more commonly of "rushed marriages, nephews and nieces, younger brothers and sisters, [or] people from the same hometown."[45] In most of the stories that I have found, in fact, existing kinship relations are recategorized, resulting in greater legal and domestic intimacies but not entirely artificial ones.

In addition, just as Natsu in "The Emigrants" has come to Brazil not out of her own desire, but in order to help her brother Magoichi, we should note the difference in agency among the members of such constructed families. Maeyama points out that it was often the case that the head of the family (usually male) was the one who had driven the decision to emigrate, while the others followed him; in fact, many of them had attempted at one point or another to resist the migration process. As a result, many spouses came reluctantly and many youths came with so little awareness of what was happening that it bordered on, in Maeyama's words, "an abduction." To make matters worse, often this unit became one's only practically accessible kin in Brazil, with a corresponding high level of dependency on that relationship.[46]

This reminds us that constructed families emerged in a state in which most "real" forms of kinship—in the sense of extended family relations—had been largely severed. As one character in "The Emigrants" puts it, "Where you work makes no difference. You know, emigrants all go to plantations they have never been to before. Most have no acquaintances in Brazil."[47] "The Emigrants" also stresses how frequently individuals entered into these constructed families precisely because they had lost the conventional kinship bonds that they needed to depend upon. Many of the characters have lost members of their nuclear families. Natsu and Magoichi, for example, had lost both of their parents. The biological kinship bond they share then motivates her to sacrifice herself in order to help her brother, migrating to Brazil as part of this constructed family.

In sum, these literary portrayals of constructed families not only remind us of this particular form of imperial kinship, resulting from a confluence of capitalist, heteronormative, and patriarchal imperialism, but also of examples of various particular formations these policies may have imposed on individual lives, with a variety of unforeseen consequences. The literary representations suggest a phenomenon that was perhaps not as common as one might expect, at least in the stark form depicted by Ishikawa; involved different degrees of agency for its participants; existed on a continuum with other decisions to form family units, which were often impacted by practical concerns; and resulted in a form of kinship at a moment when almost everyone's kinship bonds were being redefined.

We know that migration to Brazil was a process that ruptured many conventional notions of interpersonal connection. In "The Emigrants," Ishikawa presents this in a particularly stark image as the ship is leaving the port in Kobe. Natsu "flung the red paper streamer"—reminiscent of the red string that is thought to connect individuals—and wonders to herself, "Would anyone pick up the other end?"[48] As the ship pulls away, however, that question is answered: "The paper streamers were pulled taut in the wind. Then they snapped one after another. The mesh of streamers was being destroyed. So simply, each strand broke, arched in the north wind, and then fell."[49] At the same time, though, the three other stories I have described suggest that the process of migration necessitated interpersonal bonds that often became no less real than any other. We might note, in fact that this is true for "The Emigrants" as well; in the story's sequel, "Nankai kōro," Natsu agrees to Katsuji's request that she become his wife in reality. These literary representations suggest that these were not always stories with happy endings, but neither were they bonds of such transient convenience.

JAPANESE LITERATURE AS POLITICAL PROJECT

We may speculate that the process of migrating from Japan to Brazil and the concomitant disruption of many more immediate kinship ties might have brought at least an amorphous notion of "Japanese-ness" to the forefront of many of the first-generation migrants' consciousnesses. The very idea of emigration would have likely been framed within a rhetoric of departure that implied spatial changes thought to be not merely quantitative, but also qualitative in nature; the nearly two-month-long sea voyage was described by many as a strange state of suspension and anxiety marking just such a transition.[50]

If one's first sight of the port city of Santos did not sufficiently signal alterity, the bureaucratic procedures of migration surely would have. Travel documents, including many individuals' first passports, would have highlighted "Japanese-ness" as a legal status of citizenship that suddenly rendered the arriving migrants a minority population. Interaction with immigration officials once in Brazil, not to mention with non-Japanese-language speakers during the voyage, would also have reinforced a sense of "Japanese-ness" in terms of membership in a linguistic community. Once on the streets of Santos or São Paulo, migrants would have soon encountered an unprecedented level of variation in physical appearance, which many would have processed using racializing logic. Given the representations examined here, many migrants evidently also had their own sense of "Japanese-ness," this time as racial category, reinforced by this experience. This seems to be the one common element within these amorphous and multiple interpretations of "Japanese-ness": a sense of shared biological descent. Migration was surely experienced in radically diverse ways, but we should not be surprised if those undergoing it would have shared a heightened sense of themselves as "Japanese," however defined, surrounded now by so many who were not.

Yet what these authors chose to focus upon was not the difference of those they marked as non-Japanese, nor on the similarity of those they marked as Japanese. Instead, their focus is on the alterity they perceived in individuals they identified as racially self-same. The first form this took was "acquired alterity," in which a once-possessed selfsame-ness was lost through exposure to alien factors ranging from more intense exposure to the sun to the introduction of non-Japanese blood. The reactions to this acquired alterity vary here from apathy ("Settler") to dismay ("Farming") to valorization ("Tumbleweeds"). In all three cases, however, the changes are not to the implied alternate subject position with which the narrator beckons the reader to identify (one distanced from the depicted behavior, which the reader is invited to gaze upon critically, alongside the narrator), one whose identity has not itself been destabilized. It is possible, then, that acquired alterity here may function to reassure such a reader of his or her own stability amid circumstances that invite anxiety.

The second, more common form of alterity among the racially self-same explored by these writers involved a deviation from a normative expectation for that group, an imagined racial solidarity. Each of the three stories revolves around one or more moments of shock at the behavior of a "Japanese" character towards his or her own kind: Kurose betrays Ōmura, who in turn has systemically exploited his Japanese workers. Ruriko betrays her young lover in order to enter into a mutually exploitative relationship with Ōmura. Daisuke, who was sold undesirable land (by a Japanese broker?), now exploits his Japanese workers relentlessly, even as his son has disappointed and abandoned him. The waiter who mocks Luísa is only the first of many Japanese who will persecute the siblings for (non-racial, as both their parents are apparently first-generation immigrants from Japan) deviations for which they cannot reasonably be held accountable.

The shock at these examples of inhumane or unethical behavior seems always to exceed the sin of commission itself; perhaps the shock has been amplified by the sense that an ideal (which up until that point may not have been consciously held) has been betrayed. Given the dominant global racist order, emigrants would likely have left Japan prepared for ill-treatment at the hands of the racial Other. Yet what the writers describe time and again is that identity fails to guarantee more ethical or compassionate treatment than one would have been led to expect from alterity. These literary representations of this unpleasant discovery suggest that the betrayal of expectations of racial solidarity may have left an impression as powerful as, if not more powerful than, interactions with more conventional forms of alterity. It is unclear why this was the case, though one can imagine that, in part, writers may have felt freer to express frustration toward their "fellow Japanese" than toward more powerful agents of institutionalized racism. Such psychological displacement would have allowed the resentment produced by systemic discrimination to be vented against the safer object of the perceived racial self-same.

Any examination of the origins, nature, and impact of such intraracial friction would of course need to move beyond this small sample of literary representations and into the history of lived subjects. It would also have to move beyond these manifestations the preceded the Second World War and consider the greatest phenomenon of internecine violence in the community of Japanese in Brazil: the Kachigumi-Makegumi conflict between those who believed Japan had won the War and those who believed it had been defeated. Though not causally linked to the frictions that appear in these stories, it is worth noting the emergence in the 1940s of the Shindō Renmei (臣道連盟), whose members would go on to commit a series of terrorist acts within the community against those who thought Japan had lost, ultimately killing 23 Japanese-Brazilians and wounding 147 others.[51]

While neither this violence nor the tensions described in this chapter could possibly be reduced to a displaced resentment over global and local racist structures, neither are they unrelated to them. Similarly, when we consider ethnos— peoplehood constructs—as the basis for aggregating literary texts, we must keep in mind the historicity (and thus politics) of that construct. As John Lie writes,

> The categories of race, ethnicity, and nation all grope toward a social grouping larger than kinship (whether family or lineage) but smaller than humanity. They seek, so to speak, to divide people horizontally. They are categories salient in the modern era, in contradistinction to the preponderance of vertical, hierarchical categories, such as caste and status, in premodern civilizations. (. . .) Notwithstanding the salience of class stratification, the horizontal categories supersede the vertical ones in the transition from the premodern civilization, empire, or state to the modern nation-state.[52]

The construct, therefore, cannot be taken as a self-evident given that naturally justifies such a grouping; rather, it is a contingent phenomenon that emerged within history, that was shaped by and consequently shaped that history, and that remains unstable. To apply it as the organizing logic of a "national literature" is not merely to reflect a historical phenomenon, but to reproduce a political project.

5

Language

The Illusion of Linguistic Singularity, or the Monolingual Imagination

In cases such as that of Japan, it may seem obvious to group texts, and bulwark the imagination of a national literature, through the notion of linguistic commonality. Unlike the category of ethnicity, which remains a powerful logic despite frequent disavowals of it, the category of language seems far less obviously problematic; it is of little surprise that (as will be discussed below) people have turned to it as a commonsensical solution to the implicit essentialist claims that undergird the ethnic logic. It seems almost tautological to say that one aspect of anything we might call modern Japanese literature (at least in a form that we might consider "original," rather than mediated through the process of translation) is that it be written in "Japanese." This is consonant with the post-World War II forgetting, or effacement, of the multilingual and multiethnic history of Japan described by scholars such as Oguma Eiji and Leo Ching.[1] While this logic may seem sensible and intuitive when considering the historical interrelation of texts (both their production and their consumption), it is not as self-evident as it might appear, and in fact elides a great deal of complexity and heterogeneity. Though the focus of this chapter will be on the literary activities of prewar Brazil, this fact obtains in one form or another in all literary production, though in different forms and to differing degrees.

In the case of Brazil, one of the many massive upheavals experienced by emigrants from Japan was their immersion in a linguistic environment of greater complexity than most of them had ever experienced before. They were not only moving to a country in which the dominant (and official) language was Portuguese and encountering individuals (particularly at sea) who used English as their preferred mode of communication, but also coming into contact with a greater variety of idioms of Japanese than most had previously encountered. This diversity reminds us of the complexity of individual identification of the migrants, for whom self-imagining as national or ethnic subjects might have been less common in everyday life than self-imagining based on prefecture or region of origin, occupation, gender, or class, all of which had the potential to be conflated with dialectical difference. While depictions of this diversity seem to suggest that it rarely impeded mutual comprehensibility, the differences were obvious enough to be noted frequently in their fiction.

Given the complexity of this linguistic environment, it should come as no surprise that the literary works written by these Japanese speakers in Brazil—like other literary works set outside of Japan—would often address linguistic heterogeneity directly. Focusing on the specific representations occurring in Japanese-language literature written in Brazil, however, should not be taken to imply that the texts normatively thought of as "modern Japanese literature" are a monolithic collection of linguistically homogeneous texts. This is true not only of texts with settings outside of Japan or characters who are not Japanese, but also in texts that represent regional dialects or other forms of linguistic experimentation that deviates from the relatively standardized language for modern fiction (not to mention national language policy) based on the Tokyo dialect. While regional dialects are often seen as merely variations within a single language, it is valuable to recall that the divide between a language and a dialect is not as bright a line as it is often treated as being, even when one considers the most intuitive justification for such a distinction: mutual intelligibility.[2] While dialects are often (but not always) treated diegetically as comprehensible to other characters and are non-diegetically presented in a way that presumes sufficient comprehensibility to the readers of the texts, it should not be presumed that the difference goes unnoticed, or that it actually is fully comprehensible to all readers.

The monolingual (even if heteroglossic) form that most novels take—particularly when their narratorial perspective is limited to that of a single character—faces fundamental challenges when attempting to represent a multilingual environment.[3] What would fiction be for a broad audience if all of the information gaps present in intersubjective communication were somehow maintained in the literary text? While some writers minimize or ignore those gaps, many others struggle to convey them, though usually in a moderated fashion that balances verisimilitude with comprehensibility. Representing these challenges to communication in literary texts poses multiple difficulties to writers, not only in terms of the impact that they will have on their potential audiences but also in terms of the basic mechanics of inscription. These challenges remind us of the ways in which the written literary form is anything but natural and transparent, but is instead the result of technical choices that have significant impact on what can be represented, and how.

The situation in Brazil brought many of these issues into relief. Immigrants from Japan found themselves in a multilingual environment even when they resided in the Japanese-language dominant *colônias* in the interior. Additionally, their "fellow Japanese," or "countrymen" (同胞), comprised a geographically (and linguistically) diverse group of individuals, hailing from prefectures stretching from Okinawa to Hokkaidō. Living side by side, they were keenly aware of the linguistic differences in the "Japanese" language that they were using (as well as the status and cultural differences that those differences would often be taken as signaling.) Literary texts produced in Brazil regularly address these differences. These texts not only give us insight into the linguistic aspects of the migration experience, but also concrete examples of the linguistic diversity of "Japanese-language" literature and the strategies authors adopted to represent that diversity. Even limiting our discussion to the ten stories from prewar Brazil included here, we find that while that alterity is almost always present, it takes different forms from story to story. These various forms of representing the language of the Other throw into question the stability of the language from which that putative deviation is implied. The texts also help us to distinguish between the representation of a linguistic barrier and the reproduction of that barrier, even as they remind us that such a distinction will vary from reader to reader depending on his or her own linguistic competence.

STRATEGIES FOR REPRESENTING
LINGUISTIC DIVERSITY

The first tool to consider when examining representational strategies for linguistic diversity is the *furigana*. One standard translation of the term into English is "phonetic gloss," stressing the function of these supplementary scripts to provide an indication of the oral component of the primary script.[4] I use the hierarchy of "primary" and "supplementary" for three reasons: first, because of a "common-sense" understanding of them, which can be useful even if we ultimately question that insinuation of inevitability; second, because of the way in which the *furigana* is often treated as optional, and will sometimes be added or removed by editors in subsequent editions of texts; and third, because of the fact that it is often presented in ways that make it appear to be of secondary importance. This secondary importance is implied graphically in the form of smaller typefaces (*rubi*) and interlineal positioning, vis-à-vis the dominant formatting of the texts.[5] This hierarchy deserves to be questioned, but that will not be the goal of this study. Instead, the focus here will be to identify some of the ways in which these scripts are applied in this particular milieu to represent linguistic diversity.[6]

One primary way for a *furigana* to be used, consistent with the understanding of it as a phonetic gloss, is to represent (as closely as possible given the limitations of the chosen script) the way the word would be enunciated in the given diegetic context, while the primary script represents the meaning of those words in a more accessible (linguistically conventional) way. The mere presence of *furigana* suggests either that an alternative reading exists, or that some readers would require the clarification it provides. To think of *furigana* as the spoken version of the written language present in the primary script, however, is insufficient. Ultimately, what a *furigana* does is juxtapose two scripts in a way that produces more meaning than a single script alone; while convention will guide readers in determining the implications of that juxtaposition, in the end the interrelation of the two scripts is ambiguous and thus open to interpretation. This ambiguity allows for authorial experimentation in utilizing the secondary script.

For example, a *furigana* may be used to present a transliteration of a non-Japanese word and then provide a Japanese gloss for it. In some cases, the gloss is present not in the subordinate interlineal position, but in the primary position. For example, in "An Age of Speculative Farming," the gendered epithet *puta* was in its first printing inscribed "賣笑婦"; in this case, the primary script presents in *kanji* the word conventionally read *baishōfu* (prostitute), and then gives it a gloss of *puuta* (sic).[7] In a way, the primary script is not so dominant at all, in that it functions as a semantic gloss on the oral component, which is in this case the focus. The epithet appears as part of dialogue, as direct discourse, suggesting that the phonetic guide captures the (diegetic) verbal utterance, rather than merely conveying the reading.[8] Because the first portion of the same dialogue is in Japanese without any alternate gloss, implying that it would have spoken by the character in Japanese in the scene, this gloss likely indicates to us the multilingual nature of the character's verbal abuse.

We may note that the author of this story did not feel the need to provide a similar semantic gloss to a word that appears in the sentence immediately preceding this dialog: ヴァガブンド (vagabundo). This is a choice on the part of the author (or his editor); the semantic gloss provided in the previous example is, after all, optional. Perhaps the author felt that the word had sufficiently entered the vocabularies of his likely readers and thus did not require a gloss, or perhaps he felt that there was no single Japanese word that could capture the precise meaning or nuance of the term. Not surprisingly, different authors could (and did) make different choices. While this author used the term ソルベツチ (sorubecchi) in the same story with no semantic gloss, Sakurada Takeo, writing for a similar audience a little more than eight years later, chose to inscribe the same word as 氷菓子. Sakurada's primary script here presents the word typically read *kōrigashi* (ice cream) juxtaposed against the phonetic gloss (slightly different from Sonobe's) ソルヴェッチ (soruvecchi).[9] Collectively such terms are often referred to as *koronia-go*, Portuguese lexical items that were incorporated into the dialect of Japanese used in Brazil. Unglossed *koronia-go*, though differing in frequency of use from one author to another, are not uncommon in the stories.

Nishioka Kunio's "The Death of a Certain Settler" contains a similar number of non-glossed *koronia-go* terms but goes further in the demands it places on its readers' comprehension of the language. To begin with, he never accompanies any of these terms with a semantic gloss; though some readers not familiar with Portuguese might have been able to glean the meaning (or approximate meaning) from the context, the information gap would have been noticeable. This is particularly true in the cases when Nishioka made the uncommon decision to use not only Portuguese nouns, but verbs. Consider this passage:

> The following day [. . .] after the *camaradas* had gone out *carpir*, Daisuke was stacking, one-by-one, the bricks from the *terreiro* extension near the main house.[10]

The nouns would be difficult enough for a reader unfamiliar with Portuguese and the specific context of a coffee plantation in Brazil, on the one hand providing a *faux ami* in *camarada* that might be taken to mean comrade when it fact it is referring to a farm hand, and on the other presenting a term (*terreiro*) specific to the cultivation of coffee that refers to a flat, open (and in this case temporary) terrace used for drying coffee beans. It is hard to know what such a reader would make of the phrase containing *carpir* (to hoe weeds), カルピーに出た (*karupii ni deta*, gone out to hoe weeds); it seems possible that such a reader could have mistaken its grammatical function altogether, taking it as referring to a place rather than an action. Nishioka uses Portuguese verbs, as he does here, two additional times in the course of the story.[11]

The way in which Portuguese terms were used in the stories differed depending on the author. Unlike Nishioka, the author Takemoto Yoshio indicates to readers that the Portuguese term will function as a verb by following it with the Japanese "o suru" (to do X), as he does with the term *colhêr* (to pick, pluck, or gather) when he writes, "We must *colhêr* the berries, because they will fall from the trees" (珈琲が落ちるからコロアをしなければならぬ).[12] Some authors avoid the use of these terms adopted from Portuguese altogether. Perhaps unsurprisingly given the setting of the story (mostly in Japan) and the high level of formality of its language, Katayama Yōko's "Natsuyo" uses none, even when the setting abruptly changes at the end of the story to the contemporary moment in Brazil. There, when the narrator writes, "I now pass my days happily here, in the colony," the term "colony" appears as 植民地 (*shokuminchi*), rather than the more common コロニア.[13]

Sakurada Takeo's "Placement," which begins with its characters about to enter the Mekong Delta, contains no Portuguese terms until—understandably—the characters arrive in Brazil during the third installment.[14] Most of the Portuguese terms Sakurada uses in this story are, or could be taken, as proper nouns, and thus arguably do not need a semantic gloss to perform their function; the one exception is ガルガンテ (*garganta*), which also lacks a semantic gloss.[15] In fact, the use of this term might be particularly misleading to a reader possessing a familiarity with English but not Portuguese; in the passage, the speaker is comparing an old man to a large tree, which might lead one to guess that the term is a cognate of "gargantuan." Instead, it is a sudden reference to the man in question directly, rather than through the metaphor of a tree. The figurative meaning of *garganta* (blowhard or braggart), which is how it is used here, emerges from its literal meaning (throat or gargle), which in turn comes from the same onomatopoeia (of gargling) that results in the verb *gargarejar* (to gargle).

This discussion of the boastful man who is likened to a great, old tree is instructive for yet another reason: it occurs in a different form of linguistic diversity, regional dialect. A number of dialectical elements in the brief quote (*haiyottoru, desu tai, desu bai*) all suggest a speaker from Kyūshū, even if the precise origins of the character might not be identifiable to people unfamiliar with dialectical differences existing in that region of Japan. More important than the precise origins, however, is the fact that the speaker is clearly marked as linguistically Other, as compared to the "standard" Japanese-using characters who are the primary focus of the story. Along with that difference come common (often discriminatory) associations with provincialism, such as a presumed lower level of education. Thus, while most readers might not have hesitated to label this dialogue "Japanese" along with the rest of the story, it is rendered in a way that is meant to distinguish it from "standard" Japanese.

Furuno Kikuo's story "Tumbleweeds" can only be considered in this context tentatively, as the original 1940 version of the story seems no longer to be extant. The earliest version we have today, which appeared in *Bungei shuto* in June 1958 in Japan, was published with a different readership in mind. It is therefore possible that additional glosses were added for that readership, which could not be expected to have knowledge of the terms. The main text of the 1958 version provides semantic glosses in *kanji* to *katakana* in the interlinear position, which itself transliterates the Portuguese terms. There are instances in which this plays a diegetic function, as the semantic gloss supplementing the phonetic component provides information of which the speaker herself is unaware. For example, after one character recites a poem in Portuguese, a young girl (a native speaker of Portuguese who is presumably capable of some Japanese) asks what the word *saudade* means: "追憶って、なあに？" The semantic gloss, conventionally read *tsuioku* (reminiscence), provides for readers the precise information that diegetically the enunciation is meant to elicit.

Unlike previous stories, "Tumbleweeds" sees the glossing of complete phrases with idiomatic Portuguese, such as "俺 知らん" (*Eu não se*), especially in dialogue; it also occasionally drops the semantic gloss, perhaps in some cases because a translation of the original Portuguese would be considered too rude (or clumsy), as in "チェッ！プータ・メルダ！" (*Che! Puta merda!*)[16] On the other hand, there is little glossing of single terms, especially when they appear in the narrative portions of the story. This is also true in Sugi Takeo's "Revenge" (1938), though it is worth noting that none of Furuno's and Sugi's stories contains more than ten such terms.

One also sees in "Tumbleweeds" references to regional Japanese dialect, whether it is the Kyūshū accent that Akita uses when addressing his mother, or the

thick Osaka accent heard emanating from the third-class dining hall.¹⁷ While both
of these dialects are explicitly identified within the text, the first is barely represented in the dialogue (*agemassho* rather than *agemashō*), while the second is represented at greater length: "*Ma, sonai shiyaharan ka te ee dassharo, naa, anta-han,
ate kara mo owabi shimassa kai . . .*" (There's no need for that—I should apologize
too.)¹⁸ It is important to note, though, that standard Japanese, which is used almost
exclusively in narrative passages and when depicting the speech of characters who
are being elevated (in terms of education, in particular), marks dialect as something that others—and inferior others at that—have, but that the main character
and those he (most focal characters are male, with the conspicuous exception of
Katayama's narrator) identifies as peers do not have. The use of standard Japanese,
then, reflects the character's lack of awareness of his own dialectical specificity
even as it is a claim to urbanity and education. Through this language the narrator
is tacitly marked as normative while the dialect speakers are marked as deviations.

Another way that linguistic difference "within" Japanese is marked is when a
Japanese-American college student, Tani, calls out to his Japanese shipmate upon
their approach to Japan that *sakura* (cherry blossoms) and *musume-san* (young
[Japanese] women) are now visible on the horizon. The use of *katakana* to represent these two words seem to suggest that the speaker is using them, but somehow
incorrectly or unnaturally. The student's utterance as a whole is worth examining,
however:

> ハロー！ミスタ・秋田！起床々々！水平線にサクラとムスメサンが見えて
> ますよ。("Hello, Mister Akita! Wake up, wake up! You can see cherry blossoms and
> young women on the horizon.")¹⁹

The script choices seem to be implying that the Californian is primarily speaking
in English, while also employing the common Japanese terms *sakura* and *musume*.
Were this not the case, these common terms would not be inscribed in *katakana*,
when the more difficult terms *kishō* and *suiheisen* are not. Tani, the story seems
to imply, is able to use the first two terms precisely because they are common and
easy to remember. Presented in *katakana*, the implication is that Tani uses the
Japanese terms *sakura* and *musume*, but that their use is unconventional—primarily because he uses Japanese words amid an English-language statement, but
possibly also because his pronunciation is non-standard, further highlighting his
alterity. Here, the inscription choices paradoxically connote the opposite of what
they normally connote: the use of conventional Japanese orthography for the latter
indicates that those terms are expressed naturally (for Tani), and thus are (diegetically speaking) English utterances.

In "Tumbleweeds," there are also cases in which Portuguese (albeit incorrect
Portuguese) appears in the text in Roman script, such as the couplet excerpted
from the poem "Natal em Paris" by Luís Edmundo in the story "Tumbleweeds":
". . . *Oh, neve, como a saudade, caes leve, caes leve.*"²⁰ In this case, the couplet is

followed by a parenthetical translation in Japanese ("The snow falls, like a memory, so lightly, so lightly. . . .") Later in the story, Roman script appears again when the Latin "*Va victis*" (sic, "Woe to the vanquished!") appears in the story, followed by a similar parenthetical translation in Japanese.[21] This, in and of itself, is not surprising; authors in Japan had long experimented with using Roman script (inscribing a variety of languages, including Japanese) for all or part of their texts. What it does remind us, though, is that authors would have been limited by the printing capacities of their publishers as to what scripts they were able to use. There are cases of publishers in Japan being willing to create type for authors, but it is unlikely that any Japanese-language printers in Brazil would have had the capacity to do so. As a result, the writers examined here would have been limited to a conventional set of Japanese type (often purchased from Japan, but in some instances apparently purchased secondhand from Japanese printers in the United States) and a set of Roman type necessary for composing English and Portuguese.[22]

As suggested above, non-conventional orthography (and spelling) is often used to convey non-standard (sometimes non-native) pronunciation. For example, in "An Age of Speculative Farming," when the half-Japanese Hanaoka Ruriko addresses her lover, his name is transcribed in *katakana* (オームラ), whereas when it appears in narrative passages it appears in the more conventional *kanji* (大村).[23] More importantly, when his name appears in dialogue spoken by the native Japanese-speaking Kurose, it also appears using *kanji*.[24] The implication is that Kurose's pronunciation of Ōmura's name is normative, whereas Hanaoka's is somehow non-normative, and perhaps even "foreign." We might note that the script choices for the character of Hanaoka may also have the effect of highlighting her otherness; rather than using solely *kanji* or *hiragana*, her given name uses a combination of *katakana* and *kanji* (ルリ子).

Another scriptural innovation (or transgression, as it is not subsequently acknowledged by the normative center of the language's use) that is present in "Japanese-language" texts in Brazil is a domestically created character (国字), where the "domestic" space in question is not Japan, but Brazil. The primary (and perhaps sole) example of this is the character for *mil-réis* (金+千), which appears in "Placement" and which was in common use in Brazilian newspapers.[25] In the context of that story, the meaning would have been reasonably clear even for a reader who is not familiar with the character, despite the absence of either a semantic or phonetic gloss, because the sentence in which it appears states an equivalence of value of 10 of this unit at 2 yen, 50 sen; it further makes it clear that the speaker considers it an unreasonable price for one dozen daikon. The context, therefore, provides a general semantic gloss to this character that would have been very familiar to readers of Japanese in Brazil at the time, but which would have been unfamiliar to readers elsewhere.

These examples drawn from stories written in Brazil remain relatively straightforward, and do not represent a unique formation in Brazil; more complex cases exist in literary texts produced elsewhere. It is worth, then, turning to the related (but not symmetrical) phenomena of literary texts written in Japanese by bilingual Korean speakers. Kō Youngran, for example, writes about representations of multilinguality that appear in Chang Hyŏk-chu's (Chō Kakuchū) 1932 story "Gakidō" (餓鬼道). In the dialogue section that she uses as an example, the primary script provides a semantic gloss to the interlinear script, which uses *katakana* to represent phonetically the discussion that is presumably occurring, diegetically, in Korean. She notes, however, the addition of an unusual element to the dominant script lines, an element that exceeds the lines' function as semantic gloss. Here is an example:

「馬山イ。さつさと帰れよ。」 ("Maasan, go home right away.")

At first glance, this sentence seems to use the primary and interlinear scripts to convey the same sentiment in the two languages: "Masan[-i]. Ŏsŏ toragage" (Korean) and "Maasan. Sassa to kaere yo" (Japanese). At closer inspection, however, one realizes that it is not that simple. For one thing, a Korean speaker would have to understand not only *katakana* in order to access the phonetic transcription, but also the Japanese sentence in order to provide the necessary clues to decode that (rough) transcription. Additionally, for the sentence to seem natural (as a Korean utterance), the "Korean-language" reader would have to drop down from the supplementary script to the primary script in order to include the イ, without which the sentence ("Masan. Ŏsŏ toragage") seems unnatural; of course, such a reader would also have to know not to drop down and include the れよ after the second part of the phrase. Similarly, as Kō points out, for a "Japanese-only" reader, not only is the secondary script merely a collection of sounds that would be incomprehensible beyond the simple fact that it (presumably) represents Korean, but also the イ would appear as "noise."[26] It is possible that it would perform that function that Kō suggests for it—conveying the sound of this multilingual environment to readers who do not have the linguistic tools to comprehend that environment more fully—but it would carry little semantic meaning beyond that.

Writing about the particular demands on the Japanese script system in literary texts that arose from Japan's colonization of Korea, Kō explains that most scholars start from the assumption that in Korea during that period the two languages were stable linguistic spheres that did not encroach upon one another.[27] As she shows, however, not only is the use of script not that simple, but the effect differed dramatically depending on the linguistic capacities of the readerships. As a result, in examining such a text—or, I would add, any text—Kō argues that one cannot rely on an ethnocentric perspective (民族主義的遠近法) that imagines nation-states with discrete and homogeneous national languages used by ethno-national subjects.[28] Instead, one must see these authors as experimenting with the script tools available to them (linguistically or mechanically) to capture the linguistic diversity they wish to represent, in some cases cognizant that different readerships would have varying degrees of access to those representations. In the case of the stories from Brazil, the depictions of linguistic diversity would not be opaque for some, but instead would reproduce a linguistic environment that does not adhere to the putatively clear boundaries between languages; for others, the texts would reproduce its incomprehensibility.

One more point to consider is the fact that the two languages do not exist in a symmetrical relationship; there is always a pragmatic element to the code-switching, and each language carries an array of social implications. That is, the languages exist in a hierarchical relationship, though the nature of that hierarchy might shift depending on the situation and the speaker. When Luísa or João uses Portuguese in "Tumbleweeds," the implication is of their alterity, and perhaps their linguistic inability to convey the same thoughts in the primary language of their interlocutors. By contrast, when Akita uses Portuguese, that act of code-switching demonstrates his intelligence and greater range of linguistic (and, by extension, cultural) awareness. The code-switching is not only a linguistic device, but a literary device meant to reveal aspects of the characters and their relationships to one another indirectly.

Yet another point to consider is the issue of comprehension. As Naoki Sakai argues, failure of communication is not limited to interactions that occur across a presumed language barrier (with one or more of the participants operating, by definition, outside of their first language). Sometimes, however, literary texts downplay such barriers, not fully acknowledging the challenges of comprehension even when they exist in more conventional forms "across languages."[29] If the narratorial perspective implies that the reader's knowledge of events is dependent on a given character, the presumption is that such knowledge would be dependent on that character's capacity to understand the "alien" (vis-à-vis the language of the narrative itself) language. Such cases are rare in the stories examined here, for reasons examined in the previous chapter. Perhaps the most substantial example involving direct discourse attributed to a character marked as non-Japanese is the following phrase, uttered by the Baiano worker in Nishioka's "Death of a Certain Settler":

> Patrão, she didn't eat anything today either, a-and she's in her last month of pregnancy so she can't work, she's in a tough spot. I-i-is there any way you could let her have um plato of food? I will gratefully put in an extra hard day of work tomorrow in return.[30]

Given the improbability that the Baiano laborer had acquired sufficient Japanese ability, the implication is that this dialogue would have occurred diegetically in Portuguese, with the titular settler, Kaneko, then "interpreting" it in the story for a Japanese-reading audience in Brazil; presumably that audience would be comfortable with the untranslated terms patrão and um plato.

In the end, however, this is not a real multilingual situation, but a fictional one. The author is aware of what each character says, even if the narrator perhaps might not be, as each character is the author's creation. It is awareness of this fact, presumably, that invites the reader to trust the narrator's (or focal character's) understanding of those utterances. This is akin to the difference between a dramatic scene, in which the conceit is that the reader is watching the event unfold along with the characters involved, and a retrospectively reported event, in which the reader is asked to believe the account presented by a (non-omniscient) narrator. While the latter might more clearly raise the possibility of an unreliable narrator, the former—in this case, the non-diegetically interpreted utterance—might be worthy of similar scrutiny. In such scenes, when presented from a narratorial perspective that is not omniscient, we do not hear what the other (non-focal) characters say; we are told by a narrator what they said.

Language diversity might also be presented in a text with comprehension being beside the author's intended point. Nishi Masahiko writes about how other languages can be used in monolingual novels not to reveal the fissures that they would inevitably reveal in life, but rather to titillate, as mere exoticism or "local color." While Nishi does not mean that these linguistic elements are trivial, the use of such terms and the negative (and dismissive) connotations that cling to them runs the risk of devaluing a linguistic diversity that performs multiple potential functions within the texts. He likens the monolingual rendering of the multilingual environment to an invisibility cloak (隠れ蓑) that conceals fierce ironies that function in the texts that emerge from such an environment (in his case, colonial Taiwan).[31] He provides the useful thought experiment of imagining how one would handle the linguistic elements of a film adaptation of such a work. Ultimately, however, we as readers are not limited to the intentions of the author, and therefore are free to draw meaning from a text's treatment of linguistic complexity and the potential barriers to communication that might result from it. This is not only true in texts that contain scenes of multilinguality, commonly defined; it is also true of texts that "only" contain "Japanese," especially given the complex and diverse history of language practices that are grouped under that broad rubric.

NIHONGO BUNGAKU: JAPANESE-LANGUAGE LITERATURE

Despite this linguistic complexity, and the examples of unconventional representational tactics that authors have used to capture it in literary texts, such fiction (in Brazil or in Japan) remains largely monolingual or provides sufficient context to enable a monolingual reader to comprehend it sufficiently. As a result these texts, as diverse as the language environments they depict—or encode—may be, are often seen as being written *in Japanese*. It is this point of commonality that critics have focused upon in recent years when thinking of literary texts collectively, rather than through any of the logics raised in the earlier chapters, in a move toward inclusivity for authors who do not conform to a normative ethnic identity. *Nihongo bungaku* (日本語文学), or Japanese-language literature, is fast becoming the rubric employed to distinguish such texts from *Nihon bungaku* (日本文学).[32] The new category began being consciously deployed for this purpose from the 1990s, but it appeared occasionally before that as well, though then its evocation seems to have been less strategic and its meaning treated as more-or-less self-evident.[33]

One of the earliest proponents of the term was the writer Kim Sŏkpŏm.[34] Hirata Yumi describes the ways in which Kim used the term from at least as early as 1972 to explicitly comment on the ways in which Zainichi Korean literature had been marginalized from a normative notion of Japanese literature.[35] She also describes how other authors were concerned with similar issues even if they did not use this precise terminology; the example she gives is Ōe Kenzaburō in a published discussion with Gotō Meisei and others from 1970.[36] For his part, Kim felt that when Zainichi Korean writers, whose language and country had been stolen from them and who were forced to live "another's history," had no choice but to write in the language of those who had stolen those things from them, what they wrote could not be called "Japanese literature." That concept, based on the presumed unity of state-language-ethnos, which had been used to build the modern nation-state of Japan, failed to reflect the more complicated reality of writers who had come to the country by force, for economic or educational opportunity, or as refugees, but did not identify as Japanese; the concept of Japanese-language literature, in Kim's mind, more effectively problematized this history.[37]

Around the same time, two articles were published that associated the concept of *Nihongo bungaku* with the Japanese-language literature produced in Brazil. Despite not employing the phrase as an alternative to *Nihon bungaku*, the authors clearly revealed many of the same concerns that drive the proponents of *Nihongo bungaku* today.

The first, "Dying Words: The Japanese-language Literature of Emigrants to Brazil" (失われる言葉・ブラジル移民の日本語文学), appeared in the *Yomiuri shinbun* on 25 April 1969. The author, Yabusaki Masatoshi, himself an emigrant to Brazil, was born in Tokyo in 1922 and made the passage to Brazil with his family in 1933. Yabusaki was central to Japanese-language literary activities in the postwar, some thirty years after the end of the period being examined here. According to the brief biographical note that accompanies the article, in 1969 he was working at a Japanese bookstore in São Paulo and editing the literary magazine *Koronia bungaku*.

In the article, Yabusaki describes how extensive the Japanese-language literary production of the community is, given its small size: multiple daily newspapers and monthly periodicals that carry fiction, and roughly as many literary awards as there are publishing venues. With thirty to forty submissions for each award every year, he estimates that as many as one hundred works are being composed for consideration annually. Yabusaki continues, saying that the population of Japanese speakers (日本語使用人口) is estimated as being just short of 100,000, and suggesting that a notably large fraction is engaged in creative writing.[38] He then offers an interesting observation: while it is obvious from these figures that Japanese migrants are passionate about fiction, it is not at all clear what they are trying to achieve with it. Rather than being engaged in a literary endeavor that produces lasting masterpieces, he imagines that they engage in the writing of fiction in a more casual and ephemeral way, as when one tells stories of the past while sitting by a fire.

For Yabusaki, the Japanese language and its use for literature are in crisis in Brazil, partly due to a lack of influence from the language as it is used in Japan. He opines that the Japanese language used by writers there is the one they brought with them when they migrated as many as forty years earlier, and as such has long been removed from the feel of vivid daily life (鮮やかな生活感覚); the result is that the functionality of the language has deteriorated. Without interlocutors, Japanese migrants can only use the language to speak amongst themselves; the absence of true dialogue can only lead to a "deformed" (不具) version of the language. Despite the daily deterioration of the migrants' Japanese, no other language takes its place; only those who were born in Brazil or came as children can really enter the Portuguese-speaking world. The presence of two *idiomas* (glossed as 国語, and thus indicating dominant languages for their respective speakers) creates a divide between the generations, so that when migrants try to tell their stories to their children, hoping that the tales will live on in the children's memories, they discover that they cannot. When they realize this, they turn toward their homeland (故国) and think to tell their stories to the people there, but here too they fail; the result is confusion about who they themselves are, and a sense that their words/language (言葉) have become frustratingly impoverished. Only if the migrants invest the necessary labor in self-examination and restoring their dying language, Yabusaki offers, do they have any hope of someday joining a "world of dialogue" (対話の世界). In different terms, Yabusaki is claiming a form of dependence by the periphery on the center; I will return to this notion in the conclusion. To return to our present discussion, the term *Nihongo bungaku* does not appear in this article beyond its title; there it is presumably being used in a less consciously strategic sense, to denote what the article goes on to describe as "works told in Japanese" (日本語でつづられる創作) and to connote works produced outside of Japan, where the language of composition could (in theory) remain implicit.

By the time the term was used again in the newspaper, six years later, it was being used in a more intentional manner. On 2 April 1975, the *Yomiuri shinbun* ran an article titled, "Japanese-Language Literature Abroad: The Stories Told in *Nanka bungei* and *Koronia bungaku*." The author of this article was Ōta Saburō, a professor of Comparative Literature at Chiba University. In it he took up two literary journals published in the Americas: *Nanka bungei*, published in Los Angeles, which had just produced its twentieth issue; and *Koronia bungaku*, published in

São Paulo, which had already released twenty-five issues. Both journals had been established a decade earlier. Ōta refers to these as the two representative journals of *Nihongo bungaku* of the day. The article then goes on to define the phrase indirectly, as referring to the literary activities of Japanese who had migrated abroad, and naming the writings emerging from the West Coast of the United States as its earliest examples. Shortly after their arrival in Seattle, San Francisco, Los Angeles and other cities, the Japanese migrants had attained a sufficient level of economic stability, Ōta explains, to make literary activities possible in much the same way those in Brazil did a little later.

Focusing on the re-emergence of these literary activities in North America after the chaos caused by the internment, Ōta states that the dramatic gains seen recently (since the 1960s) among individuals of Japanese descent are actually limited to those who have assimilated into American society; those who instead "do not lose their Japanese consciousness and emotions, and preserve their Japanese language" are not fully assimilated. Ōta too points out that second- and third-generation Nikkei are raised speaking English, and that for them Japanese is nothing more than another foreign language. In the prewar, *Nihongo bungaku* comprised the works produced by these first-generation migrants who "lived seeing themselves as Japanese" (日本人意識に生きる). The result, according to Ōta, was works in the realist mode that dealt solely with the issues that plagued the Japanese immigrant community.[39] Ōta contrasts this with the situation as he understands it in Brazil, which saw greater continuity between the literary activities of the prewar and those of the present day (1975) thanks to less challenging circumstances for the community in the country during World War II. Ōta describes the impetus behind the creation of the literary magazine *Koronia bungaku* as being the desire to write down their experiences, as a part of a single human history (一つの人間の歴史 として), and to do so in Japanese, even as second- and third-generation Nikkei are losing their connection to the language.

Ōta argues that the very act of composing works in Japanese at its heart reveals that these individuals are powerfully conscious of themselves as Japanese. The works emerge from the experiences that Japanese only have once they are present in a foreign society, and give them the opportunity to reflect on the essence of Japaneseness. But, Ōta cautions, because these works cannot be read by second- and third-generation Nikkei, they will disappear along with the first generation, just as those migrants fear. Having said that, Ōta also offers the possibility that *Nihongo bungaku* could pioneer new territory if it follows the example set by Ōba Minako, whose works are not fixed in a given ethnicity, but instead deal in universalities. The conditions for such a development, Ōta notes, are more present in foreign countries than they are in Japan.

Ōta does see one way for these texts to live on and for them to be of value to Japanese in Japan at the same time. He urges readers in Japan to read these works, which reveal the true nature of the Japanese by depicting their experiences abroad.

The works are valuable because they allow those readers (here presumed to be Japanese) to remind themselves of what it is to be Japanese. If these texts are not read in Japan, then foreigners (外国人) will pay no attention to them. Eventually their authors will die and all trace of the works will disappear. They must be taken up "as a special area within Japanese literary history"; to do so would be to support those individuals who have developed *Nihongo bungaku.*

These two articles anticipate scholarship that begins to emerge quickly from around 1990, though there are at least two key differences: the first is that the later works are deploying the term *Nihongo bungaku* more consciously, more strategically, than do these articles, which seem to treat it more as a self-evident descriptor, even as they are clearly using it to identify a non-normative form of Japanese literature; the second is that the later scholarship tends to use the term primarily to discuss works written by writers who do not identify as ethnically Japanese, and whose relationship with the Japanese language is related to the Japanese imperial period. It is not surprising, then, that two of the earliest monographs employing this term as a central concept were themselves focused on the Japanese-language literary production of writers who identified ethnically with Korea and Taiwan, respectively.

The former was Hayashi Kōji's *Zainichi Chōsenjin Nihongo bungakuron* (1991), which was based on articles that the author published over the previous decade addressing ethnically Korean *Zainichi* writers. Given the perspicacity with which he deals with many of the relevant factors, it is worthwhile to overview some of the logical steps that he takes in laying out his argument. Hayashi begins by establishing a distinction between the language of an author's motherland (母国語) and an author's mother tongue (母語). In Hayashi's view, for resident Koreans in Japan (在日朝鮮人) the former is always Korean, though they may not be able to speak it at all; the latter is one's first language (that which one "naturally acquired from birth as one's mode of expression"), and therefore may be Japanese, especially in the case of the second and third generations.[40] For individuals such as these, Korean can become a "non-mother tongue" (非母語), which Hayashi suggests may simply mean a second language. It is interesting to note that when Hayashi uses Kim Tesen as an example, he is forced to acknowledge a further complexity to the languages involved: since Kim was born and raised (until the age of five) on Jeju Island, the Korean he uses, his mother tongue, differs from the "standard Korean of modern Korean literature" as result of Jeju Island's relation to the rest of Korea, which is similar to that of "Okinawa's position within the Japanese language sphere." According to Hayashi, for Kim, Japanese is a "pseudo-mother tongue" (疑似母語), acquired naturally from the age of five when he moved to Japan to live with his "aunt," who herself was a "pseudo-mother." It is also a "half-mother tongue" (半ば母語) that functioned as his language of daily life (生活言語). Hayashi is right to identify the political context within which there arose these subjects, the Zainichi, for whom the language of the motherland and the mother tongue were not identical. He describes various historical paths that led to this disassociation for different authors over the course of the twentieth century and is careful to note the role played by Japanese imperialism. For Hayashi, languages are products of ethnic histories; as a result, the relationship between the Korean and Japanese languages cannot be discussed without taking into account the history of Japanese invasions of the Korean peninsula. At the same time, Hayashi acknowledges that as the distance of these subjects from the Korean language increases, their relation to the language becomes ambiguous, and that their ethnic consciousness as Korean (朝鮮) approaches nil, particularly when their parents' mother tongue was Japanese. The force, in fact, that might cause them to come to possess this consciousness is social discrimination.[41]

As for how these issues related to the questions at hand, about aggregated textual rubrics, we see in Hayashi awareness of what I consider to be the key issue: if one explores the question of what the Japanese language is to Zainichi subjects, one must also ask what it is to Japanese subjects; if one asks what *Nihongo bungaku* is, one must also ask what *Nihon bungaku* is. These are not ontological questions so much as historical and political ones. Hayashi notes the centrality of the modern nation-state's project to normalize (make normative) a standardized national language to the development of modern literature as a whole. It is this process of making literature national, according to Hayashi, that resulted in modern Japanese literature becoming an "ethnic literature."[42]

It is in his use of ethnicity that Hayashi's argument becomes somewhat problematic. On the one hand, he treats the ethnicity of his authors as self-evident, as when he describes Kim Sŏkpŏm as "undoubtedly Korean" (疑いもなく朝鮮人 である), or perhaps as one who has never doubted his identity as a Korean; this is presumably the justification for all of the authors Hayashi studies having some relation with Korean as their *bokokugo*, which can then also be identified as their language of ethnic origin.[43] As the country (countries, depending on the historical moment) in question is presumed to be ethnically homogenous, one's mother country becomes the home of one's ethnic origins. In fact, perhaps it might be more historically (though not biologically) accurate to refer to this as their language of racial origin, as their common descent seems to be implied as being an essential component of this ethnic identity.

Hayashi is clear to state that ethnicities are the products of history, and that one implication of this fact is that Zainichi (在日朝鮮人) will gradually grow distinct from Koreans (朝鮮人).[44] It seems, though, that both of these identities are rooted in something essential, some sort of "Koreanness," that remains unproblematized even as Hayashi acknowledges that it seems bound to result in two distinct identities. One can imagine a number of reasons that Hayashi might choose to leave the historical origins of this (or any such) identity unquestioned, particularly as his ultimate project seems to be to acknowledge and legitimate the writers' own (diverse) relationships with that identity.

For Hayashi, ethnic identity (民族的独自性) is something that can diminish, and perhaps even be lost, as was the case (he contends) for the writers who participated in the Korea Proletarian Artist Federation (KAPF; 朝鮮プロレタリア芸術同盟), such as Kim Yonje. Ethnic identity is fluid and not a universal (or ideal, or essential) entity, he argues. One of the results of this is that for some second-generation writers, the identity (属性) that they desire is not "Korean," but Zainichi, an identity that does not oppress them, but rather feels natural. Hayashi also recognizes the material ramifications of an author's language choice, as when he discussed the author Chang Hyŏk-chu. Hayashi describes the way in which Japanese functions as a world language for Chang, allowing his works to reach a broader, global readership as part of the "commercial literary establishment" (商業文壇). The desideratum of writers like Chang was exposure to a larger public (公共性).[45] In both cases, he acknowledges the role of history, and the capacity for change.

Despite Hayashi's calls for historicization, there nonetheless remains an element of essentialization, as can be seen when he writes, "Despite the fact that today's 'Zainichi Korean Literature' is written (expressed) in Japanese by people living in Japan, there is an aspect of it that cannot be referred to as 'Japanese literature.'" He continues, "Yi Yang-ji first produced Zainichi Korean (朝鮮人) Literature when she sought for some sort of positive capacity in the fact of her Koreanness (朝鮮人である事実)."[46]

Fundamentally, however, Hayashi is committed to the capacity for historical change, even if he only explicitly acknowledges it prospectively. He also notes the presence of conservative forces that will deny the transformations that accompany the passage of time, which will withhold recognition of these new forms as literature through the exercise of authority. He also makes the following assertion:

> Whether or not it is necessary for a Zainichi Korean to identify with "Korea" (朝鮮) is a question that requires us to consider a variety of social conditions, but speaking about literature as viewed from the 'bird's eye view' of ideals, it is not necessary for Zainichi Koreans to be Korean. The value of Zainichi Korean Literature is unrelated to whether or not the author is Korean.

He makes it clear, however, that to think of literature outside of its historical context, as a universal phenomenon, is a dangerous sign.[47]

Hayashi supports Kim Tesen's argument that literature must free itself from notions of identity (帰属観念), including those toward ethnic languages (民族語), and eliminate any constraints on the choice of language used for literary expression. Once this is achieved, he argues, "modern" literatures, which were from the beginning presumed to be ethnic literatures written in ethnic languages, will be rendered obsolete; in fact, "the overcoming of modernity will begin with the collapse (破綻) of ethnic literatures." Writers, he argues, must not depend upon identification of any sort, be it with ethnicities, states, or any other large organizations outside themselves; yet the end result of this for Hayashi is a Japanese literature in which "we" (われわれ) "allow" (許容) Japanese-language literature by a variety of ethnic subjects. Who is the "we" that might allow this? From the context, it would appear to be "internationalized" Japanese subjects, but this Japaneseness seems to still be premised on an ethnic identity. Hayashi sees a dwindling of commonalities (共通項) among the works of Zainichi Korean Literature, with those of the Ikkaino (猪飼野) writers in particular being more writers of minority exoticism within Japanese Literature than of Zainichi Korean Literature. Hayashi believes that it will only be when these writers transcend Ikkaino that they will transcend Japanese Literature. Having said all this, Hayashi cautions that the bonds of "modern ethnicities" (近代民族, glossed as "nation") are not so easily severed, and that transcendence in the case of Japanese Literature will only occur when [subject unclear, but presumably] Japanese writers produce Japanese-language fiction in proper recognition of the violence (侵略性) inherent in writing in Japanese.[48]

Many of the observations that I wish to make are already present here in Hayashi, particularly when his conclusions are taken to their logical end. Unfortunately, however, he never fully subjects "Japaneseness" and "Japanese literature" to the same historicizing analysis to which he subjects his object of study. By contrast, this move of auto-critique is more present in the second work under consideration here, Tarumi Chie's *Taiwan no Nihongo bungaku: Nihon tōji jidai no sakka tachi* (1995).[49] By page seven, she has already identified the capacity of the works she is studying to "undermine the concept of 'Japanese literature' in its narrow sense." Tarumi identifies that the central goal of Japan's imperial policies was to bring the local population under the empire's full control, a process which began with assimilation and then amplified to "imperialization" (皇民化). According to Tarumi, it is this latter process that placed the burden upon the colonized subject to conform to an imperial ideal, resulting in the theme that unifies the works by *kōmin* writers from Taiwan: How can one become Japanese? It is this theme that leads Tarumi to ask the question, what is it that makes a person Japanese? Using herself as an example, Tarumi admits that she would be at a loss if she were asked to prove that she was Japanese, even as she claims that her Japaneseness is, to her, a self-evident fact.[50]

Tarumi is not merely dealing with questions of ontology; she is clearly aware of pragmatic matters of daily life, including individuals' political identities, linguistic identities, and cultural identities. She notes that while Taiwanese during the period of Japanese control were legally defined as "Japanese," the Japanese language was not their mother tongue (母語) and "Japanese culture" was not what "governed their daily lives." Yet, she notes that it is a "patent absurdity" (極まりない不条理) that it was Japanese who would declare that Taiwanese were not Japanese.[51]

Tarumi returned to the subject in 2013, and elaborated on the problem facing such writers:

From the start, the Japanese-language literature of Taiwan, born from the Japanese language education that supported imperial control, is a sort of changeling born of the politics of language. What differentiates it decisively from postcolonial literatures born from the former British colonies is the fact that Japanese itself is a language that possesses almost no marketplace beyond Japan. This means that evaluations of such works are left to Japanese people who understand the language, and the bulk of the works' messages are attended to according to the filter of the Japanese value system.

Tarumi looks forward to a day when Japan will nurture multilingual readers who can understand and appreciate the works of such writers free of such filters.[52]

The later essay appeared in one of a number of recent volumes dealing with *Nihongo bungaku*, a number of which use it in conjunction with the term *gaichi*.[53] This last term was popularized by Kurokawa Sō's publication of a three-volume collection of translations, *<Gaichi> no Nihongo bungaku-sen* (Tokyo: Shinjuku Shobō, 1996), which featured works written in the former Japanese colonies and quasi-colonial spaces of Asia. By the time Kamiya Tadataka and Kimura Kazuaki took up the term, they had decided to interpret it broadly, to include writers without Japanese citizenship who resided in Japan and those of Japanese descent in Brazil who wrote in Japanese.[54] In her 2013 edited volume, Kaku Nan'en shifts the focus to bilinguality and to the heterogeneity inherent in the Japanese language itself. In Ikeuchi Teruo, Kimura Kazuaki, Takemura Yoshiaki, and Tsuchiya Shinobu's 2014 collection, the editors responded to some criticisms of the use of the term, particularly from Komori Yōichi.[55] Rather than problematizing the relationship between *Nihongo bungaku* and *Nihon bungaku*, however, Kimura focuses on the referents of the term *gaichi*. In all three edited volumes, despite the different issues raised by the many contributing scholars, the contents all tend toward authors who somehow deviate from a normative notion of Japanese literature.

In his introduction to the 2014 volume, Kimura draws particular attention to the innovative work of Nishi Masahiko, who has offered the following definition of *Nihongo bungaku*: "The literature that emerges when Japanese-language speakers (literally, "users" [使用者]) live in constant contact with, or in the proximity of, non-Japanese-language speakers."[56] He has made this definition central to his work, though in recent years he has begun to apply it to the terms *gaichi bungaku* and *gaichi no Nihongo bungaku* more frequently.[57] In his case, he utilizes the problematic distinction between a *naichi* (inner territories) literature and a *gaichi* (outer territories), employing terms historically used to distinguish the "main islands" of Japan from its colonies.[58] For Nishi, such literature is marked by three primary elements: the suggestion of other languages, the marks of imperialism, and the presence of "overseas Japanese."[59] His particularly narrow definition of *naichi*, in which he hesitates to include Okinawa, combined with his sometimes inconsistent use of terms, appears to reinforce a notion that an unproblematic

Nihon bungaku exists, when it does not meet the criteria he lays out in the definition of *Nihongo bungaku* above.

This seems not to be Nishi's goal, as his definition leads him to characterize certain canonical works, such as Mori Ōgai's *Maihime* (1890) and Yokomitsu Riichi's *Shanhai* (1928–31) as Japanese-language literature of the outer territories.[60] Nonetheless, Nishi makes such troubling statements as: "in the same way that the literature of the United States, Australia, and India may be Anglophonic literature but not English literature, so too we can say that *koronia bungaku* is not Japanese literature (日本文学)" and "[literature by emigrants from Japan] reveals a strong ambition to blow a new wind into the literary establishment of the *naichi*, using the power of exoticism as a weapon."[61] As a result, despite Nishi's move toward inclusivity, toward bringing attention to literary texts that reach in one way or another beyond the main islands of Japan, the logic of his work may have the effect of reinforcing the normative, self-evident notion of a "Japanese literature" that can be differentiated from a "Japanese-language literature."

Similar issues arise in works that have adopted the logic of "border crossing" (越境), with national borders being the primary ones imagined (thus, "transnational literature"), but by no means excluding other possible borders. As the editor of one such volume explains it in his introduction, this approach is an attempt to undertake social critique from a global perspective.

> That is, in order to overcome a perspective based on a national language, [this approach] focuses on the postmodern postures of authors who emphasize the body and capture the foreign, and thus is able to involve an investigation into the relation between these authors' work and the current situations into which migrants have been placed. The consideration of these issues from a position that transcends those of the mainstream of world literature or ethnonational literatures is intimately connected to the postcolonial creole-related work (e.g., that of Patrick Chamoiseau and Maryse Condé, among others) and multilingual culture research that is particularly notable in Francophone studies.

Much like the works described above however, this volume too fails to deal clearly with the relationship between these non-normative literary texts and a national literature that is presumed to make up the normative form. Even as Tsuchiya claims that these "peripheral 'minor literatures' enrich the legacy of the various ethnonational literatures," with which they bear a relation, he also sees the non-normative authors and works as being Other to normative ones: "just as has been done with the excellent authors and works that have made up the ethnonational literatures, so too must attention be paid to the excellent authors and works of border-crossing literatues."[62]

The problem with using *Nihongo bungaku*—or any of these rubrics for that matter—alongside the ethnonational rubric of *Nihon bungaku* is that the former then establishes non-normative subjects who participate contingently (and peripherally) in the latter cultural totality, which it reserves for normative subjects who supposedly participate in it organically.[63] In so doing, it elides the contingent (or constructed) ways in which any writing subject participates in the imagined totality and solidly historical (rather than epistemologically inevitable) construct of *Nihon bungaku*.[64] It is not sufficient, however, to merely use the non-normative literary texts to challenge or deconstruct the notion of *Nihon bungaku* if the result is a new ahistorical conception with slightly modified contents. Instead, an examination of the history of that concept's construction, ideological function, and material ramifications is essential, with a mind to the positionality of its writers, readers, and critics.[65] As will be discussed in the conclusion, the current study is no exception.

6

Conclusions

To a discomforting extent, this study itself participates in a sort of colonial logic, instrumentalizing and objectifying the Japanese-language literary activities of Brazil in order to speak to a concern—national literature—that historically has been and might logically tend to be dominated by a metropolitan perspective.[1] It is essential to note, therefore, that prior to the Second World War, critics, readers, and writers in Brazil themselves participated in this debate, and were not lacking reflexivity. Though they rarely employed the rhetoric of "Japanese literature" and perhaps never employed the rhetoric of "Japanese-language literature" to discuss the works they produced in the aggregate, this is not to say that they ignored the issue of categorical rubrics. In fact, during the course of the more than a century that the community has existed, within it individuals have debated, adopted, created, and employed multiple alternative rubrics in ways that often structured the discursive environments in which the texts were both read and written.

When the *Burajiru jihō* announced in January 1932 that it would be bestowing a Colonial Literary Short Fiction Award, this was not the first time that such works had been thought of not only in the aggregate, but also as distinct from other literary works written in Japanese.[2] As we have seen, works produced in the colonies were not new in 1932, nor was the contest the first time that the newspaper had taken an active role in trying to encourage local literary production. In April 1922, for example, the newspaper called for reader submissions of various types, including essays on the problem of educating children, plans for encouraging youth groups, the experiences of farmers, poetry in *tanka* and *haiku* forms (on "tasteful material found in Brazil") and short fiction "whose subject matter is the lives of Japanese in Brazil."[3] More importantly for our discussion, the specific rubric of "colonial literature" (植民文藝) was already in circulation there when the newspaper adopted it.

According to Hosokawa Shūhei, a version of the term first appeared in print in Brazil in the 8 August 1925 issue of the *Seishū shinpō* newspaper in an article by its founder, Kōyama Rokurō (writing under the name K-sei). Titled "Nihon ishokumin bungei wo okosu," the article begins with the following weighty pronouncement:

> Buddhism has its sutras; Christianity has the Bible. England has Robinson Crusoe, which whet Englishmen's appetite for adventures at sea; Japan has the *Man'yōshū* and many other books that have nurtured the great Yamato race to this day, but it does not yet have a representative work of the Japanese race's expansion overseas. That is as it should be. It is likely because it must be led by those of us in Brazil.

As Hosokawa notes, in Kōyama's mind the primary function of such a literature would be "to preserve a record of the lives and feelings" of this first generation of Japanese settlers overseas.[4] What is most important to us here, however, is that Kōyama imagined this literature as a part of a specific continuum: the literary culture of the great Yamato (Japanese) race. He believed that the literature of the Japanese colonists requires its own unique name, and he wanted his fellow settlers in Brazil to be "the first Japanese colonists to have culture." Though he does not make clear how he saw the relationship of that culture to the one he imagined the land of his birth to possess, it seems likely that he believed the former to be a subset, or an expansion, of the latter. At the very least, the precise logic of the concept remained ambiguous. This can be seen in an article that appeared four years later, in July 1929, when someone calling themselves Harada wrote an article expressing confusion about to what precisely the term refers.[5] While this shows that the concept was in circulation, it also reflects its unstable referent.

"Colonial literature" (presented as either 植民文芸 or 植民地文芸) was a key categorical rubric that was actively debated and discussed by intellectuals in Brazil.[6] The 1932 award was part of a larger discourse that took place in Brazil from the late 1920s and continued throughout the 1930s.[7] The focus of the award's selection committee aligned with that of essays written in Brazil and appearing in the pages of the newspaper from as early as 1929, which called for a literature suited to the new world being created by *shokuminsha* (植民者, colonists) and *iminsha* (移民者, migrants), a literature stemming from the feelings and experiences characteristic of this community. An early definition of the term came from Imai Hakuhō in 1930: "[A]rtistic expression stemming from all areas of the lives lived by pioneers themselves and beautiful expressions of their natural observations. Put differently, it must at least be a literature built on the great nature of Brazil—as great as eternity itself; a literature that is both a record of the pioneers' precious experiences and an idealistic expression toward the future; and a literature with a rich colonial hue."[8] Critics took various positions on the concept; some of the primary examples are provided below. What all of their positions share, however, is an implicit belief that the received rubric of Japanese literature was inappropriate or insufficient for the works their community had produced and would go on to produce.

An early example appeared in 1931, when the author Kita Nansei implored his brethren (同胞) who had made new lives in Brazil not to be satisfied with imitating the homeland (故国) but instead to develop a literature rooted in their lives in the colony (植民地).[9] Throughout the article Nansei invoked a "we" (吾等) whose referent is limited to the residents of the colonies. Although he did not employ the term "colonial literature," he clearly imagined a textual identity aggregating the literary production of the colonies as distinct from that of Japan. As he wrote after conceding that the claim might be a bit excessive (囈語), "The literature of Japan . . . is no longer our literature."[10] In response to this situation, Nansei developed—over the course of three subsequent articles—an argument for the adoption of a separate focus for the literature of the colony in Brazil: peasant literature (農民文学).[11] His conception of peasant literature—a notion that Nansei was aware was also in circulation in Japan at the time—resembled proletarian literature in its motivation but differed in its nature. Nansei lamented the absence of anything that he believed should truly be called *shokumin bungei* (植民文芸) or *iminchi bungaku* (移民地文学), finding the local production thus far dominated by works of imitation and amusement, and exhorted his fellow colonists to begin "truly" producing literature. Such fiction must have, Nansei argued, an intimate connection to the lives of those in the colony (*shokuminchi*), to the special existence of individuals who lived under the rule of a sovereign country but who remained foreigners. This fact—that they were an "inassimilable people" (同化せざる国民; presented in quotes in the original)—made them a unique society, and forced them to determine what sort of literature they must have. What that literature would be is unclear; for Nansei, however, it would not be (what he considered) the strange stories of corruption, indulgence, and self-deception that dominated the Japanese literary establishment (文壇).

An article that appeared in the following year, 1932, both shows the flexibility of the terminology concerning the colony and the underlying sense that the ethnic community in Brazil was growing ever more distinct from the home country.[12] The pseudonymous author attempted to distinguish the community in Brazil from those in the formal colonies, making the point that the society of his fellow countrymen in Brazil was "not, strictly speaking, a colony," and noting that its special circumstances were causing the society of Japanese in Brazil to grow more independent of the "motherland" year by year. In Brazil, the "two-dimensional" society of sojourners was transforming into a "three-dimensional" one of permanent residents; that is, it was developing its own culture. Literature, as part of this new culture "shaped and tinged with the particular hue of the colony itself," would lead this new society in the right direction.

Sugi Takeo, an active critic as well as writer, joined the debate in 1934. In a series of articles titled "The Establishment of a Literature of the Colonies" (植民地文学の確立) Sugi calls for a literature firmly rooted in reality, the reality of the colony, not in the ideals of literature coming out of Japan.[13] To this society, works of literature from Japan—and the local pieces that mimicked them—seemed to be "the dreams of madmen."[14] He saw the demand for literature as a sign of its importance to the community, but lamented that everyone turned to works from Japan, to which (he believed) they were drawn because of the works' corrupt nature. The desires of the colonists—the emotions born of the atmosphere of Brazil and the colony—had not yet been accessed by local literature. Praise of the moon and stars meant nothing here, Sugi argued, where money dominates; a true *shokuminchi* literature must probe this, without sentimentality. Sugi's identification of these texts with those of the formal colonies becomes clear with his note that such a literature had appeared in Korea, making it lamentable that the same could not be said in Brazil.

The next year Sugi returned to the topic in an article titled "On Colonial Literature" (植民文学について).[15] In it, he argued that literature that emerges from lived reality, that is not a mere product of fantasy, necessarily differs depending on the society that produces it. He laid out a vision of a colonial literature that would take a hard look at economic structure and social system, which Sugi argued were the foundations of the ideology of the colonies. The authors of colonial literature must do this in order to expose reality, which so many are so unwilling to confront.

Ikeda Shigeji responded to Sugi in a number of articles on the topic. In his two-part "The Ideology of Colonial Literature" (植民文学のイデオロギー), Ikeda argued that a colonial literature must take up neither the class-conscious worldview of proletarian literature, nor the narrow worldview of bourgeois literature.[16] Human consciousness in the colonies, Ikeda argued, was not formed through class conflict, but through the desire to conquer nature. *Shokumin* literature, therefore, must be imbued with this ideology. He noted that peasant literature movements had appeared in a variety of countries, including Japan, but had, for various reasons, failed. *Shokumin* literature, written in "the language of the [home] country" (邦文), must grasp the specific nature of this society. Two months later, Ikeda continued his discussion in a separate series of four additional articles.[17] These praised the organization of the literary world in the colony: "It is thrilling to see this first step by the society of our countrymen [in Brazil], which has focused solely on economics, toward a society of spiritual living."[18]

While Sugi and Ikeda considered themselves to share diametrically opposed viewpoints on colonial literature based on whether it ought to be autonomous or not, what they shared was a view that such a literature existed, and that it had an important function to play in the development of the "society" of individuals of Japanese descent in Brazil. A few preliminary observations can be made about this discourse as a whole, despite the fact that individual positions differed. The first observation concerns the use of conventional deictic terms for identity, and the underlying logic of identification that those terms suggest. It is far more common to see references to *dōhō* (同胞, brethren) and *hōjin* (邦人, countrymen)—or even "we," used in explicit contrast to the population of Japan—than the proper noun *Nihonjin* when referring to the colonists.[19] The use of these deictic terms is not in itself noteworthy; it does, however, highlight the fact that the writers considered the referent absolutely clear. These were writers who premised their discussion on a shared identity with their readers. This identity, however, would appear to be based on something that either precedes the state (presumably "race") or succeeds the state ("our colonial society" [我等の植民社会]), as identification with the contemporary polity in Japan seems to be consciously avoided. Given this, the use of the commonplace term *hōbun* might suggest a notion of the language as detached from the state. At minimum, it is clear that the critics presume a fundamental autonomy of the colony from the Japanese nation-state.

The assertion of autonomy (or difference) seems to bear a resemblance to the "reactive notion of authenticity in the form of cultural nationalism" that often marks a minor culture's reaction to a major culture; what differs, however, is the absence of an overt call to tradition or essence, which is often central to cultural nationalism.[20] This seems inevitable given the shallow history of the community; yet one might argue that an incipient tradition-building process was underway, as the critics identify situational contexts that would (in their minds) inevitably lead to differentiation. A majority of the critics share scorn for (what they believe to be) the materialistic nature of their society in Brazil and see literature as offering a solution to this problem. Sympathy for the proletarian literature movement is common, but so is the belief that such literature would be inappropriate in the colony, if for no other reason than the centrality of agriculture (rather than industry) there. The writers take pride in their own grittiness, not just the robust vigor of people who survive through hard physical labor, but also the raw directness of their lifestyles. Even as there are calls for spiritual development, there are also gestures to embrace the visceral side of colonial life as part of what makes it unique.

Finally, the implicit foundation upon which all of these essays rest is a commitment to colonial society. Simply by writing these treatises, the authors present the colony as something lasting, as something that can develop, improve. As Hosokawa Shūhei points out, almost all the essays saw literature as "a spiritual and cultural undertaking" that could benefit the entire community of settlers.[21] As such, they presented colonial literature—even if just the ideal of colonial literature—as something worthy of attention and effort. This simple fact suggests a shift, from sojourners who are biding their time before they can return to their homes, to settlers who have begun a process of re-identification.

With regard to textual identity, the discourse of textual interrelation known as "modern Japanese literature" seems here primarily to be an object of either tacit or explicit disavowal. This is despite the fact that, given the significant marketplace, texts from Japan would have continued to be significant influences on these writers and critics. They perceived their literature to be one that would be fundamentally different, arising from the particular conditions of their existence and responding to the particular needs of their lives. At the same time, there was a suggestion of filiation with—if not outright participation in—a textual identity that existed outside of Brazil: the colonial literature of the various quarters of the Japanese empire.

They also shared experiences with other Japanese diasporic subjects in the Western Hemisphere, racism primary among these. Although Japanese immigrants to Brazil may have faced less discrimination than their counterparts in the United States, resistance to these communities did exist. In addition to arguments about racial inferiority, the issue of "assimilability" arose repeatedly. The most conservative elements in the Brazilian government even argued that immigration was a prelude to military invasion. Around 1938, the Japanese government began to consider its direct involvement in the colony to be a liability, particularly in light of growing nationalist sentiment in Brazil.[22] The result was rapid divestment. For example, the colonization company behind the creation and management of the Bastos colony liquidated nearly all of its holdings by April 1939, handing over control of the colony to a cooperative made up of its residents. With the declaration of war in December 1941, the semi-governmental companies behind the colonies in Brazil were forced to liquidate their remaining holdings. Deprived of all formal links with Japan, and thus the support and protection that had helped them persist, these ethnic enclaves changed rapidly. Japanese-language schools were closed in December 1938 and Japanese-language newspapers were outlawed in August 1941. On 19 January 1942, the state of São Paulo banned the distribution of Japanese-language texts and the use of Japanese in public.[23]

These developments, the isolation of the War itself, and the near-silence from Japan during its immediate postwar reconstruction dramatically accelerated the process of acculturation.[24] Although Japanese-language newspapers were re-legalized immediately after the war and emigration began again in 1953, the connection with Japan was never the same.[25] Today the migratory flow, in fact, has almost entirely reversed, with young Brazilians of Japanese descent moving to Japan for work. Japanese-language literature continues to be produced in Brazil and efforts are ongoing, though limited, to preserve the literary legacy of Japanese-language texts in the country. Nearly all of the individuals involved in that process, however, are aging first-generation immigrants who, for the most part, see themselves as custodians of a dying art.

Throughout the postwar period, the Koronia Bungakukai and its subsequent incarnations, including today's Burajiru Nikkei Bungakukai (ブラジル日系文学会) have been the key agents in preserving the Japanese-language literary tradition in Brazil. The shifting names of the organizations hint at alternative collective rubrics that have been claimed over the course of the postwar period. The Koronia Bungakukai began with twenty-six members in October 1965 in order to support Japanese-language literary activities in Brazil; it launched its journal, Koronia bungaku (コロニア文学), in May of the following year. That journal ran for thirty issues, until October 1976. The Koronia Bungakukai shut down in 1977 but was restarted in 1979 as the Koronia Shibungakukai (*Associação dos Poetas e Escritores da Colônia*) by Takemoto Yoshio. That organization published *Koronia shibungaku* (コロニア詩文学), which ran for sixty issues from September 1980 until October 1998. In February 1999, the association changed its name to the Burajiru Nikkei Bungakukai, which still publishes its journal *Burajiru Nikkei bungaku*.[26]

What marks these efforts to perpetuate this "minority literature" in (but not necessarily of) Brazil for the dwindling market of Japanese-language readers in the country, who are now vastly outnumbered by Portuguese-speaking Brazilians of Japanese descent, has been their local focus. Groups have made few efforts to reach any potential readership in Japan, focusing instead on the shrinking readership in Brazil.[27] As a result these activities become a fascinating, but likely doomed, experiment in discovering the minimal size of a reading community necessary to maintain literary activities, particularly in prose.

NAMING COLLECTIONS OF TEXTS

So, what are these texts, when thought of collectively? Are they colonial literature? Given that individuals involved in their creation called them that, one is obligated to take such a designation seriously. Yet, as we have seen, individuals involved in the production of Japanese-language literary texts in Brazil did not entirely agree on that matter (or at least on the details) when they debated it, nor did their successors find those early rubrics satisfactory. This is why other names, such as *colonia* literature and Brazilian Nikkei literature, have been used. The leading scholar on these literary texts in Japan, Hosokawa Shūhei, named them "Nikkei Brazilian migrant literature," consciously or unconsciously reversing the primacy of ethnos and place. His predecessor, Maeyama Takashi, referred to it as a "minority literature" in Brazil, which prefigured the work of recent scholars such as Ignacio López-Calvo, who reads Portuguese-language literary works by this community within the context of Brazilian literary production.[28] They could just as easily be brought into a discourse on multilingual Brazilian literature, in the vein of Marc Shell and Werner Sollors's *Multilingual Anthology of American Literature*.[29]

As for seeing it as "colonial literature," we still face the problem the author Shōken-sei identified in 1932—that Brazil was never a formal colony of the Empire of Japan—making it potentially misleading to simply refer to the texts as colonial literature. What nomenclature could differentiate these communities from the "formal" colonies of the Japanese empire? Shu-mei Shih has used "semicolonialism" to "foreground the multiple, layered, intensified, as well as incomplete and fragmentary nature of China's colonial structure," noting that it should not be taken to denote a "half," but rather the "fractured, informal, and indirect character" of the colonialism that existed in China at that time.[30] While this term could conceivably be adapted to describe the situation in Brazil, one might further distinguish it, at the risk of an awkward profusion of terms, as "paracolonial." The goal of this term would be to stress homologies and simultaneity, while also bringing into relief the contemporary perceptions among its practitioners of a relation to literatures produced under formal imperialism; at the same time, the term would identify these activities in Brazil as being distinct from—literally, "alongside"—the formal colonies.

Yet it also might be productive—as a result of being more provocative— to consider these works (and perhaps even the post-World War II production) to be colonial literature, sans distinction, working from the insights gained through postcolonial and world systems theory.[31] Such an approach would stress the ways in which this Japanese-language literary production in Brazil remains within an asymmetrical power relation that is partially a result of its position in a history of imperial expansion and colonial subordination, but is also partially a result of a contemporary world system that continues to render peripheries (variously defined) subordinate to metropoles in far more fluid and complex relationships. Perhaps the use of *Nihongo bungaku* while maintaining *Nihon bungaku* for texts produced with the normative model of national literary production achieves this. Such a model of the global economy can be applied to literary production both as a metaphor for and as a concrete description of the marketplaces within which literary commodities circulate.[32]

As the Japanese-reading population of Brazil declines precipitously in the absence of continued immigration from Japan—a condition that results from continuing economic asymmetries between Japan and Brazil—the writers of Japanese-language literature no longer find themselves in the same position as the critics from the 1930s mentioned above concerning writing as a sociocultural institution. The attitude of development marking the 1930s, when the future for Japanese-language literature in Brazil looked bright and writers and critics actively debated the direction it should take, differs dramatically from the attitude of res- ignation during the postwar phase, when migration has all but stopped and a defensive posture has been struck, in which the few remaining writers struggle to preserve and perpetuate the social potential for their literary activities. All textual identities, by definition, imply an informing past; most (if not all) also imply an informable future that must extend beyond the individual writer. Literature is, after all, a social activity, even though its production and consumption are so often imagined to be solitary. This need for literature to be a social activity is doubly important for writers without independent means, who require a minimum audi- ence/market in order to have their books printed, let alone to receive sufficient material gain to survive.

To subsume these texts into the discourse of "modern Japanese literature"— a move metonymically related to Spivak's "strategic essentialism"—might bring material benefits: it would invest a large number of readers in the literary products of this community in Brazil, allowing it to survive—in the absence of a sufficient local market—through a dependence on a "foreign" metropole, which possesses a

market of Japanese-language readers of sufficient size to sustain literary production. This would not merely be a process in which a text "becomes a commodity
whose difference is contained and consumed by those with purchasing power."[33]
Such an incorporation, even as it threatens to erase (through assimilation into
a notion of ethnocultural homogeneity) or to exoticize (through an ambivalent
application of "stranger [self] fetishism") the specificity of the texts' origins as well
as the heterogeneity of the texts' authors, would give them an audience that they
do not yet enjoy, one which might enable their continued existence. Sometimes
material realities are too readily dismissed in the search for artistic autonomy.
Even as this new marketplace might provide writers with readers—the essential
social component of the art of literature—it also provides writers with consumers,
an oft-dismissed necessity for any artist lacking the material means to support his
or her avocation.

Such materialist and instrumental considerations may seem impossibly vulgar,
missing the "true" value of literature. The motivation for focusing here on this
sort of strategic textual identification is twofold. On the one hand, it highlights
the social and historical dimensions of literary production—dimensions that, in
a capitalist economy, invariably involve commodification, whether the texts be
"pure" or "popular." On the other hand, it highlights the partial and artificial nature
of any collective identification of texts, be it national, linguistic, ethnocultural, or
regional. Simultaneously, it reminds us that the scholar is not a detached observer
of this situation; simply by raising the issue in certain institutional forums, one
draws these texts and their producers into a discourse that has particular ramifications. This raises a follow-up question. Rather than asking what identity (or
identities) should be attributed to these texts, one should ask what the ramifications are of one identification over another, when multiple choices are potentially
justifiable, but none can encapsulate every facet of even a single literary text.

Additionally, it raises the question of motivation: why name a given collection
of texts in the first place? Such a collective identification is not, after all, necessary,
nor is there a single, self-evident, overriding essence within a text from which
such an identification must be derived. To the extent that such an identification
might derive from characteristics of the text, it does so through contingent selection of certain characteristics and inevitable discounting of others. Nor is the act
of collective identification necessarily disinterested in its motivation or apolitical
in its effects. National literatures may be justifications for nations even as nations
are justifications for national literatures. In this, as in all things, "modern Japanese
literature" might be particular in its specificities, but it is not unique, and the production of these texts in Brazil is not an aberration, but merely an historically contingent event. It is not the deviation from the norm that should attract our interest
so much as the powerful disciplining function of the normative itself.

Less than it is one for the actual writers and readers of literature, this is particularly an issue for scholars, critics, historians, and—at the extremes—even political

actors, who are more likely to be engaged in a discourse of collective identity than the writers and readers we imagine to be central to the intimate act of literary exchange. Moreover, what is at stake in such discourses of literary identity is of course more than a heuristic rubric, precisely because the ultimate goal of such discourses is often actually the definition of the other elements of the holy quandrinity of the national literary imaginary. After all, more often than not, texts are defined collectively based on a community (for example, "modern Japanese literature") because of a desire to define (as Self or Other) that community ("Japan") and the living individuals ("the Japanese") who make it up, rather than because one wishes to illuminate individual literary texts.

The metadiscourse of categorically defining literary texts, then, is ultimately participating in a much broader epistemological management of the world and its inhabitants than the seemingly innocent act might suggest. It treats as ontological a question that is in fact better treated as not only epistemological, but political. This can of course be done consciously and transparently, with either progressive or reactionary political ends in mind. All too often, however, it is done as a conventional reflex, without the transparency, awareness of historicity, and care that it deserves. Lacking these, one risks reinforcing unwittingly a political agenda whose ultimate objective might not be the illumination of literary texts, but the mobilization of the power of a collectively imagined self against a configured, collectively defined Other. The application of literature to such a project misses one of the two paradoxical but wonderful capacities of literary texts: to limn individuals simultaneously in both their commensurability and their incommensurability, their identity and alterity.

NOTES

1. INTRODUCTION

1. See Mack, *Manufacturing Modern Japanese Literature.*

2. The concept of a "community" will be used as a heuristic within this book to refer to a notional group of individuals, whether of potential readers of a given text or texts, or of the population of individuals of Japanese descent. It should not be taken as a claim that such a community existed with some sort of functional intimacy, nor that its existence would be inevitable.

3. The story, "Sōbō," appears in English translation as "The Emigrants" in *The East* 21, no. 4 (1985): 62–70; no. 5 (1985): 64–70; no. 6 (1985): 62–70; and 22, no. 1 (1986): 58–65. Today, *Sōbō* (蒼氓) usually refers to a collection of three works: "Sōbō," as it appeared in *Seiza*; "Nankai kōro" (南海航路), which was published in the July 1939 issue of *Chōhen bunko* (長篇文庫); and "Koenaki tami" (声無き民), which appeared in the August 1939 issue of *Chōhen bunko*. In addition, "Sōbō" was significantly revised from its initial publication in the pages of *Seiza*; see Aoki, *Ishikawa Tatsuzō kenkyū*, 309–76 for more on these changes.

4. Ishikawa, *Kokoro ni nokoru hitobito* 51.

5. Only one piece of evidence links "Sonobe Takeo" with Inoue Tetsurō. As cited in Hosokawa, *Nikkei Burajiru imin bungaku*, 2:118n21, Masuda Hidekazu states that Sonobe Takeo was the pen name for Inoue. (See Masuda, *Emeboi jisshūjō-shi*, 227–29). Masuda does seem quite certain about his attribution, however, going so far as to address past confusion about the author's true identity.

6. The 9 July 1931 evening edition of the *Tokyo Asahi shinbun*, page 2, describes how Inoue, one of thirty-two individuals selected from all over Japan, had been taken on official visits to the Meiji Shrine, the Imperial Palace, the Gaimushō, and the Takumushō before heading to Kobe on July 8. The M'boy (later Embu; an area on the outskirts of São Paulo) agricultural training center (Instituto de Prática Agrícola de São Paulo) was founded in 1931

by the KKKK to train Japanese immigrants and formally opened in 1932. The first class of thirty-two students graduated in August 1934. *Nenpyō* 68, 70, and 78. One Inoue Tetsurō (井上哲郎) departed Japan on 14 July 1931 on the *La Plata Maru*, arriving in Brazil on 29 August.

7. *Burajiru jihō*, 21 April 1932.

8. For more on this journal and related literary activities, see Masuda, *Emeboi jisshūjō-shi*, 207–32. I am not sure how the name of this journal should be read, so I have followed convention and used the *on-yomi* of the two characters. It is possible that it should be read as *Nandi* or *Nandin*, Shiva's gate guardian bull, as these are the characters used to represent the name in Chinese.

9. Inoue, *Bapa jango*, 276. It should be noted that *Bapa jango* does not make reference to time spent in Brazil.

10. Hosokawa, *Nikkei Burajiru imin bungaku*, 2:100.

11. *Yomiuri shinbun*, 8 June 1952, morning edition, page 3.

12. Inoue, "Nihonjin Taazan shimatsuki" and *Bapa jango*.

13. I am following the selections by Takahashi Haruo and the other editors of Usui, *Sengo bungaku ronsō*, ge, 109–89.

14. Yamamoto Kenkichi, "Kokudo, kokugo, kokumin: kokumin bungaku nit suite no oboegaki," as reprinted in Usui, 123–29.

15. Komori, <*Yuragi*> *no Nihon bungaku*, 6. A similar formulation was identified by Harumi Befu in *Ideorogii to shite no Nihon bunkaron*. Although the Japanese term 国家 only refers to a state (rather than a nation-state, or 国民国家), I will use the term nation-state when my goal is to stress this imagination of the state being based in this amalgam. I do not believe that the sequence of the elements within the amalgam is relevant, so it may be presented in different order elsewhere in this text. Finally, other terms in the amalgam may vary to identify related but not identical concepts (such as "territory" for "state") when those are pertinent to the discussion. Such variation seems reasonable to me, as my goal is not to make an affirmative claim as to what "Japaneseness" actually *is*, but rather to identify what it has been *thought to be*, either implicitly or explicitly.

16. Sakai, *Shizan sareru Nihongo, Nihonjin* and *Translation & Subjectivity*.

17. Just as the concepts of "center" and "periphery" highlight the slippery notion of positionality vis-à-vis power, "production" and "consumption" are used here as broad heuristics, including both publishing and writing for the former and both purchasing and reading for the latter, but are not meant to suggest that these two acts are ever fully distinct in practice.

18. For readability purposes, the word "Japanese" will be used in this text to refer to individuals who identify as, or are identified as, "Japanese," though this should not be taken as an uncritical reproduction of an essentialist notion of an ethnos.

19. Lowe, *The Intimacies of Four Continents*, 138, 137.

2. THE STATE: LIVRARIA YENDO AND JAPANESE-LANGUAGE READERS IN BRAZIL

1. Suzuki, *The Japanese Immigrant in Brazil*, 15. Suzuki contrasts this "Brazilian period" with the "Hawaii period" that preceded it (1885–1923), when that kingdom/republic/territory received 46.6 percent of the total, and the Manchuria period (1935–45), when the puppet state of Manchukuo received 85 percent of the total.

2. There is some debate about the population of persons of Japanese descent in Brazil. The 2010 United States census saw a little more than 1.3 million people claim full- or partial-Japanese descent; the Instituto Brasileiro de Geografia e Estatística (Brazilian Institute of Geography and Statistics, or IBGE), on the other hand, reported that 1.6 million Japanese Brazilians were living in Brazil at the close of 2008.

3. Here the link between state and territory—two distinct concepts—is blurred to emphasize not only the overlapping notion of politically determined national borders, but also the coterminous spaces implied and the practical ways that movement within those spaces is facilitated.

4. For more on emigration of Japanese citizens to the Western Hemisphere, see Kikumura-Yano, *Encyclopedia of Japanese Descendants in the Americas*, which not only contains a concise overview by Eiichiro Azuma (32–48), but also annotated bibliographies of scholarship in English, Spanish, Portuguese, and Japanese. For an overview of immigration into Brazil, see Lesser, *Immigration, Ethnicity, and National Identity in Brazil*. By the eve of World War II, more than one million Japanese had migrated to thirty-five different countries; see Nihon Imin Hachijū Nenshi Hensan Iinkai, ed., *Burajiru Nihon imin 80-nenshi*, 28 (henceforth, *80-nenshi*).

5. Akira Iriye stresses the important continuum between the formal colonial projects of the Japanese state and its sponsorship of broad emigration, arguing that during the early years of Japanese expansion the distinction between emigration and formal colonization was often ambiguous. He writes, "'Peaceful expansionism' did not simply mean the passive emigration of individual Japanese, but could imply a government-sponsored, active program of overseas settlement and positive activities to tie distant lands closer to Japan" (*Pacific Estrangement*, 131).

6. Tsuchida, "The Japanese in Brazil," 332n66. While I have consulted other sources in order to verify Tsuchida's assertions, and have provided citations to other sources when relevant, I treat his work as the most reliable (and consistently documented) source available.

7. See Eiichiro Azuma, "Historical Overview of Japanese Emigration, 1868–2000," in Kikumura-Yano, *Encyclopedia of Japanese Descendants in the Americas*, 32.

8. Tsuchida, "The Japanese in Brazil," 27, 62, 68.

9. Tsuchida, "The Japanese in Brazil," 8, 17–18; Suzuki, *The Japanese Immigrant in Brazil* 12.

10. Tsuchida, "The Japanese in Brazil," 18, 22. In so doing, Italy joined a growing list of countries that had begun to block emigration to Brazil, including Germany, France, Australia, Hungary, Sweden, and Norway, among others; see *80-nenshi*, 33. The Decree brought subsidies to an end, though non-subsidized immigration to Brazil from Italy was allowed to continue.

11. *80-nenshi*, 34.

12. Tsuchida, "The Japanese in Brazil," 89. Tsuchida refers to a São Paulo Immigration and Colonization Company (SPICC); in Japanese translations of the relevant documents, it is referred to as the San Pauro-shū Imin Kaisha (サンパウロ州移民会社).

13. Tsuchida, "The Japanese in Brazil," 119–20. The Official Agency of Colonization and Labor (Agência Oficial de Colonização e Trabalho) was formed to oversee contracts and subsidies provided by the SPICC. See Decree number 1355 (10 April 1906) of the state of São Paulo, referencing article 39 of law 984, passed 29 December 1905.

14. As a noun, "Paulista" (m., f.) refers to a person from the state of São Paulo, while "Paulistano" (m.) and "Paulistana" (f.) refer to individuals from the city of São Paulo.

15. The subvention was for six British pounds for immigrants over the age of twelve, three pounds for those between seven and twelve, and one pound, ten shillings for those between three and seven; see Tsuchida, "The Japanese in Brazil," 123–24. Tsuchida states that the ten-pound subsidy was worth ¥100, though emigrants had to repay ¥40 to the employer (136). He continues that Kasato-maru migrants had total expenses amounting to ¥155, which exceeded "a Japanese farm hand's three-year income" (137). The adult fare of passage alone was ¥165, and this did not even cover the full costs (138).

16. Individual immigrants had arrived prior to this time, though perhaps no more than two dozen in number. The *Kasato-maru* group was made up of 781 individuals, 601 males and 180 females; in addition, twelve individuals came as regular passengers (see Tsuchida, "The Japanese in Brazil," 134, and Handa, *Burajiru Nihon imin Nikkei shakai-shi nenpyō*, 27 [henceforth, *Nenpyō*]). The *80-nenshi* addresses variances in the number of passengers listed in various source materials (36).

17. Tsuchida, "The Japanese in Brazil," 134–35; *80-nenshi*, 89.

18. See Tsuchida, "The Japanese in Brazil," 132–55, for details.

19. Nishida, *Diaspora and Identity*, 21.

20. Tsuchida, "The Japanese in Brazil," 157, 160–61, 164. *Nenpyō* (29) has Takemura bringing 7630 individuals in five groups between 1910–14 and Oriental bringing 6500 individuals in four groups between 1912–14.

21. Only between 74 and 230 new immigrants arrived during these years (Tsuchida, "The Japanese in Brazil," 165–68). The total number of new migrants varies depending on the sources; Tsuchida explains reasons for the discrepancies (167–68).

22. From an interview with Mario Yendo, held at his family's home in São Paulo, 23 June 2005 and 27 June 2005. According to Brazilian immigration documents, he was born on 24 January 1890; according to *Nenpyō* (141), he died on 16 April 1961. Unrestricted passengers (自由渡航者) traveled on the same ships as the contract laborers from the beginning; see *80-nenshi*, 35.

23. Endoh, *Exporting Japan*, 4.

24. *80-nenshi*, 90.

25. Toake Endoh writes, "Japan's emigration policy towards Latin America assumed a similar function as a political safety valve—selectively relocating the seeds of potential social ills overseas via government-sponsored emigration—at a crisis moment for the polity and nation" (*Exporting Japan*, 7).

26. Castles, de Haas, and Miller, *The Age of Migration*, 39–41.

27. *80-nenshi*, 90. Mainland Japanese thought that Okinawans were too ready to disrobe in public, spoke with strong regional dialects, and caused disruption by their predilection to keep to themselves. As the editors of the history point out, though, these criticisms mirrored those made by many Brazilians about the Japanese immigrants as a whole.

28. Tsuchida, "The Japanese in Brazil," 179–84. There were a number of additional arrangements that were possible: they could become *meeiros* (sharecroppers), contract farmers (*sitiantes* engaged in *agricultura por contrato*), or *arrendatários* (lease farmers).

29. Tsuchida, "The Japanese in Brazil," 131.

30. *Nenpyō*, 30.

31. Tsuchida, "The Japanese in Brazil," 131–32. *80-nenshi* (87) has them stopping in 1921. According to Tsuchida, aid from the state of São Paulo continued until 1922 (176–77).

Nenpyō, however, explains that the aid planned for immigrants in 1922 was actually cancelled (47).

32. The Society's function was to coordinate emigration from Japan to Brazil. See Tsuchida, "The Japanese in Brazil," 172.

33. The Overseas Development Company had been established in 1917 (Tsuchida, "The Japanese in Brazil," 174). The Imperial Emigration Company (皇国殖民会社), mentioned earlier, was another of the companies joined to form the Overseas Development Company.

34. *Nihon teikoku tōkei nenkan* 37, p. 71. These statistics claim that only 1378 of these individuals lived in the state of São Paulo; it seems likely this is a mistake, and that the statistic is in fact for the city of São Paulo.

35. Tsuchida, "The Japanese in Brazil," 177. Certain limited support was provided from Japan in 1923; see *80-nenshi*, 87. *Nenpyō* (54) and *80-nenshi* (87) both have the first year of subsidies from the Japanese government beginning in 1925.

36. Tsuchida, "The Japanese in Brazil," 174.

37. *Nihon teikoku tōkei nenkan* 44, p. 74. The term "inner territories" was used to distinguish the main islands of Japan from the "outer territories" (外地), or colonial holdings, of Japan.

38. Tsuchida "The Japanese in Brazil," 82, 223, 227.

39. Tsuchida, "The Japanese in Brazil," 82, 223, 227.

40. *80-nenshi*, 51–52.

41. Tsuchida, "The Japanese in Brazil," 186.

42. *80-nenshi* (87) clarifies that this company should not be confused with the Bratac that is established in 1929.

43. Tsuchida, "The Japanese in Brazil," 192 and 194.

44. *80-nenshi*, 51–52. Though their origins and the specific functioning of each type of colony differed, this study will treat these large congregations of Japanese citizens under the single rubric of "colonies," though they were not all legally treated as *colônias* in Brazil.

45. *80-nenshi*, 80. Interactions may have been more frequent than are often reported.

46. One example of this sentiment is visible in the attempt to pass the Fidelis Reis Bill, from 1921 until its eventual tabling in 1927. The bill was an attempt to impose immigration quotas on members of the "yellow race," which at the time would have meant almost exclusively immigrants from Japan (see Tsuchida, "The Japanese in Brazil," 208–20). The struggle Tsuchida describes shows that there were large numbers of advocates on both sides of the issue, but that the anti-Japanese contingent was not yet large enough to pass such legislation. Tsuchida concludes that the key difference between the situation in Brazil and that in the United States was not a higher level of tolerance, but instead "the absence of bitter economic competition between the Japanese immigrants and native [sic] Brazilians" (225).

47. *80-nenshi*, 82. The first youth organization was formed in Registro in 1921 (114). Women's organizations (婦人会) were rare (115). By 1940, there were roughly 480 Nihonjinkai throughout Brazil (116). By at least 1923, an umbrella Japanese Association was already in existence, led by Uetsuka Shūhei (53, 59).

48. *80-nenshi* 114, 55, 82.

49. *Rikkō sekai*, 1 May 1921, "Kaigai junkai toshokan shuisho."

50. *80-nenshi*, 38. One source of literacy statistics on 33,000 newly arrived immigrants' (fifteen years of age and older) level of education upon arrival (between the years 1908–1941)

has 0.3 percent illiterate, 0.2 percent with basic literacy but no formal education, 74.2 percent with a primary school education, 22.5 percent with a secondary school education, and 2.8 percent with higher education. See Suzuki, *Burajiru no Nihon imin: Shiryō-hen*, 382–83.

51. For more, see Ebihara, *Kaigai hōji shinbun zasshi-shi*, 224–28, and Aoyagi, *Burajiru ni okeru Nihonjin hattenshi*, ge, 257–69 (henceforth, *Nihonjin hattenshi*).

52. The currency of Brazil until 1942 was the "old" Brazilian *real* (pl. *réis*)—not to be confused with the "modern" Brazilian *real* (pl. *reais*). Prices are often given in *mil-réis* (often abbreviated as *mil*), or thousand *réis*. Larger amounts are sometimes given in *conto de réis* (often abbreviated as *conto*), or million *réis*.

53. Based on an advertisement from 12 November 1913 for Goshadō, which appeared in the *Nichibei shinbun*. The list included newspapers from Korea, Manchuria, and Taiwan. See Hibi, "Nikkei Amerika imin issei no shinbun to bungaku," 23–34.

54. Burajiru Jihōsha also enters the printing business as early as 22 July 1921. By 1932, not only did all of the Japanese-language newspapers have the facilities to print texts in Japanese, but also there were three independent printers in the city of São Paulo alone: São José (サン・ジョゼー), Hakuyūdō (博友堂), and Nihon/Nippon-dō (日本堂). See *80-nenshi*, 131.

55. The advertisement lists the name Suga Heikichi, presumably as the representative of the company who would be doing traveling sales in the area. An individual by this name arrived on 10 May 1914. An advertisement appearing on 8 February 1918 clarifies that Suga is the traveling representative for Endō.

56. Endō Tsunehachirō's personal calling card, which appeared in the *Burajiru jihō* on 1 January 1921, gives his address as Birigui, suggesting that that was now his base of operations; as mentioned above, this is also the city that Endō listed as his place of residence when he entered the United States at the close of 1922. At the same time, when he published his business card in the 7 September 1922 issue of *Burajiru jihō* he gave his base as the city of São Paulo.

57. *Burajiru jihō*, 31 August 1923.

58. It is not until 1928 that he begins advertising that his store "specializes in books." *Burajiru jihō*, 4 March 1927 and 30 August 1928.

59. *Burajiru jihō*, 7 September 1923.

60. *Burajiru jihō*, 13 June 1924.

61. *Burajiru jihō*, 19 December 1924.

62. Prior to 1931 the rates are as published in the *Burajiru jihō* (reported by the Yokohama Specie Bank), whereas the rates from 1931 are from the *Nihon chōki tōkei sōran*, vol. 3 (1988). Some data (November 1918–August 1920 and November 1930) are unavailable.

63. Mack, *Manufacturing Modern Japanese Literature*, 37–39.

64. Kawahara, *Taiwan shinbungaku undō to tenkai*, 260–61, and Hashimoto, *Nihon shuppan hanbai-shi*, 507.

65. The organization's own description of the events can be found in Nihon Rikkōkai, *Rikkō 50 nen*, 108–12.

66. Nagata, "Ijūchi no bunka undō," *Rikkō sekai* 1 February 1921.

67. *Rikkō 50 nen*, 110.

68. *Burajiru jihō*, 13 January 1922.

69. *Rikkō 50 nen* lists the total number of volumes as eleven thousand (111). Other sources give higher quantities.

70. *Burajiru jihō*, 2 December 1921.

71. Before being elevated to Ministry status, the organization had existed as a bureau in the Home Ministry, having been established there in 1910. The organization's roots go even further back, to the Hokkaidō Development Agency (or Colonization Office, 北海道開拓使) created in 1869.

72. Tsuchida, "The Japanese in Brazil," 230–34, 250.

73. Tsuchida, "The Japanese in Brazil," 250–51; *80-nenshi*, 52.

74. *80-nenshi*, 89.

75. Tsuchida, "The Japanese in Brazil," 253.

76. Tsuchida, "The Japanese in Brazil," 271–73.

77. The first coffee price protection plan was instituted in 1906, and the second in 1921. In both cases, the government purchased excess coffee in order to maintain the commodity price. Statistics come from Horibe, *Burajiru kōhii no rekishi*, as cited in *80-nenshi*, 72–73. See *80-nenshi*, 72, for prices 1890–1906; 72–73 for prices 1913–1927. Horibe has the prices on 219, 292, and 325–26.

78. *80-nenshi*, 73–74.

79. *80-nenshi*, 76.

80. Even in 1940 after increased migration to other states, such as Paraná, roughly 94 percent of Japanese citizens in Brazil lived in São Paulo; see *80 nenshi*, 113. Of the 202,211 Japanese in Brazil in 1939, only 4875 lived in the city of São Paulo (127).

81. *80-nenshi*, 67, as reported in the *Burajiru jihō* on 22 June 1928. The specific regions indicated by each of these districts are described in the *80-nenshi*.

82. As cited in Tsuchida, "The Japanese in Brazil," 234. It should be noted that this number exceeds the total number of immigrants from Japan, suggesting that children born of Japanese parents in Brazil (presumably but not necessarily possessing Japanese citizenship) are counted among this number. The term 邦人 ("countrymen," or Japanese) is vague in the relevant chart; other statistics in the same volume use clearer terminology, including explicit references to citizenship. See the 1930 edition of Naikaku Tōkei-kyoku, *Nihon teikoku tōkei nenkan*, 65. Note that some immigrants did naturalize; in 1940, 3830 individuals born in Japan were living in Brazil as naturalized citizens (Tsuchida, 298).

83. Tsuchida, "The Japanese in Brazil," 238.

84. As described in Irie, *Hōjin kaigai hattenshi*, ge, 379–80. See also Tsuchida, "The Japanese in Brazil," 238.

85. Tsuchida, "The Japanese in Brazil," 238–39.

86. *Dai Nihon teikoku tōkei nenkan* 56, p. 74.

87. *80-nenshi*, 85.

88. *80-nenshi*, 70, 95. Another history estimates that 90 percent of them intended only to stay temporarily (134).

89. *80-nenshi*, 113. Tsuchida explores the reasons ("The Japanese in Brazil," 297).

90. *80-nenshi*, 77, 79.

91. *80-nenshi*, 80.

92. Racism led some to fear assimilation as well. In 1921, a Brazilian Congressman said in session that "Under no circumstance, should we be so preoccupied by immediate gains as to prejudice the racial stock through miscegenation by introducing en masse inassimilable, or prejudicially assimilable, ethnic elements. . . ." While acknowledging the contribution Japanese were making to the Brazilian economy, the congressman made it clear that

Japanese immigration would not only disrupt the "bleaching" (*branqueamento*) priorities held by elements in the Brazilian government, but would also introduce a group that was incapable, or nearly incapable, of assimilation. The congressman continued, "Preferring always not to mix, the yellows will remain encysted in the national organism. They are indeed inassimilable by virtue of their blood, language, customs and religion, posing, perhaps, potential danger for the Union, as is the case in California." The congressman claimed that this was done purposefully, with immigration functioning as a component of the Greater Japanese Empire's expansionist plans. Such claims grew as rumors spread, with one Deputy claiming that Japan had territorial ambitions in Brazil and planned to send twenty million immigrants to Brazil. See Tsuchida, "The Japanese in Brazil," 212–17.

93. Tsuchida, "The Japanese in Brazil," 216, 218, 227, 294.

94. It is worth noting that while the ethnic homogeneity of these communities was significant, it was not absolute. While Bastos, for example, was largely populated by first- and second-generation Japanese immigrants, it was not exclusively so; at the end of 1933, its population was made up of 5636 Japanese (邦人) and 397 non-Japanese (伯人その他). See Mizuno, *Basutosu nijūgonen-shi*, 102 (in the PDF version archived in the online Imin Bunko, http://www.brasiliminbunko.com.br). Other colonies possessed even more mixed populations; Iguape, for example, had 4236 Japanese residents and 3590 Brazilian residents in 1932. See Annaka, *Burajiru-koku Iguappe shokuminchi sōritsu nijusshūnen kinen shashinchō*, as cited in Tsuchida, "The Japanese in Brazil," 270.

95. *80-nenshi*, 99; Fausto, *Fazer a América* 231.

96. *Burajiru jihō*, 30 April 1926.

97. Booklending, sales of older issues of magazines, and traveling libraries are only a few of the alternative means to retail sales of new books and magazines that were available in Brazil. For more information on these alternatives, see Mack, "Diasporic Markets," 163–77.

98. *Burajiru jihō*, 5 December 1919, advertisement for Segi Shōten.

99. Tsuchida, "The Japanese in Brazil," 133. The difference in sailing times from Japan to the West Coast of the United States and from Japan to Brazil was significant. Although the journey from Yokohama to Seattle or San Francisco could be completed in roughly two weeks, the journey from Kobe to Santos originally required nearly two months. The Kasato-maru, for example, left Kobe on 28 April 1908 and docked in Santos on June 18; see Endoh, *Exporting Japan*, 28. This was cut down to around forty days by 1925, when the Japanese government made the Ōsaka Shōsen South American route the official route for sending migrants to Brazil (*80-nenshi*, 88). The Panama Canal was not put into operation until 1914, which meant that a Pacific crossing between Japan and Brazil required navigating the Strait of Magellan. Although the Suez Canal was in operation from 1869, and was used for voyages between Japan and Europe, it was not used for voyages between Brazil and Japan. Instead, those voyages made multiple stops along the way, including Hong Kong, Saigon, Colombo, and Cape Town. The fact that the Japanese ships stopped in Cape Town was of key importance to the coffee producers, who counted on this method of shipping coffee there on the ships' return voyages (Tsuchida, 125).

100. *Burajiru jihō*, 4 April 1934.

101. *Burajiru jihō*, 4 March 1927 and 30 August 1928.

102. *Burajiru jihō*, 30 August 1928, and *Nippaku shinbun*, 30 August 1928.

103. *Burajiru jihō*, 19 May 1932.

104. Advertisements would presumably not list titles that were special-ordered by customers (and were therefore not generally available.) These, then, are titles that the bookstore felt might have an audience or that customers decided not to purchase after having
requested them. It seems unlikely that multiple copies of these texts were available, though
it is impossible to say. Titles rarely repeat from one advertisement to the next, suggesting
either reasonably brisk turnover or the presumed ineffectiveness of repeated advertising.

105. Endō Shōten (Shoten) from 13 June 1924 (*Burajiru jihō*) and 18 December 1935
(*Nippaku shinbun*). Half- or full-page advertisements become the norm between 1935–40.

106. *80-nenshi*, 131.

107. These conclusions are drawn from an analysis of more than 1200 titles listed in ten
advertisements between 1924–40: 13 June 1924 (*Burajiru jihō*), 19 December 1924 (*Burajiru
jihō*), 29 August 1934 (*Burajiru jihō*), 18 December 1935 (*Nippaku shinbun*), 21 August 1938
(*Burajiru jihō*), 12 August 1939 (*Burajiru jihō*), 19 August 1939 (*Burajiru jihō*), 16 December
1939 (*Burajiru jihō*), 1 February 1940 (*Burajiru jihō*), 9 July 1940 (*Burajiru jihō*).

108. Wako, *Bauru kan'nai no hōjin*, 18.

109. *Nippaku shinbun*, 18 September 1935.

110. *Burajiru jihō*, 11 July 1929. The same group had advertised a sale at all of its affiliated
stores in the *Burajiru jihō*, 30 May 1929.

111. São Paulo city (Nakaya Shōten, Endō Shōten, Nippaku Bussan Kaisha), Lins (Aoki
Shōten), Penha (Fukushima Shōten), Promissão (Iida Shōten, Suzuki Shōten), Guaiçara
(Casa Dias [カザデアス], Honda Shōten), Guarantã (Ishikawa Kawamoto Shōten,
Murakami Shōten), Penápolis (Daita Shōten, Satō Shōten), Birigui (Miyazaki Shōten),
Araçatuba (Deriha [or Ideriha, 出利葉] Shōten), Bauru (Okiyama Ryokan, Sawao Ryokan),
Duartina (Oki Shōten), Alto Cafezal (Taiyō Shōkai), Nova Europa (Higuchi Shōten),
Registro (Hirata Shōten).

112. See the following issues of *Nippaku shinbun* for advertisements listing these stores:
1 January 1936 for Nippon, 2 May 1936 for Chiyoda, 18 March 1937 for Yūmeidō, 29 October
1936 for Mikado, and 1 January 1939 for Mariria. For Yūmeidō's branch store see *Burajiru
jihō*, 20 January 1937.

113. *Burajiru jihō*, 14 May 1937.

114. Advertisement for Goseikai, *Nippaku shinbun*, 5 September 1934.

115. See Mack, "Diasporic Markets." This article also discusses a number of other print-
related ventures that arose in Brazil, some of which were not commercial.

116. Advertisement for Notícias do Brasil, *Burajiru jihō*, 7 April 1922.

117. Advertisement for Endō Shōten, *Burajiru jihō*, 19 December 1924.

118. Advertisement for Fujokai-sha, *Burajiru jihō*, 28 November 1929.

119. Advertisement for Nakaya Shōten, *Burajiru jihō*, 26 May 1932.

120. The moratorium was nominally on entry to the country by foreign passengers who
had travelled in third class (steerage), but the effect was to ban immigrants. The moratorium was limited to the extent that it did not apply to certain categories of individuals, or to
individuals in possession of 3 *contos* or more.

121. Tsuchida, "The Japanese in Brazil," 240–42.

122. Tsuchida, "The Japanese in Brazil," 243ff; cf. 279–96 for the steps leading to the
passage of this amendment.

123. Tsuchida, "The Japanese in Brazil," 245–46.

124. Apparently Vargas himself was not particularly enamored of this constitution either, and did not press for it to be enforced (*80-nenshi*, 102). He revised the constitution again in 1937, after he instituted his New State.

125. There were, however, significant numbers of Japanese in Manchuria by this time, though not as agricultural migrants.

126. Young, *Japan's Total Empire*, 352, 395.

127. See Tsuchida, "The Japanese in Brazil," 297. The census, dated 1 September 1940, was published in 1950 by the Serviço Gráfico do Instituto Brasileiro de Geografia e Estatística. Data is taken from volume two, *Censo Demográfico: População e Habitação*; Tsuchida 299, 309; and *80-nenshi*, 110.

128. *Censo Demográfico* 14–15, 12–13. The data on naturalized citizens is then further broken down by age.

129. *80-nenshi*, 113, drawing its results from Aoyagi, *Burajiru ni okeru Nihonjin hattenshi*, ge, 580–82, which are in turn attributed to the mission of the imperial government in Brazil (帝国在外公館). The *Hattenshi* states that this number (and thus the term *hōjin* itself) only includes individuals with Japanese citizenship, meaning that (for example) should a child be born to Japanese parents (literally, "is born as a Japanese child") who then only registered the birth with the Brazilian government (in accordance with the Japanese Nationality Law, which is aimed at avoiding dual nationality), then that child would not be included in this total (Aoyagi, *Burajiru ni okeru Nihonjin hattenshi*, ge, 582–83). It goes on to state, however, that it is estimated that only 2600 such children exist (and thus that the remainder were registered with both countries, and thus possess dual citizenship) (583).

130. See the 1939 *Kokusei ippan*, 200–2, for corresponding usages there. The "inner territories" were the main Japanese islands, including Okinawa but not including Karafuto (樺太), according to the 1918 Coordination Law (共通法). It should be noted that during this period, individuals identifying or identified as ethnically Korean and Taiwanese might have been included in this number. See the glosses on "inner-territory individuals" (内地人) in the 1939 *Teikoku tōkei nenkan*, 6–7, for examples.

131. Murazumi, "Japan's Laws on Dual Nationality in the Context of a Globalized World," 419–20. Anecdotal evidence, however, suggests that most children were registered, via birth registration (出生届), many well beyond the two-week limit. My thanks to Negawa Sachio for bringing this to my attention.

132. Aoyagi, *Burajiru ni okeru Nihonjin hattenshi*, ge, 583–84.

133. *80-nenshi*, 128, 134.

134. Tsuchida estimates the total to be 248,878, but he leaves out individuals born of Japanese mothers and Brazilian fathers, of whom there appear to have been a number ("The Japanese in Brazil," 298). On the other hand, the Brazilian census listed (on page 6) only 242,320 "yellow" (*amarelo*) inhabitants of Brazil. Although a significant number of respondents (41,983) declined to declare their "color" (*côr*), the "yellow" total would have included other groups as well. The total number of "Japanese" (broadly and ambiguously defined), then, probably did not exceed Tsuchida's estimate. *80-nenshi* estimates the total as 205,000 (103).

135. Instituto Brasileiro de Geografia e Estatística, *Censo Demográfico*, 19: "Persons who do not usually speak Portuguese in the home, by sex and nationality, arranged by language spoken."

136. Instituto Brasileiro de Geografia e Estatística, *Censo Demográfico*, 20. The difference between this number of Brazilian-born individuals who do not speak Portuguese at home (69304) and those from the previous chart (70476) reveals, it would seem, the small number (1172) of children of Japanese mothers and Brazilian-citizen fathers (presumably this would include Brazilian-born Nisei) who spoke Japanese in the home.

137. Instituto Brasileiro de Geografia e Estatística, *Censo Demográfico*, 21. Given that the total of these two figures (4295) exceeds the total number of naturalized citizens, we can deduce that in some or perhaps all cases, individuals were counted for either (or both) relevant category/ies.

138. Instituto Brasileiro de Geografia e Estatística, *Censo Demográfico* 21. Again, the total of these two figures (184,235) exceeds the total number of Japanese citizens in Brazil.

139. See *Nihonjin hattenshi*, jō 193–94.

140. See *Burajiru jihō*, 16 March 1928, for one of the earliest advertisements I have been able to discover.

141. See notification in *Burajiru jihō*, 20 April 1928. On 27 April 1928 a notification was printed that ownership had transferred to Takeuchi Kimi.

142. *Nippaku shinbun*, 6 July 1933, 15 November 1933, and 11 April 1934.

143. Paulista Shinbunsha, *Nihon-Burajiru kōryū jinmei jiten*, 139–40 (henceforth, *Nihon-Burajiru kōryū jinmei jiten*).

144. See Aoyagi, *Nihonjin hattenshi*, ge, 158–67.

145. *Nippaku shinbun*, 5 September 1934.

146. *Nippaku shinbun*, 11 April 1934.

147. *Nippaku shinbun*, 18 April 1934.

148. *Nippaku shinbun*, 9 May 1934.

149. *Nippaku shinbun*, 23 May 1934.

150. *Nippaku shinbun*, 18 July 1934.

151. *Nippaku shinbun*, 8 August 1934.

152. *Nippaku shinbun*, 16 October 1935.

153. *Nippaku shinbun*, 9 March 1937. Another advertisement for the book, appearing in the *Seishū shinpō* 1 September 1937, lists the publisher (発行所) as the Goseikai and the retailer (発売所) as Tōyō Shoten.

154. Advertisement in *Burajiru jihō*, 6 September 1939.

155. It ran a similarly large advertisement on 17 March 1940 and 15 August 1940.

156. *80-nenshi*, 102, 133. Apparently the *Burajiru jihō* continued to be published, illegally, for some time after this law went into effect.

157. Interview with Mario Yendo, 23 June 2005, and 27 June 2005.

3. CULTURE: SAMURAI, SPIES, AND SERIALIZED FICTION

1. Bhabha, *The Location of Culture*, 139–70.

2. Kiyotani, *Tooi hibi no koto*, 269.

3. Wako, *Bauru kan'nai no hōjin*, 18.

4. Handa, *Imin no seikatsu no rekishi*, 594.

5. For example, Maeyama, "Imin bungaku kara mainoritii bungaku e"; Arata, *Burajiru Nikkei koronia bungei*, ge; Rivas, "*Jun-nisei* Literature in Brazil"; and Hosokawa, *Nikkei*

Burajiru imin bungaku. A sample of Hosokawa's work is available in English in *Sentiment, Language, and the Arts*.

6. Anderson, *Imagined Communities*, chapter two.

7. Nagata, *Burajiru ni okeru Nihonjin hattenshi*, ge 258–59, as reproduced in Konno and Fujisaki, *Iminshi I*, 148–49.

8. Kōyama, *Imin shijūnen-shi*, 407. Note that he refers to the paper as the *Nanbei shūhō* (南米週報), but as Handa points out in *Imin no seikatsu no rekishi* (595) this is likely a simple mistake.

9. Kōyama, *Imin shijūnen-shi*, 408. *Nippaku* began to use movable type from 14 November 1919 (*Nenpyō* 44).

10. Kōyama, *Imin shijūnen-shi*, 409.

11. Konno and Fujisaki, *Iminshi I* 149–52. The newspaper launched again under the name *Burajiru asahi* from 25 July 1940.

12. On 20 October 1931, 30 March 1936, and 23 August 1937, respectively.

13. Kōyama, *Imin shijūnen-shi*, 409, and Konno and Fujisaki, *Iminshi I*, 153–54.

14. *Nenpyō*, 47.

15. The dates of the publishing schedule changes were 7 September 1931, 26 September 1935, and 23 August 1937, respectively. *Nenpyō* (78) has the paper going to a twice-weekly schedule in November 1934, when it moved operations to the city of São Paulo.

16. *80-nenshi*, 132.

17. Kōyama, *Imin shijūnen-shi*, 409, and Konno and Fujisaki, *Iminshi I*, 155–56.

18. In addition to *Duels*, this first issue also carried a short story by Wako Shungorō titled "Mori no oku," both written in and concerning Brazil.

19. Imamura was one of the most famous and powerful of the transcribers active at the time; see Langton, "A Literature for the People" 86–91.

20. Takarai, *Kan'ei gozen jiai* zenpen and kōhen.

21. Installment number two begins in the middle of page 7 in the book version and continues through mid-page 11.

22. Though under the title *Kan'ei yūshi bujustsu no homare* (寛永勇士武術之誉). Despite the title, the work followed volume 32, not volume 33.

23. 21 December 1923.

24. 20 April 1923. Takagi Takeo describes how the Asahi Shinbunsha editorial staff determined breaks for Nagai Kafū, for example, and made other adjustments to the text to alter its length. See Takagi, *Shinbun shōsetsu-shi, Shōwa-hen II*, 297.

25. 21 September 1928–11 January 1929.

26. 27 September 1918–28 January 1921.

27. In *Kōdan tsutsumi no io* (巷談坡庵).

28. A story with the same title by Watanabe Katei (霞亭) was serialized in the *Tokyo niroku shinbun* beginning 8 September 1904. The National Diet Library's Modern Digital Library has a March 1905 Miyake Seiken book version from Keibunkan. One film version was produced by the "father of Japanese film," Makino Shōzō (1878–1929), in 1914.

29. Koganei Roshū, *Kume no Heinai*; Kobayashi, *Chōhen kōdan*, volume 32.

30. The copy of the text held in the National Diet Library's Modern Digital Library has a publication date of April 1918, with the specific date of April 27 written in; the specific days of both the printing and publication of the text were left blank when the colophon was printed.

31. Takagi, *Shinbun shōsetsu-shi: Meiji-hen*, 436–37.

32. *Kokoro* ran from 20 April 1914–11 August 1914. See Honda, *Shinbun shōsetsu no tanjō* 225.

33. Ending on 29 May 1930.

34. Here I am following Langton's and Adachi's leads in using the conventional reading, rather than the original reading of Tatsukawa. See Langton, "A Literature for the People," 100n78 and Adachi, *Tachikawa bunko no eiyū-tachi*, 67–68.

35. See Langton, "A Literature for the People," 101n83 and Adachi, *Tachikawa bunko no eiyū-tachi*, 38–39, 74–75. This would also explain why the illustration used with the first installment in the newspaper does not match the illustration contained in the 1974 reprint of the Tachikawa volume.

36. This is the edition used for the 1974 reprint.

37. It might also derive from an identical reprint of the Seibundō text, published in Osaka by Shinkōsha (新興社) in 1929.

38. The first installment, for example, covers the first three pages or so of the book, ending midway through the book's first section; the second installment picks up exactly where the first left off, and then marks (with the same numbered section titles from the book) the transition from section one to section two in the course of the installment.

39. The book form has most characters glossed, whereas the newspaper glosses fewer words. In addition, the newspaper sometimes uses alternate orthographical renderings of words. For example, whereas 評 is glossed ひやう in the book version, it is glossed へう in the newspaper version; whereas 法 is glossed はふ in the book, it is glossed ほふ in the newspaper. Both of these examples are drawn from the first installment.

40. *Sandee mainichi* 4:49 (8 November 1925) and 5:8 (14 February 1926).

41. Though we should note that the conclusion of the story in *Nichibei*, which ran to 132 installments, does not match the conclusion of the *Miyako shinbun* version, which ran to 147 installments. Some documents suggest that it also ran in the *Rafu nichibei* (renamed *Shin nichibei* in 1931), another Japanese newspaper in Los Angeles owned by the same company from 1922; this may be a reference to a work titled *Naraku no nushi*, which appeared in the *Rafu shinpō*.

42. The documentation of the following exchange can be found in "Publication of a novel titled Naraku on [sic] newspaper," Diplomatic Archives of the Ministry of Foreign Affairs, Japan Center for Asian Historical Records (JACAR) reference code B03040654100 (<http://www.jacar.go.jp>).

43. *Nichibei* serialized *Daibosatsu tōge* for years. On the day Masuda wrote his letter, for example, *Nichibei* printed an installment of *Mumyō no maki*, which had begun publication in January of the same year in both the *Tokyo Nichinichi* and the *Ōsaka Mainichi* newspapers. In the earliest number of *Nichibei* that I was able to check—1 January 1919—installment 255, from *Ai no yama*, appears; this suggests that Nichibei ran the story for years, suspending publication (it would seem) with the close of the *Mumyō* chapter, on 18 July 1925. This does suggest that the letter may have had some impact.

44. More specifically, it comes from part 5 of volume 11, *Komai no tonokami no maki* (駒井能登守の巻).

45. Vol. 20, no. 1 (66–73). The reprint largely faithful to the original, though with the same sort of script and gloss variations that were apparent in the preceding cases.

46. 17 January 1934–27 July 1935 and 31 July 1935–8 January 1937, respectively.

47. The 27 May 1938 number is missing, but this date is provided by an advertisement for the serialization that appears in the 25 May 1938 number.

48. Installment 90 of *Abare* appears on 23 April, while installment 100 appears on 17 May; damage to the extant papers obscures other numbering, but the 12 May installment seems likely to have been no. 95. *Moyuru's* numbering is not very helpful, as it is clear that an installment did not run every day: 116 ran on 28 April and 125 ran on 12 May.

49. The newspaper ran until 31 August 1941, but the last weeks are not contained on the microfilm.

50. Kikuchi Kan's "Nishizumi senshachō-den," which ran from 16 May 1939 until 2 November 1939 in the *Burajiru jihō*, had previously run in the evening editions of the *Tōkyō Nichinichi shinbun* and the Ōsaka *Mainichi shinbun* from 7 March 1939 until 6 August 1939. Although there are minor differences, the text and illustrations are practically identical.

51. Torrance, *The Fiction of Tokuda Shūsei and the Emergence of Japan's New Middle Class*, 33–34.

52. Asaoka, <*Chosha*> *no shuppanshi*, 156.

53. Asaoka, <*Chosha*> *no shuppanshi*, 145–59.

54. Okazaki, "Izumi Kyōka to chihō shinbun," 45–53.

55. Asaoka, <*Chosha*> *no shuppanshi*, 146. Takagi Takeo also discusses this in his *Shinbun shōsetsu-shi: Meiji-hen*, 204.

56. Asaoka, <*Chosha*> *no shuppanshi*, 147. The original article is "Chihō shinbun shōsetsu kōdan toritsugisho no uchimaku," *Mumei tsūshin* 1, no. 8 (August 1909): 10–13.

57. Asaoka, <*Chosha*> *no shuppanshi*, 158.

58. Kawai, *Shinbun shōsetsu no shūhen de.*

59. Ozaki Hideki, "Shunbun shōsetsu no tokushitsu: Shinbun shōsetsu-ron ni furete," in Hasegawa and Takeda, *Gendai shinbun shōsetsu jiten*, 16.

60. As an imperfect comparison, we might consider the fact that around 1937, Takagi Takeo states that Nagai Kafū was paid a record seventy yen per installment by the Asahi Shinbunsha for *Bokutō kidan* (*Shinbun shōsetsu-shi, Shōwa-hen II*, 296). He also notes that one installment was not one page of *genkō yōshi*, the standard unit for calculating payment in other venues; for newspaper fiction, a single installment was usually on the order of 3 and one-half pages of *genkō yōshi*.

61. Asaoka, <*Chosha*> *no shuppanshi*, 148, 155, and 157.

62. Hirai, *Shinbun shōsetsu no kenkyū*, 23.

63. Hirai, *Shinbun shōsetsu no kenkyū*, 25–26. He was not the only critic to note the possibility that works appeared in multiple places; see 29. In both cases, though, it is treated as a kind of deception, suggesting that it was not a generally acknowledged practice. The exception to this was newspapers that were connected to the large national papers, which would often share the same works (35).

64. Hirai, *Shinbun shōsetsu no kenkyū*, 23.

65. Hirai, *Shinbun shōsetsu no kenkyū*, 26.

66. *Burajiru jihō*, 13 May 1939.

67. *Burajiru jihō*, 31 October 1939.

68. In 1937 it had been serialized in the *Hawai hōchi* newspaper in Honolulu, the *Kashū mainichi shinbun* in Los Angeles, and the *Taihoku nippō* in Seattle.

69. Tani may have been the penname of Suzuki Sadao.

70. Bellah, *Irregular Gentleman*, 2. The Chinese- and Russian-speaking Hanson, whom Bellah describes as having "the reputation of being the cleverest Far Eastern trouble shooter the State Department had produced for a generation or more" (2) is mentioned in a *Cornell Daily Sun* article ("Observer Sent into Manchuria") on 2 November 1931 as holding this position.

71. Meyer, *Life and Death in the Garden*, 84.

72. Bellah, *Irregular Gentleman*, 7, 10.

73. The first installment, translated by Yonamine Keiko, appeared in issue 56 (July 1997). The serialization concluded with installment twelve in issue 8 (July 2001) of the journal *Burajiru nikkei bungaku*, where it had been running since *Koronia shibungaku* stopped being published.

74. *Burajiru jihō*, July 3, 9, 16, and 23, 1938.

75. http://www.brasiliminbunko.com.br. As will be discussed in the next chapter, changes (either in the form of conscious edits or unintentional errors) were made to the stories at each stage of reproduction, though they remain largely consistent from their original prewar forms.

TEN STORIES FROM BRAZIL

1. Though *vagabundo* (vagabond) has a general meaning, its connotations here would have been more specific to the prewar community in Brazil, in which individuals who left the formal *colônia* and went into the cities to find their fortunes were referred to (and referred to themselves) as "vagabonds." This marks the observer as Japanese-Brazilian.

2. *Conde-gumi* likely refers to a gang associated with the street Rua Conde de Sarzedas, which runs roughly east to west on the northern edge of the Liberdade neighborhood, the center of the Japanese-Brazilian community in the city of São Paulo.

3. The advertisement is described as a *kōkoku-tō* (広告燈), which likely refers to one or more illuminated advertisements, of either neon or incandescent bulbs.

4. Conrad Nagel (1897–1970) was a film star whose career began in 1918 in a film version of "Little Women." He was also a founding member of the Academy of Motion Picture Arts and Sciences and the Screen Actors Guild.

5. The "Triângulo Histórico," which marks the historic Sé district in downtown São Paulo, is a commonly used name whose precise boundaries can vary. Here it refers to the triangle linking Praça da Sé, the Mosteiro de São Bento, and the Theatro Municipal via Rua São Bento, Rua Boa Vista (or Rua Quinze de Novembro), and Rua Direita.

6. *Momoiro-shi*; presumably a comparison to a dance card from a dance hall.

7. Tomatoes were, in fact, one of the crops that Japanese immigrants became involved in cultivating; in 1939, Japanese farms produced 9360 *contos* worth of tomatoes, as compared to 56000 *contos* worth of coffee and 367780 *contos* worth of cotton. See *80-nenshi*, 109.

8. When Ruriko says Ōmura's name it is presented phonetically, presumably to stress Ruriko's non-native pronunciation.

9. A reference to the Central, linking São Paulo with Rio de Janeiro.

10. Thatched; often thatched palm.

11. A pesticide.

12. マクロスポリウム菌; perhaps *bacillus macrosporus*. Presumably the bacteria that results in a form of leaf or fruit blight.

13. Dregs left when the oil has been pressed from the castor oil plant; used in fertilizer.

14. 複式経営, which presumably means multiple crops or maintaining side businesses.

15. 鈴掛の木—in this case, *platanus* × *hispanica*, also known as a London Plane, which is thought to be a hybrid of the Oriental Plane, *P. orientalis*, with the American Plane (American sycamore), *P. occidentalis*.

16. The name for the precursor of the Mercado Municipal.

17. A slur referring to dark-skinned individuals. When combined with the suffix -*me*, as on the subsequent page, the slur is made more vicious. I hope readers will understand my decision not to employ an obvious English slur, which I choose to avoid because I believe it would be even more noxious than this invective.

18. Company name, or city in Paraná.

19. Presumably Ōmura concedes that, since the tomatoes will be purchased for canning, they will likely be a mixture of different quality categories, thus not entirely affecting the price being discussed.

20. "Third-rate," referring to a lower grade of tomato.

21. *Kandera*, from the Portuguese *candeia* (f.) or the Dutch *kandelaar*, entered the Japanese language by at least 1717, and thus should be differentiated from other *koronia-go*.

22. Appears as *um plata* (ウンプラッタ) in the text.

23. Perhaps an indirect reference to II Thessalonians 3:10, "If anyone is not willing to work, let him not eat" (ESV) or "if any would not work, neither should he eat" (KJV).

24. Literally, "It was like encountering the Buddha in hell," a common proverb for finding help in difficult circumstances.

25. 錦を着て, referring to a triumphant return as a wealthy man. This was a commonly discussed aspiration for migrants to Brazil and elsewhere.

26. The actual proverb is "What use is a cherry blossom if you have no wine?" (*Sake nakute nan no onore ga sakura ka na*).

27. Though the word is cut off in the original, it seems likely that Daisuke was beginning to say the slur *kuronbō*.

28. Hosokawa, *Nikkei Burajiru imin bungaku*, II:34, states that Tanabe was the pen name and Nishioka was the real name. This was not the case; he was documented as Tanabe Shigeyuki when he arrived in Brazil on 14 February 1928.

29. Maeyama, *Koronia shōsetsu senshū*, 1:15.

30. *80-nenshi*, 315–16.

31. Hosokawa, *Nikkei Burajiru imin bungaku*, II:34.

32. The author is presumably using the traditional method of counting age, which means that Natsu may have been as young as thirteen.

33. The phrasing suggests that this is a reference to the Great Kantō Earthquake, which struck on 1 September 1923.

34. This is likely referring primarily to Tokyo, though it might mean either urban center and thus include Yokohama.

35. The reading of Katayama's given name, 耀子, has been rendered elsewhere as Teruko, but after consulting with the family, we believe that the reading Yōko is more likely correct.

36. Hosokawa, *Nikkei Burajiru imin bungaku*, I:68.

37. I have not discovered a "Hayashi Ise" on the rolls of arriving immigrants.

38. Arata, *Burajiru Nikkei koronia bungei*, 46.

39. Hayashi, *Ani Jun'ichirō to Tanizaki-ke no hitobito*, originally appeared in the February 1975 issue of *Shinchō*. "Senchū yobanashi" appeared in issue 23 of *Koronia bungaku* (March 1974). Hosokawa discusses Hayashi and her works in *Nikkei Burajiru imin bungaku*, II:321–25.

40. The layered bunks are referred to in Japanese as *kaikodana* (蚕棚) because of their similarity to the shelves used for silkworms in sericulture.

41. 収容所 refers to the facility where migrants were housed prior to their departure.

42. In the text is says 320 knots per hour, which is not physically possible; I have taken it to mean 320 knots per day, or around 13 knots per hour. The Kasato-maru, for example, sailed at around 14 knots.

43. "God Be with You Till We Meet Again," a hymn by Jeremiah Eames Rankin and William Gould Tomer; "Kami tomo ni imashite" in Japanese.

44. The text has 聖教徒達; I am working on the assumption that the author intended to use the homophone 清教徒達, which means "puritans."

45. A Irmandade da Santa Casa de Misericórdia de São Paulo, a large hospital in the city of São Paulo, is believed to have been founded around 1560. In September 1940, the Hospital Santa Cruz was opened by the Sociedade Brasileira e Japonesa de Beneficência Santa Cruz in São Paulo. This was the first of many large-scale medical facilities built for the Japanese community in Brazil. See *80-nenshi*, 120.

46. *Saudade*, a key concept in Brazil that is often translated into English as "nostalgia," is translated within the story using the Japanese word *tsuioku* (追憶), but with the gloss *omoide*. The result captures both the elegance of the compound, meaning a past memory, and the hominess (and accessibility) of the gloss, which has the same meaning if not the same resonances. When it appears a few lines later, the text again uses the Japanese word *tsuioku* (追憶), but now with a gloss that transliterates *saudade* into *katakana*. In this second use, however, the gloss is likely meant to capture the word actually used by the young speaker who asks for its definition, Luísa.

47. This phrase has no gloss in the original. It is a vulgarity expressing surprise and/or anger.

48. Robert B. Van Valkenburgh (1821–88) served as Minister Resident to Japan from 1866 to 1869. As the Tokugawas' control of Japan began to waiver, Van Valkenburgh began advocating that all foreign powers, including the United States, take a position of neutrality vis-à-vis the competing forces in what came to be the Meiji Restoration.

49. Likely from the poem "Home-Sickness" (ca. 1861) by Robert Bulwer-Lytton, writing as Owen Meredith, which contains the line "Dream a green dream of England."

50. 半黒; this is changed to "mulatto" (ムラト) in the 2008 DVD-ROM version.

51. Washington Irving (1783–1859) wrote in "The Voyage" (1819), "To an American visiting Europe, the long voyage he has to make is an excellent preparative. The temporary absence of worldly scenes and employments produces a state of mind peculiarly fitted to receive new and vivid impressions. The vast space of waters that separate the hemispheres is like a blank page in existence. There is no gradual transition by which, as in Europe, the features and population of one country blend almost imperceptibly with those of another. From the moment you lose sight of the land you have left, all is vacancy, until you step on the opposite shore, and are launched at once into the bustle and novelties of another world."

52. Anatole France: "All changes, even the most longed for, have their melancholy; for what we leave behind us is a part of ourselves; we must die to one life before we can enter another." From *The Crime of Sylvestre Bonnard* (1881), part 2, chapter 4, "September 20."

53. 賜暇帰朝 is a term often used for diplomats who are stationed abroad; this refers to a period during which they return to Japan.

54. Presumably a reference to the coup d'état that placed Vargas in power.

55. 原始林; a key term for the untouched wilderness that surrounded the colonies.

56. 半黒; changed to "mixed-blood" (混血) in the 2008 DVD-ROM.

57. Literally, "we will become Brazilian soil" (ブラジルの土になる). An unwillingness to leave the dead was a concern that reached beyond immediate family relations. Wako Shungorō wrote, "Abandoning the nearly twenty thousand graves here and returning to Japan is not a choice worthy of our ancestors" (quoted in *80-nenshi*, 141).

58. See Hosokawa, *Nikkei Burajiru imin bungaku*, I:219–26.

59. Maeyama, *Koronia shōsetsu senshū*, 1:35. Records remain of Furuno arriving in Brazil in August 1932, and again in October 1936. See Hosokawa, *Nikkei Burajiru imin bungaku*, I:71.

60. Maeyama, "Imin bungaku kara mainoritii bungaku e."

61. Hosokawa, *Nikkei Burajiru imin bungaku*, II:33.

62. *Nihon Burajiru kōryū jinmei jiten*, 215–16. Hosokawa, *Nikkei Burajiru imin bungaku*, I:69, lists the year as 1971.

63. For more on Furuno, see Hosokawa Shūhei's *Nikkei Burajiru imin bungaku*.

64. Kaikō (海興) was a shortened name for the Kaigai Kōgyō Kabushiki Kaisha (海外興業株式会社). Here it would presumably be used to indicate someone from one of that company's settlements.

65. The exchange rate on 10 March 1934 was 1 yen to 3.85 *mil réis*, according to the *Burajiru jihō* on the day this section of the story appeared.

66. To the best of my knowledge, a sequel was never produced.

67. Sakurada Takeo arrived aboard the same ship (the *Montevideo-maru*, which arrived on April 12) as six other individuals named Sakurada from Yamaguchi (Hatsu [ハツ], Hiroshi [博], Junzo [順三], Setsuko [セツ子], Toshio [利雄], and Umanojo [馬之丞]); all seven were bound for the Iguape colony in São Paulo, suggesting that they were likely traveling as a family, though possible a "constructed" one. Scholars have expressed various opinions about the identity of the author of "After We Had Settled"; this may be due to the fact that although the first installment of the story is attributed to him, the family name Sakurada has been conspicuously removed from the graphic that leads each of the subsequent installments, leaving only the given name, Takeo. This might explain why Maeyama writes that he was unable to determine conclusively whether the author was actually Sakurada Takeo or Sugi Takeo (*Koronia shōsetsu senshū*, 1:320). Arata Sumu states that Sakurada is a penname for Sonobe Takeo (Inoue Tetsurō), though I have found nothing to corroborate this assertion (*Burajiru Nikkei koronia bungei*, 24). It should be noted that Furuno, writing in 1949, expressed no doubt that Sakurada Takeo was the author (*Imin shijūnen-shi*, 337).

68. Maeyama, *Koronia shōsetsu senshū*, 1:55.

69. Furuno, *Imin 40-nenshi*, 337.

70. Maeyama, *Koronia shōsetsu senshū*, 1:55.

71. "Bungei jihō," *Burajiru jihō*, 2 June 1937.

72. For more on Sugi, see Hosokawa, *Nikkei Burajiru imin bungaku*.

73. Maeyama, *Koronia shōsetsu senshū*, 1:71.

74. *Nihon-Burajiru kōryū jinmei jiten*, 148.

75. For more on Takemoto, see Hosokawa, *Nikkei Burajiru imin bungaku*.

76. Low salaries (often under 200 *mils* per month) made it difficult for schools to keep good teachers (*80-nenshi*, 119).

77. The women here are not betting but performing a function similar to a dealer spinning a roulette wheel and thus producing the winning number.

78. Iracema is the indigenous woman in the 1865 novel of the same name by José de Alencar.

79. Maeyama, *Koronia shōsetsu senshū*, 1:89.

80. See Kōyama, *Imin shijūnen-shi*, 338.

4. ETHNOS: TACIT PROMISES

1. Although most (if not all) of the Japanese-language writers in Brazil during this period were born in Japan, some had come at a young enough age to be considered *jun-nisei* (proto-second-generation immigrants). See Rivas, "*Jun-nisei* Literature in Brazil."

2. This chapter takes "race" to refer to the subjective grouping of individuals based on perceived notions of commonality or difference that are linked, sometimes only semiconsciously, to an ambiguous amalgam of such elements as phenotype, language, culture, citizenship, but which always implies some biological basis produced by common descent. I do not presume that any consensus on the precise nature of a given race would be shared (between individuals, let alone among the United States, Brazil, and Japan over the course of the last century), nor that individuals would have a clear or coherent vision of their own beliefs, which would have been developed under the influence of multiple, diverse discourses and need not necessarily be consistent over time. As such, "race" should be understood here as "relational and contingent", as a product of racialization, rather than essential. See Sansone, *Blackness Without Ethnicity*, 11. For the sake of readability, the term will not henceforth appear in quotes.

3. As mentioned previously, the question of the generalizability of the conclusions drawn about these texts—that is, what these works tell us about contemporaneous literary representations, much less popular attitudes—must remain open, given that these works were selected by editors with agendas of their own.

4. In such a situation, racial, linguistic, and economic alterity can be (and historically has been) imagined in ways that reinforced a single imagined group ("Japanese"); gender alterity, of course, would have worked in a more complicated fashion. Space does not allow me to explore this important distinction sufficiently.

5. This chapter will refer to characters as they are referred to in the stories—that is, sometimes by given name and sometimes by family name. Full names are given in Japanese order. It is uncertain whether the contempt in the description should be attributed to Daisuke. Attribution of narrative passages to individual characters or to a separate narratorial voice is a challenge, as there is often a blurring between the nominally distinct narratorial voice and the focal figure. While I argue later that the overall narratorial stance

of this story is antagonistic to (and thus differentiated from) Daisuke, there are also cases of narrative as free indirect discourse, presumably associated with him.

6. *Burajiru jihō*, 19 May 1932. *Baiano*, which literally denotes the state of Bahia, is in fact a common racialized term that equates the state/region and blackness.

7. *Burajiru jihō*, 19 May 1932.

8. *Burajiru jihō*, 2 June 1932. Here the term refers to a group of *colonos* (workers on coffee plantations) who are not Japanese. When used in conjunction with Japanese immigrants, the term *colônia* (コロニア) in its narrow sense refers to the rural communities of agricultural workers where efforts were made to preserve Japanese language and cultural practices; in its broad sense, the term can also refer to the community of persons of Japanese descent in Brazil as a whole. This broader sense has fallen out of favor in recent decades. See Lesser, *Immigration, Ethnicity, and National Identity in Brazil*, 83–84, and Mack, "Ōtake Wasaburō's Dictionaries and the Japanese 'Colonization' of Brazil," 46–68.

9. *Burajiru jihō*, 16 June 1932.

10. *Colonos* too were contract workers, but the contracts were usually one-year contracts that could be renewed. See *80-nenshi*, 105–7. Also see Lesser, *Immigration, Ethnicity, and National Identity in Brazil*, 39–44.

11. That is not to say that all pejoratives indicating racial categories were edited out. The most conspicuous example is "hairy foreigners," a pejorative initially used to indicate Chinese, which was adapted to refer to individuals of European descent in the nineteenth century.

12. *Burajiru jihō*, 14 April 1932.

13. *Burajiru jihō*, 21 April 1932.

14. *Burajiru jihō*, 21 April 1932.

15. *Burajiru jihō*, 29 April 1932.

16. *Burajiru jihō*, 12 May 1932.

17. Arata, *Burajiru Nikkei koronia bungei*, 24.

18. *Burajiru jihō*, 21 April 1932.

19. *Burajiru jihō*, 29 April 1932.

20. *Burajiru jihō*, 12 May 1932.

21. *Burajiru jihō*, 21 April 1932.

22. *Burajiru jihō*, 12 May 1932.

23. See Nishi, *<Ima> o yomikaeru*, 69–89.

24. This statement of course involves exempting Ishikawa Tatsuzō's *Sōbō* from consideration.

25. The other stories can be interpreted as similarly positive, though only implicitly, through criticism of behavior that deviates from this ideal.

26. *Bungei shuto* 27, no. 6 (June 1958): 38.

27. *Bungei shuto* 27, no. 6 (June 1958): 38.

28. *Bungei shuto* 27, no. 6 (June 1958): 38.

29. *Bungei shuto* 27, no. 6 (June 1958): 38.

30. *Bungei shuto* 27, no. 6 (June 1958): 34.

31. *Bungei shuto* 27, no. 6 (June 1958): 34.

32. *Bungei shuto* 27, no. 6 (June 1958): 40.

33. The specific valences and politics of epithets over space and time of course vary; it is beyond the scope of this study to fully contextualize the meaning of this editorial intervention, or how various reading audiences might have been affected by the use of the various terms.

34. I am using the term "kinship" loosely, to capture a variety of bonds between individuals that are often thought to be based to some degree or another in biological relation and that can result in both legal privileges/discrimination and familial affections/burdens, often accompanied by real or expected affective dimensions.

35. See, for example, Lie, *Multiethnic Japan*, 91 and 98 for its use to refer to the Ainu and Okinawans.

36. The Center (国立移民収容所), opened by the Ministry of the Interior in 1928, was renamed the "Immigrants Training Center" (神戸移住教養所) in 1932. It remained open in this capacity until 1941. This chapter will only deal with the piece that won the Akutagawa Prize, and not with the two subsequent stories ("Nankai kōro" and "Koenaki tami," both 1939) that Ishikawa wrote that were then assembled as a single novel by the name of *Sōbō* (1939).

37. The "temporary" nature of the kinship bond is explained on 67, when Katsuji explains it to his concerned mother: "As soon as we get to Brazil, I'll have my name removed from the family register."

38. With the enactment of the Conscription Ordinance of 1873, seven years of military service (only three active) were made compulsory for all male Japanese subjects. This obligation was reiterated in the Meiji Constitution of 1889 and revised as part of the 1927 Military Service Law. That law required two years of service. The conscription examination, taken at age twenty, determined an individual's capacity to serve. Magoichi is to turn twenty in April and wants to leave before then in order to avoid conscription (II: 68).

39. Ishikawa Tatsuzō, "The Emigrants (I)," 67. Translation slightly modified for clarity.

40. Stewart Lone writes that the "authorities in Tokyo" pressed emigration companies to "oversee more closely the constructed families to prevent them collapsing upon arrival" (*The Japanese Community in Brazil*, 39).

41. Ishikawa Tatsuzō, "The Emigrants (II)," 65, 67. In the story's sequel, "Nankai kōro," Natsu agrees to Katsuji's request that she become his wife in reality. I have placed "fictive" and "real" in quotes in order to problematize that binary.

42. See *80-nenshi*, 89; Handa, *Imin no seikatsu no rekishi*, 44–45; and Hosokawa, *Nikkei Burajiru imin bungaku*, I:2, I:33.

43. *Burajiru jihō*, 23 February 1923. In the story it is never explicitly stated that the narrator has come to Brazil as part of a constructed family, but I agree with Hosokawa Shūhei that this seems likely (*Nikkei Burajiru imin bungaku*, I:2, I:12). See *Burajiru jihō*, 23 February 1923.

44. Hosokawa also reads the story this way (*Nikkei Burajiru imin bungaku*, I:2, I:38).

45. Maeyama, *Ibunka sesshoku to aidentiti*, 103. Relatives of some kind outnumbered complete strangers in such relations by a rate of 2:1 during the period 1913–17, 9:1 during the period 1923–27, and 20:1 during the period 1933–37 (213).

46. Maeyama, *Ibunka sesshoku to aidentiti*, 103–4.

47. Ishikawa Tatsuzō, "The Emigrants (III)," 69.

48. Ishikawa Tatsuzō, "The Emigrants (IV)," 64.

49. Ishikawa Tatsuzō, "The Emigrants (IV)," 65.

50. See Hosokawa, *Nikkei Burajiru imin bungaku*, 2:308–30 and Hibi, "Fune no bungaku—*Amerika monogatari* 'Senshitsu yawa,'" 41–49.

51. For more on this incident, see Lesser, *Negotiating National Identity*, 134–46, and the forthcoming English translation by Seth Jacobowitz of Morais, *Corações Sujos*.

52. Lie, *Multiethnic Japan*, 2.

5. LANGUAGE: THE ILLUSION OF LINGUISTIC SINGULARITY, OR THE MONOLINGUAL IMAGINATION

1. Oguma, *Tan'itsu minzoku shinwa no kigen*, and Ching, *Becoming "Japanese"*.

2. Consider the quip popularized by the sociolinguist Max Weinreich that "a language is a dialect with an army and navy."

3. This is of course not true of all novels, as a work like Mizumura Minae's *Watakushi shōsetsu from left to right* (1995) reminds us.

4. For an introduction to these glosses in English, see Ariga, "The Playful Gloss." Amino Yoshihiko writes that, historically speaking, "*katakana's* basic textual function was to record the spoken word" and that it was often used "to write down the names of things and places that had been orally described to the writer" (*Rethinking Japanese History*, 128). For a more in-depth examination of the way in which authors produce meaning using their script choices, see Lowy, "At the Intersection of Script and Literature."

5. It should be noted here that in a number of the original texts studied here, the *furigana* appears in a font of the same size as the main script, presumably because of technical limitations.

6. It is worth noting that the historical development of *furigana* is intimately connected to the transcription of linguistic diversity. See Ariga, "The Playful Gloss," 313.

7. Sonobe Takeo, "Tobaku-nō jidai," *Burajiru jihō*, 21 April 1932. In the 1975 reprint of the story, the reading is provided parenthetically after the *kanji*, despite the fact that the volume does contain interlineal *furigana* elsewhere.

8. In fact, the unconventional rendering of the word *puta* as *puuta* might not be a mistake at all, but instead an attempt to render the particular, drawn-out intonation of the term in this situation.

9. *Bungei shuto* 27, no. 6 (June 1958): 31. The precise orthography of the original version, which appeared in *Shin Burajiru* in July 1940, is unknown.

10. *Burajiru jihō*, 2 June 1932.

11. Later in the story we read, "Nowadays a person will *perde* a package of matches in a month; the pack we carried in with us lasted three years" (*Burajiru jihō*, 16 June 1932). Here the verb is conjugated appropriately for the third person and means "gone through." The third time the author uses *carpir* unconventionally as a noun when he writes, "When I was just the slightest bit strict about the *carpi* and yelled at him. . . ." (*Burajiru jihō*, 30 June 1932).

12. *Burajiru jihō*, 10 July 1935.

13. *Burajiru jihō*, 13 July 1933.

14. It is worth noting that there is another case of multilinguality in that installment, this time not with Portuguese but with Aramaic. One of the characters quotes Christ speaking from the cross, saying "Lama, lama, lama sabachthani?" (Sakurada Takeo, "Nyūshoku kara," *Burajiru jihō*, 7 February 1934). The quote is more commonly presented in the bible

(in both Matthew 27:46 and Mark 15:34) as "Eloi [or Eli] Eloi lama sabachthani." This transliteration of the Aramaic using katakana is then followed with a parenthetical semantic gloss in Japanese, "My God, why have you forsaken me?"

15. *Burajiru jihō*, 7 February 1934.

16. *Bungei shuto* 27, no. 6 (June 1958): 32–33.

17. *Bungei shuto* 27, no. 6 (June 1958): 32–33.

18. *Bungei shuto* 27, no. 6 (June 1958): 33.

19. *Bungei shuto* 27, no. 6 (June 1958): 39.

20. In the original poem, the couplet is "*A neve, como a saudade, cai de leve, cai de leve*" (*Bungei shuto* 27, no. 6 (June 1958): 31–32).

21. *Bungei shuto* 27, no. 6 (June 1958): 40.

22. Maeyama, *Fūkyō no kisha*, 216, 222. Note that this discussion of type limitations in Brazil would not have affected the 1958 printing of "Tenpō," which was published in Tokyo.

23. *Burajiru jihō*, 21 April 1932.

24. *Burajiru jihō*, 29 April 1932.

25. *Burajiru jihō*, 14 March 1934.

26. Kō, '*Sengo*' *to iu ideorogii*, 186.

27. Kō, '*Sengo*' *to iu ideorogii*, 185. A still more complicated situation is described by Ueda Atsuko in her study of Yi Yang-ji's *Yuhi*, in which the Japanese-language narrative is understood non-diegetically to be representing the Korean of the narrator; Ueda alerts us to the insufficiency of using a binarism such as "Japanese/Korean," or by extension Japanese/non-Japanese, to understand the linguistic complexity of the novel, which does not conform simply to national borders ("<Moji> to iu 'kotoba,'" 128–43). As Ueda says of *Yuhi*, "the text tells of the story of the limits of thinking of any language as a closed system (統一体, *tōittai*)" (135). Catherine Ryu also explores the ramifications of language choice for the text ("Beyond Language").

28. Kō, '*Sengo*' *to iu ideorogii*, 186–87.

29. See Sakai, "Introduction: Writing for Multiple Audiences and the Heterolingual Address," in *Translation and Subjectivity*, 1–17.

30. "Aru kaitakusha no shi," *Burajiru jihō*, 19 May 1932.

31. Nishi, *Bairingaru na yume to yūutsu*, 49, 55.

32. This move was inspired by similar developments with Francophone literature, english (rather than English) literature, Sinophone literature, and others. In English, scholars such as Faye Kleeman, Melissa Wender, Robert Tierney, Angela Yiu, Christina Yi are just a few of those who have used this formulation to study non-normative voices.

33. See Song, '*Zainichi Chōsenjin no bungakushi*' *no tame ni*, 15.

34. For more on Kim's use of the term, and the history of the term's use as it relates to writers of Korean descent, see Hirata, "'Mainaa' bungaku no seiji to gengo," 111–128. See also Textor, "Radical Language, Radical Identity."

35. Hirata, "'Mainaa' bungaku no seiji to gengo," 117, cites the afterword from Kim's essay collection, *Kotoba no jubaku*. See Kim, *Kotoba no jubaku*, 289.

36. Hirata, "'Mainaa' bungaku no seiji to gengo," 118. Kim makes it clear that his statement on the subject is not final, and that he would accept a more straightforward definition of Nihon bungaku that included any work written in Japanese, regardless of the identity of the author (*Kotoba no jubaku*, 290).

37. As quoted in and discussed by Takeuchi, *Hihyō seishin no katachi*, 329–30. Takeuchi's overview of Kim's position is a valuable one, but unfortunately she fails to problematize the nature of the identity and alterity the term is meant to highlight, seeing the ultimate goal as "learning about the self through the medium of the Other" (334), a perspective that seems to erase inherent heterogeneity even as it celebrates the value of diversity as the source of insight.

38. Yabusaki adds parenthetically that the Nikkei population is usually said to number fifty thousand, and may in fact be far larger, but that most of these are second- and third-generation Nikkei, whose "national language" (国語) is Portuguese and not Japanese. The suggestion seems to be that the number of Japanese speakers who possess a native level of mastery that would allow them to write literature is far smaller than the one hundred thousand figure, and the percentage of native Japanese speakers engaged in writing would be quite high.

39. Ōta goes on to note that the works that appear in *Nanka bungei* are quite different and reflect the different position of the Nikkei in American society.

40. See his usage of *bokokugo* on page 9, for example, and his usage of *bogo* on page 10. The quote appears on page 10. He does tacitly acknowledge that his is an unconventional use of *bogo* on that page when he feels compelled to note that "one may even refer to Japanese [being the language so acquired by some Zainichi] as their mother tongue" (10). The usage of the two terms on 34 reinforces this interpretation when discussing Yi Yang-ji's (Zainichi) character Yuhi: for her, Korean is a *bokokugo* that is not a *bogo* (at least not one that she has learned naturally from birth). The definition of *bogo* is repeated on 34.

41. Hayashi Kōji, *Zainichi Chōsenjin Nihongo bungakuron*, 58, 11, 46–47, 49, 58–59, 51.

42. Hayashi Kōji, *Zainichi Chōsenjin Nihongo bungakuron*, 12–13.

43. Hayashi Kōji, *Zainichi Chōsenjin Nihongo bungakuron*, 53.

44. Hayashi Kōji, *Zainichi Chōsenjin Nihongo bungakuron*, 51.

45. Hayashi Kōji, *Zainichi Chōsenjin Nihongo bungakuron*, 22, 51, 56, 26. Hayashi is using the term "universal" in the Platonic sense, that is, an idea in which given individual instances participate. Hence, I think it can be effectively translated here as "essence."

46. Hayashi Kōji, *Zainichi Chōsenjin Nihongo bungakuron*, 32, 53.

47. Hayashi Kōji, *Zainichi Chōsenjin Nihongo bungakuron*, 34, 57, 59.

48. Hayashi Kōji, *Zainichi Chōsenjin Nihongo bungakuron*, 60–63. Consider the fact that Hayashi is careful to note that permission of these literatures would not involve "assimilating" them, suggesting the co-existence of the various ethnic groups, with a normative ethnic subject as (benevolent) gatekeeper to the apparently stable totality of "Japanese literature."

49. As was the case with Hayashi's volume, Tarumi's monograph compiled and expanded upon a number of articles she had written between 1992–94.

50. Tarumi, *Taiwan no Nihongo bungaku*, 9–11.

51. Tarumi, *Taiwan no Nihongo bungaku*, 11–12.

52. Tarumi, "Senzen no sōsaku katsudō kara miru, Taiwan-jin sakka ni totte no 'Nihongo' bungaku," 281.

53. Including Kaku, *Bairingaru na Nihongo bungaku*; Kamiya and Kimura, *<Gaichi> Nihongo bungaku-ron*; and Ikeuchi, *<Gaichi> Nihongo bungaku e no shatei*. This move seems to follow the move toward postcoloniality in some ways but undermines itself by invoking a term that carries so much historical baggage and foregrounds territorial relations to structural ones.

54. Kamiya and Kimura, <Gaichi> Nihongo bungaku-ron, 3.

55. Ikeuchi, <Gaichi> Nihongo bungaku e no shatei, 6–7.

56. Nishi, "Shokuminchi no tagengo jōkyō to shōsetsu no hito gengo shiyō," in *Bairin-garu na yume to yūutsu*, 41.

57. For examples, see Nishi, *Gaichi junrei*, 264, 273, and 287.

58. Nishi sees such literature as primarily a prewar formation but notes that there are also postwar manifestations as well (*Gaichi junrei*, 273).

59. Nishi, *Gaichi junrei*, 267. This reference to "overseas Japanese" seems to subscribe to my notion of "acquired alterity": for example, Nishi says that "the moment a Brazilian Japanese appeared" in a story—and he does not mean a second-generation Nipo-Brasileiro, but instead someone who has "experienced the outer territories"—then that story gets caught up in *gaichi no Nihongo bungaku* (276). But what has changed in that individual that would justify categorizing the literature differently? According to Nishi, they "invariably do not resemble Japanese" from Japan; they are "transformed (変質した) countrymen" (277). He writes, "More than sixty years after the war, the places that Japanese had considered the outer territories have at some point reached to all corners of the globe and become places where these people who were once inner-territory Japanese gave up being Japanese" (278).

60. Nishi, *Gaichi junrei*, 13 and 26.

61. Nishi, *Gaichi junrei*, 28 and 287. Nishi primarily associates *gaichi no Nihongo bungaku* with the Japanese and Japanese-language-educated subjects who lived in the formal colonies of the Japanese empire prior to World War II (279).

62. Tsuchiya, *Ekkyō suru bungaku*, 8, 11–12.

63. Komori Yōichi makes this point in the specific context of *Zainichi* literature when he refers to *Nihon bungaku*, when it functions as a norm in this way, as being a "literature of the colonizer (宗主国, suzerain)" (*Zadankai Shōwa bungaku-shi*, 5:228–29).

64. Hirata Yumi raises similar concerns about reify a notion of the Japanese language itself ("'Mainaa' bungaku no seiji to gengo," 116n12).

65. Just as Hirata points out with regard to the unresolved histories of the nations of Japan and Korea ("'Mainaa' bungaku no seiji to gengo," 117).

6. CONCLUSIONS

1. An equally important question is who benefits from this challenge to a national literature framework. In many contexts, such challenges accrue benefits to the existing (cultural, economic, political, social) power structure at the expense of disempowered or marginalized groups, as in the process of cultural appropriation. I hope and expect critics of this book will identify any ways that I may be unintentionally producing such results.

2. *Burajiru jihō*, 21 January 1932. Nor was Brazil the only place where the term emerged, though its definition changed depending on the discursive context. From at least 1916, versions of the term begin to be used with some frequency in Hawaii and North America. See Nishi, *Gaichi junrei*, 8–18.

3. *Burajiru jihō*, 14 April 1922.

4. Hosokawa, *Nikkei Burajiru imin bungaku*, II:14–16.

5. Harada, "Shokumin bungaku e no dansō," *Burajiru jihō*, 25 July 1929.

6. No distinction is being drawn here between the term "literary art" (文芸) and "literature" (文学), though the former term seems to be the more commonly used.

7. Maeyama, "Imin bungaku kara mainoritii bungaku e," 314.

8. Imai Hakuhō, "Shokumin bungaku ni tsuite," *Nōgyō no Burajiru* (April 1930): 66–68, as quoted in Hosokawa, *Nikkei Burajiru imin bungaku,* II:19–20.

9. Kita Nansei, "Bungei ni tsuite no heibon naru kansō," *Burajiru jihō,* 10 September 1931.

10. Kita Nansei, "Nōmin bungaku no koto (I)," *Burajiru jihō,* 20 November 1931.

11. Kita Nansei, "Nōmin bungaku no koto," *Burajiru jihō,* 20 November, 24 November, and 27 November 1931.

12. Shōken, "Shokumin bungaku," *Burajiru jihō,* 28 January 1932.

13. Sugi Takeo, "Shokuminchi bungaku no kakuritsu," *Burajiru jihō,* 10 January, 17 January, 24 January, and 31 January 1934.

14. *Burajiru jihō,* 10 January 1934. Sugi had no profound respect for the colony, a society made up of people "who would sell their daughters to blacks to make a profit."

15. *Burajiru jihō,* 23 October 1935.

16. Ikeda Shigeji, "Shokumin bungaku no ideorogii," *Burajiru jihō,* 3 March and 10 March 1937.

17. Ikeda Shigeji, "Bungei jihyō," *Burajiru jihō,* 12 May, 19 May, 26 May, and 2 June 1937.

18. *Burajiru jihō,* 12 May 1937.

19. It should be noted that both of these terms were (and continue to be) in relatively common usage in Japan at this time as well, though often to refer to individuals who reside outside of Japan.

20. Lionnet and Shih, *Minor Transnationalism,* 9.

21. Hosokawa, *Nikkei Burajiru imin bungaku,* II:19.

22. Tsuchida, "The Japanese in Brazil," 294, 287, 264.

23. *Nenpyō,* 96.

24. *80-nenshi,* 138.

25. Kinenshi Hensan Iinkai, *Burajiru Nihon imin sengo ijū no 50-nen,* 284.

26. The journal is published for the members of the Association, who in 2008 were paying annual dues of 100 *reais,* and is available at Japanese-language bookstores in São Paulo (one recent issue was selling for 35 *reais* in 2008.)

27. Two notable exceptions to this are the works of Daigo Masao (b. 1935), which have received or been nominated for multiple awards in Japan, and those of Matsui Tarō (1917–2017), which were reprinted in Japan starting in 2010 as a result of the efforts of Hosokawa Shūhei, Nishi Masahiko, and the Kyoto-based publishing company Shōraisha.

28. For example, López-Calvo, *Japanese Brazilian Saudades* and *Peripheral Transmodernities.* Similarly, Tosta's *Confluence Narratives* reads works of individuals of Japanese descent within the context of the Americas as a whole (205–60).

29. Shell and Sollors, *The Multilingual Anthology of American Literature.*

30. Shih, *The Lure of the Modern,* 34.

31. A broader use of this term was proposed by W.E.B. DuBois; see Rabaka, "Deliberately Using the Word 'Colonial.'"

32. Early attempts at such a global study have been done by Pascale Casanova in her 1999 book, *La République mondiale des lettres,* which appeared in English translation as *The World Republic of Letters.*

33. Lionnet and Shih, *Minor Transnationalism,* 10.

Proper Names

Andō Zenpachi (安藤全八); real name Kiyoshi (潔)
Aoki Shūzō (青木周蔵)
Aoyagi Ikutarō (青柳郁太郎)
Arata Sumu (安良田済)
Arima Tetsunosuke (有馬鉄之輔)
Endō Tsunehachirō (遠藤常八郎)
Fujiyama* Nanpo* (不二山南歩)
Fukunaga Kyōsuke (福永恭助)
Furihata Fukashi (揮旗深志)
Furuno Kikuo (古野菊生); ndp. Kōenji Hagio (高円寺萩夫)
Furuta* Tsuchimitsu* (古田土光)
Gando Tarō (雁戸太郎)
Hayashi Ise (林伊勢); ndp. Katayama Yōko* (片山耀子)
Handa Tomoo (半田知雄)
Hayashi Tadasu (林董)
Hiki Takeshi (日岐武)
Hirabayashi Taiko (平林たい子)
Hirata Shinsaku (平田晋策)
Hoshina Ken'ichirō (星名謙一郎)
Ichiryūsai Teikyō (一龍齋貞喬)
Ihara Usaburō (伊原宇三郎)
Ikeda Shigeji (池田重二)
Imai Hakuhō (今井白鴎)
Imamura Jirō (今村次郎)
Inoue Jūkichi (井上十吉)
Inoue Tetsurō (井上哲朗; sometimes written as 哲郎); ndp. Sonobe Takeo (園部武夫)
Irie Toraji (入江寅次)
Ishibashi Tsuneshirō (石橋恒四郎)

Ishikawa Tatsuzō (石川達三)
Iwakami Saisuke (岩上齊助)
Izawa Minoru (井沢実)
Kagawa Toyohiko (賀川豊彦)
Kamiya Tadao (神谷忠雄)
Kanazawa Ichirō (金澤一郎)
Kanda Naibu (神田乃武)
Kaneko Yasusaburō (金子保三郎)
Kano Hisaichirō* (鹿野久市郎)
Katō Junnosuke (加藤順之介)
Kawai Yasushi (川合仁)
Kidō Isoemon (木藤磯右衛門)
Kikuchi Yūhō (菊池幽芳)
Kimura Shōhachi (木村荘八)
Kita Nansei (北南青)
Kiyotani Masuji (清谷益次)
Koganei Roshū (小金井蘆洲)
Komori Yōichi (小森陽一)
Kōyama Rokurō (香山六郎); ndp. Sokotsu* (素骨)
Kubota* Emiko* (久保多恵子)
Kuroishi Seisaku (黒石清作)
Kuroiwa Ruikō (黒岩涙香)
Kyokutei Bakin (曲亭馬琴)
Masuda Hajime (益田甫)
Miura Saku (三浦鑿)
Miyao Atsushi (宮尾厚)
Miura Saku (三浦鑿)
Mizuno Hamon (水野波門)
Mizuno Ryō (水野龍)
Moriya Yasuyoshi (守屋保吉)
Murakami Namiroku (村上浪録)
Nakamura Goichirō (中村梧一郎)
Mera Isao (米良功)
Miura Saku (三浦鑿)
Mizuki Fumio (水城文夫)
Mizuki Isoji (水城磯次)
Nagai Ryūtarō (永井柳太郎)
Nagata Mikihiko (長田幹彦)
Nagata Shigeshi (永田稠)
Nakae* Katsue* (中江克江); elsewhere it is 克巳
Nakarai Tōsui (半井桃水)
Nakaya Kumatarō (中矢熊太郎)
Nishino Kaichi (西野嘉一)
Nishiyama Satoru (西山悟)
Nomura Chūzaburō (野村忠三郎)

Odagiri Ken (小田切劒); ndp. Shōken-sei (小劒生)? (cf. *Burajiru jihō* 21 April 1937)
Onaga Sukenari (翁長助成); ndp. Hakusuirō (白水郎)
Ōkoshi Narinori (大越成徳)
Ōta Saburō (太田三郎)
Ōtake Wasaburō (大武和三郎)
Ozeki Kōnosuke (尾関興之助)
Saburi Sadao (佐分利貞男)
Sakai, Naoki (酒井直樹)
Sakaida Zenkichi (阪井田善吉); ndp. Sakaida Ningen (阪井田人間) and Nanshū (南舟)
Sakurada Takeo (桜田武夫)
Satō Kichirō (佐藤吉郎)
Satō Kōroku (佐藤紅緑)
Segi Yosoitsu (瀬木四十逸)
Shiino Hō* (椎野豊); ndp. Oka no hito (丘の人)
Shimota Norimitsu (霜田史光)
Shinshinsai Tōyō (秦々斎桃葉)
Shiroma Zenkichi (城間善吉)
Suga Heikichi (菅平吉)
Sugai* Sadame (須貝さだめ)
Suganuma Tōyōji (菅沼東洋司); ndp. Ina Hiroshi (伊那宏)
Sugiyama Hideo (杉山英雄); ndp. Sugiyama Hokage* (帆影)
Sumiyoshi Mitsuo (住吉光雄); ndp. Akino Shū (秋野愁)
Suzuki Sadao (鈴木貞雄); ndp. Tani Shin'ichirō (谷信一郎)
Tachibanaya Enzō (橘家圓蔵)
Tagashira Jinshirō (田頭甚四郎)
Takaoka Sentarō (高岡専太郎)
Takarai Bakin (寶井馬琴)
Takei Makoto (武井誠); ndp. Sugi Takeo (杉武夫)
Takemoto Yoshio (武本由夫); ndp. Takemoto Fuyu (武本夫由)
Takeuchi Yoshimi (竹内好)
Takeuchi Yosojirō (竹内余所次郎)
Tanabe Dairyū (田辺大竜)
Tanabe Shigeyuki (田辺重之); ndp. Nishioka Kunio (西岡國雄)
Tanizaki Seiji (谷崎精二)
Tani Kiyoshi (たに・きよし)
Tokuo Tsunetoshi (徳尾恒寿); ndp. Keishū (溪舟)
Tokutomi Kenjirō (徳富健次郎); ndp. Rōka (蘆花)
Tomiyoshi Kōjin (富吉好人); ndp. Nadeshiko* (石竹花)
Torii Teruo (鳥居赫雄); ndp. Sokawa* (素川) [Kōyama Rokurō's uncle]
Torii Toshio (鳥井稔夫); ndp. Teimishi (丁未子)
Tsukishima* Reiji* (月島怜兒)
Uehara Kōkei (上原幸啓)
Uetsuka Shūhei (上塚周平)
Wako Shungorō (輪湖俊午郎)
Yabusaki Masatoshi (藪崎正寿)

Yamagata Yūsaburō (山縣勇三郎)
Yamamoto Kenkichi (山本健吉)
Yokota Yūji (横田雄士)
Yonamine Keiko (与那嶺恵子)
Yoshino Jirō (吉野二郎)

* Represents an unverified reading.

Koronia-go
(loanwords from Portuguese)

Koronia-go	Portuguese	English
アグワ	água (f.)	water
アピーゾ	aviso (m.)	official notification
アマレーロ	amarelo (adj.)	yellow
アルケール	alqueire (m.)	measure of area (2.5 hectares)
アルケーレス	alqueires (m.)	plural of alqueire, measure of area
アルモッサ	almôço, almoço (m.)	lunch
アロース	arroz (m.)	rice
ヴァガブンド	vagabundo (m.)	loafer, vagabond
ヴエーニャ・アカ	venha aca	"come on!"
ウン	um (m. f.)	one
ウン・トストン	um tostão (m.)	100 réis coin
ウンプラッタ	um plato (m.)	plate (of food)
エンシャダ	enxadá (f.)	hoe
オンサ	onça (f.)	any of various wildcats
カーザ	casa (f.)	house
カーマ	cama (f.)	bed
カジミーロ	casimira (f.)	cashmere; men's suit
カッポエイラ	capoeira (f.)	a wicker basket; a large cage or coop; an area of the forest that has been cleared
カフェザール	cafèzal (m.)	coffee plantation

Koronia-go	Portuguese	English
カポイラ	capoeira (f.)	a wicker basket; a large cage or coop; an area of the forest that has been cleared
カボクロ	caboclo (m.)	half-indigenous, half-white
カマラーダ	camarada (m., f.)	hired hand
カミーザ, カミサ	camisa (f.)	shirt
カミニオン, カミニョン	caminhão (m.)	truck
ガルガンテ	garganta (f.)	a blowhard; a braggart
カルナバル	carnaval (m.)	Brazilian Carnival
カルネセッカ	carne sêca (f.)	dried meat
カルピー	carpir (v.)	to weed
カロッシャ	carroça (f.)	wagon, cart
カンポ	campo (m.)	prairie
グラマ	grama (f.)	grass
ケ、フリア　メルダ	que fria, merda	"[expletive] cold"
コーバ	cova (f.)	planting hole for coffee seedlings
コション	capim-colchão (m.)	brownseed paspalum
コジンニャ	cozinha (f.)	kitchen
コッポ・デ・レイチ	copo de leite (m.)	the Easter lily
コピンニョ	copinho (m.)	small glass, tumbler
ゴベルノ	govêrno (m.)	government, regime
ゴルヅーラ草	capim-grossura (f.)	possibly a reference to capim-gordura, or Molasses grass
コロア	colhêr (v.)	to pick, gather
コロニア	colônia (f.)	colony
コロノ	colono (m.)	tenant farmer
コンデ	conde (m.)	earl, count
コント	conto (m.)	one thousand mil-réis
コンプラドール	comprador (m.)	buyer
サッコ	saco (m.)	sack
サッペ	sapé (m.)	Brazilian sape grass
シャペウ	chapéu (m.)	hat
ジャルジネーロ	jardineira (f.)	a small passenger bus
ジャンタ	janta (f.)	dinner
シンタ	cinta (f.)	belt
セニョリータ	senhorita (f.)	young woman
セマナ	semana (f.)	week
セルベーチャ	cerveja (f.)	beer
セントラル	central (adj.)	central
ソルベッチ	sorvete (m.)	ice cream

Koronia-go	Portuguese	English
ソルベッテリア	sorveteria (f.)	ice cream shop
タマンコ	tamanco (m.)	wooden sole and leather covering shoe
タライラ	taraíra (traíra) (f.)	Wolf Fish, Tiger Fish, Trahira
タンケ	tanque (m.)	tank; reservoir; concrete wash tub
テーラ・ロッシヤ	terra roxa (f.)	purple soil
ディレイタ	direita (adj.)	straight, direct
テルセイロ	terceiro (adj.)	third
テレーロ	terreiro (m.)	terrace
ドイス	dois (m.)	two
トッコ	tôco (m.)	torch
ドミンゴ	domingo (m.)	Sunday
トリアングロ	triângulo (m.)	triangle
トレイス	três (m.)	three
トロッペール	tropeiro (m.)	driver of pack animals
ノロエステ	noroeste (adj.; m.)	northwest
ノン	não	no
パイネイラ	paineira (f.)	the silk floss tree
バイヤーノ	baiano (m.)	a person from Bahia
パウターリョ	pau-d'alho (m.)	pau-d'alho, or garlic tree
バカリヤウ	bacalhau (m.)	dried codfish
バタタ	batata (f.)	potato
パトロン	patrão (m.)	boss
パパイ	papai (m.)	papa
パルミッタ	palmito (m.)	heart of palm
バンドリン	bandolim (m.)	mandolin
ビシェーラ	bicheira (f.)	a maggot-filled sore on an animal
ビショ, ビッショ	bicho (m.)	animal, beast
ピンガ	pinga (f.)	cheap booze, usually cachaça
プータ	puta (f.)	(profanity) whore
プータ・メルダ	puta merda	"[expletive] whore"
ブーロ	burro (m.)	burro, mule
ファカ	faca (f.)	knife
フェッシャ	fecha (m.)	tumult, riot
プラッサ	praça (f.)	plaza, public square
プレット	prêto	(adj.) black; (m.) a black man
ペルデ	perde (v.)	(3p sing.) to waste
ペロボン	peroba	peroba (tree)
ホイセ	foice (f.)	scythe

Koronia-go	Portuguese	English
ボテキン	botequim (m.)	small cheap bar or coffee shop
ボルサ	bôlsa (f.)	purse, handbag, pouch
ボルソ	bolso (m.)	pocket
ボンジイヤ	bom dia (m.)	Good morning
マッシャード	machado (m.)	ax
マッパ	mapa (f.)	map
ママイ	mamai (f.)	mama
マモナ	mamona (f.)	the castor-oil plant
マモン	mamão (m.)	papaya
マンガ	manga (f.)	mango
ミーリョ, ミイーリョ	milho (m.)	maize, corn
ミスツラード	misturado (adj.)	mixed, blended; a jumble, confused
ミリョ	milho (m.)	maize; corn
ミル	mil (adj.)	thousand; abbreviation for mil-réis
ムーチョ・ビエン	mucho bien	(presumably ungrammatical Spanish) very well
ムイト・オブリガーダ	muito obrigada	thank you very much (spoken by a woman)
メーザ	mesa (f.)	table
メルカード	mercado (m.)	market
ラッタ	lata (f.)	tin can
ラランジャ	laranja (f.)	orange
リンニャ	linha (f.)	[train] line
レース	réis (m.)	plural of real, when referring to the old currency
ロッテ	lote (m.)	lot, allocation
ロテリア, ロテリヤ	loteria (f.)	lottery (or lottery ticket)

WORKS CITED

Adachi Ken'ichi. *Tachikawa bunko no eiyū-tachi*. Tokyo: Bunwa Shobō, 1980.

Amino Yoshihiko. *Rethinking Japanese History*. Ann Arbor: Center for Japanese Studies, The University of Michigan, 2012.

Anderson, Benedict. *Imagined Communities: Reflections on the Origin and Spread of Nationalism*. London: Verso, 2016.

Annaka Suejirō. *Burajiru-koku Iguappe shokuminchi sōritsu nijusshūnen kinen shashinchō*. Tokyo: Kaigai Kōgyō, 1933.

Aoki Nobuo. *Ishikawa Tatsuzō kenkyū*. Tokyo: Sōbunsha, 2008.

Aoyagi Ikutarō, ed. *Burajiru ni okeru Nihonjin hattenshi*, ge. Tokyo: Burajiru ni Okeru Nihonjin Hattenshi Kankō Iinkai, 1941.

Arata Sumu. *Burajiru Nikkei koronia bungei*, ge. São Paulo: Centro de Estudos Nipo-Brasileiros, 2008.

Ariga, Chieko. "The Playful Gloss: *Rubi* in Japanese Literature," *Monumenta Nipponica* 44, no. 3 (1989): 309–35.

Asaoka Kunio. <*Chosha*> *no shuppanshi: kenri to hōshū o meguru kindai*. Tokyo: Shinwasha, 2009.

Befu Harumi. *Ideorogii to shite no Nihon bunkaron*. Tokyo: Shisō no Kagakusha, 1987.

Bellah, James Warner. *Irregular Gentleman*. Garden City, NY: Doubleday & Company, Inc., 1948.

Bhabha, Homi. *The Location of Culture*. London: Routledge, 1994.

Casanova, Pascale. *The World Republic of Letters*. Cambridge, MA: Harvard University Press, 2004.

Castles, Stephen, Hein de Haas, and Mark J. Miller. *The Age of Migration: International Population Movements in the Modern World*. London: The Guilford Press, 2013.

Ching, Leo. *Becoming "Japanese": Colonial Taiwan and the Politics of Identity Formation*. Berkeley: University of California Press, 2001.

Ebihara Hachirō. *Kaigai hōji shinbun zasshi-shi*. Tokyo: Gakuji Shoin, 1936.

Endoh, Toake. *Exporting Japan: Politics of Emigration to Latin America*. Urbana: University of Illinois Press, 2009.

Fausto, Boris. *Fazer a América: A imigração em massa para a América Latina*. São Paulo: Editora da Universidade de São Paulo, 2000.

Handa Tomoo. *Burajiru Nihon imin Nikkei shakai-shi nenpyō*. São Paulo: Centro de Estudos Nipo-Brasileiros, 1996.

———. *Imin no seikatsu no rekishi: Burajiru Nikkeijin no ayunda michi*. São Paulo: Centro de Estudos Nipo-Brasileiros, 1970.

Hasegawa Izumi and Takeda Katsuhiko, eds. "Gendai shinbun shōsetsu jiten." Special issue, *Kaishaku to kanshō* 42, no. 15 (December 1977).

Hashimoto Motome, ed. *Nihon shuppan hanbai-shi*. Tokyo: Kōdansha, 1964.

Hayashi Ise. *Ani Jun'ichirō to Tanizaki-ke no hitobito*. Tokyo: Kyūgei Shuppan, 1978.

Hayashi Kōji. *Zainichi Chōsenjin Nihongo bungakuron*. Tokyo: Sōfūkan, 1991.

Hibi Yoshitaka. "Fune no bungaku—Amerika monogatari 'Senshitsu yawa.'" *Bungaku* 10, no. 2 (March 2009).

———. "Nikkei Amerika imin issei no shinbun to bungaku." *Nihon bungaku* 53, no. 11 (November 2004).

Hirai Tokushi, ed. *Shinbun shōsetsu no kenkyū*. Asahi Shinbun Chōsa Kenkyūshitsu Hōkoku, Shanai-yō 17. 10 May 1950.

Hirata Yumi. "'Mainaa' bungaku no seiji to gengo: Gotō Meisei ni okeru 'tasha' to no meguriai." *The Journal of Korea Association of Japanology* 111 (May 2017).

Honda Yasuo. *Shinbun shōsetsu no tanjō*. Tokyo: Heibonsha, 1998.

Horibe Yōsei. *Burajiru kōhii no rekishi*. Tokyo: Inaho Shobō, 1985.

Hosokawa Shūhei. *Nikkei Burajiru imin bungaku*. 2 vols. Tokyo: Misuzu Shobō, 2012–13.

Hosokawa, Shūhei, and Paul Warham. *Sentiment, Language, and the Arts: The Japanese-Brazilian Heritage*. London: Brill, 2019.

Hutchinson, Rachel, and Mark Williams. *Representing the Other in Modern Japanese Literature*. New York: Routledge, 2007.

Ikeuchi Teruo, et al., eds. *<Gaichi> Nihongo bungaku e no shatei*. Tokyo: Sōbunsha, 2014.

Inoue Hisashi and Komori Yōichi. *Zadankai Shōwa bungaku-shi*, vol. 5. Tokyo: Shūeisha, 2004.

Inoue Tetsurō. "Nihonjin Taazan shimatsuki." *Kingu*, February 1953.

———. *Bapa jango*. Tokyo: Dai Nihon Yūbenkai Kōdansha, 1953.

Instituto Brasileiro de Geografia e Estatística. Comissão Censitaria Nacional. *Censo Demográfico: População E Habitação*. Rio de Janeiro: Serviço Gráfico do Instituto Brasileiro de Geografia e Estatística, 1950.

Irie Toraji. *Hōjin kaigai hattenshi*, ge. Tokyo: Ida Shoten, 1942.

Iriye, Akira. *Pacific Estrangement: Japanese and American Expansion, 1897–1911*. Cambridge, MA: Harvard University Press, 1972.

Ishikawa Tatsuzō. *Kokoro ni nokoru hitobito*. Tokyo: Bungei Shunjū, 1976.

Kaku Nan'en, ed. *Bairingaru na Nihongo bungaku: Tagengo tabunka no aida*. Tokyo: Sangensha, 2013.

Kamiya Tadataka and Kimura Kazuaki, eds. *<Gaichi> Nihongo bungaku-ron*. Tokyo: Sekai Shisōsha, 2007.

Kawahara Isao. *Taiwan shinbungaku undō to tenkai: Nihon bungaku to no setten*. Tokyo: Kenbun Shuppan, 1997.

Kawai Sumio. *Shinbun shōsetsu no shūhen de*. Tokyo: Gakugei Tsūshinsha, 1997.

Kikumura-Yano, Akemi, ed. *Encyclopedia of Japanese Descendants in the Americas: An Illustrated History of the Nikkei*. Walnut Creek, CA: Alta Mira Press, 2002.

Kim Sŏkpŏm. *Kotoba no jubaku: 'Zainichi Chōsenjin bungaku' to Nihongo*. Tokyo: Chikuma Shobō, 1972.

Kinenshi Hensan Iinkai, ed. *Burajiru Nihon imin sengo ijū no 50-nen*. São Paulo: Burajiru Nihon Ijūsha Kyōkai, 2004.

Kiyotani Masuji. *Tooi hibi no koto*. São Paulo: Kiyotani Masuji, 1985.

Kō Youngran. *'Sengo' to iu ideorogii: rekishi, kioku, bunka*. Tokyo: Fujiwara Shoten, 2010.

Koganei Roshū. *Kume no Heinai*, in Kobayashi Tōjirō, ed., *Chōhen kōdan*, vol. 32. Tokyo: Hakubunkan, 1918.

Komori Yōichi. *<Yuragi> no Nihon bungaku*. Nihon Hōsō Shuppan Kyōkai, 1998.

Konno Toshihiko and Fujisaki Yasuo, eds. *Iminshi I: Nanbei-hen*. Tokyo: Shinsensha, 1994.

Kōyama Rokurō, ed. *Imin shijūnen-shi*. São Paulo: Kōyama Rokurō, 1949.

Langton, Scott C. "A Literature for the People: A Study of Jidai Shōsetsu in Taishō and Early Shōwa Japan." PhD diss., Ohio State University, 2000.

Lesser, Jeffrey. *Immigration, Ethnicity, and National Identity in Brazil, 1808 to the Present*. Cambridge, UK: Cambridge University Press, 2013.

———. *Negotiating National Identity: Immigrants, Minorities and the Struggle for Ethnicity in Brazil*. Durham, NC: Duke University Press, 1999.

Lie, John. *Multiethnic Japan*. Cambridge, MA: Harvard University Press, 2001.

Lionnet, Françoise, and Shu-Mei Shih, eds. *Minor Transnationalism*. Durham, NC: Duke University Press, 2005.

Lone, Stewart. *The Japanese Community in Brazil, 1908–1940: Between Samurai and Carnival*. New York: Palgrave, 2001.

López-Calvo, Ignacio, ed. *Peripheral Transmodernities: South-to-South Intercultural Dialogues Between the Luso-Hispanic World and "The Orient."* Newcastle upon Tyne, UK: Cambridge Scholars Publishing, 2012.

———. *Japanese Brazilian Saudades: Diasporic Identities and Cultural Production*. Louisville: University Press of Colorado, 2019.

Lowe, Lisa. *The Intimacies of Four Continents*. Durham, NC: Duke University Press, 2015.

Lowy, Chris. "At the Intersection of Script and Literature: Writing as Aesthetic in Modern and Contemporary Japanese-language Literature." PhD diss., University of Washington, 2021.

Mack, Edward. "Diasporic Markets: Japanese Print and Migration in São Paulo, 1908–1935." *Script & Print: Bulletin of the Bibliographical Society of Australia and New Zealand* 29 (2006): 163–77.

———. "Ōtake Wasaburō's Dictionaries and the Japanese 'Colonization' of Brazil." *Dictionaries: The Journal of the Dictionary Society of North America* 31 (2010): 48–68.

———. *Manufacturing Modern Japanese Literature: Publishing, Prizes, and the Ascription of Literary Value*. Durham, NC: Duke University Press, 2010.

Maeyama Takashi. "Imin bungaku kara mainoritii bungaku e." In *Koronia shōsetsu senshū*, vol. 1, ed. Koronia Bungakukai. São Paulo: Koronia Bungakukai, 1975.

———. *Ibunka sesshoku to aidentiti: Burajiru shakai to Nikkeijin*. Tokyo: Ochanomizu Shobō, 2001.

———. *Fūkyō no kisha*. Tokyo: Ochanomizu Shobō, 2002.

Masuda Hidekazu. *Emeboi jisshūjō-shi: Burajiru ni okeru paionia kyōiku*. São Paulo: Emeboi Kenkyūjo, 1981.

Meyer, Kathryn. *Life and Death in the Garden: Sex, Drugs, Cops, and Robbers in Wartime China*. Lanham, MD: Rowman & Littlefield, 2014.

Mizuno Masayuki. *Basutosu nijūgonen-shi*. Tokyo: DaiNihon Insatsu, 1955.

Morais, Fernando. *Corações Sujos*. São Paulo: Companhia das Letras, 2000.

Murazumi, Mie. "Japan's Laws on Dual Nationality in the Context of a Globalized World." *Pacific Rim Law & Policy Journal* 9, no. 2 (May 2000).

Nagata Shigeshi. *Burajiru ni okeru Nihonjin hattenshi*, ge. Tokyo: Burajiru ni okeru Nihonjin hattenshi Kankōkai, 1953.

———. "Ijūchi no bunka undō." *Rikkō sekai*, 1 February 1921.

Naikaku Tōkei-kyoku, ed. *Nihon teikoku tōkei nenkan*. Tokyo: Naikaku Tōkei-kyoku.

Naimushō, ed. *Nihon teikoku kokusei ippan*. Tōkyō: Teikoku Chihō Gyōsei Gakkai, 1940.

Nihon Imin Hachijū Nenshi Hensan Iinkai, ed. *Burajiru Nihon imin 80-nenshi*. São Paulo: Imin Hachijū Nensai Saiten Iinkai, 1991.

Nihon Rikkōkai, ed. *Rikkō 50 nen*. Tokyo: Nihon Rikkōkai, 1946.

Nishi Masahiko. *<Ima> o yomikaeru: 'Kono jidai' no owari*. Tokyo: Inpakuto Shuppankai, 2007.

———. *Bairingaru na yume to yūutsu*. Kyoto: Jinbun Shoin, 2014.

———. *Gaichi junrei: 'Ekkyō-teki' Nihongo bungaku-ron*. Tokyo: Misuzu Shobō, 2018.

Nishida, Mieko. *Diaspora and Identity: Japanese Brazilians in Brazil and Japan*. Honolulu: University of Hawai'i Press, 2017.

Oguma Eiji. *Tan'itsu minzoku shinwa no kigen*. Tokyo: Shin'yōsha, 1995.

Okazaki Hajime. "Izumi Kyōka to chihō shinbun: 'Sakuhin nenpyō to shin shiryō shōkai." *Saga Daikokubun* 18 (November 1990).

Paulista Shinbunsha, ed. *Nihon-Burajiru kōryū jinmei jiten*. Tokyo: Gogatsu Shobō, 1996.

Rabaka, Reiland. "Deliberately Using the Word 'Colonial.'" *Jouvert* 7, no. 2 (Winter/Spring 2003).

Rivas, Zelideth Maria. "*Jun-nisei* Literature in Brazil: Memory, Victimization, and Adaptation." PhD diss., University of California–Berkeley, 2009.

Ryu, Catherine. "Beyond Language: Embracing the Figure of 'the Other' in Yi Yang-ji's *Yuhi*." In *Representing the Other in Modern Japanese Literature*, edited by Rachel Hutchinson and Mark Williams, 312–31. New York: Routledge, 2007.

Sakai Naoki. *Shizan sareru Nihongo, Nihonjin: 'Nihon' no rekishi, chisei-teki haichi*. Tokyo: Shin'yōsha, 1996.

Sakai, Naoki. *Translation & Subjectivity: On "Japan" and Cultural Nationalism*. Minneapolis: University of Minnesota Press, 1997.

Sansone, Livio. *Blackness Without Ethnicity: Constructing Race in Brazil*. New York: Palgrave MacMillan, 2003.

Shell, Marc, and Werner Sollors, eds. *The Multilingual Anthology of American Literature: A Reader of Original Texts with English Translations*. New York: New York University Press, 2000.

Shih, Shu-mei. *The Lure of the Modern: Writing Modernism in Semicolonial China, 1917–1937.* Berkeley: University of California Press, 2001.

Song Hyewon. *'Zainichi Chōsenjin no bungakushi' no tame ni: Koe naki koe no porifonii.* Tokyo: Iwanami Shoten, 2014.

Suzuki, Teiichi, ed. *Burajiru no Nihon imin: Shiryō-hen.* Tokyo: Tokyo Daigaku Shuppanbu, 1964.

Suzuki, Teiiti. *The Japanese Immigrant in Brazil: Narrative Part.* Tokyo: University of Tokyo Press, 1969.

Takagi Takeo. *Shinbun shōsetsu-shi: Meiji-hen.* Tokyo: Kokusho Kankōkai, 1974.

———. *Shinbun shōsetsushi nenpyō.* Tokyo: Kokusho Kankōkai, 1987.

———. *Shinbun shōsetsu-shi: Taishō-hen.* Tokyo: Kokusho Kankōkai, 1976.

———. *Shinbun shōsetsu-shi, Shōwa-hen.* Tokyo: Kokusho Kankōkai, 1981.

Takarai Bakin. *Kan'ei gozen jiai* zenpen and kōhen. Tokyo: Shūeidō Ōkawaya Shoten, 1906.

Takeuchi Emiko. *Hihyō seishin no katachi: Nakano Shigeharu, Takeda Taijun.* Tokyo: EDI, 2005.

Tarumi Chie. "Senzen no sōsaku katsudō kara miru, Taiwan-jin sakka ni totte no 'Nihongo' bungaku." In *Bairingaru na Nihongo bungaku: Tagengo tabunka no aida,* edited by Kaku Nan'en, 275–91. Tokyo: Sangensha, 2013.

———. *Taiwan no Nihongo bungaku: Nihon tōji jidai no sakka tachi.* Tokyo: Goryū Shoin, 1995.

Textor, Cindi. "Radical Language, Radical Identity: Korean Writers in Japanese Spaces and the Burden to 'Represent.'" PhD diss., University of Washington, 2016.

Torrance, Richard. *The Fiction of Tokuda Shūsei and the Emergence of Japan's New Middle Class.* Seattle: University of Washington Press, 1994.

Tosta, Antonio Luciano De Andrade. *Confluence Narratives: Ethnicity, History, and Nation-Making in the Americas.* Lewisburg, PA: Bucknell University Press, 2016.

Tsuchida, Nobuya. "The Japanese in Brazil, 1908–1941." PhD diss., University of California–Los Angeles, 1978.

Tsuchiya Masahiko, ed. *Ekkyō suru bungaku.* Tokyo: Suiseisha, 2009.

Ueda Atsuko. "<Moji> to iu 'kotoba': I Yanji Yuhi o megutte." *Nihon kindai bungaku* 62 (May 2000).

Usui Yoshimi, et al., eds. *Sengo bungaku ronsō,* ge. Tokyo: Banchō Shobō, 1972.

Wako Shungorō, ed. *Bauru kan'nai no hōjin.* São Paulo: Wako Shungorō, 1939.

Yamamoto Kenkichi. "Kokudo, kokugo, kokumin: kokumin bungaku nit suite no oboegaki." *Riron* (August 1952).

Young, Louise. *Japan's Total Empire: Manchuria and the Culture of Wartime Imperialism.* Berkeley: University of California Press, 1998.

INDEX

Abare daimyō (Kuga), 57–58, *57*, 62, 220n48
acculturation, 202
"After We Had Settled" (Sakurada), 114–23, 166, 168, 224n, 225n67
"Age of Speculative Farming, An" (Sonobe, 1932), 2–3, 4, 70, 73–80, 165, 171; alterity and, 153; intraracial betrayal in, 158–61; Japanese-language literary activity in Brazil and, 5; *kanji* and *furigana* in, 178; nonconventional orthography and spelling in, 182
Agricultural Interpreters Association (Associação dos Intérpretes), 29
Ajia no gen'ei (Warner), 57, 63–65, *64*
Akino Shū (Sumiyoshi Mitsuo), 144, 150–51
Akira Iriye, 209n5
Akutagawa Prize for literature, 2, 3, 5, 227n36
Alencar, José de, 225n78
Aliança Colony, 129
alterity, 5, 154, 162, 177, 206; "acquired," 153, 159, 171, 172, 231n59; ethnos and, 7; extremes of, 166–71; gender, 225n4; intraracial versus interracial, 153; language differences as markers of, 8, 184; racial, 154, 155, 162, 166. *See also* Other/Otherness
Amino Yoshihiko, 228n4
Anderson, Benedict, 44
Ani Jun'ichirō to Tanizaki-ke no hitobito (Katayama), 91, 222n39
Araçatuba, 31, 144, 215n111
Araraquara railway line, 22
Arata Sumu, 91, 159, 224n67

Argentina, 45, 162
Ariansa jihō (newspaper), 46
arrendatários (lease farmers), 210n28
Asahi Shinbunsha, 52, 220n60
Asaoka Kunio, 59, 60
"Ashes" (Takemoto), 138–43, 169
Asian Exclusion Act (United States), 17

baianos (blacks from Bahia), 81, 82, 89, 154–57, 184
Ban Shinji, *57*, 58, 61
Bastos Colony, 17, 25; bookstores in, 31; Japanese population of, 214n94; land prices in, 26
Bauru, city of, 27, 35, 45
Befu Harumi, 208n15
Belém, city of, 26
Bellah, James Warner, *57*, 58, 63–65, 221n70
Bernardo Guimarães, 65
betrayal, ethnic/racial, 7, 153–54, 158–61, 172
Birigui, town of, 22
blackness, terms involving, 157, 165
Bokutō kidan, serialization of, 220n60
bookstores, 22–23; advertisements for, 29, 215n104; final purchase system, 24, 39
Brazil: abolition of slavery, 13; census (1940), 34–35, 216n127, 216n134; Constitution (1824), 35; Constitution (1934), 34; Departamento de Imprensa e Propaganda, 38; early years of Japanese emigration (1908–24), 14–24; Japanese consulate, 45; Japanese-descended population of, 11, 162, 193, 200, 202–3, 209n2, 226n8; literary marketplace in, 39; market for

247

in Brazilian census figures (1940), 34–35; Centenário (centennial anniversary) of emigration to Brazil, 70; early years of Japanese emigration to Brazil (1908–24), 14–24; economic reasons for, 16; government role in lives of, 11; "Hawaii period" (1885–1923), 12, 208n1; Japanese government financial assistance to, 16; Japanese hometowns of emigrants, 15; Japanese state-sponsored migration (1924–34), 25–33; Kobe processing facility and, 97, 100, 223n41; literacy rates among emigrants, 18, 211–12n50; Manchuria period (1933–45), 62, 208n1; moratorium on (1931), 33–34, 215n120; remittances sent to Japan by, 25; restrictions on, 15; return to Japan, 27, 109, 154, 156, 162

Emi Suiin, 59

Endō Shoten (bookstore), 22–23, 32, 36; closure and reopening of, 38; traveling reading group of, 29. *See also* Livraria Yendo

Endō Tsunehachirō, 15, 38, 210n22; newspaper advertisements run by, 21–22, 22, 212nn55–56

English language, 64, 65, 69, 175, 182; combined with Japanese, 104, 181; Japanese migrants in United States and, 188; literary works translated from, 43; terms transliterated from Portuguese and, 71; used on shipboard, 175

Escrava Isaura, A (Guimarães, 1875), 65

"Establishment of a Literature of the Colonies, The" (Sugi), 199–200

ethnos, 5, 7, 186; essentialist notion of, 208n18; "holy quadrinity" and, 11

exchange rates, yen to réis, 23, 212n62, 224n68

families: constructed, 14, 167, 168–70, 227n40, 227n43; nuclear and extended, 167, 170

family registries, 18, 35, 227n37

fazendas (plantations), 14, 15

fazendeiros (plantation owners), 34

Fidelis Reis Bill, 211n46

Five-Power Naval Limitation Treaty (1922), 32

France, Anatole, 108, 224n52

Fujin no tomo magazine, 20

Fukuoka prefecture (Japan), 15, 113

Fukushima prefecture (Japan), 15, 37

furigana, 177–78, 228nn5–7

Furuno Kikuo, 96, 102, 112–13, 150, 161, 180, 224n63

Futari Sōsaburō (Kohori), 57, 58, 62

gaichi (outer territories), 193

<*Gaichi*> *no Nihongo bungaku-sen* (Kurokawa), 193

"Gakidō" (Chang, 1932), 183

Gakugei Tsūshinsha, 60

Gando Tarō, 60, 61

Gendai taishū bungaku zenshū, 52

gender, 14, 16, 71, 161, 163, 176; gender alterity, 153; representation among immigrants, 27

Genjikan, 59, 60

"Gentleman's Agreement" (1907), 12, 13

Godōken Engyoku, 57

Goseikai Shoten, 37–38

Gotō Meisei, 186

Great Depression, 23, 26

Great Kantō Earthquake (1923), 17, 25, 95, 222n33

Guam, 12

Haha (Naoki), 30

"hairy foreigners" (pejorative term), 84, 89, 155, 156, 226n11

Hakuaikan, 51

Hakubunkan (publisher), 50, 52

Handa Tomoo, 43, 218n8

Hanson, George, 64–65, 221n70

Hasegawa Shin, 52, 57

Hase Shōten, 32

Hata (Osaka literary magazine), 2

Hawaii, 12, 45, 62, 208n1, 231n2

Hayashi Ise (Katayama Yōko), 95

Hayashi Kōji, 189–92, 230n45

Heibonsha *enpon* anthology, 52

hentaigana (alternate forms of *kana*), 48

Hibi Yoshitaka, 20

Hiki Takeshi, 56, 57

hiragana, 182

Hirano Colony, 17

Hirata Yumi, 186, 231nn64–65

Hirotsu Ryūrō, 59

Hōchi shinbun (newspaper), 20

Hokkaidō Development Agency, 213n71

Hokkaidō prefecture (Japan), 15, 84–86, 90, 91, 109, 112, 122, 128, 155, 163, 177

Hoshina Ken'ichirō, 44, 45

Hosokawa Shūhei, 197, 198, 201, 232n27

Ichiryūsai Teikyō, 55, 57

identity, 172, 206; ethnic, 191, 192; ethnonational, 166–67; extremes of, 166–71; instability of, 153; national, 44; normative ethnic identity, 185–86; textual, 6, 201–2

Iguape Colony, 17, 21, 214n94, 224n67

Ihara Usaburō, 63

Ikeda Shigeji, 128, 200

Ikeuchi Teruo, 193

serialized works: in *Burajiru jihō*, 50–58; origins of, 58–62; periodization of prewar serializations, 62
Sete Barras Colony, 17, 115, 116, 117, 168
Shanhai (Yokomitsu, 1928–31), 194
Shell, Marc, 203
Shigure hakkō (Hiki), 56, 57
Shih, Shu-mei, 203
Shimane prefecture (Japan), 15
Shimota Norimitsu, 52, 57
Shinbun Bungeisha, 60
Shin Burajiru (journal), 161
Shindō Renmei, 172
"Shin'en" (Akino), 151
Shinshōsetsu magazine, 29
Shin Waseda Bungaku, 2
Shirai Kyōji, 54
"Shi to fukutsū to on'na" (Sonobe), 3
Shōken-sei, 203
shokumin bungei (colonial literature), 3, 199, 200
shokuminsha (colonists), 198
Shōraisha publishing company, 232n27
Shūeidō Ōkawaya Shoten, 46–47
Shufu no tomo (women's magazine), 31
Shūkan asahi (newspaper), 54
Shūkan Nanbei (newspaper), 44–45, 218n8
Shun'yōdō, 52
sitiantes (landed farmers), 16, 210n28
Sōbō (Ishikawa, 1939), 227n36
Sociedade Coonizadora do Brasil Limitada (Bratac), 25–26
Soldiers Alive (Ishikawa, 1938), 2
Sollors, Werner, 203
songs, 20
Sonobe Takeo (Inoue Tetsurō), 2, 70, 158, 207nn5–6, 224n67
Sorocabana train line, 16
South American Colonization Company, 16, 26
Spivak, Gayatri, 204
spontaneous colonies, 17
state, the, 5, 6; colonies set up by, 17–18; "holy quadrinity" and, 11; state-sponsored migration (1924–34), 25–33; territory and, 11, 209n3
state-culture-ethnos-language amalgam, 7–8
Suga Heikichi, 212n55
Sugayama Shōten (bookstore), 32
Sugi Takeo (Takei Makoto), 124, 128, 180, 199–200, 224n67
Sugiyama Hokage, 65
Sumiyoshi Mitsuo (Akino Shū), 150

Tachikawa Bunko, 51, 53
Tachikawa Library, 42
Taihoku nippō (Seattle newspaper), 61, 62, 220n68
Taishō emperor, 19
Taishō nichinichi shinbun (newspaper), 20
Taishō Shōgakkō (school), 28
Taiwan, 24, 34, 185, 192
Taiwan no Nihongo bungaku (Tarumi, 1995), 192
Taiyō magazine, 20, 29
Takagi Takeo, 51, 218n24, 220n60
Takahashi Saburō-sei, 169
Takahashi Yūmeidō (Livraria dos Amigos), 31
Takaoka Sentarō, 37
Takarai Bakin, 46, 47, 57
Takei Makoto. *See* Sugi Takeo
Takemoto Yoshio, 129, 130, 139, 169, 179, 203
Takemura Emigration Company, 14, 16, 210n20
Takemura Yoshiaki, 193
Takeuchi Yoshimi, 4
Takeuchi Yosojirō, 36
Tanabe Dairyū, 46
Tanabe Shigeyuki. *See* Nishioka Kunio
Tani Kiyoshi, 65
Tani Shin'ichirō, 57, 58, 62, 64
Tanizaki Jun'ichirō, 91
Tarumi Chie, 192–93
taxation, 39
Tayama Katai, 59
Teikoku Shinbun Yōtatsu-sha, 59
textual identities, 6, 201–2
Tierney, Robert, 229n32
Tieté Colony, 25
Toake Endoh, 210n25
"Tobaku-nō jidai" (Sonobe, 1932), 228n7
Tōge on josei (Yamanaka), 56, 57
Tokuda Shūsei, 59
Tokugawa Iiemitsu, 46
Tokutomi Kenjirō, 22
Tokyo, 6, 12, 15, 39
Tōkyō Asahi shinbun (newspaper), 51
Tokyo Nichinichi (newspaper), 53
Tokyo Syndicate, 17
tomato cultivation, 74, 75, 77, 78–80, 159–61, 221n7, 222n19
Torrance, Richard, 59
Tōyō Bungei Kabushiki Kaisha, 59
Tōyō Shobō (bookstore), 36
Tōyō Shoin [Livraria Oriental] (bookstore), 36–37
Tōyō Shoten (bookstore), 32, 36, 38

translations, 9, 65
"transnational" literature, 194
Três Barras Colony, 25
Tsuchida, Nobuya, 17, 209n6, 209n12, 210n15
Tsuchiya Shinobu, 193, 194
Tsurumi Yūsuke, 30
"Tumbleweeds" (Furuno), 102–12, 161–66, 171; koronia-go (Portuguese loanwords) in, 184; linguistic diversity of, 180–82

Ueda Atsuko, 229n27
Uetsuka Shūhei, 211n47
United States, 12–13, 34, 162; Immigration Act (1924), 17; Japanese migrants in, 188, 202; newspaper syndication services in, 48; stock market crash (1929), 27. See also California; Hawaii

"vagabonds" (vagabundos), 73, 88–89, 158, 161, 178, 221n1
Van Valkenburgh, Robert B., 106, 223n48
Vargas, Getúlio, 23, 26, 33, 34, 216n124, 224n54
Vida Secas (Ramos, 1938), 65
"Vortices" (Takemoto), 70, 129–37, 144
"Voyage, The" (Irving, 1819), 221n51

"Wakareta hito e: futatabi kokoku no K-ko ni" (Takahashi), 169
Wakayama prefecture (Japan), 15
Wako Shungorō, 45, 218n18, 224n63
Waseda bungaku magazine, 20, 29

Watanabe Katei, 218n28
Wender, Melissa, 229n32
women's magazines, 31, 33
women's organizations, 211n47
world systems theory, 204
World War I, 16, 64
World War II, 36, 64, 172, 188, 202

Yabusaki Masatoshi, 186–87, 230n38
Yachiyo Bunko, 46, 47, 48, 49, 50
Yamada Bimyō, 59, 60
Yamamoto Kenkichi, 4
Yamanaka Minetarō, 56, 57
Yashiju (literary journal), 129
Yendo, Mario, 38
Yi, Christina, 229n32
Yiu, Angela, 229n32
Yi Yang-ji, 191, 229n27
Yokomitsu Riichi, 194
Yokota Yūji, 60–61
Yomiuri shinbun (newspaper), 186
Yonamine Keiko, 221n73
Yorozu chōhō (newspaper), 20
Young Men's and Women's Associations, 18, 126
youth groups, 24, 126, 197
<Yuragi> no Nihon bungaku (Komori, 1998), 4

Zainichi Chōsenjin Nihongo bungakuron (Hayashi, 1993), 189
Zainichi Korean literature, 186, 189–92, 230n40, 231n63

Founded in 1893,
UNIVERSITY OF CALIFORNIA PRESS
publishes bold, progressive books and journals
on topics in the arts, humanities, social sciences,
and natural sciences—with a focus on social
justice issues—that inspire thought and action
among readers worldwide.

The UC PRESS FOUNDATION
raises funds to uphold the press's vital role
as an independent, nonprofit publisher, and
receives philanthropic support from a wide
range of individuals and institutions—and from
committed readers like you. To learn more, visit
ucpress.edu/supportus.